DATE DUE

Freedom Writer

Virginia Foster Durr
Letters from the Civil Rights Years

Edited by Patricia Sullivan

The University of Georgia Press
Athens

Paperback edition published in 2006 by
The University of Georgia Press
Athens, Georgia 30602
by arrangement with Routledge

Originally published in 2003 by Routledge,
an imprint of the Taylor & Francis Group

Edition © 2003 by Patricia Sullivan
The letters herein are published with the permission
of the children of Virginia Foster Durr

Printed in the United States of America on acid-free paper.

10 09 08 07 06 P 5 4 3 2 1

Library of Congress Cataloging-in-Publication Data

Durr, Virginia Foster.
Freedom writer : Virginia Foster Durr, letters from the civil
rights years / edited by Patricia Sullivan.
        p.   cm.
Includes bibliographical references and index.
ISBN-13: 978-0-8203-2821-8 (pbk. : alk. paper)
ISBN-10: 0-8203-2821-9 (pbk. : alk. paper)
1. Durr, Virginia Foster — Correspondence. 2. Durr,
Clifford — Correspondence. 3. Civil rights workers — United
States — Correspondence. 4. Lawyers' spouses — United
States — Correspondence. 5. African Americans — Civil
rights — History — 20th century. 6. African Americans —
Civil rights — Alabama — History — 20th century.
7. Alabama — Biography. I. Sullivan, Patricia. II. Title.
CT275.D8848 A4 2006
323.092 — dc22   2005025333

To the memory of
Clifford Judkins Durr

Contents

Acknowledgments

More than a decade ago, Virginia Durr suggested that I consider editing a book of her letters. We spent time reviewing a batch of letters one summer, and I was hooked. Other projects and demands crowded my time, but I continued pursuing the network of friends who were the recipients of Virginia's bountiful correspondence, a paper trail that led to archives and private collections around the country and in England. It is a pleasure finally to thank all who helped to make this book possible.

I am deeply grateful to Ann Lyon, Lucy Hackney, Virginia "Tilla" Durr and Lulah Colan, the daughters of Clifford and Virginia Durr. They shared memories, answered my many questions, and provided generous support over the years. Much of the early work on the letters was done in the kitchen of Lucy and Sheldon Hackney's home on Martha's Vineyard, where Virginia presided in her favorite window seat, positioned to observe all the comings and goings in that busy household. Ann and Walter Lyon's home in Harrisburg, Pennsylvania, was a favorite research destination, thanks to Walt's role as the family archivist as well as his and Ann's warm hospitality.

My appreciation goes to all the libraries that made Virginia Durr's letters available to me, particularly the Schlesinger Library at the Radcliffe Institute of Harvard University. Several archivists were especially helpful in tracking down letters and other information not readily accessible and deserve special mention. They include: Michael Parrish, the Lyndon Baines Johnson Library; Alexander Rankin, Special Collections at Boston University; Mary Wolfkskill, the Library of Congress; and Norwood Kerr, the Alabama Department of Archives and History.

Virginia, a friend remarked, "was good at collecting people." Her friends and political comrades span several generations, from veterans of early movement years during the New Deal era through the civil rights movement and beyond. I am thankful to all who shared memories, recollections, and letters for this book. They include: Pete Seeger, Studs Terkel, Marge Frantz, Dorothy Burnham, John Hope Franklin, Shelagh Foreman, Constancia "Dinky" Romilly, Andrew Roberts, Johnnie Carr, Anne Braden, Lois Eliot, Catherine Galbraith, John Kenneth Galbraith, Harris Wofford, Anthony Lester, Jonathan Steele, Nicholas Bosanquet, Robert Cassen, Julian Bond, William Styron, Rose Styron, William Preston, Myron Thompson, Bryan Stevenson, Robert Smith, Deborah Ellis, Randall Williams, and Olivia Turner.

As the project began to take shape, friends and colleagues read sections of an evolving text. Their comments, suggestions, and insights, along with ongoing discussions, helped enormously as I worked to craft a book from a sea of letters. I am deeply indebted to Dan Carter, Blanche Wiesen Cook, Missy Daniel, John Dittmer, Sheldon Hackney, Leon Litwack, Waldo Martin, William Preston, Susan Reverby, Anne Firor Scott, Larissa Smith, and Michele Stoddard.

Other friends and colleagues shared ideas and research and provided support and assistance in innumerable ways. Ray Arsenault shared letters he uncovered during his own research on the Freedom Rides, and his tribute to John Hope Franklin inspired the title for this book. I would also like to thank Susan Ashmore, Donna Bohanan, Randall Burkett, Robert L. Carter, Bettye Collier-Thomas, Catherine Fosl, Edwin Furshpan, Raymond Gavins, Eugenia Guinier, Walter Jackson, Martha Jones, Catherine Macklin, Melissa McKee Hackney, Richard Newman, Barbara Savage, John Simon, Frank Smith, Peter Sussman, Martha Swain, and William Taylor.

I am, as always, grateful to my parents, Thomas and Doris Sullivan, for their inspiration, encouragement and loving support.

There are several others I owe special thanks to. Scott Shostak provided generous advice and help on several aspects of the book. Lewis Bateman has been a supporter of this project from the start; Virginia and I both deeply appreciated his early and unstinting enthusiasm. Eileen Sullivan hosted Virginia and me during several trips to New York. Steve Milder has provided tireless and invaluable research assistance. Marge Harris helped me bridge the distance between my home (and files) on Martha's Vineyard and Berkeley, California, where I finished the book. Rhoda Litwack's generous friendship during my time in Berkeley made all of the difference.

I have been a fellow at the W.E.B. Du Bois Institute for Afro-American Research at Harvard University for most of the time that I have been thinking about and working on this book. Here, as part of a vibrant community of scholars, writers, and students, I have gained a deeper understanding of the way in which race informs the American experience, a subject that was at the core of Virginia Durr's social and historical interests. I will always be grateful to Henry Louis Gates, Jr. for this opportunity and for his generous support of the project. A fellowship from the National Humanities Center provided support during the later stages of this work. My thanks go to the center and its staff and to my friends on The Glen in Chapel Hill.

Bountiful thanks to my agent, Ellen Geiger and to Karen Wolny, my editor at Routledge. Ellen was enthusiastic about the idea of the book when we first discussed it; her cogent advice and active support have been formative. Karen's keen appreciation of Virginia Durr's significance and of the story her letters tell has made this a better book. I am also grateful to Jaclyn Bergeron and Nicole Ellis. They guided me through the publication process with patience and good cheer, while maintaining a rigorous schedule. The timely publication of *Freedom Writer* on the eve of the hundredth anniversary of Virginia's birth is due to the extraordinary efforts of Karen Wolny and her colleagues at Routledge.

My greatest debt is to the late Virginia Durr. I was a graduate student seeking information on the New Deal era campaign for voting rights in the South when I first met Virginia in May 1978. She was living at the Pea Level in Wetumpka, Alabama, in the house that Cliff built. He had died three years earlier. Their's was an extraordinary union. In the spirit of the partnership that unfolds in these pages, this book is dedicated to the memory of Clifford Judkins Durr.

A Guide to Correspondents

Ann   Ann Durr Lyon, eldest daughter of Virginia and Clifford Durr

Anne   Anne Braden, regional field organizer for the Southern Conference Education Fund (SCEF) and editor of the *Southern Patriot*, SCEF's newspaper

Ava Helen   Ava Helen Pauling, peace activist, board member of Women's International League for Peace and Freedom; wife of Linus Pauling

Clark   Clark Foreman, one of Virginia's oldest and closest friends; a founder and former president of the Southern Conference for Human Welfare; director of the Emergency Civil Liberties Committee in New York, 1951–1968

Corliss   Corliss Lamont, wealthy benefactor of civil liberties causes, including the Emergency Civil Liberties Committee

Dec/Decca   Jessica Mitford, a friend of Virginia since 1939; executive director of the East Bay Civil Rights Congress in Oakland, California during the 1950s; in 1960 she began a successful career as a writer and lecturer

Esther   Esther Gelders, native of Montgomery, Alabama; widow of Joseph Gelders; lived in Berkeley, California

Hugo   Hugo Black, brother-in-law; U.S. Supreme Court Justice

Jim   James Dombrowski, director of the Southern Conference Education Fund

Mairi   Mairi Fraser Foreman, wife of Clark Foreman

Marge	Marge Frantz, daughter of Joseph Gelders; worked and studied at the University of California, Berkeley during the 1950s and 1960s, while raising her children; active in peace, civil rights and civil liberties causes
Max	Maxwell Geismar, literary critic
Otto	Otto Nathan, refugee from Nazi Germany; economist and peace activist based in New York
Tex	Arthur Goldschmidt, a member of Virginia and Cliff's circle of friends and associates in Washington during the New Deal era; worked at the United Nations and lived in New York during the 1950s and 1960s
Vann	C. Vann Woodward, historian and teacher
Wicki	Elizabeth Wickendon Goldschmidt, friend from New Deal days, and a social welfare policy expert

Introduction

Early Thursday evening, December 1, 1955, Virginia and Cliff Durr had just returned home from Cliff's law office in downtown Montgomery, Alabama, when a call came from E. D. Nixon. Nixon worked as a pullman porter and was one of the city's most prominent black political leaders. He told Cliff that Rosa Parks, a 42-year-old seamstress and NAACP Youth leader, had been arrested. The police refused to provide Nixon with any information. Cliff telephoned the jail and learned that Parks had been arrested for violating a city segregation ordinance. He called Nixon back, and the two men agreed to meet at the jail. Virginia assured her daughters, Tilla and Lulah, that they would return soon. Then she grabbed her coat and hurried out to the car behind her husband.

Virginia Durr had met Rosa Parks shortly after settling in Montgomery in 1951, and the two women had become friends. Remembering that night, Virginia described the "terrible sight" of Parks "being brought out from behind bars . . . this gentle, lovely sweet, woman." After Nixon posted bail, the Durrs followed Nixon and Parks back to Parks's home, where they discussed her case. Rosa Parks had been arrested for refusing to give up her seat to a white man on a city bus. Cliff was confident that he could have the charges dropped because the bus driver had not followed the procedures prescribed by the city ordinance. The other choice was for Parks to challenge the constitutionality of the segregation ordinance, a course that her husband Raymond Parks strongly opposed. "Rosa, the white folks will kill you," he told his wife over and over. But Nixon encouraged Parks: this was the chance they had been waiting for. Finally, she agreed. Fred Gray, a 25-year-old lawyer and local legal representative for the NAACP, would represent her, and Cliff would assist him.[1]

In response to Parks's arrest, black community leaders in Montgomery joined in organizing a citywide bus boycott, igniting what would be one of the longest mass protests in U.S. history, now viewed by many as the event that launched the modern civil rights movement. Virginia and Cliff Durr were among a handful of whites in Montgomery who actively supported the protest. For Virginia, the boycott created a world of possibility that had been beyond imagining when she had reluctantly returned to Alabama four years earlier. It was, as one friend put it, "the break in the dam" for a middle-aged woman who had devoted more than a decade of her life to the struggle against the South's racial caste system.[2] Her earlier activism had taken root in the vibrant climate of New Deal Washington, D.C., far from the ingrained segregationist culture of the Deep South.

A native of Birmingham, Alabama, Virginia Foster Durr had lived with her family outside Washington during the 1930s and 1940s. After escaping the confines of Southern society, Virginia had no intention ever to live in Alabama again, but in spring of 1950, the Durrs sold their house in Alexandria, Virginia, their family home for sixteen years, and looked for new prospects. For Virginia, this marked the end of a remarkable sojourn. Since arriving during the early days of Franklin Roosevelt's administration, the one-time Southern belle had become a seasoned political organizer and a leading advocate of civil rights causes. Virginia and Cliff thrived on the energy and possibility that percolated through the nation's capitol during the New Deal era. Their rambling farmhouse was the scene of legendary gatherings that mixed government officials, labor organizers, and young radicals.

Life in Washington changed with the advent of the Cold War. In 1948, Cliff Durr left his position with the Federal Communications Commission (FCC) in protest against President Harry Truman's loyalty order, which required that federal employees be investigated for evidence of Communist sympathies or affiliation. Durr opened a law office and struggled to make a living, fighting the loyalty-security program and the rampant abuses of the FBI. His fledgling practice defended government workers, teachers, scientists and others caught in the net of hearings and faceless informers sponsored by federal loyalty boards and Congressional committees. Cliff finally conceded the futility of it all; it was, he said, "like trying to walk against the Niagara Rapids."[3] Tired, discouraged, and sickened by the fog of fear and suspicion that hung over Washington, Cliff and Virginia were ready to leave. He was 51 years old and she was 46.

Cliff longed to return to Alabama. He had few illusions about the difficulties that awaited them there, but it was home, a place of refuge in an uncertain time. Virginia dreaded the prospect, though, so Cliff looked elsewhere for work. Late in April 1950, as he prepared to go to Denver to interview for a position with the National Farmers Union, Virginia wrote to their daughter Ann about her fear of returning to the Deep South: "I hope and pray [Daddy] will get this job with the Farmers Union . . . I am frankly terrified of going to Alabama. I think I could manage all right, but only by suppressing myself constantly and conforming to a pattern which I think is utterly evil."[4]

It was the day-to-day evilness of segregation that rotted relationships and repelled Virginia's sensibilities. In her letter to Ann, she described an episode during a recent visit with Cliff's brother John and his wife Annie Paul in Birmingham—a simple exchange with a black postman:

> When I was staying at Annie Paul's the postman came to the door and asked if I didn't used to live over on Niazuma Ave. I didn't remember him and asked his name. He said Jim or Bob or something Edwards. I said I am glad you remembered me "Mr. Edwards." . . . He told Pie [the cook] that I had called him Mister—she told Annie Paul—she told John and he told Daddy that he wondered if I could live down there when I did things like that. Well that just shows how terrifically difficult the situation is—and how careful I would have to be. I honestly have gotten to the point where to call an educated strange Negro man by his first name is impossible and I just can't do it. To treat people with such calculated disrespect so as to destroy their hope of manhood seems like murder to me—and even if I don't do it I feel I am an accessory to it—and yet if Daddy is to make a living I would have to pretend to conform all the time.

Virginia's response to a situation that was part of the natural order for most white Southerners offered a measure of how much she had changed since leaving Birmingham for Washington in 1933. At that time, Cliff, aged 34, was an unemployed corporate lawyer. Raised among Birmingham's elite, Virginia had busied herself with volunteer work as a young wife and mother and had served as vice president of Birmingham's Junior League. As for many of their generation and social position, the Great Depression had challenged the sense of security and privilege they assumed to be their birthright. For Virginia and Cliff, uncertainty about the future yielded to the possibilities created by the New Deal.

Washington was a hothouse for Virginia's inquisitive nature, vibrant personality, and simmering resentments. While her upper-class background allowed her to move easily into the social life of Washington's policy elite, she was drawn to the vortex of democratic activism fueled by the depression and the New Deal. Her political development was guided by her attachment to the South as well as by a desire to break free from the conventions that bound white Southern women. Virginia's rejection of racial segregation was part of a broader personal transformation on the cutting edge of New Deal politics. It was an extraordinary change for a woman of her generation.

Virginia Foster was born on August 6, 1903, in Birmingham, Alabama, the industrial hub of the New South. Her father, Sterling Foster, was minister of the prestigious South Highland Presbyterian Church. Her mother,

Anne Patterson Foster, was the daughter of Josiah Patterson, a Confederate hero who served under Nathan Bedford Forrest, the celebrated Civil War general who founded the Ku Klux Klan. "The Confederacy was still sacred when I was young," Virginia recalled. She worked as a page at the annual state Confederate reunion held in Birmingham, and remembered the whisky-scented kisses of the old veterans, "not pleasant . . . although it was the kiss of Heroes." Socialized in the strict racial and class codes that governed most aspects of Southern life, Virginia was raised on the mythology of the Old South. Among her most vivid childhood memories were summers spent on the old Foster plantation in Union Springs, Alabama, presided over by her grandmother, Virginia Heard Foster, for whom young Virginia was named. She "had always been surrounded by servants or slaves . . . and never had to do anything in her life but be charming."[5]

The innocence of Virginia's early years was shattered when church members accused her father of heresy. Foster, who had studied at Princeton Theological Seminary and at the University of Berlin, refused to accept a literal interpretation of the Bible story that Jonah was swallowed by a whale and spewed up whole three days later. He was tried, found guilty, and expelled from the South Highland Presbyterian Church. After losing his parsonage, he attempted to make a living selling insurance. Virginia was ten years old. From then on, she recalled, there was "always a sense of insecurity, [of] not knowing what was going to happen next." Income from the Union Springs plantation enabled them to "keep the best foot forward."[6]

The Fosters moved to Niazuma Avenue in a fashionable section of Birmingham, joined the country club, and pursued their social aspirations through their children. Virginia's education in Birmingham's public schools was interrupted by a year at Miss Finch's Finishing School in New York, and later a year at the Cathedral School for Girls in Washington. She was a curious child and avid reader who caused her father to worry that his "bookish" daughter might never marry. Hugo Black, then a young labor lawyer who was courting her older sister Josephine, encouraged Virginia's interests. He brought her history books and, as Virginia recalled, "He would talk to me like an equal."[7] She was delighted when her sister married Black in the summer of 1921. That fall, Virginia enrolled at Wellesley, a women's college near Boston.

Wellesley was a formative experience for Virginia; she described it as "the greatest adventure of my life until then." Discussions about religion, economics, and the roles of women in society tested her provincial attitudes. Seeking connections with other young Southerners, she joined the Southern Club in Boston and met Clark Foreman, then doing postgraduate work at Harvard University. Foreman, whose grandfather owned the *Atlanta Constitution* newspaper, provided a link to other young men at

Harvard, including Corliss Lamont, son of the prominent banker Thomas Lamont, a partner of J. P. Morgan. Foreman and Lamont not only enhanced Virginia's social life in college; these youthful encounters would have important consequences later.

Virginia found that "being a Southern girl from Alabama [was] an asset." She was popular with her classmates and young men from neighboring colleges. But her Southern values were abruptly challenged at the start of her sophomore year, when she was assigned to share a table in the dining hall with a black student. "Of course," Virginia recalled, "I had been surrounded by black people all my life . . . But to eat with them at the table, this was social equality and it meant breaking a taboo I had been trained in all my eighteen years." Filled with embarrassment and some anger, she immediately informed Miss Harrison, the head of the house, that her seating assignment must be changed. Harrison said that was not possible. When Virginia insisted, she responded that Virginia could either accept her place at the dining table or withdraw from the college. She spent a sleepless night trying to resolve her dilemma. "To give up all the joys of college . . . the dances and parties and above all . . . the boys! It was impossible." Finally, she reasoned that what worried her most was what her father would think, and she decided not to tell him. She took her assigned place at the table, and she soon realized it was not "the Negro girl I was afraid of," but rather the guilt associated with violating the mores of her family and community. Though this was not a moment of epiphany, a doubt had been planted.[8]

Nonetheless, Virginia's time at Wellesley was soon cut short. As she put it, "the boll weevil ate up my education." The boll weevil infestation of the early 1920s sent cotton prices and land values plummeting in the South, diminishing the Fosters' primary source of income. Virginia withdrew from Wellesley at the end of her sophomore year. The trappings of status lingered, however. After returning to Birmingham in 1923, she made her debut and immersed herself in a whirl of parties and teas. Soon thereafter, she got a job as a librarian for the county bar association to help pay the family's bills—a source of great humiliation for her parents.[9]

Financial worries were compounded by her parents' concern about Virginia's marital prospects. At the ripe age of 21, she had not yet found a husband. However, she soon met Clifford Judkins Durr at church and was instantly attracted to this tall, blond young man who wore English suits. A former Rhodes scholar, Cliff was from Montgomery and worked for the leading corporate law firm in Birmingham. Their courtship was brief. Cliff wrote and informed his mother, "Virginia and I like each other well enough to believe that we can spend the next fifty or sixty years together without being bored." They married on April 7, 1926. Their first child, Ann, was born a year later.[10]

Cliff's career prospered; he was soon made a partner in the law firm. Virginia was active in her church and the Junior League, played bridge, and belonged to a sewing circle. Meanwhile, economic conditions in Birmingham steadily worsened. The Fosters lost nearly everything they had, and finally they moved in with Cliff and Virginia. Her mother sank into a deep depression and was temporarily hospitalized. The impact of her family's losses was compounded by Virginia's first encounter with the raw face of poverty. As a Junior League volunteer, she accompanied Red Cross workers to the steel mill villages on the edge of Birmingham to investigate families of laid-off steelworkers and determine their eligibility for relief. "All of a sudden," she recalled, "Birmingham broke on me and I just couldn't believe it. I had never been in these mill villages before. It was absolutely horrible."

By the early 1930s, unemployment rates had climbed to 60 percent in Birmingham. The Tennessee Coal and Iron Company (TCI), a subsidiary of U.S. Steel, allowed unemployed workers to stay in the company houses, but turned off the electricity and water. Republic Steel, Virginia reported, evicted families from the company houses and threatened to shoot them if they returned. Many of these workers sought shelter in "the coke ovens . . . the brick beehives where coal [was] smoked to make coke." People were starving, she recalled. "[They] were cold, they were sick, and so many children had rickets which I thought was a form of cerebral palsy . . . They couldn't walk simply because they didn't have any milk." What bothered her most was that "these poor people blamed themselves for their situation. They never said, 'We are destitute because the U.S. Steel Company doesn't treat us as well as they treat the mules.' . . . There was no wrath or indignation . . . They were full of guilt about themselves."

The desperate poverty and the callous indifference of the steel companies provided her "first ineradicable lesson on the injustice and inequalities . . . of society." This experience, along with the hardships her parents suffered, caused her to question some fundamental assumptions. "[Until then] I had been a conformist, a Southern snob. I actually thought the only people who amounted to anything were the very small group I belonged to. . . . What I learned during the depression changed all of that."[11]

For both Virginia and Cliff, the depression changed how they viewed themselves and imagined their future. They read and studied in an effort to understand the causes of the economic collapse, and their sense of social responsibility deepened. In a letter to her college friend Corliss Lamont, Virginia expressed interest in his views on socialism and said she was going to hear Socialist Party leader Norman Thomas the following week. "The depression has shown that no one group is omnipotent," she wrote, "and that when the powers and the money get concentrated in a few hands that all the rest of the people are bound to suffer. I believe we are bound to see in the next few years some startling changes."[12]

At Cliff's law firm, junior members and support staff began to bear the brunt of declining revenues. Early in 1933, the senior partner fired a number of people just as scarce relief money was drying up. Cliff protested the firings and proposed that the partners take a cut in pay in order to avoid further dismissals. His colleagues rejected the idea. It is not clear whether Cliff himself was then fired or whether he resigned, but he was soon out of a job.

In April 1933, barely a month after Franklin Roosevelt's inauguration, the Durrs sold their car and retired to a fishing cabin on a river near Clanton, Alabama, while Cliff contemplated what he would do. They had been there a week when he got word from his brother-in-law Hugo Black, who had been elected to the U.S. Senate in 1926, that the Reconstruction Finance Corporation (RFC) was seeking to hire corporation lawyers. Cliff immediately left for Washington for what he thought would be a temporary position. Virginia and their six-year-old daughter, Ann, joined him at the end of May when it became clear that his term would be indefinite.

Arriving in Washington from Birmingham, Virginia recalled, "was just like light after darkness." Until then, she remembered, "I didn't have a framework for the way I felt . . . I was almost completely apolitical." That changed dramatically in the excitement of the New Deal. Cliff worked day and night at the RFC on the reorganization of the banks, delighted at being "part of the big experiment." He was among the legion of young lawyers, economists, and social workers who flocked to Washington to "help right the wrongs that had befallen the country," as one of them put it. Virginia absorbed the energy and optimism that pulsed through Washington. It was infectious and, for her, irresistible.[13]

The Durrs settled into an old white farmhouse on Seminary Hill in Alexandria, Virginia. Though only six miles from Washington, it provided a rural retreat for their growing family and allowed Cliff to indulge his deep attachment to the land and his passion for digging and planting. Clifford Jr. was born in September 1935, followed sixteen months later by Lucy; in September 1939, Virginia gave birth to her namesake, who was called Tilla. Nine years later, Lulah was born. The Durrs were the first New Dealers to move to a community dominated by old Virginia families and teachers at the Episcopal Seminary, but Hugo and Josephine Black soon followed, and before long Seminary Hill was home to several other families who shared the Durrs' passion for Roosevelt and the New Deal. They included Massachusetts Congressman Tom Eliot and his wife Lois, economist John Kenneth Galbraith and Catherine Galbraith, and BBC Washington correspondent Charles Siepmann.

Life on Seminary Hill was pleasant enough, but Virginia longed to be a part of the wider world of Washington politics. After meeting Eleanor Roosevelt at a garden party hosted by her sister Josephine Black, she volunteered with the Women's Division of the Democratic National Committee.

Around this time, the Women's Division undertook a study on voting in the South, focusing on the poll tax as a barrier that kept many poor white Southerners from voting—particularly women. Virginia had experienced these restrictions at first hand: after she married Cliff, he had paid $15 in accumulated poll tax in order for her to vote. For a family of lesser means, such an expense was prohibitive, and it was often limited to securing the ballot for the man of the family. When the Women's Division initiated a campaign to eliminate the poll tax, Virginia recalled, she "plunged into the fight . . . with the greatest gusto." Long-gestating resentment of the restrictions that bound white Southern women had found an outlet. Instead of two days a week, she began going to the headquarters every day.[14]

Washington's social scene was also a major venue for Virginia's political development. Various circles opened to the Durrs through family connections, Cliff's work in the Roosevelt administration, and Virginia's eclectic approach to social networking. Hugo and Josephine Black introduced them to people from the upper echelons of government. Black was a powerful voice for organized labor and one of the New Deal's leading supporters in the Senate before joining the U.S. Supreme Court in 1938. Through Cliff's work with the RFC, they met Tom Corcoran and other bright lights of Roosevelt's team. Most significant, Virginia renewed her acquaintance with Clark Foreman, who worked under Harold Ickes in the Interior Department.

Virginia sought Foreman out after seeing a short profile on a "Mrs. Clark H. Foreman" in the society page of a local newspaper. She was delighted to find that Mairi Fraser Foreman was indeed the wife of her friend from college days. As Virginia and Clark became reacquainted over dinner at the Foremans' home, she was shocked to learn that he had used his new position as special advisor to Interior Secretary Harold Ickes on the Economic Status of the Negro to integrate blacks into the Roosevelt administration. Foreman was the only white administrator to employ a black secretary; he also hired Robert Weaver, a young, black, Harvard-trained economist, as his assistant and ultimate successor. Dismayed, Virginia accused him of betraying the South. Foreman, as Virginia recalled, shot back that she was just "a white, Southern, bigoted . . . provincial girl." But their association continued. "The fact that he was so enthusiastic and absolutely believing . . . had a tremendous effect on me," Virginia recalled, and on Cliff as well.[15]

Through Clark and Mairi Foreman, the Durrs met other Southern New Dealers. There were Aubrey and Anita Williams; Aubrey was Harry Hopkins's deputy assistant on the Works Progress Administration (WPA) and director of the National Youth Administration. Arthur "Tex" Goldschmidt worked with Clark in the Interior Department, and his wife, Elizabeth "Wicki" Goldschmidt, was Aubrey Williams's assistant. Newly elected Congressman Lyndon Johnson and his wife, Lady Bird, became part of their circle. This group gathered frequently, sometimes joined by folk singer Pete Seeger and Alan Lomax, who at that time was creating the Library of Congress's Archive of American Folk Song. We "got to be a community," Virginia recalled. Close friendships were formed around shared Southern roots and an abiding interest in what the New Deal meant for that benighted region. Clark Foreman, Cliff Durr, and Tex Goldschmidt were architects of the 1938 *Report on the Economic Conditions of the South*, a manifesto for reforming the South's economic and political system.

In January 1937, Virginia's personal experiences and political interests merged when the LaFollette Committee turned its spotlight on Bessemer and Birmingham, Alabama, and the anti-union practices of the Tennessee Coal, Iron and Railroad Company. Chaired by Wisconsin Senator Robert LaFollette, the Special Committee on Civil Liberties investigated and exposed the illegal and often violent tactics used by businesses and manufacturers to crush labor-organizing efforts, in direct violation of the 1935 National Labor Relations Act. Virginia, who had just given birth to Lucy, was riveted by accounts of the massive show of force that met efforts to organize workers in the mill villages she had visited just a few years earlier. She was startled to learn that most of the men named in the hearings were fathers of her childhood friends, the "leading citizens" of Birmingham. She wrote letters to all of them, she later recalled, "asking them to deny it and I can remember so well the evasions they wrote back." Each wrote back and vouched that he had nothing to do with the beating of labor organizers, but was just "trying to . . . save Birmingham from riot and revolution."[16] Virginia probed deeper. She was intrigued by testimony of one of the victims, Joseph Gelders, a former University of Alabama professor turned labor organizer, who was beaten by the head of the TCI police and left for dead. Cliff had gone to the University of Alabama with Gelders, and Virginia knew his younger brother. She wrote to Gelders and arranged to meet him during her next visit home to Birmingham.

Virginia was instantly attracted to Joe Gelders, a tall, slender man who impressed her as a person of "total integrity." She met with Joe and his wife Esther in a park near his office because Gelders was certain that his office was under surveillance. "There was such a contrast between 'riot and revolution' and Joe and Esther," she later recalled, "whom I thought were the kindest and sweetest people I ever met . . . I suppose meeting Joe was the one event that really changed my life." She was fascinated by the story of his journey from apolitical physics professor at the University of Alabama to labor and human rights activist. Like her, Gelders had been deeply disturbed by the abject poverty he witnessed during the depression and wanted to understand its causes. He studied economics, ultimately finding the most convincing explanation in Karl Marx's analysis of capitalism. Gelders soon became affiliated with the Communist Party and investigated and exposed the violent repression and often illegal arrests of labor organizers. Undeterred by the terrible beating he had suffered, he continued his work in the South. He was, Virginia recalled, "prepared to give his life . . . he was struggling, trying to get something accomplished." The two developed a deep and enduring friendship.[17]

In the spring of 1938, tragedy struck the Durr family. At two and a half years of age, Cliff Jr. died. He had become ill with a stomachache and the family pediatrician failed to diagnose appendicitis. Cliff and Virginia finally took him to the hospital. The doctors operated, but it was too late; his appendix had already ruptured. In the days before penicillin, there was no way to contain the infection. Ann, who was just eleven, remembered that her parents were "absolutely devastated" by young Cliff's senseless death. They spent hours alone in their room. Virginia hardly ever spoke of her loss. In the following months, she began attending the LaFollette Committee hearings and became more deeply immersed in politics. "Staying at home was so painful for me," she recalled. The hearings helped "to take my mind off my little boy's death, at least during the day."[18]

Virginia became enthralled by the LaFollette Committee's continuing investigation and was soon traveling into Washington every day to attend the hearings. "That was where I got my education," she later explained. For most of the summer, the committee focused on the efforts of the Steel Workers Organizing Committee to establish unions in major steel-producing areas in Ohio, Pennsylvania, and Michigan. Witnesses told how Republic Steel officials mobilized public and private resources to crush the strikes, precipitating what historian Jerold Auerbach described as "one of the bloodiest and costliest conflicts" in American labor history. Accumulated testimony offered stark evidence of the ways in which powerful interests used the cloak of "law and order" and charges of communism to justify a wholesale assault on union organizers and their supporters. For Virginia, the hearings provided a concentrated course of instruction on the economic and political relationships at the core of the struggle around the New Deal. They also introduced her to a radical group of New Dealers and labor activists. Throughout the summer, she frequently lunched with members of the committee's staff: Charles Kramer, Robert Lamb, John Abt, Luke Wilson, and others—brilliant young lawyers. Some were members of the Communist Party and some were not—but all were staunch advocates of the labor movement.[19]

That same summer, Joe Gelders and Congress of Industrial Organizations (CIO) publicist Lucy Randolph Mason sought Virginia's assistance in organizing a conference to rally Southern support for the right of workers to organize and to promote the expansion of political democracy in the region. Virginia advised Gelders and Mason to contact Cliff, Clark Foreman, and other Washington-based Southerners who had prepared the *Report on the Economic Conditions of the South*. Issued that spring, the report was part of Franklin Roosevelt's effort to mobilize liberal voters in the South and "purge" anti–New Deal Democrats during the 1938 primary elections. Virginia agreed to do a study of Southern press coverage of the La Follette hearings in preparation for their meeting. It was a sobering introduction to how the media distorted, misrepresented, or simply ignored the labor struggle in the South. She also wrote a report on the poll tax. In five years, Virginia's ideas about the South had changed dramatically. She joined with a small band of fellow Southerners in one of the most ambitious efforts ever to confront the region's repressive economic and political systems.

Over Thanksgiving weekend in 1938, the streams of Virginia's political life came together in her hometown of Birmingham at the conference that resulted from Gelders's and Mason's efforts. Eleanor and Franklin Roosevelt endorsed the gathering, which was organized with the help of Clark Foreman. The *Report on the Economic Conditions of the South* guided the group's deliberations. Labor organizers, WPA workers, state and federal government officials, members of Congress, newspaper editors, students, and business executives were among the 1,200 people who gathered in Birmingham's Municipal Auditorium; more than two hundred black people attended. Among the participants were Eleanor Roosevelt, Mary McLeod Bethune—a noted black educator and head of FDR's "Black Cabinet"—and Supreme Court Justice Hugo Black. It was a vibrant expression of support for the New Deal by the many constituencies that had benefited from its expansive approach to government, just as conservative Southern Democrats were mounting opposition to Roosevelt's reforms. For Virginia, it was "a wonderful sort of love feast because it was the first time that all the various elements from the South had gotten together. And we were not segregated."

Conference organizers did not intend to make an issue out of segregation; a few non-segregated meetings had been held in the Municipal Auditorium before. On the second day of the four-day meeting, however, Police Commissioner Eugene "Bull" Connor informed the gathering that he would enforce an ordinance barring integrated meetings or he would shut down the meeting. Not wanting to disband, the organizers of the conference agreed to comply with the order. The auditorium was divided in half, with blacks on one side and whites on the other. When Eleanor Roosevelt returned to the meeting hall, she sat down with the black participants. A police officer informed the First Lady that she could not sit in the "colored" section; it was against the law. In response, Roosevelt took her chair and placed it in the middle of the aisle separating the two groups. It was a powerful gesture. The organizers of what became the founding convention of the Southern Conference for Human Welfare (SCHW) vowed that all future meetings would be integrated. This caused many of the initial supporters—businessmen, elected officials, and segregationist liberals—to fall away, but the Roosevelts remained committed to the Southern Conference, and Eleanor Roosevelt gave it her active support.[20]

Virginia attended the Birmingham meeting as a representative of the Women's Division of the Democratic National Committee. For her, the gathering represented the spirit of the New Deal and filled her with optimism. But her mood was tempered by the response of her closest friends in Birmingham, who were bitterly opposed to Roosevelt. The disturbance over segregation at the meeting confirmed their fears that racial equality was a part of the president's agenda. They dismissed her efforts to defend the New Deal. People she had known since childhood labeled her "an outright traitor, an outlaw. It was very painful for me to see all of my friends against me," she recalled, "but I never had a moment's doubt of where I stood."[21]

The SCHW became a major venue for Virginia's political activism over the next decade and for her subsequent participation in the civil rights movement. By 1938, Virginia's thinking about race had changed. She could not point to any one event or incident that marked her transformation from a segregationist to an opponent of segregation: "Just by osmosis, mainly," she later explained. In Washington she met African Americans socially at dinners hosted by the Foremans and through her work on the antipoll tax fight, which brought her into contact with Mary McLeod Bethune. Bethune in turn introduced Virginia to Charles Houston and William Hastie, NAACP lawyers who were leading the fight for black voting rights in the South. Virginia's personal experience gave the lie to the beliefs about black inferiority that had been part of her upbringing. This conviction reinforced her involvement in the movement to democratize Southern politics, for she quickly realized that black Southerners were critical allies in this effort.[22]

Initially the SCHW's executive council voted to concentrate the organization's minimal resources on a campaign to abolish the poll tax. They established a committee on civil rights to carry it forward, with Joe Gelders as executive secretary and Virginia Durr as chair. As a result of their efforts, California's Democratic Congressman Lee Geyers introduced legislation that would ban the poll tax in federal elections. Although the bill never made it out of the House Judiciary Committee, it was the first shot in what would be a nearly three-decades-long battle to break down voting restrictions in the South. Conservative Southern Democrats responded in kind. "All hell broke loose," Virginia recalled, when Geyers introduced his bill in

October 1939. Powerful Southern conservatives viewed any federal tampering with voter restrictions as the beginning of the end. Democratic National Committee head James Farley immediately ordered the Women's Division to stop all work on the poll tax issue. Virginia left the Division in protest and began working full time in Geyers's congressional office, while Gelders divided his time between Washington and fieldwork in the South until enlisting in the army in 1941.

Virginia Durr emerged as one of the most effective organizers of the anti-poll tax movement. Working through her growing network of contacts in the labor movement and in Washington, she and Gelders built a broad coalition of support for legislation, and in 1941 a bill passed the House, only to be blocked by a filibuster in the Senate led by Southern Democrats. Virginia developed a close working relationship with Eleanor Roosevelt and consulted with the First Lady at the White House on political strategies, particularly on their efforts to get a Southern sponsor for the legislation. Through Roosevelt's intercession, Senator Claude Pepper of Florida agreed to cosponsor the bill in the Senate. During these early efforts, Virginia met C. Vann Woodward, then a young professor of Southern history at the University of Florida. Woodward's recently published book, *Tom Watson: Agrarian Rebel*, had become a handbook for Southern New Dealers eager to learn from the experience of the biracial Populist movement of the 1890s. After enlisting Woodward's help in the publicity campaign, she wrote him confidently: "I have an invincible belief that if the right people ever get together something is bound to happen."[23] This remained a guiding principle.

In 1941, the National Committee to Abolish the Poll Tax (NCAPT) replaced the SCHW's Civil Rights Committee and served as a clearinghouse and center for anti-poll tax activity. Durr was its sole staff member and continued to work as an unpaid volunteer. The NAACP was prominent among the NCAPT's allies, lending legal talent and lobbying support to the campaign. Other major supporters included the AFL and the CIO, as well as national civic associations, women's organizations, and religious groups. Durr had a knack for enlisting other volunteers to aid in a very low-budget operation. Young congressional staffers—led by Palmer Weber, a recent graduate of the University of Virginia—volunteered to work after hours for the NCAPT, and college students showed up to stuff envelopes and run the mimeograph machine. As a student volunteer put it, the poll tax fight was *the* issue among politically active students she knew then; it represented "the crying inconsistency in the country . . . it was just natural for Antioch students in Washington to go to the poll tax office."[24]

The crusade against the poll tax gave full rein to Virginia's talents. A tall, striking woman with a loud, clear voice and an easy laugh, she seemed to command a room effortlessly. Virginia could easily play the part of the Southern belle with her gracious manner and flirtatious blue eyes, but she had a penetrating mind and a disarming directness. British-born writer Jessica Mitford first met Virginia at a breakfast in Washington in 1939. The woman in the huge white hat, Mitford recalled, "spoke in a soft scream happily devoid of the slight whine I had come to associate with Southern voices." Virginia introduced herself to Mitford and "as soon as she learned I was English she fired question after question at me"—about Neville Chamberlain, the appeasing prime minister, about English country life ("what in the world did you *do* all day long"), and about Jane Austen, one of her favorite authors. "Mrs. Durr made me feel outnumbered, as though I were being cornered by a roomful of reporters." Mitford found that Virginia applied her "direct-question method to all without discrimination, no matter how delicate the subject." And few resisted. "She was a real spellbinder," Mitford wrote, "whose peculiar charm lay in her enormous curiosity about people, her driving passion to find things out, to know about the details and the motives, to trace big events to their small human beginnings."[25]

Virginia loved entertaining and, as Marge Frantz recalled, she was "the bee everyone gathered around." Friends and political allies, old and new, would come together at the Durrs' home on Sunday afternoons. The fare was simple; Virginia "put on meals, she didn't cook." It was the conversation and interesting combinations of guests that drew people. Mitford, a frequent participant, described the "the kaleidoscopic mix of people" that turned up each week and included "judicial dignitaries, Southern legislators—who Virginia was forever trying to proselytize for the anti–poll tax cause—New Deal functionaries, earnest young radicals." Lyndon and Lady Bird Johnson were among the regulars. Mitford recalled a particularly memorable scene of the Johnsons and the Durrs relaxing barefoot on the lawn and "chinning" away in what to this young Englishwoman was "their near incomprehensible patois about the ins and outs of Southern politics."[26]

The initial meeting between Virginia and Jessica Mitford blossomed into a lifelong friendship and a political camaraderie fueled by a constant exchange of ideas, even when separated by long distances, as they later would be. Virginia was enchanted with "Decca" (as Mitford was called) and her husband, Esmond Romilly. They were an enormously attractive young couple, the first English people Virginia had ever known, and passionate about life and politics. Romilly had recently returned from fighting with the Loyalists in Spain. Mitford, a leftist who rejected her family's fascist proclivities, was the renegade daughter of Lord and Lady Redesdale. Decca and Esmond, Virginia later wrote, "came into my life at a time when I was sinking under the strain of family troubles and feeling I was to blame." She told Decca, "You and Esmond not only cheered me up but you made me realize that my new found ideas were *not* so terrible after all, not only that you made me feel there was a new world [in the] making and I was not caught forever in melancholy and failure and pretense and 'Southern tradition.'"[27]

In the summer of 1940, Esmond went off to join the Canadian Air Force to fight Hitler, and Decca moved in with the Durrs temporarily. Their daughter, Constancia Romilly, was born that fall. She had already been nicknamed Dinky Donk after the symbol of the Democratic Party during the adventures of Virginia and the pregnant Decca at the 1940 Democratic national convention. The following November, Esmond's plane was shot down over the North Sea. Decca and "the Donk" remained a part of the Durr household for nearly three years.

The pull of politics and the urgency of the anti–poll tax fight competed with the demands of domestic life and a growing family. Neighbor Catherine "Kitty" Galbraith wryly observed, "a compulsive housekeeper and over-solicitous mother she was not." Stories about Virginia were legendary among her friends, such as the time when Vice President Henry Wallace announced that he was coming out to see a bedridden Cliff Durr, and Virginia hurriedly pulled out the vacuum and cleared a path from the front door upstairs to their bedroom. Virginia's children were often left in the care of others—either her mother, who came to stay with the family for an extended period, or the housekeeper; eldest daughter Ann also bore increasing responsibility.[28]

Virginia's daughters remember their mother as an active if not constant presence in their early lives. Most of the neighbors sent their children to private school, but Virginia was a firm believer in public education and was actively involved in the Lee Jackson School, which Lucy and Tilla attended in the 1940s. As head of the Parent Teacher Association, Virginia led the effort to get a cafeteria and play equipment for the schoolyard. The girls had piano lessons and took ballet, with Virginia driving them to and fro. She often read to them, sharing her love of writers like Louisa May Alcott and Charles Dickens. Children were very much a part of the Durr household and not shunted off during parties or other social gatherings. "We roamed freely," Lucy recalled. The vast variety of people coming and going, Tilla said, "made me feel included in the whole world." Still, they craved their mother's attention. One of Lucy and Tilla's fondest childhood memories was of a bout of scarlet fever when they were quarantined with their mother for a week or more. "It was just great because she couldn't leave and we had her all to ourselves."[29]

A woman of boundless energy, Virginia worked to balance the many demands on her time and attention, but politics in the service of changing the South was her passion. It engaged her keen intellect while providing an outlet for her restless spirit and insatiable social appetite. During the war years, as the anti–poll tax bill and other liberal legislative efforts stalled, her activities extended beyond Capitol Hill. Starting in 1944, the SCHW expanded its program to include local and state affiliates around the South. As chair of the group's Washington committee, Virginia participated in efforts to desegregate public facilities in the nation's capital. She also joined the Arlington, Virginia, branch of the NAACP and served as cochair of the SCHW's Committee for Virginia with Luther Porter Jackson, a professor at Virginia State College, a black college in Petersburg. Jackson was also director of the Virginia Voter's League, the statewide black voting rights organization. In a state where less than 12 percent of eligible voters were registered, the Virginia committee worked with labor unions, local NAACP chapters, and other civic groups to promote voter registration and organize coalitions of black and white Southerners around a program of progressive political action.

In many ways, Cliff and Virginia were a study in contrasts. He was conservative by nature, quiet and deliberate, and she, as Jessica Mitford put it, was "one of nature's rebels." But their political beliefs and values developed in tandem. Cliff, like Virginia, was greatly influenced by his experiences in Washington. Although he had never imagined a career in public service, his opportunities within the Roosevelt administration and his participation in the broader social life of New Deal Washington nurtured his transformation from corporate lawyer to active proponent of the public interest and stalwart defender of civil liberties. Cliff's brother-in-law Hugo Black and new friends like Clark Foreman and Aubrey Williams had an important influence on him. As biographer John Salmond writes, "They took him far from the world of banks and stocks into the world of people, of social programs, and of social possibility."[30]

Cliff's distinguished career with the Reconstruction Finance Corporation was capped by his critical role as an architect of the financial and industrial plan that prepared America for entry into World War II. In 1941, President Roosevelt appointed Durr to the Federal Communications Commission (FCC), where he became a pioneer in the development of public radio and television. With the advent of television and a trend toward monopolization, Cliff fought to hold the power of commercial broadcasters in check and to secure greater public control of the airwaves. He promoted the broad educational possibilities of the newly available frequency modulation (FM) and was largely responsible for securing 15 percent of FM frequencies for educational purposes. Through his initiative and largely under his direction, the FCC established clear standards for program balance and diversity by which applicants for radio licenses and renewals would be measured, outlined in the report *Public Service Responsibility of Broadcast Licensees* (also known as "the Blue Book").[31]

Early in his tenure at the FCC, Cliff encountered the shadowy politics of loyalty when he was assigned to oversee an internal investigation of Goodwin Watson, a Columbia Teachers College social psychologist recently hired by the FCC. Democratic Congressman Martin Dies of Texas, chair of the House Un-American Activities Committee (HUAC), charged Watson with being a Communist or a Communist sympathizer. Under Dies, HUAC became a vehicle for Republicans and Southern Democrats to discredit New Deal reforms by hunting for subversives in the Roosevelt administration and the labor movement. Cliff's investigation revealed that the charges against Watson had no basis in fact, and the FCC voted to retain him on the staff. Conservative House members responded by tacking a rider onto an appropriations bill that barred the payment of Watson's salary. Cliff successfully lobbied the Senate to strike the rider. But before the Watson case was settled, Cliff became the subject of an FBI investigation himself. According to J. Edgar Hoover, the FBI had received a complaint about Durr—anonymous, of course, but likely filed by a member of the House Un-American Activities Committee.

Several years later, Cliff confronted the FBI head on. In the summer of 1946, a group in Hollywood applied for a license to operate a commercial station. What appeared to be a routine procedure stalled when FBI director Hoover informed the chairman that he had found that "the majority of these individuals are members of the Communist Party or have affiliated themselves with the activity of the Communist movement." Hoover complied with FCC acting chairman Paul Walker's request that he provide material relevant to the review of the group's application, with the proviso that it be kept confidential. The information, drawn entirely from unidentified sources, listed memberships held and alleged statements made by several of the applicants, but it offered no evidence of Communist Party affiliation or subversive activity. Pursuing its own investigation, the FCC failed to find any information that would justify denying the group a license, yet, fearful of offending the FBI, the Commission decided not to act on the application.

Cliff publicly expressed his opposition. Speaking to the National Association of Educational Broadcasters in October 1947, he departed from his prepared text to attack HUAC, then in the middle of a highly publicized investigation of communism in the film industry. But at least HUAC operated in public view, he noted, and was subject to some scrutiny. "The hidden activities of our military organizations and of the FBI," however, were far more dangerous, and he warned that broadcasters themselves were vulnerable. He revealed that the FBI was already "furnishing unsolicited reports on individuals connected with radio and I can assure you that if you should be told the kinds of things contained in many of these reports you would dismiss the information as baseless gossip."

Columnist Marquis Child was one of the few who praised Cliff for challenging the climate of fear that was enveloping the country. His colleagues on the FCC, however, quickly disassociated themselves from Cliff's statement; in a public letter to Hoover, they assured the FBI director that they welcomed any information he thought would be of interest to them. Commenting on his colleagues' letter, Cliff agreed that the FCC should invite information that assisted it in discharging its duties, but he insisted that its decisions must be based "on substantiated, relevant facts, and not on rumor." Furthermore, Durr maintained that the FCC could not deny a license to anyone except after a public hearing, which meant that evidence must be given on the record and under oath, not by nameless informers.[32]

As Cliff fought the politics of loyalty within government, Virginia became embroiled in the battles that divided liberal and progressive groups with increasing frequency during the 1940s. Liberal anticommunism grew out of factional struggles among labor unions and liberal groups that heightened in the late 1930s. In part, this was a response to the American Communist Party's support of the 1939 Nazi-Soviet pact; it also served as a way to appease the "red-hunting" sponsored by HUAC and the FBI. In 1940, the American Civil Liberties Union (ACLU) adopted a resolution that effectively barred Communists from its board and staff, leading to the expulsion of founding member Elizabeth Gurly Flynn. Several members of the SCHW pressed that organization to adopt a similar policy, but the majority on the board refused, contending that "a red-baiting, negative, undemocratic policy" would undermine the organization in its effort to expand democracy in the region. Such a blanket policy, as civil rights lawyer Charles Houston argued, also ignored the fact that members of the Communist Party had been in the forefront of civil rights and labor organizing efforts in the South. Regardless of the varying motives that caused people to join the anticommunist crusade, Virginia believed that it reinforced "a unified and coordinated effort . . . to simply liquidate the small gains that the New Deal had made on the grounds of communism," and she opposed any compromises with it.[33]

After Winston Churchill's famous "Iron Curtain" speech in March 1946 marked the start of the Cold War, Harvard historian Arthur Schlesinger, Jr., a founder of the Union for Democratic Action in 1941, helped launch the postwar drive to rally liberals to the anticommunist cause with a widely publicized article in *Life* magazine. Schlesinger warned that Communists were a corrupting force in the body politic, spreading "their infection of intrigue and deceit" wherever they went. He described the patterns of infiltration—in labor unions, Hollywood, and government, from the Truman administration to congressional offices and staffs, and he warned that the party "was sinking its tentacles into the NAACP." Whether the Communist

Party posed "a fifth column threat" to the United States, Schlesinger could not say for sure; that, he wrote, was a matter best left in "the competent hands of the FBI." Several months later, Schlesinger was among the founders of Americans for Democratic Action (ADA), an expanded version of the Union for Democratic Action. The ADA proposed to lead in building a new liberal coalition free of the taint of communism.[34]

The drive to root communists out of American life became a national crusade early in the spring of 1947, when President Harry Truman issued an executive order establishing a loyalty security program. The order aimed to mobilize the public behind the recently issued Truman Doctrine, committing the United States to containing the spread of communism abroad. It was also designed to defuse the growing potency of anticommunism as a Republican tool. Truman's program called for a sweeping investigation of all federal employees and targeted as a security risk anyone associated with the Communist Party. Such associations were broadly defined to include "membership in, affiliation with, or sympathetic association with any foreign or domestic association, group, or combination of persons," designated by the attorney general as totalitarian, fascist, communist or subversive. Here, wrote historian Henry Steele Commager, was "guilt by association with a vengeance."[35]

Cliff Durr dissented from the administration's policy. He argued that the loyalty program would impair the national security it was devised to safeguard. By focusing on attitudes and associations rather than on wrongful behavior, by relying on nameless accusers, and by giving the FBI power over government employees, the program was fraught with "potentialities of injustice, oppression, and cruelty." It was likely to confuse conformity with loyalty. At a time when "new and unorthodox ideas were desperately needed to cope with new and unorthodox problems, the federal loyalty program tended to force all social, economic, and political thinking into orthodox patterns." Although confidence in the government was of vital importance, the order tended to destroy confidence by implying that the government could not be trusted because there were subversives in its ranks. Whatever good the loyalty program was designed to advance, Cliff believed, was far outweighed by the evils inherent in its conception. He refused to cooperate with its implementation within the FCC.[36]

As the Cold War escalated, the SCHW became a major target of efforts to enforce a strict anticommunist line. In a bitter battle, Virginia led in defeating a move to oust suspected Communist Party members from her state committee. She explained: "My position on the Communists is as it has always been—that they represent the extreme left of the political circuit, and I often disagree with their programs and methods. But I see so clearly that when one group of people is made untouchable the liberties of all suffer, and our Democracy is on the way to ruin. I see and feel so clearly how it has crippled the lives and hopes of both the Negro and white people of the South." The SCHW continued to maintain a non-exclusionary policy that left membership open to all who supported and worked toward the goals of the organization. In May 1947, on the eve of a rally the SCHW sponsored for former Vice President Henry Wallace, HUAC issued a report charging that the SCHW was "perhaps the most deviously camouflaged communist front organization" in the country, whose sole purpose was to serve the aims of the Soviet Union.[37]

Henry Wallace was a leading critic of Truman's Cold War policies. His demonstrated commitment to racial equality also distinguished him among national political leaders. Through his exposure to the South as secretary of agriculture, the Iowa-born agrarian developed an interest in racial issues and brought a commitment to civil rights and racial justice to his vision for democratic reform. As vice president, he articulated an uncompromising program for political and economic democracy regardless of race, color, or gender. His bold challenge to the power of conservative Southern Democrats ultimately cost him his place on the Democratic Party ticket in 1944. In 1947, Virginia Durr, Clark Foreman, and other SCHW leaders arranged several tours through the South for Wallace as part of a national effort to challenge Truman's policies, and also to test Wallace's viability as a presidential candidate.

After Wallace announced his candidacy for president on the Progressive Party ticket in December 1947, leaders of the SCHW joined with labor and civil rights activists to organize support for him in the South. Palmer Weber, then working with the CIO Political Action Committee, and Louis Burnham of the Southern Negro Youth Congress codirected Wallace's Southern campaign, building on the inroads made in the region during the previous decade by labor and civil rights groups. It was organized around domestic issues, including a revival and expansion of New Deal-style programs, abolition of the poll tax and unrestricted access to the ballot, labor rights, and an end to racial segregation. Wallace took several tours of the South, challenging segregation from Virginia to Mississippi, resulting at times in violent confrontations that captured national headlines. Both black and white candidates ran for office on the Progressive Party ticket in most Southern states. Virginia Durr served as state chairperson of the Virginia Progressive Party and ran for the U.S. Senate on the Progressive Party ticket in Virginia, challenging Harry F. Byrd.[38]

Her candidacy and that of the four Progressive Party candidates running for Congress in Virginia attracted local attention to Wallace's presidential campaign, while also challenging the dominance of Harry Byrd's machine in state politics and bringing critical local issues to the fore. This was Virginia Durr's only campaign for public office, and it provided her with a platform to speak freely on the issues that concerned her. During this time, she was serving as president of the Northern Virginia PTA, and a major focus of her campaign was the abysmal state of Virginia's public school system, which ranked behind every Southern state, save Kentucky, in support for public schools. She spoke mostly before small community forums and in black churches. Reporting on Virginia's active schedule of campaigning, Cliff observed to their daughter Ann: "I suspect you realize that your mother is a rather exceptional person, with a first class mind and more than one person's share of guts. And she has faith!" After a campaign that was either ignored by the mainstream press or smeared as communist-inspired, Virginia won nearly 6,000 votes, twice as many as Wallace tallied in the state.[39]

Despite Virginia's role in the Wallace campaign, Truman offered Cliff a second term on the FCC in the spring of 1948 and enlisted Hugo Black in an effort to persuade Cliff to accept. He declined, explaining to the president that he could not remain part of an administration committed to the loyalty program. Cliff had been considering leaving the FCC since 1947. Increasingly isolated on the commission, he doubted that he could accomplish much if he remained. In recent years, Cliff had received inquiries from several universities interested in hiring him, and his hope was to secure a teaching position.

Shortly after Cliff left the FCC, he and Virginia traveled to Europe under the sponsorship of the One World Committee, an organization established in memory of Wendell Willkie, the 1940 Republican candidate for president. Cliff was among a handful of people the committee selected as representing Willkie's internationalist ideas. Others included Albert Einstein, former Justice Department lawyer O. John Rogge, and broadcaster Norman Corwin. Einstein sent his good friend, the economist Otto Nathan, in his place. It was Virginia's first trip out of the United States. Their travels abroad confirmed the Durrs' skepticism about the direction of American foreign policy. A peace conference in Poland was the group's primary destination. There they had opportunities to talk with Poles about the horrors of the war experience and the extermination camps, and they viewed the devastation and destruction at first hand. The group heard criticism of the Soviet domination of Poland, but this was surpassed by the rampant fear of the United States and its policy of rearming the Germans as a bulwark against the Soviet Union. Afterward, the Durrs traveled to Prague, Rome, and Paris, and there too they became aware of the resentments and fears generated by the United States' aggressive ratcheting up of tension with the Soviet Union.[40]

Cliff returned to an uncertain future. He contacted Princeton University and several other institutions that had tried to recruit him less than a year earlier, but no offers were forthcoming. By 1948, his public opposition to the practices of the FBI and HUAC had marked him as a target of suspicion, and in the charged atmosphere of the Cold War, this deterred universities that had once been eager to hire him. With no alternatives, Cliff opened a law office in Washington. He took loyalty cases regardless of the ability of his clients to pay; most of those accused had already lost their jobs. To take such a case, Cliff said, "was simply part of the responsibility of being a lawyer." He was also one of the few lawyers in Washington who would represent former Communists who were unrepentant, like his client Frank Oppenheimer, physicist and brother of Robert Oppenheimer, who headed the wartime Manhattan Project that produced the atom bomb.[41]

In 1949, Cliff became president of the National Lawyers Guild, an organization founded by New Deal liberals and radicals ten years earlier as an alternative to the conservative American Bar Association. For Cliff, the Guild provided an institutional base for continuing his challenge to the activities of the FBI and the excesses of the loyalty-security program. Under Cliff's leadership, the Lawyers Guild undertook an investigation of the illegal practices used by the FBI in the case of a former Justice Department employee and documented the Bureau's policy of targeting individuals purely because of their political opinions. The day before the Guild released its report, California Congressman Richard Nixon, acting with information obtained from the FBI's surveillance of the Guild, launched an attack on the Lawyers Guild, charging that it was a tool of the Communist Party and calling for a HUAC investigation of the organization. Starting around this time, the FBI put Cliff under surveillance. That surveillance would continue for nearly twenty years.[42]

Cliff had no shortage of clients, but his law practice could not support his family, and he saw no future for himself in Washington. He acknowledged in a letter to his daughter Ann that "independence of mind can be an expensive luxury. Unhappily," he conceded, "I am so constituted that I regard it as a necessity."[43] By March 1950, with debts mounting, the Durrs reluctantly sold their house on Seminary Hill, and Cliff began to seek opportunities beyond Washington. To Virginia's great relief, he obtained the position of general counsel with the National Farmers Union in Denver, and the family moved to Colorado in June.

Commenting on the vast Western landscape, Virginia admitted that she was much more "at home in the world of people than . . . in the world of Nature." Still, she was grateful that Cliff had a job, and they had a place to live. The family settled in a modest house that she described as "a fine refuge from the storm." Cliff, who had long suffered from back problems, underwent surgery to repair a ruptured disc shortly after they arrived, which left him in a cast from his shoulders to his knees and bedridden for a month. Virginia swore off any kind of political activity until they got established, resigning herself to domesticity. "Time seems so long out here," she wrote Mairi Foreman. She wondered if she would ever "be able to do anything but wash, iron, cook, and nurse."[44]

Careful not to jeopardize Cliff's position, Virginia held her political impulses in check and avoided public activity. Through her correspondence, she carried on an extensive debate with Clark Foreman about America's role in the Korean War, disagreeing with Foreman's support of U.S. intervention there. When she received a postcard signed by the noted chemist and peace activist Linus Pauling, she thought nothing of responding by adding her name to a petition opposing the escalation of the war. Within weeks, however, the right-wing *Denver Post* headlined a story "Wife of General Counsel of Farmers Union Insurance Corporation Signs Red Petition," placing Virginia in the position she had tried so hard to avoid.

Virginia's innocent signature became ammunition in the paper's effort to smear the National Farmers Union. James Patton, Farmers Union director, was desperate to appease his critics. He demanded that Virginia publicly withdraw her support of the American Peace Crusade, sponsor of the petition. That she was willing to do. He also insisted that she repudiate the organization and its leaders. She would not agree to that. Describing the ordeal to Clark and Mairi Foreman, she wrote "To live today you have to compromise so much, but to save yourself by throwing other people to the wolves seems to me to be the one really heinous crime."[45] Her husband would not have let her sign such a statement even if she had considered it, she noted. Cliff then resigned from his position.

The prospect of further "decisions and moving and adjusting" was more than Virginia could contemplate. She admitted to the Foremans that she longed "for my remembered surroundings," a place where "I will hear the sound of rain again . . . my hair will curl again, and I won't wake up gasping for breath." Besides, she wondered, "where is it any better as far as the political and spiritual climate today?" After a brief visit in Washington for Ann's wedding to Walter Lyon in May 1951, Virginia, Cliff, and their three daughters returned to Alabama, to the home of Cliff's mother in Montgomery.

Exhausted from the battles of the past several years, Virginia initially found some comfort in being back in the South. She and Cliff were absorbed by the immediate challenges of making a living and getting settled in the community. After their experience in Denver, she knew that she must avoid public activity for the time being. Their dependence on Cliff's family, all staunch segregationists, and the lack of sympathetic companionship wore away at her normally resilient spirit. She became consumed by a sense of loss and isolation, comparing her life in the cradle of the Confederacy to "living in a closed room, simply struggling for air."

Virginia fought loneliness through an outpouring of letters to friends from New Deal days. Hungry for news, she wrote nearly every day and often answered letters immediately to hasten a response. The correspondence connected her to a world beyond the confines of Montgomery and enabled her to sustain the friendships, political engagement, and constant dialogue that had been at the core of her life in Washington. Here she could speak freely about the place she had come home to. She described the painful adjustments to life in the Deep South as she struggled to understand it and searched for signs of change. Her letters became her lifeline—her air.

Time and place conspired to broaden the context of Virginia's meditations on the South. With the start of the Montgomery bus boycott in 1955, she was writing from the front lines of the civil rights movement. Through her letters, she created a rich account of life in Alabama from the last days of segregation through the tumultuous years of the late 1950s and the 1960s. She brought a rare insight to this era, sharpened by her marginal status. While she acknowledged her roots in the South, she completely rejected the racial premises of white Southern society. Her allegiances were with the plight and struggles of black Southerners. She developed friendships with several black women and men in Montgomery, but social interactions were limited by rigid racial boundaries. Blacks had an extensive network of organizations, clubs, and churches that supported a rich social life, and there was little common ground for interracial socializing. Virginia lived on the borders of both communities. As she often explained, her burning desire to end segregation in the South was driven by her longing to feel at home there.

Virginia brought a longer view to the events of the 1950s and 1960s than did most contemporary civil rights activists. Her experiences during the 1930s and 1940s shaped her approach to race and civil rights. She recognized elements of fascism in the white supremacist ideology and the state-sanctioned violence and police terror that supported the segregation system. Though acknowledging that there would be other battles to fight, Virginia believed federal protection of voting rights was critical to restoring democracy and the rule of law in the South. She shared the view that racial discrimination was primarily a function of economic exploitation, and that core issues of economic inequality and injustice could be effectively met only by interracial political alliances. Her experience in the New Deal era had demonstrated that this was possible, but it also underscored the difficulty of overcoming the deep racial divisions and prejudices that structured American life.

Written from the jagged edge of daily experience, Virginia's letters contradict the inevitability that is so often attributed to the civil rights movement. Like a Civil War diary, they capture the fragile nature, halting progress, and great drama of a movement that changed the South and the nation. The total collapse of law and order in the South after the Supreme Court's decision in *Brown v. Board of Education* is vividly portrayed here as a conspiracy that united all branches of government in Alabama and other Deep South states. The reign of "the lawless law," as Virginia fittingly described it, was accommodated by a reticent federal government that failed to register significant involvement with the Southern scene until after the 1961 Freedom Rides. She touted the student protests of the 1960s as the best thing that happened to the South since the 1930s; her home became a way station for young people traveling in the Deep South. Virginia's perspective on the nature of the struggle and the limits of change steadily evolved in response to a shifting political landscape which, by the mid-1960s, was punctuated by the rise of George Wallace, the growing appeal of Black Power, and Lyndon Johnson's descent into Vietnam.

The bulk of Virginia Durr's correspondence was with her closest friends, most notably Clark Foreman and Jessica Mitford. Other friends she corresponded with included Marge Frantz (the daughter of Joe Gelders) and Anne Braden. These letters convey Virginia's voracious appetite for news about friends and their families and are expressions of the deep bonds of friendship that she tended with devotion. She roams freely, discussing children, mutual friends, aging, and all kinds of personal matters, mixed with observations and commentary on the local scene, the latest outrage, and her family's ongoing struggle to survive in Montgomery, along with appeals and suggestions of how Northern friends might aid the movement. Often the letters go on for two or three typed pages, single-spaced. Anne Braden recalled how she and Jessica Mitford were amused that Virginia would type to the very bottom of the page, and then when there was no space left, abruptly sign off, "Love, Va." The arrival of one of her letters at the Foreman household was cause for excitement, Shelagh Foreman recalled. Out in California, Marge Frantz and Jessica Mitford would swap the latest missives they received from Alabama.

Virginia's friends saved her letters, and many of them have been archived at the Radcliffe Institute's Arthur and Elizabeth Schlesinger Library at Harvard University. Unfortunately, Virginia was not their match as a letter-saver. Walter Lyon, her son-in-law, once retrieved a letter from Lyndon Johnson from the wastepaper basket—a letter in which Johnson acknowledged the Durrs' influence on his commitment to civil rights.[46] This book, therefore, is drawn exclusively from Virginia's writings, with some notation of other correspondence when available. Such an approach, however, works well for a book of this kind. Virginia's letter-writing also served as a form of journal-keeping and provides a stream of thought that fashions a narrative about a particular place and time.

Virginia was at once intrigued and repelled by the contours of race relations in this Deep South city, but she resigned herself to the sidelines. "Even in a battle the wounded are entitled some rest," and for the time being, she acknowledged, "our ammunition has plumb run out."[3] Her attention was absorbed by the needs of her family and a desperate desire to restore order and security to their lives. While Cliff spent most of the summer of 1951 in bed completing the recovery from his back surgery, Virginia tended to the needs of their daughters—Lulah, age four, Tilla, several months shy of twelve, and Lucy, fourteen—and prepared herself for a wage-earning job. She enrolled in the local business school to learn typing and shorthand. Commenting on her adjustment to life in Alabama, Virginia wrote a friend from New Deal days: "For the time being my 'public' life is at an end. I resigned from everything I belonged to and haven't joined anything else, and my one great desire now is to get to be a first-class secretary and not have to do my letters over."[4]

Getting established in Montgomery proved challenging. Virginia confided to her daughter Ann, "We feel so out of touch with the community." Cliff worked to get acquainted with life in Montgomery. He taught a class at the University Extension School in an effort "to find out what people are thinking about," but Virginia reported, "there seems to be no pattern or form that we can find." He also led a discussion group on "The American Heritage" at the public library and spoke to local civic groups, including the Junior Chamber of Commerce. In October 1951, the *Montgomery Advertiser* ran a major feature story on Cliff, profiling his career in Washington.[5]

Early in 1952, Cliff opened a law office in Montgomery, and Virginia went to work as his secretary. Their difficulty in building a law practice reflected how isolated they were and deepened their dependence on Cliff's family. After a year in Montgomery, the Durrs had established a very small circle of friends. Prominent among them were Aubrey and Anita Williams, old friends from Washington. Aubrey was a native Alabaman. He and Anita had moved in 1945 to Montgomery, where Aubrey published *The Southern Farmer*. The Durrs also established friendships with relatives of Esther Gelders, wife of Joe Gelders, who had grown up in Montgomery. They included Esther's sister, Sadie Franks, and her cousin Dorothy Lobman and Dorothy's husband, Bunch. That sparse social network provided a scant buffer to the harsh adjustments that life in Montgomery demanded.

The Durrs anticipated a short-term stay with Cliff's mother, but it stretched to nearly three years. Such an arrangement, less than ideal under most circumstances, bred pressures that Virginia found increasingly difficult to bear. She and "Mother Durr" were both strong-willed women, a natural source of tension. As their situation in Montgomery failed to improve, Virginia was plagued by the feeling that Cliff's mother blamed her

for her family's predicament, and particularly for Cliff's "failure" to succeed as a lawyer. At the same time, the general tenor of life in Mother
Durr's home represented grim aspects of Southern life that Virginia
thought she had escaped long ago. In her letters, she describes the household as a microcosm of the larger society—a repressed and threadbare culture held firmly in the grip of the past.

Virginia's growing despair was heightened by the gap that seemed to be
developing between her and Cliff. He had a deep affection for Montgomery
and was determined to spend the rest of his life there. While this was in large
part a function of family ties, Virginia also realized that it exposed a fundamental difference in their characters. As she explained in a letter to Corliss
Lamont: "Cliff . . . has . . . much better technique than I do in dealing with
people and situations . . . But since he has never felt an outcast, he cannot
feel the abyss of bitterness and frustration that I feel. He has always belonged,
and what he does he does out of his own generous heart and mind and he
wants it done in an orderly way. But for reasons that would take too long to
tell, I have so often felt the outcast, and felt the bitterness and the frustration
and the hatred, and wanted to tear down the walls that bound me."[6]

While she tried to accept that this was her life for the foreseeable future,
Virginia struggled to get her daughters out of Montgomery for at least
short periods. Lucy recalled that her mother desperately wanted them to
be exposed to the larger world. "She really was suffocating [and] she was
afraid for us." In order to create these opportunities, she had to reach out to
friends for help. She succeeded in getting Lucy and Tilla off to camp for
several summers, with a combination of scholarships and work arrange-
ments. When it was time for Lucy to go to college, Virginia was determined
that she would not go to the University of Alabama, which was all they
could reasonably afford. After Lucy was accepted at Radcliffe, Virginia and
Lucy obtained a work arrangement for room and board that, along with
scholarships, enabled Lucy to attend.[7]

Virginia was sustained by the belief that the future of Montgomery
rested with the black community. Even as she encountered the unyielding
nature of segregation in Montgomery, she was confident that change
would come. She continually looked for signs of movement, though at one
point she wrote, "It's like watching a glacier move." Virginia followed the
legal groundwork being laid by the NAACP and was attentive to the scattered efforts of blacks around the South to register and vote. She became
acquainted with local black civic activists, particularly E. D. Nixon, head of
the Progressive Voters League, and Rosa Parks, a seamstress who served al-
ternately as secretary of the NAACP branch and head of its Youth Council.
Charles Gomillion, leader of the voting rights effort in Tuskegee, also became a friend and confidant. Virginia frequently drove Mary Harris, her

mother-in-law's cook, to church out in the country, and she observed the interchange between rural Southern blacks and visiting relatives from up north as a hopeful development. The great challenge, as she saw it, was to broaden voter registration efforts beyond the middle class and reach the great mass of black people—a subject she wrote about for a special issue of the *Nation* in 1952.[8] While she identified with the nascent civil rights movement and drew strength from the spirit of resistance she encountered among people like Gomillion and Parks, she feared doing anything that would jeopardize their fragile base in the community.

Living quietly, however, was impossible under the national spotlight searching out Communists and their sympathizers during the early 1950s. Late in the summer of 1953, headlines in the *Montgomery Advertiser* linked Cliff to the National Lawyers Guild after Attorney General Herbert Brownell added it to his list of subversive organizations. Brownell called the Lawyers Guild "the legal mouthpiece of the Communist Party." Cliff defended the organization as one of the few that spoke out against the "inquisition methods" used by Senator Joseph McCarthy and others. Although he had not been involved with the organization since he had left Washington, he explained that was because there were no chapters in the South. He emphasized that he was not in any way disassociating himself from the organization, and that as far as he was concerned, there was no reason to believe that there was any subversive activity in the guild.[9]

Six months later, Virginia was subpoenaed to appear before the Senate Internal Security Subcommittee chaired by Senator James Eastland at a special hearing in New Orleans. Staged on the eve of the *Brown v. Board of Education* decision, Eastland's inquisition sought to link the civil rights activities of Virginia, Aubrey Williams, and other Southerners to the Communist Party as a way of smearing the desegregation effort. The hearings, which focused attention on Virginia's early civil rights activities and her relationship to Supreme Court Justice Hugo Black, were front-page news for several days. As she noted, few people in Alabama believed she was involved in espionage. But now, she wrote, "the fact that we are against segregation is blazoned forth to all the Southern world, and in the minds of most Southerners that is tantamount to being subversive if not actually insane."

The publicity surrounding the hearings threatened further to diminish Cliff's struggling law practice and placed him under severe strain. After nearly three years, their place in Montgomery was still tenuous. "He feels wretchedly lost and ill lots of the time," Virginia told a friend. "I cannot help but think that the conflict of his family and me and of his principles and the fear of not making a living are the cause of it all." But she felt helpless in the face of it. "The conflict lies in him and he is the only one who can resolve it." She had faith that he would find his way out of it "and make up which side he is finally on."[10]

For Virginia, the Eastland hearings had a liberating effect of sorts. "In a way," she recalled, "I was glad that my cover as a nice, proper Southern lady was blown by the hearing, because . . . I could begin to say what I really thought."[11] The *Brown* decision followed two months later, and Virginia became captivated by the responses of whites and blacks to the historic ruling. She began attending meetings of the Council on Human Relations, at that time the only interracial group in the city, and her involvement with the local NAACP branch deepened. She spoke to the Youth League on the importance of voting and arranged for Rosa Parks and several Youth League members to attend a workshop at Highlander Folk School during the summer of 1955. Founded as a labor school in the 1930s, Highlander was one of the only interracial organizations in the South that actively supported school desegregation. The sprouting up of White Citizens Councils to hold the line against integration suggested a long road ahead, but her letters convey hopeful anticipation of change.

In March 1955, Claudette Colvin, a 15-year-old high school student, was arrested for refusing to give up her seat on a city bus in Montgomery. As Virginia's letters reveal, Colvin's arrest and trial galvanized Montgomery's black community as nothing had in recent memory. When Fred Gray, the young black lawyer representing Colvin, asked Cliff to assist him in the case, Cliff did not hesitate. He went on to play a critical role as a legal advisor behind the scenes during the Montgomery bus boycott and worked on scores of civil rights cases over the next decade.

As their positions came into alignment, Virginia and Cliff settled into a partnership that placed them firmly within the orbit of the burgeoning civil rights movement. In the rigidly segregated Montgomery of the 1950s and early 1960s, this meant a life on the margins. Greater difficulties and challenges were to arise as racial tensions and violence heightened. By the end of 1955, however, Virginia and Cliff had begun to establish a place for themselves in Montgomery—one that was increasingly defined by their relationship to the movement and their isolation from Montgomery's white community.

Virginia once described Clark Foreman as "blood of my blood, bone of my bone." White Southerners born to privilege, both rejected the values and traditions they were raised with. Clark had a formative influence on Virginia's political development. Their experiences building the Southern Conference for Human Welfare, working for Henry Wallace in 1948, and fighting to maintain civil liberties in the wake of the Cold War forged a deep bond. After returning to Montgomery, Virginia wrote to Clark and his wife, Mairi, nearly every week, and sometimes more than once a week.

The Foremans and their three children—Shelagh, Joan, and Hugh (known as Geno)—moved to New York in 1949. Mairi Fraser Foreman, a

Canadian-born journalist and artist, had been active in the interracial movement in Washington. Clark held a Ph.D. in political science from Columbia University and had extensive experience as a government official and political advisor. Still, like many others who had been active in the Henry Wallace campaign, he was having a difficult time finding a permanent position.

The following letter, written shortly after the Durrs returned to Montgomery, describes the household of Cliff's mother, Lucy Judkins Durr, which included Lucy Durr's sister, Willalulah Judkins (known as "Little Auntie") and Willie and Mary Harris. The Harrises had worked for the Durrs for many years and lived in a cabin behind the main house.

June 1951

Dearest Mairi and Clark:

How can I begin to list all the things I have to thank you for? I suppose first of all it would have to be for your long and faithful friendship that has stood the test of years and many trials and tribulations. It was wonderful to have you there at the wedding*. . .

I am glad to think of it as we have had pretty rocky going since we got here. We met Cliff in Montgomery and he was having a good deal of pain—so he went up to Birmingham to see the Doctor and he put him to bed and said he would have to make up his mind to be quiet . . . for ten months time to a year. He is staying in Birmingham with his sister now and getting the very best attention and I am here with the children. I have started a business course as I feel I must do something and unfortunately all the jobs I have ever done have been non-paying jobs. So I go every morning from nine to twelve and take the children swimming in the afternoon. It is a good thing I have something definite to do for if I simply sat here and was waited on by Willie and Mary† I would be as fat as an elephant. I had forgotten all the joys of Southern cooking and I have to exercise the most terrific will power to resist it. The household is not difficult because the pattern is so far behind the time and so remote from reality that there is no discussion or friction. Mrs. Durr is 86 and Little Auntie is 74 and Willie and Mary about 70—so everyone has ac-

---

*Marriage of Ann Durr and Walter Lyon in Washington on May 18, 1951.
†Willie Harris worked as a caretaker and gardener and Mary Harris was the housekeeper and cook.

cepted life as it is here long ago and there is no use talking about it. Mary grumbles all day and we all pretend not to hear—but she has a good time ruling the household and knowing she is indispensable. Willie hates all women and is always threatening to bash Mary's head in but never does. To make up for his frustration he goes "rambling" every night as Mary calls it and comes home in the morning subdued. We have family visitors every day and the talk is all of people long dead or somnolent . . . I feel as though I were in a house with a storm raging outside and if I don't look out of the window I won't feel the force of it . . .

I know we are lucky to have a refuge during this time, although I sometimes feel cut off from the actual world. I have seen Aubrey [Williams] twice but that is difficult as the family regards him as Satan himself. Don West* came to call and they thought the "preacher" was charming, not knowing his ideas . . .

I wish I knew how to send you all the love and gratitude I feel for you.

Lots and lots of love, Va.

Virginia met Otto Nathan during her trip with Cliff to Europe in 1948. They developed a friendship that was sustained through correspondence. Nathan had been a professor of economics before fleeing Nazi Germany in 1939. A lifelong socialist and pacifist, he was one of Albert Einstein's closest friends and served as executor of Einstein's literary estate.

August 29, 1951
Dearest Otto: . . .

I must give you a brief review of our family . . . Cliff is improving after having had a bad back and having to spend more than six weeks in bed . . . On the whole his spirits stay pretty good and he has been doing a lot of reading—Lincoln Steffens and Mark Twain—and now he is reading Morris Cohen. He cannot help but have periods of depression with the world in the state it is in, and feeling so helpless to do anything. But his good sense and sweetness of character help him to make the best

---

*Don West, Georgia-born poet and Vanderbilt-trained minister, was a cofounder of Highlander Folk School with Myles Horton and James Dombrowski in the 1930s and a militant labor activist and supporter of racial equality.

of a necessary situation . . . I am going to Business School and I take short hand and typing—both of which I need a lot more work on—but I am learning and in another two or three months I will be a good secretary. I like going back to school and find it very interesting and am pleased that I can learn a new skill. The children are all well . . . All the family here are very kind to us—and we could not be treated with greater kindness—which makes it harder for me to say that I am frequently attacked by spells of claustrophobia and feel I must break out. The complete lack of any sympathetic companionship and the feeling of being out of touch with the living world is hard . . . It is hard to even carry on an intelligent conversation as the whole basic premises are so different. Of course it is a constant pain to see the steady and continuous and taken for granted oppression of the Negroes. It is like seeing a great stone lying on them—but it lies just as heavily on the white people too—and I feel so continually guilty that I am not doing anything about it. The only Negroes I have any direct contact with are the cook and her husband in the house and I have several times taken her out to her home in the country and met her family—and then I begin to have some hope. They are so healthy and there are so many of them—and they are more and more educated—and there is the constant intercourse between Detroit and Alabama as they go up there to work in the plants but continue to visit back here, and keep their homes too. Also the Tuskegee Institute although very conservative in many ways is putting on a voting campaign and that is the cause of great consternation.* I think the Negroes are stirring and they won't be held down much longer—but I don't see how they will ever forgive us for what we have done to them. And yet we must learn to live together here and in the rest of the world. I puzzle over it a great deal to see if I can find a crack or an opening but I know all the time that the real difficulty is that I want to help them but not at the price of being thrown out of my own group—which is what it amounts to here, just complete ostracism and loneliness, and then too

---

*The voter registration campaign in Tuskegee began in the mid-1930s under the leadership of Charles G. Gomillion, a professor at Tuskegee Institute, and was organized through the Tuskegee Civic Association. Virginia followed developments in Tuskegee closely and became a close friend of Dr. Gomillion.

no way to make a living—but all this is old stuff to you. Perhaps after Cliff gets well, and I get a job, we will see some opening. Right now I do the best I can and hope for better times to come.

Do write Dear Otto—With much love.

November 5, 1951
Dearest Otto:

Thank you so much for sending us the copies of the *Compass** and other material. I especially enjoyed the articles by Izzy,† who seems to get better and better . . .

Personally our life goes on as before. Cliff has improved a great deal, although the Doctor still does not give him permission to go to work. He is going over to the University this week to give some lectures. He has spoken several times and seems to be very effective. People will listen to him, and they know he is honest and he makes them think, and at least makes them a little doubtful of the clichés. He is considering opening a Law Office here, and yet I think he would far rather teach if he could find an opening. He likes the contact with young minds, and he is so patient and so careful he impresses them . . .

The children are well and are becoming fairly well adjusted and so on the whole we are getting on very well. I am still at the Business School . . . and hope to be finished by January. I will get whatever job I can find until I get some experience. I am not as lonely here as I was in Denver—just because the environment is more familiar, and I like the rain and the green and the physical environment, and I like the people too, but I cannot deny that I am terribly lonely. For so many years—so long that I had begun to take it for granted—I have been in communion with people that believed and worked for a solution to the ills of the world, and honestly believed, whatever their differences among themselves, that there was a solution, so that however terrible the present was . . . there was hope for the future. Now I am utterly cut off . . . I listen to the conversations here and it is sometimes like a long dirge. Sick-

---

*A progressive newspaper published by Ted O. Thackery in New York from 1949–1953.
†I. F. Stone, the liberal journalist and publisher of *I. F. Stone's Weekly* and outspoken opponent of the Cold War and domestic loyalty measures.

ness—death—sorrow—drunkenness, despair, madness, faithlessness, brutality and corruption. There is a general assumption that the world is an evil place . . . Of course, as always, there is hope among the children and on a personal basis both love and charity but amid so much arid desert of despair. Cliff is a stronger person than I am, and he is not so much affected, and then perhaps doesn't expect so much as I do, he is always surprised and delighted when he finds even a glimmer among the people we see. I think it is so dim . . . The sullen repressed resentment of the Negroes—the bleak despair of the poor whites—and the frustrated cheapness of so many people who have a certain amount of economic security but no moral security whatever—and what we see so often among the "old families" is the resigned acceptance of despair and tragedy and often madness . . . unless I can find some means of working to change it, or at least helping in some way however small, I think it would drive me to despair . . . I hope dear Otto you will forgive me for pouring my troubles on you.

In the following letter, Virginia refers to the trial of W.E.B. Du Bois. Earlier in the year, the 83-year-old civil rights leader had been indicted by the Justice Department for failing to register as a foreign agent in his role as chairman of the short-lived and by then defunct Peace Information Center. John Rogge, the government's chief witness against Du Bois, served as an attorney with the Justice Department during the early years of the Roosevelt administration and had been active in many left-wing causes before turning informer. It was Rogge who had invited Du Bois to chair the Peace Information Center.

November 30, 1951
Dearest Clark and Mairi:

It is such a joy to hear from you that I hasten to answer so I can get another letter . . .

I see you do not even admit within your range of possibilities the one of returning to the South. It is difficult—no doubt—but every place is now—and at least we understand it, and I love it in the way you love your family—and yet want to shake them for their blindness. They want to shake me no doubt too. The big question will come when we are out on our own and have to make a living. Then we will face the test of whether we will be allowed to live or not. So I suppose I do not yet have a complete picture of what that is . . .

I have been absolutely amazed at the Du Bois trial and John Rogge. I am glad Marc* got him off—and feel much safer to think that being for "Peace" doesn't ipso facto make you a traitor. God knows after our experience in Denver, I felt driven by the fear that they might brand us all as traitors to our country. But for John to be the Government witness is beyond my scale of comprehension. I thought after Lee [Pressman]† that I would never be shocked anymore—but I am. There seems to me to be an enormous difference between having to be quiet and try to survive, and turning on your former associates and helping send them to their destruction . . .

I often think of where would I be if you had dismissed me as impossible when I was impossible? If you had not hung on like grim death during so many of my . . . worse times—that is why I think you should come back South—you can speak their language and if you will be willing to accept the humble place we find we must occupy, still you can do some good. That is if you can make a living . . . I feel you have contributed so much and done so much good and if we are going through a dim period I don't think it will be forever. Perhaps you and I had to learn to walk softly and learn patience and humility—but that does not mean that what we did was not right and courageous and I am proud of it. We are caught in a situation that is hard to bear, but I think we pushed the course of history a little further along and I know if it had not been for you and your forthrightness and courage I would never have dared break out of my shell.

Do write me again and tell me all you know about our mutual friends—I do get lonesome for word of them.

---

*Vito Marcantonio, former congressman from East Harlem in New York (1935–36; 1939–50); he was a leading supporter of civil rights legislation and sponsor of an anti-poll tax bill.

†Lee Pressman had been a leading labor lawyer during the New Deal era, and served as general counsel to the CIO and to the Steel Workers Union until 1948, when he joined the staff of Henry Wallace's Progressive Party. In 1950 he testified before HUAC that he had been a member of the Communist Party, and named several other associates as having also been party members.

Virginia reports on the death of her sister, Josephine Black, and considers the ultimate tragedy of her life and that of her mother. Josephine had a rheumatic heart and suffered from bouts of depression. She died on December 7, 1951, at age 52.

December 31, 1951
Dearest Clark and Mairi:

I was so glad to find your letter upon my return. I went by Charlotte and stayed with my Father a week after I left Washington and just got here on Christmas Eve. Ann and Walter drove down from Washington and they picked me up in Charlotte. They just left yesterday and I am able to write some letters for the first time.

As soon as I heard the dreadful news my first instinct was to pick up the telephone and ask you both to come down—and then I thought of all the expense and difficulty it would involve and did not do it . . . She had been so well the last few months, although she had a very bad cold and had just been down to see my Father who is recovering from an operation for cataracts. I know she was deeply worried over his misery and helplessness, but on the whole she seemed quite well and they were planning a trip to New York and one to Florida. She died in her sleep and her doctor said it was just a failure of her heart. I think the long years of anxiety she had gone through—and the vast quantities of sleeping pills and sedatives she had to take were no doubt contributing factors . . . But from all the evidence at hand it does seem as though the last few years she had attained a measure of peace and happiness and of course her painting had been a lifesaver to her. She had you all to thank for that and I think it did her more good than anything else. But on the whole and in spite of her many sided interests, I think her life was a tragedy as was my Mother's, and I increasingly hate and despise all the fetters that bound such lovely and gentle spirits.

I think if Sister had ever been able to hate evil as I do she might have been saved, but she never could. And perhaps that is not the way to salvation—but at least it gives you an outward target for your angers and they are not turned inward.

I was glad to get the better news of your family as I worry over you as you know. Do let me know anything cheerful that happens to you . . .

The children are well and fairly happy and so we are doing all right considering the situation we are in.

Except for the Lobmans and the Williams* we have not found any congenial friends—even Aubrey is not always a pleasure as you know, as he is so terribly contradictory and inconsistent—but at least they speak our language. I think the thing that would impress you most if you settled here is that no one knows you have been gone—or where you have been, or what you have done, or gives a damn. It is the immediate—the present and the familiar that interests them, and except for the people over at the University we might as well have spent our time away from Alabama in the Sahara Desert writing in the sand. While very deflating to the ego, it is very restful for a time.

Lots of love and do write again soon, and tell me in detail what your prospects are. Did you take the job Izzy was talking about?†

In a letter to her daughter and son-in-law, Ann and Walter Lyon, Virginia provides a glimpse of life in her mother-in-law's house.

January 14, 1952
Dearest Ann and Walt:
We were delighted to receive your letter . . . I look to see the house a vision of beauty the next time I come, and . . . I promise I won't get mad about the checked curtains. Just my old dictatorial spirit rising.

I must say I have a hard time dictating here as not only does my family resist, but I have four other disputants for the title. I think there was never such a small place ruled over by so many people, and each with their own inviolate territory. This last week I caused a real upheaval by raking the lawn, and it has not calmed down yet. It seems that is Willie's bailiwick but as I told you he was stabbed and shot in a whore-house and is laid up. But he seemed to think I was taking advantage of his illness. Then Mary took umbrage as part of the cleaning up was her snuff cans and all the eggshells and orange peels she throws out in the backyard, and when they were all assembled it was monumental. Then

---

*Dorothy and Bunch Lobman and Aubrey and Anita Williams.
†Directorship of the newly formed National Emergency Civil Liberties Committee, which Foreman did take.

Mother Durr took alarm as she said I was raking up the leaves with the trash as they were her fertilizer, and I should pick the trash up with my hands, which I did. Then when the pile was assembled in the middle of the driveway I began to burn it, and that caused wild commotion and everybody rushed out to tell me I would set the house on fire, and so I had to dig a hole and bury it in the back garden. It seemed to me typical of the whole backward part of the South—full of trash and needing so desperately to be cleaned up and everybody objecting. That did not cause the real upheaval though. Last night some one called for "Mrs. Harris" and Little Auntie who answered the telephone said no "Mrs. Harris" was there—that if they wanted to speak to their cook "Mary Harris" they could. So the person [hung] up but must have informed Mary of it, as this morning she was a thundercloud, and said she would have to leave as she was afraid she would kill Little Auntie, and sometimes I am afraid she will too . . .

Daddy is up in Birmingham on this case he has, and I hope he will be back today . . . [He] has a calming influence over the household, as he simply does not notice anything askew unless it bursts out into flame.

Virginia reports on a letter she received from Charles Gomillion inviting her to speak at a meeting organized by the Tuskegee Civic Association (TCA). Gomillion, a professor of sociology at Tuskegee Institute, was the leader of a black voter registration movement organized through the TCA, which was founded in 1941. Virginia and Gomillion became good friends and were frequently in contact from here on.

January 25, 1952
Dearest Otto:

I have been meaning to write you ever since I saw you in Washington to tell you how very much I appreciate the *Compass*. I keep up with all my friends and I enjoy it very much indeed . . .

I am enclosing a letter I received from a man at Tuskegee* that impresses me very much. I have promised Cliff to refrain from public ad-

---

*Charles Gomillion.

dresses until we achieved a little more of a foothold in the community so I will not be able to do it. I don't feel so badly as I know I would not be of much influence at present. But this battle for the Vote is the thing I believe in most strongly and the brave men that are fighting for it I admire wholeheartedly. I do not see any solution of the other problems until that is solved as the dreadful fact is that disfranchised as the Negroes are—they are nothing but a liability to any politician . . . As soon as they get the vote the situation changes at once, then they have something tangible to offer in support of their friends. I wish I knew of some way to impress upon all the people that work in the North how serious and important it is and now that the Party down here is splitting (I mean the Democratic Party) I think their vote would be sought if they had it. The NAACP only touches the topmost layer and the mass, at least here in Alabama, is untouched. It is not stressed enough by the Negro press and by all the organizations that work in the field. The power of the Negro community lies in the North—and they take the right to vote for granted and look down on their benighted brethren from the South . . . They do not seem to realize that their own future is bound up with what happens here. The Marxist analysis that the crux of the problem of the Negro lies in the Black Belt is true, but as you know their solution even theoretically of a "Negro Nation"* I reject absolutely . . . I do not think the National Question is a problem in the U.S. although it is in Africa, but I do think the equal application of the Law is a tremendous one, and here you have a large section and a large portion of the population living outside the Law. Of course things are changing a little . . . but as in Africa the Black Mass is almost untouched here in the South—and how to touch them and what forces influence them I am trying to figure out. Maybe Mr. Gomillion at Tuskegee is as baffled as I am by their not voting when they can, although of course here it is very hard. I mean in Ala.

Lots of love dear Otto—do write and tell me what is happening.

Devotedly Va.

---

*Refers to the Communist Party's assertion that African Americans in southern Black Belt counties constituted an oppressed nation and possessed the right to self-determination.

In a letter to Hugo Black and his daughter Josephine, Virginia refers to the many letters she received regarding the death of the elder Josephine Black. She also reports that Cliff had opened a small law office in Montgomery with Red James, who had worked as Cliff's assistant at the FCC. Virginia tested her newly acquired skills by working as his secretary.

January 29, 1952
Dear Hugo and Jo Jo: . . .

I was glad to get your letter Hugo, and I know what an immense task you have to answer all those many letters. I have had so many too, and am still answering them. I have sent some of them to Daddy, and some I will send to you. It is a comfort to know that she left such a beautiful and happy memory and brightened the lives of all the people whom she touched, in spite of all the suffering she went through.

The news from this part of the Family is very good. Cliff continues to improve, and has opened an office at 17 Molton Street, a suite which he shares with Red James. He is doing some business already, and we hope he will do a great deal more. I am acting as his secretary for the time being, but am in daily and hourly danger of being fired. At first I was very confident and demanded at least 50 c [cents] an hour which is the rate apprentice stenographers get, but the second day I came down to 30 c, the third day I offered to work for nothing, and now he claims he should pay my tuition for teaching me. Never having worked in an office before I find there are whole worlds I know nothing about, but it is fascinating and I enjoy it very much, and if I can just hold on to my job I hope in time to work up to a paying one. I go for a shorthand class every day as well, as it is the shorthand in which I am so slow.

The children are doing well, and seem happy in their school. Lucy is full of dates and dances and clothes and bobby pins, and Tilla seems to be getting just like her. They spend hours over their hair and complexions, and take baths constantly as they listen to the Radio so much that they are convinced that they smell bad, and the only way they can avoid total ostracism is to be 99½% pure and clean. Other than those manifestations of teenagitis they do beautifully. Lulah is always a joy . . .

We all hope you will come down before long when Jo Jo has her Spring vacation.

Devotedly—Jinksie*

The following letter responds to a letter from Patricia Frank, a friend of Virginia's from Washington, and wife of Lew Frank, who was Henry Wallace's campaign manager. Now living in Detroit, Frank apparently sought her advice regarding a specialty shop she had recently established. In the course of her explanation, Virginia describes the close relationship between blacks in Detroit and in Macon County, Alabama, and speculates on how this might help stir greater political interest and activity among rural Southern blacks.

February 13, 1952

Dear Patty:

I was delighted to hear from you and I will have to take up your letter section by section since it was so interesting.

As for the Business end of it. The best way to get the information you want is to write to the State Department of Conservation, State Capitol, Montgomery, Alabama or the State Chamber of Commerce. That is where I got my information in the first place and they will fall over themselves trying to get some rich Yankee to spend a little money down here—especially the flowers. Right now there are yards full of camellias and magnolias and narcissus, and there are so many they must be fairly cheap. Of course there is an enormous part of Detroit that comes from the Black Belt, but I don't know if they would have the money to buy flowers and would think it a legitimate expense. Perhaps crackling bread and chitterlings and black-eyed peas and grits are more of a reminder of their home which is not Heaven on earth. I must say in spite of its disadvantages that the people that move to Detroit come back at least on visits quite often. I took the cook out to her church meetings all summer and I never got over my surprise to see these big fine cars in the churchyard and to meet somebody who was steward in Local 66 or 600 or Business agent in the Union. There is not one single voter in all that part of Macon

---

*Virginia was called "Jinksie" by her family and friends in Birmingham. She started going by "Virginia" after she arrived in Washington.

County. The only voters in the whole county (I mean Negro voters) are right around Tuskegee Institute, and the people who still live in the country live a primitive life to put it mildly, and yet there was the juxta-position of the most advanced labor point of view and the prosperity and the big cars, and union sentiment and political savvy, and yet they don't seem to translate one bit of it back home, I can't see why. Unless they know it is so much easier to vote in Detroit than in Macon County. But they have such influence on the stay-at-homes and if they would use their influence and encourage them to vote and become citizens it would help a lot. They (I mean the Emigres) try hard to get members of their families up to Detroit, but so many of them, and particularly the women feel about it the same way I did about Denver. That they just as soon be dead as live there they say. So dirty and crowded and close and they have no place to hang out the wash. This is a beautiful country, and so green and so warm and lush and full of flowers and sunshine and rain. I don't blame them for wanting to stay in spite of the difficulties as it is as much home to them as it is to me, and they seem to feel just the same way about it in spite of the discrimination.

The Durr Family is looking up . . . We did have a dirty deal in Den-ver . . . God how I hated it. This place is just like it has always been and very familiar and as queer as Dick's hat band, but the kind of queerness and horror I am familiar with. It would be here whether we stayed or went—I mean the horror and the queerness, and perhaps before we die we might be able to make it a little less so, but I am not sure. I really love the land and the people and the climate and the food, and if sanity should ever return here it would be marvelous. I do worry over the chil-dren and I hope we can get them away often so they will see other parts of the country and know other ways. But I must say that whether you look east or west there is the same cuckoo's nest . . .

Do write again . . .

Lots of love Va.

April 30, 1952

Dearest Otto:

I am not sure who owes who a letter, but I always feel I am the one that should write you since you are willing to take the time and pains to send me the *Compass* which I enjoy so much . . . I think Izzy gets better and better, and I am always amazed at the amount of news I get out of it . . .

From here I do not see that the flame of War shines less brightly. The physical and psychological build up goes on and on, and here where there is such a huge military installation, the coming War is taken for granted, at least by military officials. Also it is interesting to see at first hand how wholly phony and false are the reported "integrations" in the Air Force. The segregation is as complete as ever and all the Lillian Smiths* to the contrary notwithstanding—there is no breach the size of a dime in the Wall. Strict segregation is practiced by all the Labor Unions except for one or two that have left wing affiliations and are outside the CIO and constantly being attacked by the CIO. The churches never say a word and the only place there is even a tiny crack is among some of the women's organizations. For example, the Alabama Nurses Association is not segregated professionally—I don't mean the Negro nurses are called to the white hospitals, but they have the same organization. That is of course not true among the teachers. Tuskegee has meetings of various kinds to which certain professional people go, but the contact does not extend beyond campus. I think people like Lillian Smith do a great deal of harm to even say things are getting better—there is a long and fierce struggle ahead and I think it will be another South Africa, in a different way. I am still convinced that the VOTE is the central issue.

While I often feel imprisoned and have mild claustrophobia here, especially since I am not yet in a position to take a positive stand and fight against the evils, still I think we are in the right place and may in time do some good. For example, we have far more contact with the Negro community than we ever had in Washington or Virginia, not socially as we did there and in organizations, but as clients. The various cases take in the whole range of behavior and are very interesting. I think we will build up a law practice in time, but it is slow of course . . .

I think of you often, Otto, and of the wonderful and hopeful world we saw together . . .

Much Love, Va.

---

*Lillian Smith was a Georgia-born novelist and essayist whose exploration of the cultural and sexual dimensions of white racial fears and violence won national attention. Smith was an outspoken and active opponent of racial segregation.

Virginia was concerned about how the narrow atmosphere of Montgomery limited the experiences of Lucy and Tilla, and compared it to Ann's experience growing up in Washington.

May 27, 1952
Dearest Ann: . . .

I took Lucy and Tilla and forty-five other girls on a house party up the River from Friday to Sunday night, and it was simply exhausting. They did not sleep at all the first night, and the noise and confusion were terrific, but they were mostly very sweet young girls, and I suppose it is only natural that they should not think or talk of anything else but boys. Tilla is going to Memphis on the 10th of June for two weeks, and I am also trying to get her a job at the Girl Scout Day Camp as Junior Swimming aide when she gets back. She is really a wonderful swimmer and is beginning to learn to dive as well. She rode the skip jack on the river better than anyone else. Lucy is very popular with the boys and they are around the house all the time and she is silly on the subject. I don't see any counteracting influences here to give them a wider view of life and the world and the people in it. Reading, studying, music, athletics, nothing has any validity aside from being "popular" and I think it is a very unhealthy atmosphere, but I don't know it is any different anywhere, do you? I think you did have all the different kinds of people coming to the house, and the opportunity of hearing and seeing a wide variety of people, but living as we are of course they have no chance of that and they are confined to such a small and narrow group of people whose ideas don't take in but such a tiny part of the world.

Early in 1952, Clark Foreman became director of the newly established National Emergency Civil Liberties Committee (ECLC), founded to provide an aggressive defense of civil liberties, particularly for those individuals and groups that the ACLU would not aid because of its anticommunist policy. Journalist I. F. Stone, Yale law professor Thomas Emerson, Judge Hubert Delany, Palmer Weber, and attorney Leonard Boudin were among the founding members. With this letter, Virginia began her effort to draw the attention of Foreman and the ECLC board to the South to help promote black voter registration and aid in the fight to broaden political par-

ticipation in the region. Virginia also sought the Foremans' help in finding
a way to get her daughters out of Montgomery during the summer.

February 26, 1953
Dearest Clark and Mairi: ...

I have a serious suggestion for you and one I want you to consider
with your board—of course based on the premise that you can get some
money to do it. But Corliss must have inherited several more millions ... with his Mother's death and I don't see how it will take so
much money anyway.

Now you know my thesis has been for years that the easiest and
quickest way to change the political complexion of the country was to
get the South voting, as I think lurking under all the devilment they are
by nature and experience bound to be on the progressive side. Hell they
have to progress, there is nothing to go back to but more misery. Now in
spite of our feeble efforts they still Don't Vote and don't let the Eisenhower vote kid you as the Eisenhower crowd are just the old Dixiecrats
dressed up a little and not much at that. The NAACP of course is doing
things, and I keep up with that through Aubrey, but not very much
really to get down to the masses of the people—just the top layer of the
Negroes, and I am doing some work with the League of Women Voters
but they barely scratch the surface and nothing else is done and if you
will examine the American Heritage group figures you will see it is the
same old thing—23, 24, 29 percent and so on. All the baloney about the
Poll Tax amendment is sheer eyewash. They may get rid of it, and that
helps of course and all our work there was worthwhile, but the Boards
of Registrars, the apathy and the ignorance remain and they grow
greater. Now what I think should be done and how many thousands of
times have you heard me say it, how many board meetings of the SCHW
have I interrupted and been called down, but still I think the idea is
good, and that is to establish Voter Service Clubs. Make people pay to
join—two bits and fifty cents—and do the same kind of thing on a mass
base that the League of Women Voters does on a selective basis. Start in
the South and it may spread to the rest of the country, and when you
consider the need for political education it seems to me it is a golden
opportunity. Don't let it be partisan if you can help it, and be as demo-

cratic and open and easy to understand as possible, but no matter how nonpartisan it may be it is bound to have a terrific progressive impact. Of course I think Palmer* would be ideal for it as he gets on with the masses of people, but I suppose there are others, and it seems to me that the brainy people on your committee would see it. Let them read Key's book†, Nick Comfort's book from the U. of Okla., but why should they when (sorry to write on back but paper is so damned expensive) all they have to do is read the voting record, and see how this vermiform appendix of the South is swollen and tight with green, nasty, filthy, smelly pus and germs, can infect the whole nation if we don't operate on it. When the Big Brass and the Big Boys and the Respectable fronts get tired and can't operate openly, the South will be their tool to destroy us, since they control it and the opposition is weak. [Senator Joseph] McCarthy is awful and horrible and disgusting and so is McCarran,‡ but what are they compared to [senators] [James] Eastland, [Herman] Talmadge, [John] McClellan, [Richard] Russell, [James F.] Byrnes, and the whole slimy crew, and they control to a far greater extent than McCarthy and McCarran . . .

My spirits range from 110 in the shade to forty below, but on the whole stay within fairly normal range. I am sometimes seized with a shuddering horror of this society . . . The girls are alright. If you know of any work Camps or scholarships to Camps or any way to get them out of this for the summer it will be appreciated. I hate for them to lose touch with the larger and saner world.

You know how much I love you, but I will say it again for the record. Devotedly Va.

---

*Palmer Weber, who had worked with Virginia on the anti-poll tax campaign and served as codirector of Henry Wallace's Southern campaign. Weber moved from Washington to New York in 1950.

†V. O. Key, *Southern Politics in State and Nation* (1949).

‡Democratic Senator Pat McCarran from Nevada, sponsor of the Internal Security Act, passed in 1950, requiring all Communist and Communist-front organizations to register with the federal government, and chair of the Senate Internal Security Subcommittee, which sponsored hearings to expose Communists and their sympathizers.

April 14, 1953
Dearest Clark and Mairi:

I know I dismay my friends by answering their letters so promptly. Don't feel you in turn have to do so, as I know the pressures of time and business make it hard. As for me, I love to write letters as you know, and only find the difficulty in stopping, and it also no doubt provides an outlet for my frustrated literary leanings.

You sounded tired in your letter . . . I am sure that life is not easy with you any more than it is with us, and advancing years certainly do make a difference. It is hard to realize that I am now middle aged, and Lulah is always asking me what we did in the "olden days." I still make a spasmodic attempt at youth, put henna in the rinse water, and use lipstick and eye shadow, and try to sit up straight and hold my head up as Mairi taught me, but often I feel older than the hills . . . I have lost about fifteen pounds which I could well afford to do and am trying to lose ten or fifteen more. Since our diet is largely starch and cream and ham, etc. it is difficult, but I have done it simply by not eating and that makes you feel limp so often. It is not vanity but health that prompted me, and one fortunate consequence is that when Ann went to Siam I could inherit all of her clothes.*

The news here is not much different than when I last wrote you. Cliff's practice keeps him busy and he has several cases that if they pay off will be wonderful but on the whole it is not a profitable business yet. Red James with whom he has been sharing an office is going to Texas with Roy Hofheinz and that raises new problems about the office . . . I think I told you that I passed both the Grade I and Grade II of the State Civil Service for a stenographer, and I have been offered several jobs— one at Kilby prison, but under all the circumstances it seems best for me to stay on down here at the office, and so after Red leaves I can take on the whole job if necessary. I am really getting pretty good, and turn out all kinds of interrogatories and complaints and petitions and so on. I like legal work very much as it interests me and of course everything I

---

*Ann and Walter Lyon were on their way to Thailand (then called Siam) for Walter's job with the U.S. Public Health Service.

do I feel a deep personal interest in, so the office is really a very pleasant place if we would just make some money. But in spite of that, Cliff is determined to live and die in Dixie and here he has taken his stand, so I must make the best of it and I try to do it . . .

We see Aubrey real often and he was mad yesterday because they are having a big shindig at Tuskegee and didn't invite him—or me either. They did invite some the most reactionary people in town, but that still does not make me lose faith in their ultimate cooperation with progressive elements. We just don't have enough strength to do anything for them, and I am not doing any cooperating myself right now. The Negro community here has just put on a "mock" election for Mayor and the amount of interest it aroused was phenomenal. I think it is a wonderful idea. It looks as though the Poll Tax might really get abolished this term in the legislature, but the League of Women Voters that is backing it never invites me to participate although I belong to it. Goodness what a very dangerous woman I must be! Very flattering . . .

Give my love to all and write me again when you can . . . Va.

Marge Frantz, the daughter of Joe Gelders, was one of Virginia's regular correspondents. After World War II, Joe Gelders settled in northern California. He was studying biophysics at the University of California at Berkeley on the G.I. Bill when he died in 1950 at the age of 52, after suffering a series of heart attacks.

Virginia had known Marge since she was a child, and they worked together in the SCHW and in the Wallace campaign. Marge was married to Laurent Frantz, a lawyer who had also been active in civil rights and voting rights efforts in the South. The Frantzs moved from North Carolina to Berkeley, California in 1951, and had stayed with the Durrs in Denver on their way west.

April 29, 1953

Dearest Marge: . . .

The news here is just about the same. I am still working in Cliff's office and love it. We have lots of clients, and such nice ones, but all poor, so we are still completely without money. But we have several cases which if they pay off will help a lot. I am here almost all of every day, and then I fix breakfast and supper and sew and look after the children to the best of my ability and that is about all. I have tried to work with the local League of

Women Voters but that has not come to much as they are working for the repeal of the Poll Tax on a "it doesn't mean Negroes will vote, and we can tighten up the election laws for the Boards of Registrars, etc." I protested this line, and they didn't like it, and say I am unrealistic, and actually they don't want me to have anything to do with it. Just a repetition of the League in Washington. When the going was tough they would not touch it and now that it is respectable they claim it as their own, but what the Hell, as long as we did the job that is all that matters . . .

Give my love to Joe and the Baby and to Laurent and write again soon.

Devotedly—Va.

During the summer of 1953, Virginia began corresponding with Curtis MacDougall, a journalism professor at Northwestern University who was writing a history of the Progressive Party campaign of 1948 and Henry Wallace's third-party candidacy for president. He sought information from Virginia about her involvement in the Progressive Party. MacDougall published a three-volume history of the Wallace movement, *Gideon's Army*, in 1965. In this letter, Virginia reflects back on the 1948 campaign and speculates about its consequences.

July 13, 1953
Dear Mr. MacDougall:

I read your letter with great interest and while I don't think we ever met, I have heard of you too, and I hear you are a very "honest" person and I will try and give you an "honest" account of the Virginia Campaign of the Progressive Party as I saw it.

It is rather painful I am bound to confess to go back over the ground as it was not very much of a success as you know, certainly it was not in Virginia and the South, and it is hard at this time to know if the pains and penalties were worthwhile for the small success we achieved.

It is impossible to give you the story of the Virginia Campaign without giving you the background out of which it came, and of this I have no idea how much you know. I am sure you have or will interview Palmer Weber, Louis Burnham and Clark Foreman, all of whom are living in New York and who played a much larger role than I did.

The best way to understand what we did in the South and what we built on is to read *Origins of the New South* by Professor C. Vann Woodward of Johns Hopkins University who tells in detail of the Populist movement in the South. That movement was destroyed not by "red-baiting" but by "race-baiting" and unless you count the Wilson era as a liberal period, the South stayed almost wholly conservative until the advent of Roosevelt and the New Deal. Then started the CIO drive as well as all the political measures that were aimed at correcting the old time abuses of the South and both met with great reverses. The CIO drive was met with injunctions and terror, and the political measures were met with the Republican-Dixiecrat alliance. Beanie Baldwin* at this time was in the forefront of the Southern fight with the Farm Security Administration, which had a profound effect on the South. Mr. Roosevelt after the failure of his "purge" authorized the publication of "The South, Economic Problem No. 1" which Clark Foreman and a group of Southerners in the New Deal authored. You should certainly get a copy of that as it was the beginning of the fight in the South. Out of that group and the CIO group and the NAACP group and other various groups, came the Southern Conference for Human Welfare which was active in the South for a number of years. When the NCPAC† was formed they did not come into the South, but simply cooperated with the SCHW, and when the NCPAC played such a big part in the 1944 campaign, a number of the SCHW people such as Jim Dombrowski, Palmer Weber, Clark Foreman, etc. worked in the [NCPAC] headquarters with Beanie. That was a glorious time and a glorious victory, and we felt that the future was ours, but with Roosevelt's death came the Big Change. We became increasingly disgusted with Truman and his policies, and Henry Wallace came more and more to represent to us the continuation of the Roosevelt policies and when he broke with the Administration our sympathies were all with him. The SCHW had a chapter in Virginia on which was represented all the various New Deal

---

*C. B. "Beanie" Baldwin, from Radford, Virginia, joined Henry Wallace's staff in the Department of Agriculture during the early days of the New Deal. He directed the Farm Security Administration, and later worked with Sidney Hillman in the CIO Political Action Committee. Baldwin directed the Progressive Party campaign.

†NCPAC—the National Citizens Political Action Committee, a coalition of liberal individuals and groups, formed in 1943 to work with the CIO Political Action Committee (CIO-PAC) to promote voter education and registration, and organize support for liberal and pro-labor candidates.

groups in Virginia. Among the Negroes, Dr. Luther P. Jackson, Dr. L. H. Palmer, and Mr. Oliver Hill were our chief supporters, all very fine men. In the CIO Charlie Webber was our staunch friend, and Brownie Lee Jones of the Southern Workers Educational Foundation. We worked mainly on the franchise, but also took action on other matters as well. Wallace came into Virginia the Spring before the Convention and we had a very fine meeting for him at Norfolk,* the credit for which should go to a young man that was head of the CIOPAC whose name I have for the moment forgotten . . . That meeting was the only really inspiring moment of the Wallace movement. We had it in a big municipal Hall, and we thought that the police had agreed to a non-segregated meeting, but when it opened they threw in about a hundred policemen, and told us that all the people would have to separate. It was a huge Hall and a huge crowd and both races were all mixed up. It looked for a minute as though there would be serious trouble, and Wallace had not come so there was nothing to hold them there, and the Negroes sent word that if they were to be separated they would walk out. I was presiding and as I went on the stage to open the meeting the Police told me to announce that all the people in the Hall would have to separate. Backed up by Clark Foreman I opened the meeting by calling for the Star Spangled Banner, and after all four verses (very feeble the fourth) I then called on Charlie Webber to pray (Charlie was a preacher). Charlie prayed and prayed, for the brotherhood of man, and especially for the police, but then his breath gave out, and it looked as though the police would move in, when Henry appeared walking down the center aisle. He gave a magnificent speech, and after it was over the people took their children up on the stage to meet him and to shake his hand, so they could say that they had met a great man, and certainly at the moment we all thought he was.

When he announced and was nominated the SCHW split and some of us formed the Progressive Party, but the CIO and the NAACP which had been the very backbone of our strength did not go along with us, and what is more they turned on us and began the vicious red-baiting that

---

*This meeting occurred in November 1947, during Wallace's tour of the South prior to declaring his candidacy.

marked the whole campaign. It was difficult to understand how people who only a few months before had been working and fighting with you, would so suddenly turn on you and the whole Progressive Party. I still think it was nasty business. I am sure we made numerous mistakes ourselves, I well remember and blush when I think of it, passionately telling a group of Negro peanut workers about the bombing of Warsaw and its destruction (I had seen it that summer) and calling on them to vote for Wallace and World Peace. It was all true but so utterly alien to their experience, and I might as well have been talking about Mars.

In any case, we had small successes, I think Henry got about 3500 votes [in Virginia] and I who was on the ballot for Senator got about 6000. One curious footnote was that the Communist candidate who was running for Congress in the Richmond district, a crew-cut Harvard lad, got five times as many votes as Henry and three times as many as I did! I often wished I could know the explanation of that . . . In any case the voters did not vote for us, and the idea of running local candidates which was really an idea of trying to get publicity for Henry did not work very well, and it might have been better if we had not tried to do it, but this I don't know either.

I think the great question that comes out of the Progressive Party Campaign is would it have been better to stay in the Democratic Party and fight for a better foreign policy and Civil Liberties, or to have gone and formed a new party as we did. Frankly I don't know the answer. Here in the South it is hard to see any good we did. We are out of the Democratic Party and there is nothing else. The Negroes have the Progressive Democratic Party which they control entirely, but there is no longer any political group where they meet together. The SCHW is no more, and the CIO PAC stays strictly to itself, and the alliance that was the backbone of Roosevelt's strength is broken and gone, at least they [blacks and whites] go their separate ways. But at the time there did not seem to be anything else to do, and I never doubted then that I was on the side of the Angels, and I think I was, but I am not sure that Angels are necessarily good political organizers . . .

There is always hope that someday the seeds we planted with so much hope will sprout, as the seeds of the Populist Party sprouted in the New Deal which did actually change the face of the South and made the beginnings of a new country. We still have a long row to hoe, but I think we made a beginning and perhaps one day we will know that it was not wholly lost.

Virginia continues her discussion with Curtis MacDougall about the Progressive Party (PP), particularly the role of the Communist Party (CP) in the Wallace effort. Virginia explains why, although she once thought that being a Communist "was the only way to salvation," she never joined the party.

August 17, 1953
Dear Mr. MacDougall: . . .

I am sorry that you did not see Mrs. [Sarah] d'Avila* as she worked very hard and could have told you a lot of things about the Campaign in Virginia. I know Mike [Straight]† so well and he is so violently anti-Communist that I always take what he says with a grain of salt, several . . .

I certainly would like to see the CP [Communist Party] account of the PP [Progressive Party] and hope it will be sent to me. I can't figure out what you say about the CP not claiming any credit for helping with the PP. They wrote about it fully and claimed *all* the credit for it at times. Read the files of *Political Affairs* and you will get it all there in black and white. I think it was intended to be a Popular Front thing to try and stop the drive toward War, and they were perfectly willing to put up with Henry's anti-Marxism and his fuzziness to get his strength toward stopping the belligerence that was so manifest in Washington. As for the wheels within wheels, that Mike went on about, starting it, only to sabotage it, that seems silly to me. I am convinced from my own experience with the Russians and from what I saw in Poland, that in their devastated and exhausted state, they were frantic at the thought of having to start arming again, and they would take *anything* to get a few years breathing space. You would have to see Warsaw and the people in it, and see Poland to realize how horrible it was. My husband saw Russia too (sent by the State Department for Telecommunications conference) and he said it was just about as bad as Poland, if not worse. I may be simple but I am of the opinion that people love life better than death, and most people want to live and that horror, suffering, starvation, ruin

---

*Secretary of the National Committee to Abolish the Poll Tax from 1941 until the committee was dissolved in 1948, and also worked with Virginia in the Progressive Party in Virginia.
†Publisher of the *New Republic*.

and devastation is just the same to Communists as to all other people. In fact that is my besetting sin. I think Communists are human, some good, some bad, some smart, some dumb, some heroes, some cowards, some bright guys, some stinkers. Communists were not considered so awful in the 1930s in Washington, and I knew some good ones, and of course they were in the Labor movement, and in the Civil Rights movement, and it is silly to say they were not. At one time I even thought to be one was the only way to salvation, and the reason I did not become one was not that I did not believe in Socialism, I do. But I think their political approach for this Country was all wrong. From the days of the Know Nothings, to the Ku Klux Klan, all secret societies have been suspect and have frightened people. I think they should have concentrated on building a political party as they have done in France and Italy and to some extent England, and not had all these phony organizations, and thought that one Communist in an organization made a Spring. I think their political tactics for this country were awful, and they are paying for it, and unfortunately a lot of others [are too]. But I did not think the PP was that kind of a false front business, but a straight out cooperative venture. The head of the [Communist] Party in Virginia, a Mrs. [Alice] Burke, who was a very nice woman came to see me and offered to cooperate, but they did not have much to promise. That is another [problem] with it, they promise more than they can deliver. I told her that I thought the two groups should stay distinct and separate and if they wanted to vote for Wallace, well fine. But after the PP was formed and the big split came in the CIO and the NAACP, the groups that the CP had some influence in were just about the only ones that were receptive, this is not wholly so, but the FTA* and the Peanut Workers (maybe they are the same) were just about the only organized groups that gave us any real support . . . Personally the reason I decided I simply could never be a Communist is that I could never agree to agree to something I disagreed with. I thought the CP made a terrible mistake about calling the War "a phony War" before Hitler attacked the USSR. It was silly in my opinion to equate England with Germany. I know the Tories are awful, but not like the Nazis . . . But beyond that single instance there are

---

*Food, Tobacco and Agricultural Workers Union.

numbers of others, I could not be a member of an organization that said I had to be for something I was against, and support it. My whole Scotch Presbyterian ancestry revolts at the thought. But perhaps I could not be a member of a Union either, or any political Party or disciplined group. I want Socialism but I want a free conscience too. I want to be able to say what I please, and think what I please, and write what I please. But now I haven't got Socialism and I can't speak or write either. I make an honorable exception of writing to you. But some of the Communists in the South have been real heroes, martyrs, who have died for people. I wish I could write the story of one of them—Joe Gelders who was as near a Saint as I will ever know. I am confused about this, as many of the Jesuits were saints too in many ways, and yet the Catholic Church congealed into oppression. These are the kinds of questions that need to be discussed and talked and written about, but with the kind of censorship we have it is difficult . . . I agree with Palmer that the CP issue wasn't important in the South, it was Wallace's standing for Negro rights, and refusing to speak to a segregated audience, and that was grand and noble, and did good I know, and I think drove that two bit punk Harry Truman to make promises he didn't deliver, but he made them and he gave the Negroes hope and now Eisenhower has to make them, so in that way I think Henry did a lot of good. In that one way I think he made a *terrific* contribution . . . Yes, I do adore Marc.* He is a real politician and a good one, and I trust him completely. In fact it was only after he said that you were OK that I dared write you so fully. I suspect a lot of people think you are from the FBI . . . I write in such haste as I have so much to do, so forgive the lack of punctuation.

In the summer of 1953, Virginia and Cliff rented a little shack on a nearby river where they went to swim and often spent the night. It provided a place where they could be alone as a family. After two years in Montgomery, Cliff was still struggling to build a law practice. Alabama senators Lister Hill and John Sparkman, men they had known well and worked with in Washington, avoided them, although Cliff and Lister Hill had been friends since their college days. And it did not look like their prospects were about to improve any time soon. The U.S. attorney general

---

*Vito Marcantonio.

had recently added the National Lawyers Guild to his list of subversive organizations, and the *Montgomery Advertiser* ran a front-page article on Clifford Durr and the guild.

September 16, 1953
Dear Clark: . . .

I am feeling much better from my low point of despair when I faced another winter like the others and could see no prospect of relief. I think the shack on the River has done more than anything; at least it is a refuge . . . and some place we can go and have some family life. I still see no bright prospects for a flourishing law practice, but I will continue to do all I can to make it come true if possible, but I think we are going to be doomed to the same isolation that Aubrey lives in. Personally I think people like us, at least a good number, and yet we have gone outside the tribe and broken the taboos and they won't take us back in unless we do penance and confess our sins, and we don't and we won't and so that is that. I think after this winter Cliff will have his mind definitely made up if he can make a go of it or not, and will be willing to at least look for something else. Red James has gone to Houston to be the legal advisor to the Mayor of Houston, Roy Hofheinz. Although Red was certainly never even "pink" and was benighted about race relations, still he did have a labor practice and as they got weaker the practice did too, so he got a well-paying job with Roy. The Unions down here, at least in Montgomery are practically wiped out already. Cliff just drew up a contract to sell the Textile Workers Union Hall, as they are flat busted and out of business.

Even John Sparkman and Lister [Hill] are on the defensive, and as they get more scared and the opposition gets stronger, they draw in their horns more and more, and we have only seen Lister once in the two and a half years we have been here, and John not at all. Now after the long article the paper carried on Cliff and the Lawyer's Guild, I am sure they will avoid us more carefully than ever, if that is possible. So I really don't see where the practice is coming from . . . If we did not have the small retainer from the Durr Drug Company, out of which we have to pay the office expenses and our personal expenses, I don't know what we should do, and as it is the going is tough to say the least . . . I think it is a hard blow for Cliff, and will be a harder blow to take if he has to leave, to realize that all the personal affection, and uncles and cousins, and relatives of all sorts and descriptions, still does not add up to a law practice. He has always thought and still thinks that character and personal relations and personal affections are stronger than economic interests and political ideas, and I am afraid he is having a rude awakening. I hope I will turn out to be wrong for his sake and mine as well, as if we could just make a living and have any kind of home of our own, I think I could live down here very happily, in spite of the few people who have similar ideas. I love the physical surroundings, the hot sun and the rain and the river, and I am fascinated by the point-counterpoint of the two races, and the small gains that are made and the rationalizations that are made, and the political scene with the emerging Negro vote is also of greatest interest but, and it is a big BUT, where are the clients coming from? Since we have no ties except personal ones, and they are with the most conservative group in the city, I simply don't see where we fit in as far as clients are concerned, and I can only hope that some miracle will occur.

Lots of love and do write more fully about the [National Emergency Civil Liberties] Committee and what the plans are and who is helping your plans along and who is blocking you and all about it. Give my love to dearest Mairi, and as always I am,

Your devoted, Va.

With McCarthyism at its peak, the web of investigations, hearings and subpoenas expanded and soon came south. Virginia's family and friends were among the targets, and she ultimately would be one herself. She was stunned when her son-in-law, Walter Lyon, became the subject of a security investigation. Lyon had been working for the U.S. Public Health Service in Thailand for nearly a year as a consultant in environmental health, and Ann was teaching English in a local school. With little explanation beyond a vague reference to his security file, his supervisor told him that he and Ann were being sent back to the United States. Virginia worked through her various channels to uncover the reasons for this action.

November 6, 1953
Dear Hugo:
Mike Straus called us this morning, and he had found out some further information regarding Ann and Walter which I am sure you would like to hear.

The Public Health Service was as much in the dark as they were. Said there was nothing in Walter's record that was in any way derogatory. He has been cleared three times for full security and the last clearance is only six months old. BUT when Mike got to Mr. Ross at the Foreign Aid Organization he said . . . that he had been given the order for their return, that THE RULES HAD BEEN CHANGED and that on the basis of the new rules, they were not entitled to clearance on the basis of the new information they had obtained. What the information is he was not able to tell Mike, and said there WAS NO WAY AND NO AGENCY THAT COULD GIVE HIM THE GROUNDS AND THAT THEY HAD NO OBLIGATION TO DISCLOSE THE INFORMATION.

Mike thinks he will have to face a "Loyalty" hearing on his return, or perhaps will even be fired from the Public Health Service as a security risk without ever having a hearing or even knowing why he is a risk.

Cliff talked to Lister [Hill] again and called John [Sparkman] and he said he would write Stassen too. They are both mad and say that they are cleaning out all the Democrats and their friends in this fashion. Cliff could not help but tell them that he had said exactly this would happen, but that is small comfort to be right, when you know that your daughter will have to come back to this sort of thing.

Well it is a Mess but I know Ann and Walter will take it all right, and I suppose he can get a job somewhere. I wonder if they would be safer to stay in Europe, since he is a German Jew they can revoke his citizenship if they want to under the McCarran Act.* Cliff thinks they would not be better off there than here, and he says the only thing to do is kill the scoundrels.

Love Jinksie

November 13, 1953
Dear Clark: . . .

We have just heard from Ann and Walt that they are being sent back here, with no reason given. Until we know more about it we will just assume it is an economy move, and replacing all Democrats with Republicans, but it could easily be something more sinister. Anything can

---

*The McCarran-Walter Immigration Act (1952) broadened the power of the attorney general to deport immigrants even after they had become naturalized citizens.

happen these days, and I am getting either punch drunk or more philosophical, any rate I am not going to let the God Damned Bastards kill me with worry, and I hope to live to see the day they burn in Hell.

Devotedly your friend, Virginia

November 24, 1953
Dear Clark: . . .

Ann and Walter will arrive in New York on the 29th on the *Constitution* and I do hope you all can meet them as we can't, and it will be wonderful if you can. I am so furious at the goings on that I for a time thought it might be wise for them to stay in Europe . . . I suppose you have seen . . . that Hummon Talmadge* has announced that ALL the Committees are coming to Georgia to do a job on the Reds in the South. The *Atlanta Journal* (Hearst paper) has already started out on Jim Dombrowski and Aubrey and also on Louis Burnham.† Aubrey and Jim had a meeting in Atlanta with your friend Mr. [John Wesley] Dobbs and he and they have decided not to release any of the SCEF mailing lists or contributors or anything like that. Aubrey is right worried about it, but not too much so. Cliff spoke at the Negro College here on the Rights of Citizenship and they loved it and in their publicity they billed him as a "Business and Financial Tycoon" which has caused much amusement to all the people who know our precarious finances.

I know I always reply much too soon and write much too long letters, but I love so being in touch with you and how else can I express my devotion?

November 28, 1953
Dear Hugo:

Lister [Hill] called Cliff over to his office yesterday and told him that he had heard through John Horne, who is John Sparkman's secretary, that he (John Horne) had gone over and talked with the Security Officer of the Mutual Security Agency, and the Security Officer had told him in

---

*Herman "Hummon" Talmadge, governor of Georgia.
†James Dombrowski, long-time labor and civil rights activist, was executive secretary of the Southern Conference Education Fund. Louis Burnham, a leader of the Southern Negro Youth Congress during the 1940s, had been co-director of Henry Wallace's campaign in the South in 1948.

confidence what the charges against Ann and Walter were. There are none against Walter of any kind, except that he is married to Ann, and against her they have the following charges: 1. That while in college she had a friend (unnamed) who was a Communist. 2. That she wrote a letter to Judge Medina or Judge Kaufman either protesting the conviction of the Communists under the Smith Act, or protesting the death sentence of the Rosenbergs. 3. That she had applied for a scholarship to Charles University in Prague in Checho-Slovakia upon her graduation from Wisconsin.

We have no knowledge of the first actions on her part, but as far as the scholarship that was simply an inquiry as she wanted to get abroad and at that time in 1949 they were trying to get American students, but they did not give her one and the whole program was dropped. There may be other and more serious charges against Cliff and me, but I am sure they must have had a lot of trouble digging up these on Ann. Of course I do not think any of this makes any sense unless they are trying to get at you, for you are the only target they might think worthwhile, but I hardly see how they could use anything as stupid and puerile as this against you.

I would feel better about the outlook if I saw anything that gave hope that it might be stopped, but except for you and Bill [Douglas] and sometimes a few of your colleagues that still believe in the rule of Law occasionally, I don't see any opposition. Truman simply fell into the trap they dug for him, and if that is going to be the principle of the Democratic Party, then the whole concept of a legal society is gone, and anybody can be caught with any lie somebody wants to trap them with . . .

I will keep you informed as to any other developments . . .

Affectionately, Jinksie

In the midst of Ann and Walter's troubles, Virginia received word that Jessica "Decca" Mitford had been subpoenaed to appear before the House Un-American Activities Committee during a major probe of Communist Party activity in the San Francisco area. Decca and her daughter Dinky had moved to San Francisco ten years earlier. Robert "Bob" Treuhaft, a labor lawyer, followed Decca west and they soon married. Decca and Bob joined the Communist party in 1943 and were active in labor and civil rights struggles in the San Francisco Bay area. By 1953 they had moved to Oakland, and Decca was executive secretary of the East Bay Civil Rights Congress.[12]

December 2, 1953
Dearest Clark, . . .

Dec wrote me that she was up before the Committee, simply thrilled to be on television apparently, said she had a new hat and hoped to get a movie contract. I know she will spit in their eye. Laurent Frantz is the lawyer for her . . . and I hope he keeps her out of jail because I am committed to Dinky Donk if she goes . . . but I don't think I could take her now.

ca. December 1953
Dear Marge and Laurent: . . .

Since I last wrote you . . . Ann and her husband have been recalled from Thailand for a "Hearing."* As you know both of them are conservative in their thinking and have tried to lead respectable lives and not take any chances. And now this happens to them! Cliff on account of his Lawyer's Guild experience is officially declared "subversive" by Mr. Brownell and now Ann. Well it has done one good thing at least, it has made the whole family (I mean my family) aware that it wasn't Mama's crazy ideas that got the family in trouble and that this was something that had to be fought tooth and toenail. I really feel a great sense of relief now that the family is so mad about Ann, and realize that the witch hunt is based not on fact but on pure and unadulterated persecution. I am very much afraid Walter will be deported if they can pin anything on him, as he is an immigrant and a victim of Hitler who will no doubt next be canonized along with Whitaker Chambers†. . .

Talmadge has announced that he has called *all* the Committees to Georgia to hunt for Reds and they will start as soon as they fulfill other engagements—so we will have a lively show and the Hearst paper in Atlanta has already started on Aubrey and Jim. You know Aubrey debated Talmadge on television on the question of segregation in the schools

---

*Walter and Ann returned to Washington at the end of December. Walter decided not to challenge the order that led to his recall from Thailand. There was no hearing and he went back to work with the U.S. Public Health Service in Washington.
†Gained notoriety by identifying Alger Hiss as a Communist. Chambers's bestselling autobiography, *Witness*, was published in 1952 to critical acclaim.

and it made him so mad that is what got him started I believe, that and the fact that Dr. Clement* got elected to the Atlanta Board of Education with a lot of white votes.

Lots of love and do write and soon. Va

February 1954
Dearest Marge:

I loved your letter but do not have time at this moment to answer it properly as I am doing this in an interim when Cliff is talking over the telephone. Strictly against the rules of the office.

I have gotten a job for July and August as Assistant Cook at a Camp in Vermont and in payment they are giving Tilla her tuition and Lulah too. I am so thrilled over the chance to get them in a good inter-racial camp where they will have healthy surroundings. It is run by a Quaker named Kenneth Webb . . . I got it through the recommendation of my Quaker friends that I made by my peace stand. I am looking forward to it almost as much as the girls, as I have to confess that Montgomery, Alabama gets me down. Death, decay, corruption, frustration, bitterness and sorrow. The Lost Cause is right. The only gay and bright and coming spirit is among the Negroes and I am almost entirely cut off from them although I do bootleg a little bit. They will inherit the South and they should, as they have the vitality and the love of life. But you know it all as well or better than I.

Lots of love and I will write a full letter when I have time.

By the start of 1954, the South was thick with discussion about the pending *Brown* decision, and segregationists increased their efforts to link civil rights activities with the subversive influences of the Communist Party. Aubrey Williams and James Dombrowski were prime targets for a Southern witch hunt. Williams was president of the Southern Conference Education Fund (SCEF), an outgrowth of the old SCHW, which had disbanded in 1948, and Dombrowski was the executive secretary. SCEF and the Highlander Folk School were the only Southern-based interracial organizations active in the fight to end racial segregation. As the NAACP cases on school desegregation made their way through the Supreme Court in the early 1950s, SCEF sponsored several South-wide meetings to build support for

---

*Rufus Clement was the president of Atlanta University.

school desegregation. By 1953, Williams had distinguished himself as one of the leading white Southern opponents of segregation and was invited to debate Herman Talmadge, one of its leading defenders, on national television.

Early in 1954, the Senate Judiciary Committee's Subcommittee on Internal Security turned its attention to SCEF. On March 6, Aubrey Williams received a subpoena to appear before the subcommittee at a special hearing in New Orleans on March 16, chaired by Senator James Eastland of Mississippi.

March 7, 1954
Dearest Ann:

Your letter came yesterday and we are always simply delighted to hear from you . . .

I never know when I write to you whether I should be cheerful and untruthful or truthful and uncheerful, and I try to be both if possible, but sometimes I am not able to be . . .

The real problem is the fact that by principle and sympathy and experience we belong in one world and live in another and that could not help but create problems. I am afraid they will come to a head very shortly as Aubrey has been served with a subpoena by the Jenner Committee and has to appear in New Orleans on March 16, and Daddy is going to represent him before the Committee. Daddy never hesitated and did not even pause for breath, but went right to work getting ready for the Hearing. There is no use trying to dissuade him as you will only create more problems for him as he is going to do it. What effect this will have on his family I don't know, or his law practice, or anything else, but he seemed shocked when I asked him if he thought he could do it. Of course I think he is right and being himself could do nothing else, but I don't know that the family will feel that way. But it is his family and he will have to deal with them. I just hope that Marshall Field and Jim Warburg put up a good fee for him, but I doubt it . . . But I simply am not going to face all these problems until they come to a head. I have learned that to survive I can't look ahead all the time . . .

Please darling, don't worry. You have had so much to worry you and I think we will win . . . yet.

Lots of love, Mother

Aubrey received his subpoena on a Saturday. Virginia spent most of the weekend trying to talk Cliff out of going to New Orleans, terrified that he might not survive the experience. He had a mild heart condition and he was still recovering his strength after his back surgery. She enlisted the help of the doctor, who warned that Cliff should not go to the hearing under any circumstances. Cliff remained determined; he would not let Aubrey go alone.

They were still arguing about it when they arrived at their office on Monday morning. A federal marshal was waiting with a subpoena for Virginia. Virginia, a former board member of SCEF, had resigned from the board in 1950 when they moved to Denver. She cut her ties with all other political organizations, and along with Cliff was trying to lead a quiet life, focusing their attention on making a living, looking after their family, and getting reestablished in Alabama. Now, with the spotlight of a Congressional hearing on them, these efforts were completely undermined.

As they prepared to go to New Orleans, Virginia went into high gear. She recalled that Aubrey and Cliff took "the elevated southern gentleman attitude about everybody in Washington" and would not think of seeking help from anyone who failed to offer it. She, however, did not have such "high class feelings." She got on the phone immediately and began calling everyone she knew in Washington, starting with Lyndon Johnson, then serving as minority leader in the Senate.

Failing to reach Johnson at his office, she called his home late into the night until she finally got through to Lady Bird. Lyndon was asleep, but Virginia insisted on speaking to him. She and Aubrey had been subpoenaed by Eastland's committee, Virginia explained, and she needed to talk with Lyndon right away. Virginia later recalled Lady Bird's response. "Bird said, 'Honey, I don't know what it's all about, but I know you and Aubrey are good people.' That's exactly what she said, 'I know you are good people.' You see, this was getting down to character, not ideology. So she went and waked Lyndon up, and he got on the telephone." Virginia went on to recount her conversation with Lyndon:

> I said, "What do you mean letting this happen? You're the Minority Leader of the Senate, and sending this Jim Eastland down to rake us over the coals this way?" [He said,] "Well honey, I didn't know one thing in the world about it." I said, "And you're the Minority Leader of the Senate and you didn't even know what was going on." He said he really didn't and I think he was probably telling the truth. So he said, "What can I do?" I said, "Well Lyndon, in the first place, you can see that no Democrat comes with Eastland. Let Jim Eastland come by himself, but don't you let a lot of Democrats come down."

Virginia reasoned that if Eastland came alone, the chances that they would be held in contempt of Congress were lessened. Although Johnson didn't commit himself, he assured Virginia, "Well sweetie pie, I love you. I'll do what I can." She called everyone else she knew in Congress—George Bender, a Republican Congressman who worked with her on the anti-poll tax effort, William Langer, chairman of the Senate Judiciary Committee,

Senators Claude Pepper, Lister Hill, Estes Kefauver, and others—to alert them to what was going on, and to urge them to see that no other senators accompanied Eastland to New Orleans. When the hearings opened in New Orleans on March 16, Eastland presided alone.

Eastland's investigation of SCEF and its possible communist activities received wide coverage in the Southern press. In addition to Aubrey Williams and Virginia, others subpoened to appear before Eastland's subcommittee included SCEF executive secretary Jim Dombrowski and board member Myles Horton, who was also director of Highlander Folk School. In press reports surrounding the hearings, Williams and Dombrowski emphasized that SCEF's work was focused on the abolition of racial segregation and discrimination, and charged that Eastland sought to destroy the organization by linking it to Communism. Virginia recalled that few in Montgomery thought she was a Communist. But now the fact that she was an opponent of segregation was fully aired in newspapers across the South, which was at least equally damning.

On the morning of March 17, Virginia took the witness stand, represented by Montgomery lawyer John Kohn, who volunteered his services. Initially she had planned not to answer any of the questions as a display of her utter contempt for Eastland and for the proceedings, but given Hugo Black's position on the Supreme Court, she concluded that she had to answer two questions: Was she a member of the Communist Party? Was she under Communist Party discipline? No, was her response to both queries. She would answer no others, ignoring Eastland's insistent demand, "Answer that question." Virginia merely said, "I stand mute," and occasionally opened her compact and powdered her nose.

Paul Crouch was the subcommittee's principal witness. Crouch, a former Communist who had been a party member for 17 years, was employed by the Immigration Service in Hawaii as a consultant on subversive activities and worked as an "expert witness" for numerous Congressional hearings. Crouch charged that Virginia used her contacts with Eleanor Roosevelt and Hugo Black to aid the communist movement, and was part of an espionage ring that reached into the White House. Her home, Crouch reported, "was a frequent gathering place for people connected with the Soviet infiltration of Washington." Crouch said that he doubted she was an actual member of the Communist Party, implying that she was too important to be linked to the party in that manner.

That afternoon Crouch testified against Aubrey Williams, spinning another tale of intrigue and subversion within the New Deal. Cliff Durr, serving as Williams's counsel, asked Eastland for permission to cross-examine Crouch and, in a move highly unusual for a congressional hearing, Eastland granted it. As Cliff began to question Crouch, Richard Arens, counsel for the committee, suddenly interjected, "Is Mr. Durr a Communist?"

Crouch replied that he didn't know if he was still a member of the party, but he had been in the past, and went on to recall meeting Cliff at several high-level meetings of party officials in New York. Cliff insisted that he himself be sworn in as a witness to answer the charges. He was, and he stated categorically that he was not then and never had been a member of the Communist Party. Then he turned to Eastland and said that as chairman of the committee it was his responsibility "to see that one or the other of us is indicted for perjury." Nothing was done.

Tensions were running high when the hearings concluded the following morning. As the courtroom began to clear, Cliff and Crouch came face to face. As Cliff later recalled, something snapped. He vaulted over the jury railing and lunged for Crouch, shouting, "You God damn son of a bitch. Lying about my wife that way! I'm going to kill you!" Federal marshals quickly separated the two men. Cliff's friends insisted that he rest on a bench, and they summoned a doctor. After checking his heart, the doctor sent him to the hospital immediately. He remained there for a week and underwent tests. Then he and Virginia went to the Gulf Coast to rest for two weeks before returning home, with the support of Ethel Clyde, a wealthy benefactor of SCEF.[13]

Writing from Gulfport, Mississippi, Virginia reported on the experience to Eleanor Roosevelt and Esther Gelders, the widow of Joe Gelders. These letters are followed by others written from Montgomery, describing the aftermath of the hearings.

March 31, 1954
Dear Mrs. Roosevelt:

A friend sent me the column you wrote defending Aubrey Williams and myself against the charges of Paul Crouch before the Subcommittee of the Senate Internal Security Committee in New Orleans. I want to express to you my very deep thanks. It takes real courage these days to stand up for one's friends and acquaintances in the face of the fear and hysteria of the times.

I cannot express to you too strongly my sense of shame and indignation that your name and the name of your husband should have been dragged into these "Hearings" by a paid perjurer and that such testimony should have been allowed into the Record by a so-called "Democratic" Senator . . .

To say I was a "party to an espionage ring operating in the White House from 1938 to 1942" is an absolute lie, as you well know. Of the five people named, I was never at the White House with any one of them. Two of them, Mr. Lash and Mr. Parkes, I never even met to my knowledge. The other three, Mr. [Malcolm] Dobbs, Mr. [Howard] Lee and Mr. [Joseph] Gelders, I knew in the Southern Conference, and from my knowledge of them I do not believe that any one of them was a spy, or a traitor to his country.

The few times I was ever at the White House, other than at official receptions, was when I came to ask your help on the various Anti-Poll Tax bills. Because you believed in a free franchise you did help, and it was a great inspiration to me personally. Because I also believed so strongly in a free franchise, I gave years of my life to this cause. The records of the Southern Conference and of the Committee to Abolish the Poll Tax are in the archives of Atlanta University, which requested them for future scholars of the long fight for a free vote in the South. There was no need of a "Hearing" to establish facts that are open and plain to anyone that can read and do research.

This was a political maneuver pure and simple. Senator Eastland thought he could win votes in Mississippi by attacking an organization that is opposed to segregation, and lent himself to a further attack on the Roosevelt Administration on the "twenty years of treason" charge.

But, Please, Mrs. Roosevelt, do not think that this man speaks for the South. Southerners are loyal to their friends, and we know that both you and your husband were friends of the South and wanted to help us . . .

Come and visit us and see for yourself and you will find that the name of Roosevelt is still held in love and honor in the South.

Thanking you again, I am,

Sincerely yours, Virginia Durr

April 6, 1954

Dearest Esther:

We are still in Gulfport, but will go home Thursday if Cliff continues to be all right. His heart condition is improved but it will be some time before he is OK and then only if he takes care of himself. I am sure you know what that is. There is no actual heart disease, only a constriction that could be serious if he does not get relaxed and off the tension. How to do that is my problem which I do not yet see the solution of.

I am sending you the clippings that dealt with Joe. At least all I can find. It was such a madhouse . . .

If you have not been through one of them, it is hard to describe the horror of it. It is the idea that your own Government of your own country doing such a thing. Using paid liars, perjurers and paying them to go around the country and do their dirty work.

The background of the Hearing is very clear. There have been a good many southern voices raised to speak against segregation. Some of the boys at the U. of Ga. [University of Georgia] wrote a fine piece in their paper and Herman Talmadge got busy and said he had gone to Washington and ALL the committees had agreed to come down and hunt "subversives." Then shortly thereafter he and Aubrey Williams debated the subject on television and I think Aubrey got the best of him. Then pronto his pal Eastland announces that he is coming South to find subversives and the SCEF is the nesting ground. I resigned from all of everything when Cliff got sick and we came here to stay with his family, but of course Eastland could not pass up the chance to get a headline out of Hugo so I was called up too. At first I did not want to come at all, defy them all the way, but then things got hot and the pressures began to mount. I agreed to come but not answer any questions, then the pressures really got heavy and I finally agreed to answer The One, which I think weakened my position of defiance and also everybody else's. I sent you a copy of my statement too. I think it was pretty good considering the circumstances. In any case it was the best I could do or so it seemed. There is nothing to do with these characters but kick them in the teeth as hard as you can . . . Please read this to Dec and Marge and tell them I will write when I possibly can.

April 16, 1954
Dear Hugo:

I appreciated your letter so much and thank you for it. I am so sorry that you have had to go through another headline hunting spree and I was glad to learn from Ann that you were not taking it too hard. It was a horrible experience and when I think that it has been repeated over and over again, it makes me fear that our country is headed for fascism, in spite of your wonderful decisions. Locally the response has been very good, and the idea seems to be that a home-town boy has been wrongfully attacked, but what it will mean in terms of a law practice remains to be seen. It was a delicate growth at best, and I hope this does not wither it. If it does, we will have to try it somewhere else.

Cliff is much better and I think if he will take care of himself and does not have any further excitement for a time, he will be all right. He has been under a terrible strain and for a long time . . .

Lots of love, Jinksie

May 1, 1954
Dearest Dec:

Please excuse my long delay in answering your telegram and your letter and also the resolution that Bob got for Cliff. I have thought of you often, but the pressure of events has been heavy. We were sort of shell-shocked after it was all over, and then Cliff was a week in the Hospital and two weeks on the Coast . . . He has not had an actual heart attack, but some pretty grim warnings that if he did not watch out . . . he would have, so we have been trying to rearrange our life so that he will get some peace and quiet. We have rented an apartment and are in the process of moving in now . . . Cliff still wants to stay here if it is possible in any way—he dreads to leave and feels that this is his proper place. Most of the people here have been wonderfully kind and friendly on a personal basis . . . What is more encouraging to me is the fact that the Southern Negro community has come to our defense and have written letters and drawn up protests and have done what was in their power to do. They certainly want us to stay and Aubrey and anyone that they feel is friendly. Actually they are the only help we have. The group here is working on the northern organizations to protest to the Jenner Committee any possible contempt citations and also the other Hearing that is supposed to be held in Birmingham in June under Eastland's chairmanship. Aubrey, Cliff, Jim, Myles and I are all in contempt of the Committee, and I most of all. Even so I don't think I was in enough contempt since I answered the $64 questions and I think that is giving in to them. I hope you saw a copy of my statement which was published in the *Washington Post* and got a good response on an individual basis, although the *Post* did not have any editorial . . .

Mrs. R. wrote a nice column in my defense and also a nice letter to me personally. We have gotten wonderful letters from all over the country, and I think there is some awakening, but there is a hard road ahead. The horror of the sort of thing we went through is that it is done under Government auspices, and the use of perjured testimony is deliberate, and the complete lack of any fairness or due process—and the deliberate intention of trying to lynch you publicly, but you know all about it.

Just two months after the New Orleans hearing, the Supreme Court ruled in *Brown v. Board of Education* that segregation in public schools was unconstitutional. Virginia was cautiously optimistic about the implications of the court's ruling.

May 19, 1954
Dear Hugo:

Well the Great Decision came on yesterday and has caused far less excitement than anyone thought it would. A lot of Lucy's friends were at the apartment when it came through and they took it calmly and said they did not see how the Court could have ruled any other way. A few vicious people could cause a lot of trouble, but if they can be kept under control I think it will work out without too much violence, at least in the cities, it is the country where there seems to be the most fear and resentment. Cliff's truckers in the Baggett case are the most violent in their resentment, especially the ones from Mississippi.

Cliff is better but still has to be more careful. If we can just win these pending cases and get a little money ahead, I think he can be cured easily.

May 25, 1954
Dearest Clark: . . .

The reaction here on the decision is calmer than I had thought it would be, but still that might simply be the calm before the storm. Talmadge of course is sounding off and Eastland, and even John and Lister, and so on, but while there is a lot of talk about it, I don't think any violence is imminent.

But then I don't think any integration is imminent right now. There will be endless lawsuits and so on.

After the Eastland hearings, the future of Cliff's struggling law practice looked even less promising. Nevertheless, Virginia insisted that they move to an apartment of their own. "We didn't know what the effect of the hearing would be," she recalled, "whether we would be attacked or there'd be crosses burned." And the pressures associated with living in the home of Cliff's mother had become harder to bear after New Orleans. They moved to an apartment house nearby, at 2 Felder Avenue.[14]

In the following letters, Virginia discusses the after effects of the hearings. Ironically, it appeared that the partial elimination of the poll tax in Alabama through a voter qualification amendment approved in December 1953 helped to undermine plans for another set of Eastland-style hearings in Birmingham. Liberal Jim Folsom handily won the Democratic primary election for governor.

June 3, 1954

Dearest Marge and Esther,

I have not dared to write you fully as we have been so closely watched, mail opened, telephone tapped and so on. As long as the Birmingham hearings were hanging over us and you were likely to get a subpoena, I did not want them to have anything to quote, and for a while I think it better to send any personal letters to our new address—2 Felder and put no return address on them.

We understand from reliable sources that the Birmingham hearings have been called off and that is a great relief. Actually the New Orleans hearings were the build-up for the Birmingham hearings . . . The Birmingham hearing was going to shoot the works and from the notice we had of it, Tex, Polly, Alton, and all of you were to be subpoenaed.* But it looks sometimes as if there is justice on account of the Poll Tax in Alabama being repealed for all over 45 and reduced to $3.00 for all under, there was a 200,000 increase in registration and John [Sparkman] and Jim [Folsom] got in on the first primary. Another thing the Negro community of the South really went to town for us in protesting to the Committee and we got a lot of support from them in the North too and what came out of it was that when the show-down came the Negroes had more political power than the Dixiecrats, and even more than [Richard] Arens and the Twenty Years of Treason boys,† which does make me feel that we have succeeded in what we were trying to do.

---

*Malcolm "Tex" Dobbs, Polly Dobbs, and Alton Lawrence had all been active in the Southern Conference for Human Welfare's Birmingham chapter.

†"Twenty Years of Treason" was a charge leveled by right-wing Republicans against the Roosevelt and Truman administrations.

Personally we are pretty well shot still, huge debts and no money and business practically at a standstill, and Cliff still sick, but he wants to hang on and stay here, and IF we can, I have begun to think it is the best thing to do. Everybody with any decent ideas gets driven out of the South, and there is no bridge between the two races, or at least a very tenuous one, but the going is tough and no doubt about it. Aubrey has lost $40,000 in advertising already since the New Orleans business and we seem to have lost our clients. But we are going to stick it out this summer and see if we can make it.

Write me and tell me what you think, and don't be afraid to write me frankly.

Lots of love, Va.

[p.s.] Just since beginning this the Presiding Bishop of the AME Zion church has come in with some business that will mean a good fee—so maybe we can make it.

June 1954

Dearest Dec: . . .

Cliff is a little better but the dilemma of our situation remains the same and I don't see the solution in sight right now. He simply has not been able to make a living down here and has to draw on his inheritance which I can't see is so awful, but it makes him feel a total failure and of course the family considers him as such and "Poor Cliff" is their theme. Of course they think if he hadn't married me he would not have strayed so far from the orthodox ways and would now be solvent, prosperous and successful. What he has stood for, fought for, believed in and I think influenced is nothing but foolishness in their eyes. I think my sister-in-law expressed it perfectly the other night when she said about someone with unorthodox opinions who was having a hard time, "But he has no right to express his opinions when he can't make a living for his family." I feared it would be like this and it has been. They don't influence me so much—at least now that I am out of the house, but they influence Cliff a great deal because he is so fond of them. But essentially it is Cliff's own conflict which he has never solved that is the difficulty, and he will have to solve it in his own way. He himself is so tolerant and can take such opposite points of view without getting enraged, that he does not realize that for most people this is impossible. To represent Aubrey Williams on the one hand and the

Durr Drug Co. on the other means that we fall between the two stools and belong neither to the one nor to the other . . . His heart condition is purely nervous so far, but it can kill him just as quickly. I don't know the answer for I don't know any place where we can go and make a living without him changing his whole approach to things and I don't think he will do that. The horror of the hearing in New Orleans, and all the publicity was awful for him, and the sense of burning outrage and injustice, but honestly I think the thing that is killing him is simply that he feels such a failure because he can't make a living for his family down here. I keep hoping that he will make some effort to get away into a more congenial atmosphere but he keeps saying there is no place to go, and for the time being, he is sick and worried and there is nothing to do but stand by him and try and get him well so he can make decisions.

The Durrs spent most of the summer away from Montgomery. A couple named Wilcox who admired their stand in New Orleans sent them money to travel north, where they visited with them and several other friends in Massachusetts. On the way back to Alabama, they spent time with the Foremans in New York and with Ann and Walter in Harrisburg.[15]

They returned home to find Cliff's nephew, Nesbitt Elmore, in the midst of a school desegregation case. In the first effort by blacks in Alabama to enforce the *Brown* decision, 23 black students from the Abraham Vineyard School attempted to enroll in the all-white William R. Harrison School in Montgomery. The Abraham Vineyard PTA organized the challenge, independent of the NAACP. Nesbitt Elmore, Cliff's nephew, served as the group's attorney, and Aubrey Williams, Jr. supported the students. Nesbitt, who shared Cliff's law office, was considered a renegade by the rest of the Durr family owing to his involvement in civil rights and police brutality cases.

September 8, 1954
Dearest Mairi and Clark:

I must write and thank you again for the hospitality that was extended to us in New York . . .

We got home to find all Hell had broken loose, as Cliff's nephew had brought suit for 23 Negro children to get in a white school, and he and young Aubrey have been threatened and had anonymous calls and there have been editorials in the paper, blaming all of it on big Aubrey of course, and "feeling is running high" as they say. It looks as though the NAACP may not take part in it, but it is all in such a state of flux that no one can say what will happen. In the meantime anything may happen, as there has already been a big fight in the Negro community and the ringleaders of the attempt have been put in jail and Nesbitt is trying to get them out, and a wonderful southern touch! One of the ringleaders in this attempt has worked for years for the Hills* (the anti-Lister Hills), and so while the Hills are the chief bulwark of segregation and are trying to work out methods to evade [desegregation], still they are in the suit to get their old time servant out of jail for being a ringleader in the fight against segregation. What a life this is, so full of contradictions, but awfully interesting.

A special legislative committee recommended that Governor Gordon Persons call a special session of the legislature to abolish Alabama's public school system in the aftermath of the *Brown* decision, but few political leaders in Alabama felt such a sense of urgency, since the court had not yet ruled on an enforcement plan. Persons, who was in the final months of his administration, declined to act and left the matter for his successor, James Folsom.

September 24, 1954
Dearest Mairi and Clark: . . .

I keep hoping each day to hear from you, although I know you must have been terribly busy getting the children off to College. We are over that hurdle now as they just go across the street [to Lanier High School], and it is still hot as Hell and summer has not gone by any means . . .

The segregation business is still boiling and the papers are full of it and the Legislative Committee has brought out a "Mississippi Plan" to do away with the public schools, but Jim Folsom says he thinks that might "discriminate against the White as well as the Negro children" (what I call a masterpiece of understatement). Lister [Hill] is here but after all his kindness to us in Washington we have not seen hide nor hair of him here and when Cliff called his office they said they "would let him know when he could see him" and that has not yet been. Also for the first time, we are meeting with some studied oversights and coolness, which is painful but to be expected. A big family wedding—in

---

*T. B. Hill, prominent conservative lawyer.

law—to which we were NOT invited—but if that is all we have to suffer we will be lucky.

September 30, 1954
Dear Clark and Mairi: . . .

The Segregation issue gets hotter and hotter—and the papers are full of it. It looks as though they are trying to work people up to some point of violence. Our next-door neighbors have stopped speaking to us, but that is a small loss, although unpleasant and it may not be that issue at all. But here there is being built up the most determined opposition to any integration all of which makes no sense as all the Federal installations are integrated, and they are begging for more, and then too the Catholic Hospital is integrated and they *say* they are going to integrate the school. Then too I went down to give some blood and a Negro man was just ahead of me and we went into the cafeteria after we gave it and the "best" people in town served him and me although at separate tables but right next to each other—so it all goes askew and contradictory. If our views—which have now been so publicized—just don't keep us from making a living—that is all that bothers me, which is quite a lot of course. I am hoping that when Jim Folsom comes in he will not add fuel to the flames but of course no one knows. He has objected to turning over the public schools to private groups and yet he says that it will be settled voluntarily and that the Negroes don't want it either—which of course is simply not true.

In response to the *Brown* decision, business and political leaders organized resistance to desegregation through the White Citizens Council. The first Citizens Council was founded in Sunflower County, Mississippi in July 1954, and chapters quickly sprang up throughout the Deep South.

December 13, 1954
Dearest Marge:

This is to wish you a Merry Christmas and hope that all goes well with you in the New Year. I know the going is rough even if you do have loving and congenial friends around you, and I think you and Laurent have been wonderful to brighten the corner where you are and to stick by your principles and raise your children and manage to keep going . . .

While I still long to escape to greener fields, still until there is some place to escape to, there is no use in being so miserable myself and making all the family so miserable, although I still cannot see any future for us here that is either pleasant or profitable, simply an existence until times get better . . . The White Citizens Councils here in Alabama have flowered all over the Black Belt and so far they have had it almost all their own way, with no protest from anyone else. The only restraining influence seems to be that those planters that have Negroes on their plantations are afraid they will get so frightened that they will run away. The slogan is that "the end of segregation will mean unlocking the bedroom doors of our white women to Negro men" which in itself is a revealing side-light on the way they regard "their women." Feeling down here is very high right now, although the general impression is that Jim Folsom won't join with Talmadge and the others in abolishing the Public School systems. But only time will tell. It is a curious and frightening feeling to meet seemingly nice, well-intentioned, intelligent people and then have them display on the subject of "race" a vindictiveness and fury of feeling that is awful. But you know all this as well as I do if not better.

Lots of love to all of the Frantzes and what I cannot send in the way of gifts, I send in the way of affection.

December 30, 1954
Dearest Clark and Mairi:

It was so nice to hear from you over the Holidays and we enjoyed Clark's letter and also Mairi's card. Also the splendid issue of *Rights** . . .

We had dinner with Lister Hill night before last and he seemed in fine fettle, he will be the Chairman of the Senate Labor and Welfare Committee—he and Henrietta both looked well, they have a new grandson and they both seemed better adjusted and more in harmony than I have ever seen them. Lister takes great pride—to us—in keeping us all out of jail for contempt. He thinks Talmadge was behind . . . the Hearing and that he and Eastland had cooked up a whole series of Hearings all over the South—but that after our Hearing, it was all called off. The horrible ones

---

*The quarterly journal of the National Emergency Civil Liberties Committee.

in Miami are the House Committee. I think what happened was that Lister helped him get re-elected in Mississippi as the price of calling off the Hearings—helped him in the TVA area, but this is gossip and rumor.

While Lister recognizes McCarthyism as a political evil and is agin it and voted for censure etc. still I did not get the impression that he was full of moral indignation at the violations of civil liberty and the horrors that are taking place—but it was simply a party and gay and convivial and so not the place for deep discussions. Upon going out in "Society" again I was struck anew with something that always did disgust me, and that is the vileness of the jokes that are told by "nice" southern men—I remember how Stella used to comment on it, but this time it struck me with redoubled force. Actually I think it is a good indication of the corruption that exists in the relationships of men and women . . .

John Welsey Dobbs* is coming over to speak on New Years Day and there is to be an Emancipation Day Celebration at the big Negro church here and they have asked me to come and be a guest. All within the framework of what is possible to do and still exist. That is always the debating point. How to survive and still not simply dry up. Of course we have lots of people that don't like us and disapprove of us but that would be true anywhere else too, I suppose . . .

Well let us hope that the New Year will bring us all some more peace and good will than we have now and that we will find things easing up a little, although personally I don't think anything but long and unceasing and unremitting struggle against the forces of evil will do any good.

Virginia was guardedly hopeful about Jim Folsom, the newly inaugurated governor. Folsom had served as governor from 1947 to 1951, during which time he promoted black voter registration by appointing sympathetic registrars. However, the racial climate had changed markedly in the aftermath of the *Brown* decision, and most Southern politicians found it difficult to resist the growing pressure to defend white supremacy.

---

*Grand master of Georgia's Prince Hall Masons and a founder of the Atlanta Civic and Political League.

January 26, 1955
Dearest Clark: . . .

The feeling on the Supreme Court decision is running high to say the least and it is a rare person with whom we don't have to avoid all ticklish subjects. I am not sure what Jim Folsom had in mind. He said that he is not going to "force" whites and Negroes to go to school together and I don't think he will. He is urging the Negroes to get out and vote and says he will see to it that they get registered—but even he can't get them registered in some of these Black Belt counties, I am sure. His Inauguration was terrific and he seems in complete command of the situation, has the Legislature eating out of his hand, and even the papers are being more polite. Hugo [Black] is the one that gets it day in and day out—they make some nasty remarks about him almost every day. These people down here are so paradoxical—so gracious and kind until you hit the race question and then they are as hard as iron. But the big Federal military installations are going right ahead with integration and no trouble at all.

Virginia had known Corliss Lamont since her college days. From a prominent banking family, Lamont was a socialist and a major benefactor of civil liberties causes. In 1953, Lamont ended his 20-year-long association with the ACLU after his renomination to the organization's board of directors was rescinded under pressure from other board members who were opposed to Lamont's ongoing challenge of the ACLU's anticommunist policies. After he was dropped from the ACLU board, Lamont joined the board of the National Emergency Civil Liberties Committee and in 1955 became vice chairman of that organization.[16]

Responding to a copy of a speech he had sent her, Virginia apparently took issue with Lamont's assumptions about the relationship of personal economic security to the struggle for freedom. She argued that some measure of economic security was essential, and pointed to Montgomery civil rights leader E. D. Nixon, a man who had an economic base independent of local whites, to support her point of view. The Durrs had become friendly with Nixon and Rosa Parks, leaders of the local NAACP branch.

February 9, 1955
Dear Corliss:

This debate of whether freedom or food comes first is the one that is shaking the world, and I want both, but I am of the opinion that a necessitous man is not a free man and that when every waking moment is taken up with surviving that the ordinary man has no time or strength left over for fighting for freedom, and only will do so when he sees he can't survive unless he does.

The only point at which I take issue is your remark that your speech was made to "a middle class audience of intellectuals, most of whom do have some kind of permanent economic base." I'll bet not three of them have any kind of base, and know that when or if their salary is cut off that they are bound to be on the community in less than three months. I get a lot of letters from all over the country from the many friends we made during our days in Washington and most of them are simple re-countals of the ways in which they are surviving—or not surviving, and these were people who were all active and effective in good works, but with the change in the climate they simply have become outcasts, and to survive at all takes all of their time and strength and energies. Perhaps this is rationalizations, but this is the way it seems to me. That is why I have always been of the opinion that the only way a progressive or lib-eral party can be built is on the basis of the trade unions as that is a guarantee that the people have jobs, or most of them, and if the Union is any good, they are protected in their jobs. Here in Montgomery the most effective as well as the bravest fighter for equal rights is a Negro named E. D. Nixon, who is an active member of the Brotherhood of Sleeping Car Porters, and is supported by them in any dispute over his job and they have tried repeatedly to get rid of him (I mean the Rail-roads) and he is also an active member of the NAACP and is supported by them in his fights, and that also gives him strength and support. He probably has more support on a national basis than any man in Mont-gomery, and is more effective politically than any other Negro here. Same is true of John Wesley Dobbs. This is not to say that I don't think the lonely hearts do good and make valuable contributions, as I do think so, and they often blaze the trail as you are doing—BUT to be ef-fective politically you have to have an economic base of some kind to sustain the troops.

It is such a pleasure to discuss things with you . . . because I am so fundamentally in accord with you.

During his first term as governor (1947–1951), James E. Folsom, a Pop-ulist-style politician and a "radical democrat," proved sympathetic to the appeals of Charles Gomillion that the fundamental guarantees of democracy be extended to the black citizens of Macon County seeking to register and vote. Folsom's appointee to the Macon County Board of Registrars, Herman Bentley, applied voter registration requirements fairly, and as a consequence the number of registered black voters in Macon County quadrupled to approximately 600. After Sam Engelhardt, Jr. was elected to the state legislature in 1950, following a campaign that promised to maintain white supremacy, Bentley was ousted from the Board of Registrars and black voter registration slowed to a trickle. Four years later, Folsom was elected to another term as governor. Shortly after his inauguration, he and Engelhardt came to blows over Folsom's efforts to pass a large bond issue for road construction, which Engelhardt and other conservatives opposed. Folsom's alleged threat, described below, was used by Engelhardt to consolidate support for aggressive resistance to black voting.[17]

February 17, 1955
Dear Hugo:

I am delighted that you are going to be able to get to Florida again and get some sunshine . . .

From down here it does look as if the tide were turning just a little—not much but some.

Yesterday I received a telephone call from one of the professors whom I know at Tuskegee* and he asked me if I thought you would be willing to come down and speak at the Institute. I told him that I could not speak for you in any way, shape, or form, that you made your own decisions and spoke for yourself at all times and under all circumstances. I did add that I thought it was your practice not to make public speeches during the terms of the Court, but that in any case I was not the proper person to make inquiries of, as our relationship was purely personal and I could give him no idea of what your reaction would be. I hope I handled it all right. Cliff was here and heard me and he was satisfied. As you have probably seen by the papers, there is a big row going on between the Governor and the Senator from Macon County on the issue of registration—and the Senator claims that Folsom said "I'm going to register every damn nigger in Macon County if you don't go along with my roads program." I doubt very much if he said this, but there is no doubt that the issue of reg-

---

*Charles Gomillion.

istration has become very hot, as the Macon County Board of Registrars has simply stopped registering anybody at all, and Folsom has promised that he would see to it that the Negroes got registered and were allowed to vote. With the rise of the White Citizens Council the whole situation is explosive—but the curious thing is that integration goes on at Maxwell and Gunter [Air Force bases]—no segregation of any kind, and no trouble of any kind either. Also at the Catholic Hospital here and Mrs. Walter Bragg Smith who is the Secretary of the Alabama Nurses Association and a lovely woman has managed to integrate the Association with no trouble of any kind and no publicity—but Mr. Hearin says the whole matter is hotter than I realize—as hot as it can be.

On March 2, 1955, 15-year-old Claudette Colvin was arrested for refusing to give up her seat on a city bus to a white person when ordered by the driver. Fred Gray, the young black lawyer who represented Colvin, sought the assistance of Cliff Durr. Cliff did not hesitate to aid Gray, a gesture that seemed to resolve Virginia's concern about where he would stand as the racial divide deepened. Virginia, meanwhile, worked through her contacts around the country to publicize the incident and raise money for the case, which was a prelude to Rosa Parks's defiance of the city's segregation law later in the year and the beginning of the Montgomery bus boycott.

ca. March 1955
Dearest Clark: . . .
    The last few months have been the best months we have had, and if this will just keep we will feel that we are seeing daylight for the first time. If we do succeed in establishing a law practice here in Montgomery, Alabama it will be a miracle of the first order as our situation is just as it would be if you went back to Atlanta, sick, broke, smeared all over, and had to start from the beginning to build a business . . . Socially we are still lonely but the people that come to the office don't seem to care about anything except the fact that we give good service. He [Cliff] is working with a young Negro lawyer on a bus case right now—helping him out with it. A young fifteen year old Negro girl was told to "move back" and refused as there were no seats available, and under the law she was right, but the bus driver and Three huge big policemen dragged her off the bus, handcuffed her, and took her to jail. Southern chivalry at its highest. God what brutes we breed down here. How the

exceptions do stand out and how wonderful they are. But actually it is not the brutes that do the damage—it is the vast mass of people who do nothing, take no stand, and just let the brutes have their own way.

ca. March 1955
Dearest Dec: . . .

The Bus case has been occupying a lot of our time as the young Negro lawyer that has been handling it has come to Cliff for advice on all points and still does on the appeal. I went to a meeting for the girl and she was wonderful—little, thin, childlike creature—sort of like a gosling and just had broken through the shell and yet she stood her ground in the face of the big burly white bus driver, two big white policemen and one big white motor cop. They dragged her off the bus, handcuffed her, and put her in jail and the most marvelous thing about her was that the two other young Negro girls moved back, the woman by her moved back, and she was left entirely alone and still she would not move. She was crying all the time, and the policeman hit her with his billy club on her rump and when they got her to the jail the chief or the presiding policeman said that all she needed was a good "whupping" but they didn't give it to her. I asked her what made her stand her ground and she said "I done paid my dime, they didn't have no RIGHT to move me." Isn't that thrilling to think that one little fifteen year old girl could have the courage to stand up to all that? The Negro community is raising money and any money or encourage-ment you can send would be wonderful. Send it to Claudette Colvin in care of Mrs. Rosa Parks, Cleveland Court Apartments, 634 Cleveland Avenue, Montgomery, Alabama. She is head of the NAACP group that is helping out in the case. Send Cash . . . I spoke at the [NAACP] Youth Camp last Sunday. I try so hard not to do anything and then sometimes I can't help myself, and only hope we won't be run out of town. Our tenure here is very feeble, but I am beginning to hope we can stay. If we can only hold on this is the place for us to be, as what little we do here is worth ten times more than any place else.

April 8, 1955
Dearest Dec: . . .

Claudette Colvin . . . was tried in the Juvenile Court and found guilty of breaking the Alabama segregation law and put on probation, and it was felt by the Judge that he had been very lenient. The NAACP is financing the appeal of the case and I think they are going to try and take it up to the Supreme Court if possible. Money is badly needed for the appeal and the donations from you and Buddie were much appreciated. Mrs. Parks said she was going to write you about it. I hope she did . . .

I was invited over to Tuskegee last night to a big banquet and went and saw and heard the dish that is being handed out by the leaders. There must be an end to discrimination and segregation because we must join the free world in the sacred fight against totalitarian dictatorship, etc., etc. It made me think of what one old sister down in the country near there said to me about Tuskegee—"Those folks at Tuskegee aint no better than the white folks." They certainly seem to make their main aim to be as much like them as possible in all ways, but that is not true of the friends I have made here in Montgomery. They have a real pride and independence—curious world, isn't it.

April 25, 1955
Dearest Clark: . . .

The news here is that Lucy is graduating and there is wild excitement on every hand. She is going to thousands of teas and we are making dresses and so on . . . With the graduation . . . I had so much to do that I was getting snowed under so we have gotten a girl to come into the office in the afternoons so I can be home with the girls and it is working out fine . . .

I have been very much interested in the case here of [Claudette Colvin] . . . I have raised a little money for it and turned it over to the local NAACP and they hope to make a test case of it. It shows so clearly the matter of course brutality that this system breeds. She is only fifteen . . . clean, tidy, and neat—so there was absolutely no reason for her to "move back" except color—and yet because she stood up the full fury of the system was turned against her. I cannot imagine how she had the courage to stand firm in the face of the bus driver and the three policemen but she did . . . The awful thing too is that it happened in a crowded bus and no one either white or Negro came to her defense. She bore it all alone . . .

One good thing to come out of it was that the brother of the bus driver was running for City Commission and he of course took the side of his brother and the case got to be an issue in the campaign—AND—the City Commissioner got beat and was replaced by a much better man.* The Negro vote did it without a doubt, and they worked and voted solid. This has made quite an impression.

May 5, 1955
Dearest Dec:

I was so glad to hear from you and Mrs. Parks is going to write and give you the list of names and she is enthusiastic about a Committee, the only BUT being that it has to be endorsed by the local NAACP since they hope to take this case up to the Supreme Court and if they do they will need the backing of the National NAACP . . . The group here is fine and wonderful people and they don't redbait themselves or even pay attention to that kind of thing, but they do take the orders of the National without question and Mrs. Parks and the head of it have a "List" of proscribed organizations put out by the Attorney General that they check against as a matter of course. Isn't that awful—I mean the matter of factness that has come to be taken for granted by so many people of a total black list. The case came up in the Circuit Court on Tuesday, a closed hearing was adjourned until tomorrow—Friday—as the Bus Company said they didn't have their witnesses handy to try the case. I think they are trying to figure out ways to get off the hook as the case is so foolish and puts them in such a silly and ridiculous light as well as brutal and sadistic. Imagine having to press the claim that a little, thin, frail fifteen year old girl committed assault and battery against four big white burly men to the point they had to handcuff her and put her in jail. But they might go that far—brutality toward the Negroes has been taken for granted for so long that they don't even see how absurd they are. You should read some of those speeches in the Legislature and from the White Citizens Councils about how if the Supreme Court decision is carried out that "the bedrooms of our women will be open to black men, etc. etc." They seem to have a terrible inferiority complex that if they have to compete with black men they will lose out—and also that their women can't say no to any black man. Underneath southern life

---

*Frank Parks.

there is a sort of swamp—such deep corruption, that it seeps through all the crevices and crannies of life. I find it interesting and I think to see the Negroes putting up such a wonderful fight is thrilling and to help them just a little is wonderful. But until it changes I could never like it. It is like living in a closed room all the time and simply struggling for air . . . I suppose under all my attempts to like it and to fit in again and to make friends, this distaste and horror and revulsion must come through, because we are still very much isolated and always will be, I am afraid. I am not complaining—I am simply stating a fact—and I don't think it is so odd that a healthy minded person would not like living here. The only time I like it is when I am doing something to change it— and that little bit does give me great satisfaction and it seems to give my Negro friends satisfaction too. But don't think the letters and the money have been unappreciated for they certainly have not and the little girl as well as Mrs. Parks got the most terrific thrill out of them. Some are wonderful letters and I think they have gotten forty or fifty dollars. But she is waiting to see how the trial tomorrow comes out before she writes you.

May 6, 1955

Dearest Dec:

I thought you would like to hear how the Claudette Colvin case turned out this morning. They dropped the charges of her breaking the segregation laws and found her guilty of ASSAULT AND BATTERY. Can anything go to more extreme limits of stupidity and absurdity and horror as that? They were so scared that the appeal on the constitutionality might be sustained that they dropped all the charges on the segregation issue and just left the one charge that this little, thin, frail fifteen year old girl committed assault and battery against the policemen and so they sustained the sentence and put her on probation.

She is terribly disappointed and so is her lawyer but I think some way might be found to appeal the case and I will let you know what develops. This has created tremendous interest in the Negro community and made them all fighting mad and may help give them the courage to put up a real fight on the bus segregation issue.

One of the things I have had to learn the hard way is that the Negro leaders themselves have such a hard time arousing the mass of the Negro people to put up any kind of fight for themselves. They have been beaten down so long that they are afraid to do anything for themselves—but that is changing—and all the help and support they get from other places does help a lot to help them feel that they have a chance to win. It is hard to make people fight when they think there is no chance that they will win the fight. To give them hope is the important thing.

After Cliff had served as an informal adviser to Fred Gray on the Claudette Colvin case, Gray asked Cliff to join him in a case involving the death of a 12-year-old black boy who had been killed by a white man driving a Jaguar at high speed. Cliff agreed, and noted in a letter to Clark Foreman that the case might set some kind of precedent, commenting "it will be interesting to see how a Black Belt jury will react to the Negro-white legal combination."

May 18, 1955
Dearest Clark:
    The case got set for the Friday before the Saturday of the meeting. I agree with Cliff that the precedent of a white and Negro lawyer trying a case together in Montgomery is startling and I don't know how Montgomery will react. Cliff is so astonishing—he won't commit himself verbally at all—and tries hard to keep me from committing myself verbally and then goes and acts in such a fashion that his sentiments are clear to all. If we survive down here it will be a miracle. He has lots more determination and courage to stick it out than I have. I like to belong and feel a part of things and not outside of the group. I am not a lonely martyr and want lots of other martyrs around, but he seems to go on and find Montgomery the best place to live in spite of the fact that we are not "in" at all, but that doesn't seem to bother him at all. The only thing that really gets him is my unhappiness and I cannot find Montgomery a very homelike place although we do have a few friends, but since he wants to stay here and is determined to, I try to make the best of it, although I frequently fail. *It is interesting* [though]—the fight of the Negro for his rights as a man, and the reactions of the white people, all this makes a fascinating pattern and I love to see the changing patterns emerge, but it is the isolation that I mind, and the lack of any group to belong to, the lack of any feeling of being part of the community and yet perhaps that is everywhere, and at least it is not hard and

cold and rocky as Denver. These days all of our old friends seem to be suffering from this same sense of isolation from the community, at least according to their letters.

The debate in the Legislature as reported by this morning's paper is almost unbelievable. The subject was Jury service for women, which did get passed. The opposition to it was led by the Black Belters as usual, who quoted the Bible and Paul to bolster their point that women should not be "heard" and that this would hurt their feminine charm—but the crowning argument as always was that it would mean that a pure white southern woman would have to sit perhaps between two black Negro men on a jury and that would be worse than putting her between two pole cats. The sex argument always comes up. It is some kind of fear that is all prevailing and while the cause is known it always comes as a shock to know that men can sink to such a low level.

Virginia reported on the growing white resistance to desegregation, organized largely through the White Citizens Council.

June 20, 1955
Dearest Esther:

I was sorry to hear from Sadie that you had been sick again and with boils of all things! It is too bad for that kind of affliction to hit you when you already have so much to bear. I hope you are better now and nothing will prevent your going to Europe which I know will do a world of good . . .

Old friends from the past come through the office and we are always glad to see them. Claude Williams* came through the other day. He had just been given the boot by the Presbyterian Church for daring to believe that man could save himself from Hell by his own efforts and did not have to depend on the "Grace of God" (literally these were the charges against him and which convicted him of heresy.) . . .

We had supper out at the Williams last night with Bee and Harry and we are thinking of going over to Selma Wednesday night to see and hear Herman Talmadge preach to the White Citizens Council—which is a

---

*Southern radical preacher and labor activist whom Virginia knew through the Southern Conference for Human Welfare.

more refined version of the Ku Klux Klan—and is led by Preachers and prominent citizens of all kinds—and is pledged to prevent integration by means of economic pressure and denial of credit or services to any Negro or White man who dares to be for Desegregation. They are very vicious and already one Negro in Mississippi has been killed* as a direct outgrowth of their activities. Aubrey says if we go they will run us out on a rail but I don't think we would be recognized as we look so much like everybody else.

I cannot help but feel that I am living in Enemy territory and it is hard, but I am trying hard and it is a comfort that we do have some friends and allies and the struggle is not lost yet down here by any means. Jim Folsom is being a . . . strong Governor and he does not go along with the WCCs at all and might save the day yet. In any case there is no Utopia anywhere and at least here I see happening what I have worked for [for] so long . . . Don West has a paper in Georgia that is good and he too has gone with the Church of God and he says that in Georgia, in spite of Talmadge, that there is a lot of resistance. The issue seems to be coming down to the one simple fact of either doing away with the public schools, or having them integrated and of course there are a lot of people that would rather be ignorant and have their children ignorant than "go to school with niggers." But there are lots of them that feel that is too high a price to pay . . .

Did I tell you . . . that Lucy has gotten into Radcliffe? . . . I just worked and worked on it and hoped and hoped and I am so thrilled that she will have this wonderful chance to go although she might only go one year and get married like Marge did.

I did not mean to write so long a letter just to tell you that I was so sorry you still were not well, that I loved you and always will, that I think of you and Joe at least once a day and probably oftener, and that I hope you will soon feel better.

Virginia became acquainted with E. Franklin Frazier, the noted black sociologist and Howard University professor, during her time in Washington. They worked in the Henry Wallace campaign together, and Frazier served on the board of the Southern Conference Education Fund. Virginia

---

*Rev. George Lee, leader of voter registration effort in Belzoni, Mississippi, was murdered on May 7, 1955.

had taken a class with Frazier at Howard in 1949 on intercultural race relations. He was one of the scholars who contributed to the NAACP's brief for the *Brown* decision, which won him the attention of Senator Eastland of Mississippi.

Eastland had delivered a lengthy speech on May 26th in the Senate attacking the *Brown* decision and charging that it "was based upon the writings and teachings of pro-Communist agitators and other enemies of the American form of government." He claimed that the Court had been "brainwashed" by pressure groups and called for an investigation by the Senate Judiciary Committee of the Court's citation of authorities with Communist and Communist-front records.

June 27, 1955

Dear Dr. Frazier:

I have just read with fascinated interest the recent speech of Jim Eastland in which he accuses you of being the chief "brain washer" of the United States Supreme Court and then recites lengthy tales of your sins. The whole speech is simply fantastic and I hope you haven't missed it.

Well it is nice to have company and I am glad that you have joined the company of the damned—damned by Eastland—which is in my opinion honorable company. I think we should have degrees of the damned though and until he gives you the full television, radio, and newspaper "inquisition" I will be vain enough to think I belong to a lower degree of his Hell than you do, and that of course makes me just a little higher than you in Heaven—same old White, Southern prejudice operating still—you see!

Well after four years I still find living in the South difficult and making a living is even more difficult, but it has its compensations, not the least of which is seeing the theories and dreams and plans translated into actual reality, and knowing the people who are making this epic fight for freedom, which I think is also freedom for all of us here in the South. I wish some proper homage and honor could be paid to the people here who in spite of Hell and High Water are holding up the banner of liberty and fighting for their rights and in a very intelligent manner too. I have come to know them well and only regret my inability to help them as I would like to. It is not the scholars [and] not the school men (except for the honorable exception of Dr. Gomillion of

Tuskegee who is wonderful) but it is the people who while living by the work of their hands are still working in their spare time to make it all come true—a pullman porter, Mr. Nixon, a tailor's assistant, Mrs. Parks, and others just as splendid. It makes you proud to be human to see how the human spirit can rise above oppression and work for glory—these people are making me proud to be a Southerner. Come and see us.

Early in the fall of 1954, C. Vann Woodward, the noted historian and friend of the Durrs, delivered a series of lectures at the University of Virginia on the history of racial segregation in the South. Woodward explained that the Jim Crow system was a relatively recent invention—not, as widely assumed, part of the region's immutable folkways—and he anticipated that Southerners would abide by the *Brown* decision. The lectures were published as a book, *The Strange Career of Jim Crow,* which quickly became a primer for civil rights activists. In response to the following letter, Woodward acknowledged that he was probably "a little optimistic," explaining that the lectures had been "written in the immediate afterglow of the Supreme Court's decision."[18]

December 5, 1955
Dear Vann:
Could you do me a favor and get me a copy of the speech William Faulkner made to the Southern Historical Society in Memphis several weeks ago on the subject of Segregation? Or tell me where I could write to get it. I long to see it. It was announced in the paper and then blank silence.
I have distributed your "Jim Crow" book as widely as I could and think it is a splendid book but a little optimistic from the point of view of Montgomery, Alabama, which is, I admit, better than Mississippi, but still determined to resist to the last . . .
The actuality of living in Montgomery and trying to make a living . . . and raise children in such an atmosphere is difficult to put it mildly, but Cliff is determined to stay, as I think he feels that if he is "run out" that it will mean a victory for Jim Eastland that low down skunk.
Lots of love to you both . . . and let me have this information if you can.

On December 1, 1955, Rosa Parks was arrested for refusing to give up her seat on a city bus to a white man. When the police at the jail rebuffed E. D. Nixon's inquiries about Parks, Nixon phoned the Durrs, as

Virginia explains in the following letter. With the start of the Montgomery bus boycott, Virginia felt guardedly hopeful that the tide had finally turned.

December 7, 1955
Dearest Clark:

Well it always seems darkest just before some break comes your way and while our personal fortunes are still precarious still the most wonderful thing has happened right here in Montgomery, Ala.

It may have been in the papers up there but in any case what has happened is that the Negroes here have organized a boycott of the buses in protest against the arrest of Mrs. Parks and it is almost 100 per cent effective and they are carrying it on in the most orderly and disciplined way and with the utmost determination.

The custom here in the buses is that the Negroes fill up from the back and the whites from the front and if there are no whites then the Negroes can sit as far forward as there are seats, but if any white person gets on they are ordered to get up and give them their seats. Of course as you can see this creates endless difficulties and irritations and bad feelings, as no whites are ever ordered to get up and give up their seats.

Last spring a little fourteen year old [sic] Negro girl got arrested because she refused to move and the local NAACP was going to make a test case out of it, BUT she got pregnant . . . and her Mama made her drop the case because she didn't want her to be shamed by going into court. So the local head of the Youth Branch of the NAACP—Mrs. Parks—refused to move last Friday night and she got arrested and was fined and found guilty and the NAACP is going to take up her case as a test case and as a measure of protest the entire Negro community is boycotting the buses, at I don't know what the cost to themselves in terms of difficulties and troubles. While only a few of us are in sympathy with it, still the whole population has been very much impressed by their determination and courage. It is still going on and has been so far absolutely orderly and disciplined.

They called us to get her out of jail which Cliff did, but then the local NAACP attorney took over the test case, a young and very intelligent Negro, Fred Gray, who adores Cliff and consults with him on every move he makes and uses our library. The heroine of the occasion—Mrs.

Parks—has sewed for me ever since I have been here and we have become fast friends and last summer I got her a scholarship to Highlander and she was thrilled by it as for the first time in her life she was treated as an equal. She is a lovely person and very intelligent and brave. She asked me to speak at the meeting on Sunday afternoon, which I did, and I must admit rather trembled at the thought of it being in the papers the next morning but it wasn't. Aubrey is out at four in the morning taking passengers. I think he is thrilled to death as it seems to be a vindication of all his work and faith in the Negroes. It has really been astonishing.

Even over in Georgia the boys are really mad now about the Governor trying to stop them playing at the Sugar Bowl. This is the best lesson in the cost of race prejudice they have ever had.

Of course the "best people" here explain it all away by saying that the Negroes are intimidated that is why they are not riding the buses—and when "Poor Cora" doesn't run to work until ten o'clock they say it is because she is so frightened. But the whole town is impressed and they know after this that they have a united group to deal with.

Well that is about all the news around here that I know of. It is mighty interesting down here . . . now if we can just hang on.

PART 2

The Montgomery Bus Boycott and After
1956–1960

From the earliest days of the boycott, Virginia sensed that she was witnessing a historic shift. She strained to find words to convey the new spirit reflected in the protest that united 50,000 black people in the challenge to segregation. "It has a quality of hope and joy about it that I wish I could give you," she wrote Jessica Mitford. "I feel like I am in touch with all the rising forces in the world and the end of fear and slavery is in sight. I know this is just a moment, but . . . it only takes a moment for a new world to be conceived."[1]

Virginia's letters chart the course of the protest and reveal how deeply the boycott affected her and her marriage. She confided to a friend that since it began, she and Cliff had become closer than they had ever been. "It is no longer a matter of theory to him, but an actual situation, and when it gets down to that he does just the right thing."[2] Cliff assisted Fred Gray, the young lawyer who represented Rosa Parks, in drafting the legal challenge to bus segregation that Gray took to the Supreme Court; Gray referred to Cliff as his "silent partner."[3] Virginia often typed the legal briefs they prepared and drove for the carpool that helped carry people to work each day, mostly black women working as domestics. "To be able to help just a little," Virginia wrote, "has changed my entire point of view."[4]

The hopefulness inspired by the boycott was tempered by a defense of racial segregation that hardened into a united front of white resistance to any breach in the color line. Two months after the boycott began, Autherine Lucy entered the University of Alabama under court order, the first

African American to attend the school. Several thousands rioted at the university, threatening to kill Lucy and promising to "keep 'Bama white." The university's board of trustees suspended Lucy "for her own safety" and later expelled her. A revived Ku Klux Klan policed black ambitions with a campaign of arson and bombings while the more "respectable" White Citizens Council wielded economic pressure and public exposure to enforce white allegiance to the pro-segregationist cause. As historian J. Mills Thornton has observed, Montgomery "slipped into a surreal dimension in which only extremist views were publicly voiced among whites and any hint of deviation from white supremacist orthodoxy . . . incur[red] both active harassment and social ostracism."[5]

Defiance and obstruction were sanctioned by the South's highest elected officials and bolstered by a flurry of laws and resolutions. Alabama Senators Lister Hill and John Sparkman were among the region's congressmen and senators who issued the "Southern Manifesto" in March 1956, which declared that *Brown* was unconstitutional. They commended the states in their determination "to resist forced integration" and pledged themselves "to use all lawful means to bring about a reversal of this decision." John Patterson, Alabama's attorney general, led the movement to drive the NAACP from the South, issuing an injunction in June 1956 that effectively barred the organization from operating in the state. City and state leaders tightened segregation laws and the Alabama Senate resolved to study a plan that would promote black settlement in the North.[6]

The 381-day boycott ended on December 21, 1956, after the U.S. Supreme Court ruled that bus segregation was unconstitutional. Although the fight to desegregate the buses was ultimately won in the courts, the boycott had created a potent force for change. As its undisputed leader, the Reverend Martin Luther King, Jr. attracted national attention and came to symbolize a new kind of black protest. Virginia readily acknowledged King's brilliant leadership in unifying the black community, but she had reservations about his ability to build an effective political movement. Her letters provide a critical assessment of the young King while also reflecting her own discomfort with the spiritual grounding of his appeal and the adulation that quickly grew up around him. Virginia felt more closely allied with seasoned political activists and community organizers like E. D. Nixon, Charles Gomillion, and Rosa Parks. Still, she sensed King's unique power, acknowledging to Clark Foreman, "I should see King as the great historical figure he will no doubt be and stop seeing his flaws on the home scene."[7]

While recognizing that nonviolence and moral suasion had injected the movement with renewed vitality, Virginia continued to believe that voting was the critical lever for loosening the grip of segregation. "The South won't be safe until the elementary rights of free citizenship are enjoyed here," she wrote. After that, there would be other battles, but "now" she contended, the fight for the ballot "is the most important one."[8] In the face of massive resistance, blacks, she believed, understood better than anyone "the vital necessity of getting the vote if they are to survive the assault on them." Virginia lobbied friends in the North to support the efforts of "indigenous Negro groups" to mount voter registration drives, emphasizing the importance of the black vote in "building a countervailing force against the reactionary power in the South." Aubrey Williams shared her sentiments, and the Southern Conference Education Fund (SCEF) devoted increasing attention to voter registration. He hired Anne and Carl Braden, white civil rights activists from Louisville, Kentucky, as SCEF field workers to aid with fundraising to support black voter registration campaigns, while also organizing white Southern support for desegregation.[9]

Montgomery officials and commentators concurred with this assessment of the black vote. In a 1957 editorial, breaking down the number of potential black voters in every county in Alabama, the *Montgomery Advertiser* cautioned, "The rock bottom race issue in the South is not race mixing in the schools but the registration of Negro voters."[10] As the number of registered black voters slowly climbed in Tuskegee, Alabama, a place where blacks greatly outnumbered whites, state representative Sam Engelhardt introduced a bill that shrank the city limits, excluding nearly all black voters. Engelhardt's bill easily passed the state legislature in the summer of 1957. Blacks in Tuskegee, under the leadership of Charles Gomillion and the Tuskegee Civic Association, organized a boycott of white businesses in protest. Attorney General John Patterson responded by leading a widely publicized raid on the offices of the Tuskegee Civic Association to uncover "evidence of violation of our state laws and evidence of subversive activities which are designed to create disorder, strife, and the destruction of our government." Patterson charged that the boycott was in violation of state law, and he also contended that the TCA had "connections with foreign organizations whose purposes and aims are not in the best interest of the state."[11]

In 1958, John Patterson ran for governor with the open support of the Ku Klux Klan and defeated George Wallace, the favored candidate, by a large margin. Wallace had run on a strong pro-segregationist platform and enjoyed the support of the White Citizens Council, but Patterson's embrace of the most reactionary elements in Alabama proved a more effective strategy. Patterson banned black marching bands from his inaugural parade, and few blacks attended the event. In his address to a nearly all-white crowd, the new governor promised that he would dedicate himself to the maintenance of segregated schools. Referring to a recent plan announced by Martin Luther King, Jr. and the Montgomery Improvement Association (MIA) to press for school integration in Montgomery, he warned blacks that he would close the schools if such a challenge was brought and that blacks would bear the burden for many years to come. The recent closing of all of the city parks in response to a desegregation suit by the MIA suggested that Patterson would follow through on his threat. Under pressure from black teachers and others in the black community, the MIA suspended its school campaign, and King soon left Montgomery for Atlanta.[12]

Growing pressure from liberals and civil rights groups for federal action in the area of civil rights began to yield some results. Senate Majority Leader Lyndon B. Johnson and President Dwight D. Eisenhower joined forces behind a civil rights bill to provide federal protection of the right to vote. The Republicans entertained the possibility of making inroads among black voters, while Johnson was anxious to broaden his appeal to Northern liberals as he eyed a future presidential run. After much debate and trimming of the bill's provisions, topped off by a 24-hour filibuster by South Carolina Senator Strom Thurmond, the Civil Rights Act became law in August 1957. It expanded the investigative powers of the Justice Department through the establishment of a civil rights division and a Civil Rights Commission empowered to investigate voting rights abuses, but it failed to strengthen the federal government's power to prosecute voting rights violations. Still, through investigations and hearings, particularly the televised hearings held in Montgomery in December 1958, the Civil Rights Commission helped to expose the blatantly illegal methods used by registrars to bar blacks from voting.

President Eisenhower was sympathetic toward white Southerners in the area of school desegregation, commenting, "We cannot erase the emotions of three generations overnight."[13] During the debate over the 1957 Civil Rights Act, he said he would never use federal troops to enforce school integration in the South. But just a few months later, Eisenhower's hand was forced when Arkansas Governor Orval Faubus called out the National Guard to block the court-ordered entry of nine black students to Little Rock's Central High School. The *Montgomery Advertiser* praised Faubus's action as the ultimate form of nullification—"backed by force and [a] candid defiance of federal authority." Eisenhower responded by sending in federal troops to oversee the enforcement of the court's order. Faubus had tested the limits of obstruction and secured his political future with Arkansas's white voters. The federal government's intervention at Little Rock proved to be an isolated and fleeting victory for supporters of school desegregation.[14]

The momentum of the Montgomery movement flagged in the face of a seemingly impenetrable wall of white resistance and no sustained countervailing pressure from outside the region. Virginia continually urged friends in the North to mobilize support for the Southern movement. She pressed Senator Lyndon Johnson to turn his attention to the treatment of black soldiers stationed in the South and made appeals to Eleanor Roosevelt to help put some backbone in the Democratic Party. The national party's appeasement of Southern Democrats resulted in a watered-down civil rights plank in the 1956 party platform that pacified all but the most rabid segregationists, and presidential candidate Adlai Stevenson avoided any serious engagement with the race issue. Such a strategy, Virginia warned, left the party in an extremely vulnerable position that was being exploited by Vice President Richard Nixon. She watched with amazement as Nixon wooed Martin Luther King, Jr. and earned King's qualified praise. As the 1960 election approached, it appeared increasingly plausible that many black voters would cast their ballot for the likely Republican candidate for president, Richard Nixon.

Nixon was a leading red-hunter who worked hand in glove with J. Edgar Hoover to undermine Cliff Durr and the National Lawyers Guild, and Virginia could find no redeeming qualities in him. He was, in her mind, the "#1 public enemy." She understood his appeal for King, given that no leading Democratic official had made similar overtures to the civil rights leader; locally, it was Democrats who barred blacks from voting. Yet Virginia viewed Nixon's gestures as cynical and manipulative, particularly in light of his administration's failure to do anything of substance to enforce the *Brown* decision or to protect members of the U.S. armed forces stationed in the South from the humiliations of Jim Crow. What she feared most was that the "unholy alliance" of Republicans and Southern Democrats, born in opposition to the New Deal, would exploit Southern white disaffection to create a strong national political movement that linked prosegregationist, anticommunist, antilabor, and antigovernment forces behind the Republican Party's corporate agenda. And this, she believed, was Richard Nixon's ultimate goal.

By the late 1950s, the Durrs had secured a fragile place in Montgomery. "We live on a narrow edge of tolerance," Virginia wrote. Cliff's work with black clients steadily increased, and whites stayed away. He prosecuted cases against loan sharks who charged illegal interest rates and won a major case against an insurance company that had used deceptive methods to invalidate contracts with its mostly black clients. Cliff routinely prosecuted cases of police brutality, a major component of the apparatus that sustained the racial status quo. He assisted Fred Gray on a variety of civil rights cases, including the legal fight to overturn the state's injunction against the NAACP, and on death penalty cases. The latter frequently involved black men who had been charged with rape and were convicted by juries drawn from all-white jury pools, often on flimsy or compromised evidence. There were a few courtroom victories, and with pressure kept on the police, their abuses seemed to abate somewhat. Still, Virginia acknowledged that it was "like trying to sweep the sea back with a broom."

"It was the everydayness that was so hard," Tilla Durr explained, recalling her parents' lives in the 1950s, particularly in the aftermath of the boycott—being ostracized, not belonging, financial worries, silences, living in the midst of family who disagreed and disapproved. After Cliff inherited ten acres of land in rural Elmore County in 1956, he spent most weekends at the Pea Level, as it was called, clearing the land, planting, and gardening. Cliff much preferred the beauty and stillness of nature to the social whirl that Virginia felt so at home in; the Pea Level was his refuge. Virginia, in contrast, was persistent in her efforts to find and connect with kindred spirits. She belonged to an interracial prayer group, one of the only places where black and white women came together socially. "We used to meet and pray and sing and hold hands and have a cup of tea afterward," Virginia recalled. By the fall of 1958, praying together was viewed as a subversive activity, and arch-segregationists succeeded in breaking the group up through harassment and threats of economic reprisals directed towards the women's husbands.[15]

The most difficult part of it all was feeling powerless to protect their children from the open hostility of the community—particularly Tilla, who was fifteen when the bus boycott began. Lucy had gone off to Radcliffe that fall, and Lulah was only eight years old. Tilla was, as she remembered, "old enough to know what was going on" and empathized with what her parents were going through. She supported the movement and attended mass meetings with her mother. Virginia wrote Hugo Black, who was often reviled by white Southerners, that Tilla "got the full blast of the criticism and from her teachers in school and she stood up and defended and fought for all of us, Cliff and me and you." Finally, she refused to go to school, feeling alienated from her peers and from the teenage culture of the 1950s. With money borrowed from Jessica Mitford in the spring of 1956, the Durrs enrolled Tilla in the Cambridge School in Weston, Massachusetts, where she completed her junior and senior years of high school.[16]

In the years following the boycott, Virginia's letters describe a society teetering between social transformation and wholesale political reaction and terror. She explores the patterns of white resistance to change, probing the tangle of racial fears and hatreds rooted in the region's past and nurtured by the insularity of white Southern culture, brilliantly described in Wilbur J. Cash's 1941 classic, *The Mind of the South*. At the same time, she was aware of the islands of integration that had grown up in Montgomery since World War II on the two local Air Force bases, which provided some of the best-paying jobs in the city. Here, where federal policy prohibited segregation, whites and blacks worked together, ate together, and even swam together, suggesting that folkways could yield to economic incentives and government mandates. By the late 1950s, however, the defense of white supremacy reigned, bolstered by the power of state and local governments and the effective silencing of dissenters. Virginia wrote plaintively to a friend, "We have such a feeling here that we have been abandoned by the rest of the country to the tender mercies of the Citizens Council and the Ku Klux Klan."

On February 1, 1960, four black college students took seats at a whites-only lunch counter in Greensboro, North Carolina, ordered coffee, and refused to move. Their action ignited a sit-in movement that heralded a new wave of protest that captured the attention of the media like nothing else since the Montgomery bus boycott. *U.S. News and World Report* stated, "The battle of the lunch counters had . . . spread into six southern states, into more than 20 southern cities, and into several big cities in the North" by the end of February. The magazine described "the sit down movement" as "the biggest racial issue in the South since the U.S. Supreme Court set out to end segregation in the public schools."[17]

Virginia's response to the sit-ins was decidedly more sober than the hope with which she greeted the bus boycott. She embraced the spirit of the youthful protests as a sign that black aspirations could no longer be contained, but she feared that they would be met by the power of the state and the unrestrained fury of whites determined to extinguish any challenge to segregation. When blacks tried to march on the state capital in Montgomery in support of a student sit-in there, they were beaten back by hundreds of police and deputies on horseback in what Virginia described as "the most awful demonstration of brutality I have ever seen." For her, the police massacre of blacks protesting apartheid in Sharpeville, South Africa, on March 21, 1960, offered a horrific glimpse of what the future might hold if the nation left the South to work out its own destiny.[18]

Nevertheless, developments during 1960 ensured that racial conflict in the South would command increasing national attention. The sit-in movement grew into an organized force that linked black youth throughout the South and resulted in the formation of the Student Nonviolent Coordinating Committee (SNCC) in April 1960. The student protests drew the national media back into the South, and this time there would be no retreat: direct-action protests escalated from the sit-ins to the Freedom Rides and a full-scale assault on Jim Crow. Montgomery Police Commissioner L. B. Sullivan was not far off the mark when he warned in the spring of 1960, "Not since Reconstruction have our customs been in such jeopardy."[19]

The presidential election of 1960 also helped set the stage for a new approach to civil rights at the national level. In the last weeks of a very tight race, John F. Kennedy's sympathetic telephone call to Coretta Scott King following the imprisonment of her husband in Georgia halted the slide of black voters to the Republican Party and added to John F. Kennedy's slim margin of victory of some 120,000 votes. Although the Kennedy administration was not prepared to provide aggressive leadership in the area of civil rights, the heightened expectations that greeted the new Democratic administration, along with escalating protests, ensured that civil rights could no longer be ignored.

Finally, on November 15, 1960, Charles Gomillion, the Tuskegee Civic Association, and the NAACP won a major victory in the U.S. Supreme Court when the court, in a unanimous ruling, overturned the gerrymander of Tuskegee implemented by the Alabama legislature and ordered that the original city boundaries be restored. *Gomillion v. Lightfoot* was a major departure for the Court, which had previously avoided questions of legislative motive in establishing voting districts. The court ruled on the obvious racial intent of Alabama's action, ushering in an era of court activism in the area of voting rights.[20]

Despite these promising developments, the forces of white resistance in the South were firmly entrenched in 1960. While Virginia held onto the belief that change would ultimately come, the events of the late 1950s seemed to push it further beyond reach, and it became increasingly difficult to imagine the form it might take.

January 3, 1956
Dearest Dec: . . .

The bus boycott still goes on and on and it is simply wonderful that the Negroes have kept it up in spite of rain, cold, and distance. It is almost 100% effective . . . The White Citizens Councils are acting horrible and so is the Bus Company and they are trying their best to stir up violence and bad feeling, but I do think a lot of people are for the Negroes on this. All the people that have written letters have been called up and insulted and asked if they have "nigger blood." The combination of race feeling and the fact that so many of the men have Negro mistresses and one of the prominent White Supremacists not so long ago had a heart attack at the home of his Negro mistress and the doctor said he could not be moved but he said he would have to be moved, so they took him to the hospital and he died on the way. You saw the full horror of it in Mississippi in the Willie McGee case* and it creates a particular atmosphere of corruption and evil and real horror that only Faulkner has caught—and by the way he has finally come out of his ivory tower and has made a speech denouncing the murderers of the Till boy and saying that integration was inevitable and a lot more that I have only heard about.†

[...]

Lots of love and do write.

Rosa Parks acknowledged that her experience at Highlander Folk School during the summer of 1955 had been formative in her growing determination to challenge segregation. As the boycott gathered steam, Virginia reminded Myles Horton, director of Highlander, and his wife Zilphia of their contribution.

January 30, 1956
Dear Myles and Zilphia:

I just received a communication from there giving a summary of the past year's activities and I think you should add how much you had to do with the Montgomery Bus Boycott which is really making history and is of the deepest significance. LIFE, TIME, CBS, NBC, and countless other papers have been down here covering it . . . I think it is the first time that a whole Negro community has ever stuck together this way and for so long and I think they are going to win it.

But how your part comes in is through the effect of the school on Mrs. Parks. When she came back she was so happy and felt so liberated and then as time went on she said the discrimination got worse and

---

*The Willie McGee case garnered much publicity in the late 1940s. A white woman in Laurel, Mississippi, accused McGee of rape; McGee claimed that the two had been having an affair. He was tried and sentenced to death. Due to the efforts of Rosa Lee McGee, McGee's wife, and the Civil Rights Congress (CRC) the case won national attention. Jessica Mitford, who headed the CRC's Oakland branch, led a three-woman delegation to Jackson, Mississippi, where they petitioned the governor to commute the death sentence and helped organize a mass protest. After five years of protests and appeals, McGee was executed in May 1951.

†Probably refers to "American Segregation and the World Crisis," a speech Faulkner delivered at the annual meeting of the Southern Historical Association, November 10, 1955, but Faulkner did not mention the murder of Emmett Till in this speech.

worse to bear AFTER having, for the first time in her life, been free of it at Highlander. I am sure that had a lot to do with her daring to risk arrest as she is naturally a very quiet and retiring person although she has a fierce sense of pride and is, in my opinion, a really noble woman. But you . . . should certainly take pride in what you did for her and what she is doing.

All OK here, I think things look good although Aubrey doesn't. Lots of love to all and come see for yourself.

February 9, 1956
Dear Clark:

I had just mailed my letter to you when your letter came in the mails—two minds with but a single thought . . .

The firm of Durr and Durr is very much pleased as I wrote you with our victories but so far no money has come in at all and they are trying to beat it down to nothing and it looks as though we would have to try it again almost to get anything out of it.* I was amused at your suggestion that we go to Europe. Even if we get a good fee or any fee at all, we will have to use it to pay back our creditors. We have cut our living expenses way down but still it is the damned doctors, dentists, etc. that take the money. If we clear $300 a month we think we have done well indeed and that is by the hardest kind of work and taking all kinds of little piddling cases that bring in $5.00 and $10.00 but in spite of the difficulties and the social isolation I am glad we were here during this time as I do think we have been of a lot of use and the Negroes trust us and come to Cliff for advice all the time and this whole experience has made us "oner" than we ever were before, as Cliff avoided the race issue and now he has been plunged into the center of it and, as usual, he did just right. This all has been terrible for Tilla and she comes home and cries every day and can hardly wait to get out, she is the only one in the school that speaks out and even her teachers castigate the Negroes and Hugo [Black] and she feels so isolated and alone. The high school students have been burning crosses, shooting water pistols at Negroes and throwing fire-

---

*Cliff won a major usury case against the First National Bank of Birmingham on behalf of truckers who were charged interest rates far beyond the legal limit set by the state.

crackers and it has gotten to the point that finally even the school officials have had to do something about it. But how can you blame them
when their teachers, the papers, the radio and everybody they come in
contact with goes on screaming about the "niggers?" . . .

I have gotten used to being unpopular now and don't mind it so
much, although it was hard to get used to as like all southern girls as you
well know, I wanted to be "popular" above all else, and each additional
snubbing hurt . . . If I can only get Tilla out into a civilized place, I can
take it all right, but to see her suffer is terrible.

In the ten days leading up to a White Citizens Council rally on February
10, the homes of Martin Luther King, Jr. and E. D. Nixon were bombed,
and white mobs rioted at the University of Alabama following the court-
ordered admission of Autherine Lucy to the university. Senator James Eastland called on the estimated 15,000 people gathered at the rally at the
Alabama Coliseum to mount a "massive grass-roots campaign against
racial integration." Virginia wrote about the upcoming rally to Esther
Gelders, who grew up in Montgomery, and her daughter Marge Frantz.

February 10, 1956
Dearest Esther and Marge:
I thought you all would be interested in seeing some hometown news.
Boy it has been Hot here and it gets hotter all the time. I don't know what
is coming off after that big speech tonight by Eastland. I am longing to go
but Cliff says that it will just make him sick and he had rather see it on
the TV so we are going over to Dorothy's and watch it there IF she can
take it, as she says she has butterflies and doesn't know if she can take it
or not. It has been awful but very exciting and I have been thrilled by the
way the Negroes have stuck together in spite of it all, they have been magnificent and I may add that I have been delighted and thrilled that we
could be of any use. They come up here and consult with Cliff all the
time (keep it to yourself) he drew up the Petition to the Court to declare
the Bus laws unconstitutional.* Also they report to us every day on what
is going on and really seem to trust us. Also some, (very few) of the white

---

*On February 1, Fred Gray filed a petition in federal court challenging the constitu-
tionality of city and state segregation laws.

people have been wonderful too, a young Episcopal minister, Tom Thrasher, a young Lutheran minister, Rev. [Robert] Graetz, Rev. [Robert] Hughes of the Southern Regional Council, Aubrey of course, Juliette Morgan, and even Mrs. Myron Lobman wrote a fine letter after which she got terrible phone calls. The telephone calls have all been vile and threatening and after the bombs were thrown they called and said it was just the beginning, next time they would aim to kill. Of course the ADVERTISER has been weak but some of the Radio commentators have been fine. We have been so immersed in it all that we have not had time to think of anything else. But I do send lots of love.

February 13, 1956
Dearest Dec: . . .

I thought your article was very good and I am so glad you are writing again and hope you keep it up. I think you have a talent there and should develop it . . .

We have been so immersed in the bus strike that I haven't thought about anything else . . . If you can raise any money to send to Mrs. Parks that is the thing to do. She has lost her job and is having a very hard time . . . She is the main figure in the boycott and her case will come up soon and she has to stay here and is having a hard time getting work. Things here are getting very bad. Of course you knew about the bombings and then on Friday night Senator Eastland had a huge throng to cheer him, over 15,000 people, and you never heard such rebel yells and so much horrible anti-Negro speech in your life and the papers are full of it. The worst part of it is what the young high school students are doing, they go hunting for "Game" as they call it, which means any helpless Negro they can find and they throw rotten eggs and potatoes and squirt water pistols and scream at them "nigger, nigger" and throw firecrackers at them, just like young Nazis and as completely unfeeling. You can imagine the atmosphere when they would treat anyone as they did that young woman at the University. That awful yell, "Hey, Hey, Ho, Ho, Autherine gotta go." "Keep Bama White." Here you see southern chivalry at its highest.

One thing is that as bad as it is some people have come out of their holes and spoken out, but not many. But a saving few at least. But the general sentiment is to blame it all on the NAACP. But I am proud of the ones that have had the courage to speak up and take action and particularly of Cliff who has given his time and legal talents unsparingly and also of Aubrey who has been magnificent and a few of the churchwomen here and two ministers and so the picture is not all dark, although I will have to admit it is frightening to a degree. I have a tendency to vomit when I read the paper but that is getting under control, as I think personal feelings can only hinder any constructive efforts. But all these things add up to something and every slight effort that has been made has borne some fruit . . .

Do try and raise some money for Mrs. Parks who has the heaviest burden to bear and who is wonderful, really wonderful and so brave and good. They also raised her rent.

In 1956, John Hope Franklin was appointed chair of the History Department of Brooklyn College, becoming the first African American to chair a history department in a predominantly white college. Virginia first met Franklin in the fall of 1949, while she was a student at Howard University. At the end of this letter, she expressed her shame at the treatment Autherine Lucy received at the University of Alabama.

February 17, 1956
Dear Dr. Franklin,

I read with so much pleasure this morning that you have been appointed to the Chairmanship of the History Department at Brooklyn College. This is encouraging news and delights me.

I am sure it will delight Vann Woodward too. You and he are my favorite historians.

We are certainly living through history here in Alabama and I only hope it will turn out better than last time when we had a crisis. There are some encouraging aspects of the situation but also many discouraging ones. Eastland and his ilk are on the rampage. We were his first victims which I am proud of. I think he and his like can be stopped IF they are not able to find allies among the fascist minded in the North, and the center of the infection will narrow little by little, BUT if the rest of the country lets them get by with it then we are sunk. I hope justice will be done in history to the magnificent spirit and courage the Negroes have shown down here. It makes me proud to be a Southerner again and an American . . .

I remember with such pleasure how kind you and all the other people were to me during my brief period at Howard. I am so ashamed and sorry about what happened at the University.

On February 21, a Montgomery County grand jury indicted 89 bus boycott leaders, including 24 ministers, for violating a 1921 Alabama anti-boycott law. This stiffened the resolve of the black community, while drawing more national attention to the boycott. Virginia's mood was hopeful as she described the heightening tensions in the following letter and appealed to her friends—Clark Foreman, Palmer Weber, and Corliss Lamont—to help rally support.

February 24, 1956
Dear Clark, Palmer and Corliss:

I am waiting for Cliff to get back from Court and thought I would write you and tell you what is going on down here and how exciting and thrilling it is. I am so sorry that I missed you when you called up the other night.

It is really wonderful. Sort of a second Emancipation. And taking place in the Cradle of the Confederacy. It makes you feel that every little effort, every little push has been worthwhile. When we came here five years ago E. D. Nixon who is the leader of the Negro community in politics . . . told us then that it was not the "White Folks" that were the trouble. The trouble was that the Negroes were all split up and jealous of each other and divided into cliques and you couldn't get them together on anything. We went to a few meetings and they were rather sparsely attended and what he had said was absolutely true. I think the change started when they arrested that little Claudette Colvin girl last spring . . . and then Mrs. Parks took up the fight and refused to move and got arrested. She is simply wonderful, calm, composed, cool and collected. She is so brave, and so intelligent and so determined. So as the Negroes said when they "messed with her they messed with the WRONG ONE" and the whole Negro Community united over night and with each stupid and vicious attack on them they got madder and madder and more determined and instead of a handful you now have forty or fifty thousand simply determined to stick it out until Hell freezes over. To arrest all of their leaders was the very thing that was needed to make them more determined and especially to arrest their preachers. I have picked up and carried [many who are boycotting the buses] . . . and they all express the same determination. One old lady said last night that she simply got tired finally of "greens and cabbage and wanted something different."

All the big newspapers have people here and the Radio and TV and *Figaro* and the *Manchester Guardian* and that of course is a big factor in giving the Negroes the feeling that they have support all over the world and certainly the papers in the rest of the country have done a good job of coverage. I think with the horrors in Mississippi and all the grim, discouraging goings-on that this burst of hope and fight back and unity is encouraging to even the most case-hardened reporter. Also the Negroes are so good laughing and cracking jokes and hugging each other and all the Preachers had their flocks—there was a sort of holiday air about it all. Clark and Palmer know what I mean and I wish Corliss could have seen it too. All laughing and slapping each other and saying "Man, Man, where you bin, must have slep late" and then all dying laughing. Even the deputies and the police officers were laughing and being nice.

BUT there is another side to the story. There were a lot of cars parked around the jail and a lot of youngish thug-like-looking men sitting in them, some with overalls on, and all mean-looking with their feet up and not saying anything, just waiting and watching and of course the White Citizens Councils grow apace day by day and there is a real blackmail going on. They work the blocks and buildings and ask each one to join and if they don't—Well, there is no doubt you get on a black list. One of the fairly liberal people we know here left town today, said if he didn't join the WCC he simply could not make a living here at all and as much as he has ever done is to go to a meeting of the Southern Regional Council. Fortunately we have been on the black list so long that we are more or less used to it. There are a number of unpleasant things to put up with as people whom we see every day say the most horrible things. "But they *smell* so bad, so dirty, so unmannerly, so ugly, so obnoxious in every way BUT just let them get a toe hold and none of our white women will be safe, miscegenation, intermarriage, etc." They never see the contradiction and if you point it out they get mad. All of you read *The Mind of the South* again by W. J. Cash. Anchor has it now in paper and it is better than it has ever been.

Cliff will write you about the legal situation and the money etc. The main thing to do is to be sure that they are not sold out as they were before and no Hayes-Tilden deal* is done on them. If the National Government were sincere, they could stop all this fooling around simply by saying they were not going to put any more Federal installations in the South until it complied with the law, but I don't think they are sincere at all, and the worst Racists in town are also Eisenhower Republicans and the Democratic Party seems to be affected with paralysis and poor Big Jim† does his best and I think does pretty good in spite of fumbling sometimes, and don't believe the papers about him, he never did say the NAACP agitators were behind it all, that is a lie. He is still the best hope of any decency, but they were afraid to send the National Guard Boys to the University because they were afraid the National Guard would join the rioters. You must remember the National Guard is strictly Jim Crow . . . If the National Guard was not Jim Crow the Negroes would have some protection, now they have absolutely none at all.

I bet I have bored you with this long dissertation, but we have for so long been working on this and now it has worked and like some ever-flowing spring I don't think it can be stopped up again.

Lots of love to All, Va.

March 2, 1956
Dearest Dec: . . .

I saw Mrs. Parks yesterday and she has gotten enough money for herself to relieve her own personal difficulties and she thinks that the women should now turn their efforts towards raising money for the Protest (they are not calling it a Boycott any more since they were indicted for boycotting) and if they can work with the Preachers that will be fine and make it broader and more dynamic. It takes a lot of money to keep it going in terms of gas for the cars and after all there are forty or fifty THOUSAND that are involved and while tremendous numbers of them walk—still some of them simply have to be transported and all of

---

*Refers to the Compromise of 1877 that settled the contested presidential election and marked the final withdrawal of federal troops from the South, leaving white southerners to dismantle the gains of the Reconstruction era and resolve the race issue on their own terms.
†Governor James E. Folsom.

that takes money, and then too there is the money for the trials and the legal fees and the court costs and the bail, etc. Also the expressions of support and unity are wonderful and help keep up their spirit and it is this feeling that the country and the Negro community is behind them that helps to keep up their wonderful spirit . . .

I agree that this is far more than just a local protest. It is bigger than Montgomery and involves the conscience of the whole country, and the fact that the Negroes have been so brave and so calm and good natured and determined and above all so UNITED shows what they can do. The bus Company is losing about $1500 a day and they can't keep in business here indefinitely at that loss, and they have privately told the Negroes that as far as they are concerned they are willing to meet their demands for equal seating but the City Commission stands in the way of course, but IF the Bus Company would only let their position be known publicly then I think the City Commission might come to terms. The City Commission does not want to have to take on the Bus Company when it is losing money at this rate, and it may end with having no bus service at all, which a great many people here will accept for the keeping of the principle of segregation. I cannot tell you how incredible they are, they have no . . . idea of how they appear to the rest of the country, they think they are heroes standing by the Confederate Flag and the more awful they are the prouder they are of themselves. I am sorry in a way for Cliff to be so disillusioned about his own people and mine too but after all disillusionment is the beginning of wisdom. There are a few, a very few that are wonderful. But it is really hard for Cliff to accept the low down skullduggery of which expelling Miss Lucy is the latest—on the part of the leading citizens of the State. Then too his own family while they stay silent for the most part when we are around are heart and soul with the other side and his Aunt who is completely outspoken about the "niggers" thinks they should all be sent back to Africa. She told Mary who bathes her, rubs her back, cleans up after her . . . feeds her, nurses her when she's sick . . . that "you niggers are not citizens of this country, you ought to go back to Africa if you don't like it here." And Mary with her eyes simply snapping said "Well when the Lord wants to send me back just let him send a chariot to take me, but when he takes us all back to Africa I don't know who is goin' to look after the white folks." That is what makes the whole thing so completely and obviously and wholeheartedly ridiculous that the White South rests on the Black South and now the Alabama Senate is trying to get the Negroes to "move to the West" (as they did the Indians), [and] they are simply pulling out (but only in words) the foundations of the economy, but I must say that reason has flown out of the window and nothing is left but hysteria—pure hysteria. My only hope is that like a bursting abscess it might clear up the body politic, but then on the other hand it might infect the rest of the country and there will be a meeting of the Racists and the Anti-Reds and we will go to Hell in a bucket. I think it is terribly important that the rest of the country be aroused and try to get as much white support as you can and the politicians put on record and an issue be made of it. Because if these two forces in our lives coalesce, then Fascism will cease to be a word and become a reality . . .

Thanks a lot and lots of love and encourage your women out there to begin putting the politicians on the spot and get it in writing and make it an issue and especially that low down SOB [Richard] Nixon.

March 15, 1956
Dearest Clark and Mairi,

How wonderful to receive the material for the new dress, just when I wanted something pretty so badly . . . Mrs. Parks and her mother are going to make it for me. Mrs. Parks got over $500 from the various letters I wrote . . .

Fortunately the Boycott is being well financed since they arrested all the Preachers, all the big Negro churches are raising money for it and in one day they got in over $12,000! But keep it quiet, as they never know when or if the money will be impounded. They have tried every known means to break them up and the more they do the more they stick together. It is the unity and determination that is so wonderful and no one would have dreamed it could have happened and among the whole Negro community is a sort of rejoicing that extends down to the most ignorant and humblest.

I know Clark does wish he was here and Palmer too and all the Southerners that have fought for so long for this to happen, and I am sorry you have to miss it in a way, but it would never succeed without the help that is given from the outside. I think one of the best things that could be done is to put the big National Organizations on the spot and ask why they succumb so limply when they come to the South. The League of Women Voters, the YWCA, the YMCA, the National Council of Churches, the Churches themselves, the Unions, the Republican and Democratic Parties, they all sound off so fine and then as soon as they come up against a situation here in the South, they give in completely and say that "they must preserve their usefulness." It makes the few of us who do stand firm or try to absolutely alone for the most part. The Women's Division of the Democratic Party did have a meeting in Tennessee and had several Negro delegates and two from Bessemer, due to Asbury Howard* I am sure, and the Alabama National Committeewoman refused to go and the ones that did came back furious and said the white women of the South had been insulted by having them there, but the Negro women themselves said they were treated wonderfully well and received well and had no trouble at all. But that is Tennessee, but after all it is right next to Alabama and I am proud of it. That is why I am for [Estes] Kefauver,† he is after all a Southerner and Tennessee has behaved so far very well indeed and has stood out like a light in the South.

March 16, 1956
Dearest Dec:

Mrs. Park has been asked to come out to Seattle to speak on . . . the 28th of this month. She is going to speak at an NAACP meeting there and they are paying her way.

I think if your group of Negro women would ask her that she would very likely stop by there either coming or going. She is a big figure in the NAACP . . . and so no doubt check with the branch there . . . I think the Minister's association you mentioned might be interested. She is speaking this weekend in Detroit to the Local 600 of the UAW. It is all simply

---

*Asbury Howard worked in the mines in Bessemer, and had been active in labor organizing and civil rights activities since the 1930s; he organized support for Henry Wallace in Alabama in 1948. During the 1950s, Howard was president of the Progressive Voters League and active in the Bessemer branch of the NAACP.

†U.S. senator from Tennessee who was seeking the Democratic nomination for president in 1956.

thrilling for her . . . She is going to speak for the Highlander Folk School in New York this spring.

Things here are still going well. No one is riding the bus. The spirit is good and money is coming in. The trial is on Monday and the NAACP is in charge of that.* This is the first successful movement of this kind that has ever taken place in the South and it has attracted worldwide attention and people are pouring in.

I certainly do wish there was some way you could come to visit and if you can think of any way let me know . . . Now they have started a rumor from Walter Winchell† that the Socialist Worker's Party is in town and they are screaming for an Alabama Un-Alabama Committee to investigate the NAACP. Life is not dull but it gets rather trying to say the least, so much to do and so much opposition, but it looks to me as if this is the place where the battle will be won. I do hope I am not too hopeful.

February-March 1956
Dearest Dec: . . .

One thing people are doing is to send shoes as walking does wear the shoes out. . . . Another thing is to remember always that this started with the Negroes, it is run by them, they have the controlling say and while our help can be offered, they are the ones to say what and how and who and everything else, as they are bearing the burden. They had rather their help comes from their own organizations, churches, etc., and all of us who want to help them can only get them in touch with each other. That is what is so wonderful, it is so spontaneous and so purely out of their own history and background and they are being so brave and so joyful and so patient and good with it all. I almost feel I am getting religion after hearing the Negro preachers, they always preach "Love your enemies" and don't let "hate get you down." So far it is so free from any bickering or bad feeling or jealousy and they are so united.

---

*Martin Luther King, Jr. was the first of the indicted leaders to be tried. He was convicted and fined $500.
†Winchell, famous gossip columnist and radio broadcaster who, by the 1950s, had become a strident anticommunist. In his March 4th broadcast, he claimed that the Socialist Workers Party had assigned its most important figure to Montgomery "to keep the racial conflict there raging."

Do you know the spiritual, "I got shoes, you got shoes, all God's chillun got shoes."

Tell the ladies to write to Mrs. Parks or to Mr. Nixon and forget your worries and let them handle it and you can help them. BUT THIS IS THEIR SHOW, THEY HAVE SHOWN US THE WAY IN MY OPINION.

Early in 1956, folk singer Pete Seeger, a longtime friend of Virginia, wrote to her inquiring about the music of the Montgomery movement.

March 1956
Dear Pete:
I received the copy of *Sing Out* which I enjoyed so much. Thanks for sending it to me. I am no musician, but I am so much interested in folk music as the repository of the history of a people, both emotionally and politically and all other ways. I have always thought it would be fascinating to take a definite period of history and relate the events and changes that took place to the songs that arose out of it . . .

Now as for your questions about the music in connection with the Bus Boycott. I called Mrs. King, the wife of the Rev. M. L. King . . . She is a musician herself and sings very beautifully and knew of you and was glad to give me the information.

Yes, there is a great deal of singing at the mass meetings. Both Hymns and Spirituals. The hymns come mostly out of the standard Hymnals, such as *Broadman's Baptist Hymnal,* and they sing hymns like Leaning on the Everlasting Arms, What a Friend We Have in Jesus, Onward Christian Soldiers, Pass Me Not, O! Gentle Savior, and then they also sing spirituals.

She says the ones she remembered being sung the most are: Steal Away, Old Time Religion, Shine on Me, Study War No More, Swing Low, I Got Shoes (this has been sung a great deal and a lot of people have sent boxes of shoes here for the walkers), I Got a Home in That Rock and

Rich Man Dives lived so well,
When he died he went to Hell,
Poor Man Lazarus, poor as I,
When he died he had a home on High.

She says you are absolutely right, that these songs were and are sung as songs of struggle, and that even in the time of slavery they were, but had to be allegorical and they had to use symbolic meanings to survive, and had to conceal what they wanted to say. The church has been, and is, the center of their lives and it was only when the NAACP militants got the churches behind them that the movement developed into a mass movement.

It is still going strong and looks as though it would keep on. But they need lots of help to keep it going, money for the transport system mainly, and even with that the walkers bear a big burden, and with the hot weather coming it will be heavier. I wish I could write a song about the beauty of these patient Negro women, their heads tied in scarfs, walking morning and night, to and fro. It is like some deep, dark silent spring welling up out of the bowels of the earth, and as irresistible and as compelling, some of them old, some of them fat, lots of them with their feet hurting, and walking no matter what—rain, cold, sleet, ice, heat—nothing stops them.

March 24, 1956
Dearest Dec: . . .

It is wonderful about the Committee out there and I talked to Mrs. Parks yesterday and she thinks she will go to Seattle and is also seriously considering coming to Oakland . . .

I am so thrilled that the Montgomery boycott is arousing interest all over the country as I think it shows people what they can do if they will unite and sacrifice. Do not think in spite of it all that there has not been a great deal of sacrifice, especially among the women who walk to work for miles in all kinds of weather, and naturally are cut down on their hours at home so the work there is doubled. But still they do not ride the bus no matter what the weather. Some of the old women almost have to creep along on their poor old feet, and I pick up all the ones I can, and as they never know whether you are a friend or foe, they always refuse to say anything about why they are not riding the bus except that "I usually walks, just a little late this morning. I comes with my son but he had to go to work real early this morning." If you can convince them that you are in sympathy with the boycott then they will sometimes open up and tell you all of their grievances which are many, deep and bitter and have been burning for generations. The wonderful thing now is that they have such good leadership.

April 16, 1956
Dearest Dec:

Mrs. Parks has come back and she had a wonderful time and loved the "ladies in Oakland" and especially you. She said some "snoopers" were trying to cause trouble on your account but the "ladies in Oakland" all liked you very much and did not appreciate [that] at all. It is like a fairy tale, orchids, flowers, presents, banquets, and speaking to audiences of 3000 people. She is going to New York next month too. Just think this is the first time in her life that she ever went anywhere . . . She is going to speak in New York for the Highlander School. I got her a scholarship there last summer and she loved it. Poor Zylphia Horton* died very unexpectedly, of some kind of kidney poisoning, very sudden and fatal and so sad, as she was such a vital person. I am sure you remember her.

The White Citizens Council set the tone for the 1956 Democratic primary elections. Governor Jim Folsom suffered a major defeat when state representative Charles McKay, a leading segregationist, outpolled him in his run for Democratic national committeeman. Even though Senator Lister Hill campaigned to uphold segregation, retired Admiral John Crommelin, a white supremacist and anti-Semite, won more than 100,000 votes in his challenge to Hill.

May 7, 1956
Dearest Clark: . . .

I think we get so narrow living down here in the midst of all this and thinking that the current of life is eternally flowing in the wrong direction. God—the last elections were terrific. Jim Folsom in spite of his foolishness has been good on the race business and although he made some concessions to segregation in his campaign still he (compared to the Miss. and Ga. governors) has said and done wonderful and brave things, and evidently the Negroes thought so as they voted for him en bloc. But he got clobbered and this McKay that was running could not

---

*Folk musician and wife of Highlander Folk School founder Myles Horton.

be worse. Then too the crazy Fascist—John Crommelin—that was running against Lister, who not only is violently anti-Negro but violently
anti-Jew and simply flooded the city with the vilest kinds of anti-
Semitic stuff, he got 112,000 votes and while Lister beat him two to one
still Lister had to come out with the most abject segregation statement,
pointing to his record against Civil Rights Bills and the Poll Tax Bill!
And how he had filibustered like all good Southerners, but then compared to Crommelin he is an angel of light. All the people that were running with the Folsom endorsement got clobbered too. It was a clean
sweep almost for the White Citizens Councils. And yet evidently Jim
Folsom must think that the Durrs and the Williams are too radical for
him as he has never so much as answered any note we wrote to him or
shown any sign of recognition of us and that certainly leaves us on a
mighty small base when even the Folsom crowd thinks we are too radical for them. But now that he got beat so badly he might think that all of
us have got to stick together, on the other hand he might do like Tom
Watson* and go all the way with the bastards, but I really don't think so.

On the other hand on the specific issue of the Bus Boycott, we are
doing well. The Bus Company, in Chicago (I don't know whether old
Aubrey's prodding and all the people he could get there to prod had
anything to do with it or not) but in any case they came out . . . and said
Hell we are not going to act as policemen any more and we are NOT
going to enforce segregation and told their drivers that, and then I understand the Bus Drivers Union which has been awful came around and
said they would uphold the Bus Company and THEN the damned old
City Commission and the Police Commissioner went to Court to get an
injunction against the Bus Company to make them enforce the City and
State segregation laws and now Judge [Walter B.] Jones . . . has it under
consideration, but at any rate the Bus Company has changed lawyers
and now has Truman Hobbs and John Godbold who are liberals of a
sort, and while they don't go so far as to endorse the school decision
they are willing to go along with the bus business of desegregation for
which we are thankful.

---

*Populist leader in Georgia who, in the face of electoral defeat, abandoned his appeals
for interracial cooperation and became a vehement white supremacist.

Now the big case comes here on the 11th of May when the Negroes go before the three judge federal court and try their case, but since the shift in forces, they will have the Bus Company on their side and the Bus Drivers Union and will only have the State and the City and the Public Service Commission on the other side. Cliff has seen the Brief (confidential) and says it is splendid and so if the local Federal Court upholds the Law then I don't see what those bastards can do except to withdraw the franchise from the Bus Co. which they will likely do or else simply use force and violence.

It is all very interesting and exciting and Cliff does do a lot to help in my opinion, but we are so few and of course with the Negroes we have some strength and I think it will grow, but it is like walking a tight rope and I am not one for subtlety as you know and to be cautious and discreet is hard, but I am learning fast!

May 1956
Dearest Clark and Mairi: . . .
I am glad Mrs. Parks made a good impression, I wish you could know her better because she is so quiet and repressed that you have to know her well to appreciate her. She is getting invitations to speak from all over the country, but could have accepted none of them except for the money that was raised for her home expenses . . . The leaders here are pure Negro for the most part, right out of Alabama. [Ralph] Abernathy comes from Lowndes County and so does [James E.] Pierce and of course [E. D.] Nixon is from right here. They are big, dark, determined and full of good humor and natural leaders. King is the more sophisticated and educated type, Ph.D., and extremely clever and well-read, and has a beautiful wife with a lovely voice. I wish someone could have her sing up there as she is very attractive. They all laugh at me when I praise them and say they are fighting for my freedom as much as for their own. "We Got to save white folks too." One of them after an SRC meeting about "love and more love" and so on, turned to me and said "I declare, Mrs. Durr, you white folks done just about loved us niggers to death." . . .

The other night I took the Unitarian preacher [Rudy Gilbert] from Denver . . . who was visiting us, and they had one of the worse kinds of old-fashioned screaming acting preachers that danced and sweated and intoned and went on in the old-fashioned way, which is just awful in my opinion, and the Unitarian had never seen anything like it and was quite shocked. But in any case Dr. King said to me afterwards that they take the churches in rotation [as locations for mass meetings] and don't miss a one, old-fashioned or not, and even the little Church of God has gotten a new station wagon [to help transport people]. By the way, Mrs. Parks gave me one of the pairs of shoes you sent her and they are fine! They get shoes, clothes, food, station wagons, etc., and really have gotten a feeling of uplift that only comes once in a lifetime. This is an experience I would not have missed for anything.

Cliff Durr's happiest memories from his youth were of summers spent with his maternal grandfather James Henry Judkins on his farm in Wetumpka, Alabama, in Elmore County, 20 miles outside of Montgomery. After inheriting ten acres of the land from his aunt, Cliff built a small cottage on his piece of land, known as the Pea Level because peas once grew there in abundance. Corn Creek, a winding stream and favorite place for cooling off in the summertime, was nearby. He spent as much time as possible at the Pea Level cultivating the land, tending to his gardens, and fixing up the cabin. It was where he felt most at home.

May 23, 1956
Dearest Dec: . . .

I am so disappointed . . . that you don't think you can come to visit us as we had really looked forward to that . . . I think we will be here all summer. Little Auntie gave Cliff ten acres up on the Creek (where we went to picnic) and he and we are building a shack up there and will spend lots of time there I know this summer. I think he would like to live there all the time, but I hold out for water, but in time we may. At least it is a refuge if things get worse, we can always grow something, or perhaps he can. I was never very good at farming but might learn . . .

It is getting to be like a straitjacket, just one wild rebel yell, but the Negroes are standing firm in spite of all of it and the handful of whites that are sympathetic, and it is only a handful literally, there may be more but they are too frightened to speak, or as Adam has so kindly put it, "apprehensive." Apprehensive is right. There is a regular spy system here—although not official as there is in Mississippi—and anyone making any remark or showing any out of the way sympathy for the Negroes is put on the black list. It all makes life interesting and what little you can do seems larger than it would be any other place—but it is like walking on eggs all the time, and trying to build a law practice is about as tough as you can imagine, but I think that after this the Negroes might start leaving the old line lawyers that they have been going to for "protection" and coming to us or a Negro lawyer—he had a terrible time until the boycott, the Negroes literally buy protection by going to the worse SOBs in town who have "influence" . . .

I do so long for a breath of freedom from this ever present and ever pressing feeling of being hemmed in and suffocated by the crowding walls of prejudice, but the Negroes have had it much worse and they are struggling to free us all . . .

Dearest Dec, do try and write more if you can and only postcards if nothing else. Tell Marge to write too if she can. I do love you both so much and long so to see you and talk to you and feel the sense of communion.

May 29, 1956
Dearest Clark: . . .

Mrs. Parks returned simply glowing with delight over her trip. She had never been to New York before and she got a wonderful reception . . . It simply goes from day to day. Now they have subpoenaed the records of the station wagons and they are harassing them in every way possible and young Gray calls him [Cliff] up everyday on something. I think too that in this particular situation that only a person such as Cliff could function well, as he does not want any recognition or any claim to fame or any share of the credit, and the Negroes are so proud of the fact that this is an all-Negro movement, led, financed to a large degree and activated by Negroes. I think Aubrey feels a terrible sense of being left out of it—although he has been very helpful and done all he possibly could, but publicly he has not received any acclaim at all, and in fact except for Pastor Graetz who has a Negro church no white man or woman has received any recognition. I can understand how Aubrey feels as this is the fulfillment of his dreams in a way and the thing he has fought and suffered for, and when it comes, he is left out, but Cliff fully understands that this is a Negro movement and has to be one and they have to have the pride and knowledge that they can do it by themselves. Then too while he knows people know he has helped them, still as long as it is not publicized, he can function as a lawyer, although naturally he is criticized. In fact I would say that at least ninety percent of the white people are either afraid or opposed. When Dr. [Ralph] Bunche* spoke here on Sunday, the papers had nothing but a tiny little notice on an inside page and then there were only about five white people in the audience. I went and went to the reception and thought he made a fine speech, although of course he always brings it down to the level of this is the way to defeat totalitarian communism, etc., but then he forgets his dignity and remembers his indignities and tells about the segregated rest rooms in Birmingham and the segregated drinking fountains. I suppose there is really no worse indignity than to be considered as a race to be diseased and to smell bad and to be so physically repugnant that other people can't stand you. But then the WCC goes on to say that if the Negroes have a chance all the white women will marry them! I do get so ashamed of the white southern man, God! How can they sink to the depths of degradation as they do, and reveal themselves not only as brutal but as so weak and insecure. Your hatred of them has to be tempered by both pity and contempt.

. . . I think these next few years are going to be crucial not only in the South but in the country and if things here go too badly then the South could be and might be still the breeding ground of a real fascism for the rest of the country. Last night "Judge" Tom Brady of Mississippi spoke here for the WCC and the whole City Commission announced that they had gone on the Board of the WCC. He spoke not only about the Negroes and segregation and integration but went on and on about "socialism" and England and what we are having here was a sort of "creeping socialism" such as they had in England. Now that they have the Communists on the run they are beginning on the "English Socialists" . . .

Lots of love and Thank you a thousand times my best friend (male).

Virginia's frustration with the national Democratic party reached a boiling point in the summer of 1956. The failure of party officials even to

---

*Ralph Bunche, first African American to win the Nobel Peace Prize (1950), was then serving as undersecretary general of the United Nations.

acknowledge Aubrey Williams's request to appear before the platform committee at the Democratic national convention that summer triggered the following letter to Eleanor Roosevelt.

July 24, 1956
Dear Mrs. Roosevelt,

Aubrey Williams sent us a copy of the letter he wrote to A. Philip Randolph* and also your reply to his letter to you. Let me say first how wonderful it is to have someone like you to write to and to count on and how much your loyal and honest support has meant to us.

Second, I would also like to say at some length that I know Aubrey is totally correct in what he says about the situation of the southern liberal who has to fight not only against the prejudice of his immediate neighbors, but the prejudice of the organizations in the North that should support his efforts and who in many cases seem to go along with Eastland instead. In the case of the NAACP there is no doubt that they sent down word for the local chapters not to have "anything to do with Aubrey Williams" although I will say that to the eternal credit of the southern Negroes, there are a lot of them that paid it no mind at all. Can you think of a more ridiculous situation than for a man who has given his life to the cause of justice for the Negro to be redbaited by the NAACP because he has been attacked by Eastland. Of course the same forces that attacked Aubrey are now attacking the NAACP. I hope it teaches them a lesson that they badly need to learn.

But Mrs. Roosevelt, what I want to say might pain you, but it is this. I do not blame the NAACP for their behavior, nor the CIO, nor the AFL, nor the Farmers Union nor the ADA. All of these great organizations that had such a fine record of fighting for what was right, and who, under your husband, were the foundation of the Democratic Party, were perverted from their true course by the Truman Administration who made "anticommunism" the very touchstone of its policies both here and abroad and turned what was a great forward liberal and democratic movement into a sterile and defeated force. To have turned this country and the Democratic Party from its great course and into this

---

*President of the Brotherhood of Sleeping Car Porters union and among the most prominent civil rights leaders during this period.

kind of blind alley is to my mind one of the greatest tragedies of our age. I do blame Mr. Truman who both on the foreign and on the domestic stage made "anticommunism" the main point of his policy and who succeeded in bringing the Democratic Party to defeat thereby. To see how evil it has been, how far it has gone, how many innocent people have suffered, how disruptive it has been, we only have to read the daily press and look around us. I think Mr. Truman was a stupid and ignorant man who was used by evil forces, particularly Mr. [John Foster] Dulles, and who fell in the trap that McCarthy and the Republicans dug for him and in trying to deny their "twenty years of treason" insanity went them one further by establishing the loyalty order and starting the whole business of faceless informers, confidential informants, blacklists and perjured and paid for government witnesses, and turned people against each other, each afraid of his neighbor and let suspicion and slander run rife so that people to protect themselves had to agree to something that most of them knew was wrong or evil. The more they yell "Peace" and "Civil Rights" the more they chop away at the very foundations of what we have thought was the glory of this country and they are laying the foundations of a police state in their pretended efforts to prevent it from being one.

For nearly twenty years Aubrey Williams has been fighting for simple justice for the Negro people—the right to vote, the right to a job, the right to an education, the right to live unsegregated as a human being. He has hated the injustices and wrongs of dictatorship wherever they occurred. Long ago he used to rail at the Communists for being so blind in defending the abuses of the Soviet Union . . . He fought them face to face as he has always fought for what he believed in. But now he is fighting ghosts because there is nothing against him he can fight but the dreadful fact that he is "a man who has been investigated." Men such as Lyndon Johnson whom he helped to make, men he worked with and helped for years not only never rose to defend him but now don't give him the courtesy of a reply. He has been trying to get to appear before the Platform Committee of the [Democratic] Party and they don't even answer his requests. Eastland gets far more consideration in the Democratic Party than a man like Aubrey. Here is this whole farce of the Civil Rights bill being sent to Committee to be buried by Eastland after fine speeches. What a farce and how hypocritical. I am ashamed of the Democratic Party. Aubrey and Cliff are still loyal to it and I would like to be but what is there to be loyal to anymore? You and you alone are all that remains of its former glory. I hope you will be able to speak to them and arouse their consciences when you do. They keep you as a symbol of the Roosevelt Era when they let Eastland bury it. How can we feel sure of Stevenson when he comes South and pussy foots and gets all the white supremacists to endorse him and then goes to California and speaks out so boldly. What does he really believe? We will have the Republicans in forever or something worse.

I may have written too frankly and if so I am sorry, but I have had the taste of gall and wormwood in my mouth too long and I must get it out of my heart.

Sincerely yours, Virginia Durr

July/August 1956
Dear Corliss: . . .

I think you are a darling to think of us and you have certainly saved our life and our usefulness here for the present. The pressures of the WCCs and now the KKK and just the general prejudice of the people make things difficult and will for a long time to come, and actually our only hope of making a living is to build a good practice among the Negroes, and hope that we will get a few white clients from time to time. But the really great handicap here is that the law, as all else, is run on strictly personal lines, and both the Judges,* who are old classmates and fraternity brothers of Cliff's, are still so biased that he usually loses in the lower courts and wins on appeal. In fact he has a 100 percent batting average in the Court of Appeals, which is unprecedented, but that does not mean that he will win with Judge Jones always on the other side.

The only hope here is to get out the bulk of the vote, both white and Negro, and change the political complexion. I do not honestly believe that court orders will be obeyed until the people, both white and Negro, have the political power to get rid of these—well, I will try and be a lady and not use such words. Now I don't think there will be so much oppo-

---

*Walter B. Jones and Eugene Carter were the two circuit court judges in Montgomery.

sition to the bus decision as after all unsegregated transportation has been accepted in every other field, but I think of the kind of things that send the blood pressures up, such as schools and swimming pools. There is going to be a long and very tough fight . . .

I am of the honest opinion that the kind of wild and aggressive foolishness that brought on the Civil War is again abroad in the land here, and will certainly bring violence of some sort. In light of the situation who in the world are you going to vote for for President? I simply cannot make up my mind to either [Adlai] Stevenson or [Dwight D.] Eisenhower, and [Averell] Harriman makes me simply shudder, and I am afraid they have knocked [Estes] Kefauver out of the race with such very dirty tactics.

October 15, 1956
Dear Mrs. Roosevelt:
Thank you very much for your letter which has just come. I do appreciate it very much as I know how busy you are campaigning. I came back from a visit to New York and Philadelphia and Washington quite discouraged as I found most of my Negro friends voting for the Republicans in protest against Eastland, and if they do vote Democratic finally I think it will be almost entirely due to you.

While I am wholeheartedly for Stevenson and Kefauver, still I can understand their "pessimism." The enclosed clipping will tell you more than I can, and that is that the South seems to be winning the counteroffensive. It only took the resignation of about 15 local chapters for the PTA* to give in, and both the Republican Party and the Democratic Party still are segregated here and all of the big national organizations such as the Churches, the Federal Council, the YMCA, the YWCA, the League of Women Voters, etc. Every one of these organizations has passed the most wonderful resolutions and never live up to them, and the Democratic Party here in Montgomery is using the argument that [we must] keep the Democratic Party in power so we can have the power to block any Civil Rights legislation. How can the Negroes here

---

*Several local chapters of the PTA had resigned after the National Congress of Parents and Teachers adopted a resolution urging local PTAs to support school desegregation.

have any confidence in that kind of Party as they see it on the local level? Also when it is Democratic officials that deny them the right to vote?

I know you don't have time for a long letter so I will write one and send it on to you later to be read after the election. I have a good idea which only you can carry out.

I hope we will come to some meeting of the minds about "violence." When the enforcement of a law is met with "violence" as it has been in Texas, Kentucky and Alabama and Tennessee (and only in Tennessee are the Negro children still in school) I think the victims of that "violence" should be protected and I cannot see how this can be construed as using "force and violence." Every Sheriff's writ has to be backed by force of some kind and every law has to ultimately depend on some kind of enforcement and cannot simply rest on consent.

Sarah Patton Boyle, a white Virginian, spoke out in support of integration and became the target of harassment, including a cross burning, in the genteel university community of Charlottesville; her husband was a professor at the University of Virginia. She wrote about her experiences in the *Nation,* and about her determination to continue speaking out. Virginia was interested in whether Boyle's family suffered financial repercussions, and wrote directly and asked her. Boyle responded that a bill was introduced in the state legislature calling for her husband to be fired, but it was not enacted.[21]

October 24, 1956
Dearest Clark:

I am always sorry when I write you a whining letter as I am sure you have troubles enough as it is and don't complain nearly as much as I do. It is not that the troubles are not real, just read Sarah Patton Boyle's article in this week's *Nation* . . . The thing about her article that is lacking is how does it influence her husband and his job? It is the lack of any financial backing and fear of losing their livelihood that scares most people more than anything else and makes them stay silent.

Yesterday I went to see Professor [Lawrence] Reddick at the Alabama State Teachers College who is writing a book about the Montgomery Boycott. He is the ex-Librarian of Atlanta University and has all of the Southern Conference stuff and Anti-Poll Tax stuff stashed away there.

Do you know anything about him? He seemed very nice and intelligent and quite fair minded. He wanted to write something about the part that Cliff and I had played in the boycott and asked my permission but how could I give it to him? Let us be written up as having played a part, however it may seem to History, simply means that our tenuous hold here is lost for good. He understood it finally but I hated to have to tell him that History cannot feed your children or pay your school bills.

I have been thinking more about the Meeting and wonder how it would be to have a Joint Southern Meeting, let Highlander, SCEF and NAACP (if they would) share in it and in the proceeds and launch a drive for Two Million Negro votes in the South, make it dramatic and perhaps this way some of the overlapping could be minimized and something could get done which would be constructive down here. It is all such a drop in the bucket, it does seem so silly to have all the overlapping and so much futility.

It looks from here as though Alabama might go Republican but that is the Montgomery outlook which is always as bad as possible, but North Alabama might be a different story.

On November 13, 1956, the Supreme Court upheld a special three-judge federal court's June 5 ruling on *Browder v. Gayle*, striking down Alabama's bus segregation laws. A final appeal from the Montgomery City Commission delayed implementation of the ruling until December 20.

November 20, 1956
Dearest Clark: . . .

We are no more unpopular than we have been and actually we are not so unpopular personally as we are just "suspect" as being heretics. We are no longer members of the tribe and there are penalties attached to that as you know, mostly economic ones, but so far we survive and that is a real triumph. The Supreme Court is the arch enemy according to the papers and the WCC movement is still strong and getting stronger, but somehow there is not as much ginger to it as there was at first. "Mongelization" and "race mixing" seems to lose a little of its potential rabble rousing value after they use it day after day ad nauseam. The latest proposal to get around the Bus decision is that a law shall be passed giving a woman a right to refuse to let ANY man sit beside her, not just a Negro man, but any man, as the proposer of the law went on to say that even among members of her own race, she would be likely to be insulted by a strange man sitting beside her, and this way she can protect her pure white womanhood from any man. These are the kinds of things that are discussed seriously . . . Cliff goes on giving good advice to the Negroes and they come up and ask him all kinds of legal questions . . . and they trust him and like him and he just does it as a matter of course, although he knows it makes his position worse and worse. Aubrey is fine too and he too goes ahead and works with them and carries them in his car and gets abused almost every day in the paper . . . I think you know from John Wesley [Dobbs] how grateful they are and that is a lot of thanks and makes you feel good, although I have never acted from benevolence but from a burning desire to change the South so I could be at home in it. . . .

I still think for Montgomery County to go Republican was simply the result of no work and no leadership and letting the Negroes with their 2500 votes to be snubbed and despised . . . I wish there was some way to get Mrs. R[oosevelt] and Senator Lehman to form a Committee for the South and get the national organizations that have branches in the South to cooperate and see if they can't bring some integration to those groups. If the Army and the Air Force would make some protests about their personnel being segregated that would help more than anything as the South certainly does not want to lose all of those federal installations and the idea of a Negro officer coming here to Staff School and then coming to town and being Jim Crowed is disgraceful in my opinion. Don't you think so? The Federal Government, certainly the Military could change the picture overnight if they wanted to and there would be no more bucking it than there was over the integration of the Army. When I was in New York I tried so hard to interest people in setting up some kind of a Committee that would also work on getting the Negro registered. The NAACP is outlawed and the SRC [Southern Regional Council] can't do anything political. The SCEF is also bound by tax restrictions as I recall. I think that another two or three million Negro votes would change things quicker than anything I know of except the Federal Government but I have said this so often I say it in my sleep and

I have said it so long and everyone agrees but nothing much has been done since the demise of the old SC [Southern Conference for Human Welfare].

A weeklong series of workshops and mass meetings were held in Montgomery from December 3 to 9 as part of the Institute on Nonviolence and Social Change to commemorate the boycott movement's first anniversary. White author Lillian Smith, an outspoken opponent of segregation, was scheduled to address a mass meeting on December 5, but was unable to attend because of a recurrence of cancer. Local black civic leader Rufus Lewis read her speech, "The Right Way Is Not a Moderate Way," to the gathering.

Virginia wrote to Smith describing the evening. She and Smith had known each other through the Southern Conference for Human Welfare but had never been friendly. Smith resigned from the SCHW in 1945, charging that the organization was run by a handful of people (Virginia Durr was among those named) and that several board members followed "the Communist line."[22]

December 6, 1956

Dear Lillian:

While the memory is fresh in my mind I want to write you about the meeting last night . . .

The church was packed and people were standing on the outside and bulging in the doors and windows. So far as I could see my friend and I and two ministers were the only white people there and the Negro group ranged all the way up and down the ladder of the social order. First there was some singing by the choirs with the lovely, plaintive minor note that is so much in the Negro singing and after various introductions Mrs. [Irene] West introduced you. We did not know that you were not there . . .

Then Dr. Lewis came forward . . . and told them that you were ill and that he was going to read your speech . . . It was the most wonderful speech and so full of love and truth and at the end when you thanked them for what they were doing to free the South and the white people of the South from their fear and prejudice, you could hear a deep sigh go all over the audience.

You said so beautifully what every "good" Southerner thinks and the response was almost ecstatic. They announced that they were going to print 50,000 copies to be distributed. I am so glad as I think it is a message that should get around as widely as possible. You said it so graciously and gratefully.

It was the high point of the meeting . . . Of course I as a white southerner feel that it lifted a little of the load of guilt off of our shoulders and at least let these brave people know that there is *one* at least who thanks them for unbinding her spirit.

The distress over your illness was deep . . . *I am so sorry* that . . . we were divided and did not ever become friends. How silly it seems now in the light of what has actually happened. We should have known that the Negroes in the end were going go find their own way and that what we did and thought could only come to fruition in what they did. The fact that they have chosen the way of love and forgiveness and nonviolence is, I think, a great step forward in the thinking of us all. Thank you for broadening our view and translating your grace into words that we can all keep.

With the desegregation of Montgomery's buses imminent, Virginia believed that black voter registration was critical to laying the foundation for real change in the South. She looked to Clark Foreman and Palmer Weber to help raise support in New York to help aid Rosa Parks and E. D. Nixon, who were organizing a voter registration campaign in Montgomery. She also encouraged them to consider supporting similar efforts around the South by contacting black civic activists they had worked with ten years earlier through the Southern Conference. Weber's apparent suggestion that there were more pressing issues facing the Emergency Civil Liberties Committee (ECLC) infuriated Virginia; she soon went to New York herself to lobby for the cause.

December 7, 1956
Dearest Clark:

I am simply furious with Palmer. Aleine Austin wrote me two letters explaining why all my lady workers in New York could neither contribute nor work for the project of helping Mr. Nixon and Mrs. Parks open a Registration and Voting office. She said he said "I could get more respectable money and there were so many unpopular causes that the progressives needed to support." I would like to know what is more unpopular than a Negro voting in Montgomery and who these "respectable" sources are. But the thing that makes me really angry is that with his old Virginia charm he makes me feel he is still my best friend and . . . he will help me, and THEN never saying a word to me about his change of mind (if he ever did agree) and goes on and blows up my plans without a word to me and Aleine writes as though after Palmer had spoken the last word had been said and that was it. I cannot understand her being so weak minded either.

I wrote Palmer after I heard from her thinking that he must have some ideas to meet the situation and he has not answered. So Rosa is left with nothing to do and no office and Mr. Glenn Smiley has the floor with LOVE LOVE LOVE.* I could really go on for a long time but I won't, but I do think this is why "progressive" movements fail. New York always has to say what is what and the people out in the field have nothing to say about anything. I am really boiling mad and it is a good thing that NY is 1,000 miles away.

December 17, 1956
Dearest Clark: . . .

Well Palmer wrote me and said he had not intended to bust my balloon and no doubt there are just too many people coming to the well with dippers. I always get furious with people I love and trust and Palmer like you has become one of the foundation stones of my life, so in direct proportion as to how much I like people and trust them, so do I get furious with them. Not a happy characteristic . . . You and Palmer are blood of my blood and bone of my bone and Cliff says that when I get mad at him I blame him for every white southern liar I ever knew, so I do with you and Palmer. Certainly I cannot put all the sins of the white southern male on you when you all are among the few I know who don't deserve to be blamed for the ills of the South. But in any case the time has now gone by, I am afraid, for Mr. Nixon to start the voting office. I think the MIA will do it on a big scale and it should be a great success but Mrs. Parks won't have a job there (the jobs all go to college people) and Mr. Nixon won't be in charge. Perhaps Mr. Nixon can start the Progressive Democrats again . . .

---

*Glenn Smiley was a white pacifist who represented the Fellowship of Reconciliation and went to Montgomery to advise King on the principles of nonviolence.

I hope the parties were a great success and lots of money was raised and you can go ahead and rescue even more people from despair . . . If in the spring you find that you can do and want to do something for the South and know what you want to do I will come and talk myself hoarse for you if it will be in private gatherings and not news items for the *Advertiser*. Living with the *Advertiser* is like living with a loaded gun to your head. I am glad Cliff is not with the FCC although God knows they need good men. He would either be dead or mad by now if he had to put up with the deceit in Washington. Here at least he knows his way around and is not deceived and has come to have a clearer understanding and deeper anger on account of the Negroes than any of us. Cliff has to deal with fact not theory and he has done far more good than anyone else in the present situation, I mean among the white people. He is now trying a lot of little police actions as the Police are harassing the Negroes so on traffic violations and Fred Gray sends them up to him as he thinks Cliff will have a better chance than he would to get them off. Of course they don't pay anything but every satisfied client may lead to another. But practicing law with the Courthouse in charge of the WCC is hard to put it mildly and we struggle from month to month.

January 7, 1957
Dearest Clark:

Thanks so much for your sweet letter which I appreciated a great deal. I think my state of mind *is* better and has been for the past year in that I have been able to function a little although not much, but with the boycott and the chance to help the Negroes, if only a little, I feel I am at last making some use of myself, and while I do not discount the personal life I lead and the use I am to Cliff and the children, it is painful in the extreme for a person such as I am to live in a situation such as this one is and do nothing about it . . . To be able to help just a little has changed my entire point of view . . .

I will be delighted to come up in April . . . I only want my expenses paid and $25.00 a week to get someone to take my place here in the office in the morning. . . . I would want what money I raised to go to the ECLC but with the proviso that it be used for work in the South and I hope on VOTING. My idea is that you renew your contacts with people such as John Wesley [Dobbs] and Mrs. [Mojeska] Simkins and whoever else you still know well and inquire into the chances of establishing offices for voting and registration.* Let it be local and let it be run by them and we can only help but for God's Sake let's get going on it as there is the key to this whole thing and until it is done nothing else will be. I figure that an office of that kind can be run for about $250.00 a month including office, secretary and telephone. Now the one here is about to get going and it will be run by Mr. [E. D.] Nixon with Mrs. [Rosa] Parks as Secretary and will be the office of the PROGRESSIVE DEMOCRATS as Mr. Nixon says he is not non-partisan. Of course Asbury Howard in Bessemer is also a wonder and he has the Negro Voters League. They have done wonders on no money but think what they could do with some. Does this make sense to you? As you well know speeches, prayers, exhortations etc. do not take the place of block by block canvassing and having a central place and a voter's list and someone to keep after people all the time . . .

I think the main thing we have to work out in this kind of a deal is exactly what and why and HOW what money I can beg borrow and steal will be used. Nothing vague or fulsome but concrete. The reaction is the thing I don't know or cannot figure out. I always feel about New York that it is a vast Merry Go Round and when you go there for a day or so they give you one whirl and after you leave they go on and forget you were ever there. The NAACP under the name of a State Coordinating Committee has some kind of voting machinery or registration machinery but Mr. Nixon does not think it functions at all well, and also there are these church and local groups, but this would be specific and local and city by city and it might be that John Wesley and Mrs. Simkins and Mr. Nixon and Mrs. Parks would do better than I. I never know how much undercutting and red baiting the NAACP will do, certainly they do not want anyone else in on the act . . .

I don't think it ever occurs to people that the Republican Party and the Democratic Party do not function with the Negroes nor does the League of Women Voters nor the Fund for the Republic. I think I wrote

---

*John Wesley Dobbs's Atlanta Civic and Political League led a major voting rights drive in the 1940s and became a key factor in Atlanta politics. Mojeska Simkins was a long time civil rights leader in South Carolina; she lived in Columbia.

that their contribution was sending Boy Scouts around with tags to tie on door knobs "HAVE YOU VOTED?"

Cliff is in Wetumpka on a case for the morning so I am evidently taking the morning writing to you and am sorry it is so long. Lots of love to you and Mairi and be thinking along these lines and thinking hard and let's have no more crossed wires.

Following the desegregation of the buses on December 21, snipers fired on city buses, wounding one black passenger and causing the city commission to suspend evening bus runs temporarily. Early on the morning of January 10, six bombs exploded in Montgomery, damaging four black churches and the homes of the Rev. Ralph Abernathy and the Rev. Robert Graetz.

January 23, 1957
Dearest Dec: . . .

We are just getting over the bombings here. They were frightening as they were so completely vicious and without rhyme or reason and then too most people like us think either the Police did them or protected the people that did them. In any case, it is a real collapse of law and you know that you have no protection against people that hate you and want to do you evil. Of course the Negroes have had that a long time but I am just beginning to know what it is like.

February 1957
Dearest Clark: . . .

Two young teenagers who go to our Church whose grandfather is one of the big wheels in our church (used to be Cliff's Sunday school teacher) were arrested and convicted in Federal Court for burning a cross and threatening the wife and child of the Federal Judge here.* They were put on probation, and I heard from good authority that the reason they did it was that they were inflamed by the words of their grandfather (. . . he has a disease called the black tongue and it is well named.) . . . These two young boys seemed to think they would be heroes and when they got the FBI after them and they were caught and arraigned and brought to trial, THEY were surprised . . .

---

*U.S. District Judge Frank M. Johnson.

Of course there is very great doubt that the Bombers will be convicted. They have gotten John Blue Hill* to defend them and a Committee has been formed for their defense, in fact two Committees and $60,000 is being raised for them and the Prosecutor will be Billy Thetford who will know that he is signing his political death warrant if he prosecutes them very vigorously. It is a City Offense and will be prosecuted by the City and it looks right now as if they will all get off. That is why I say this thing has GOT to be brought down on a local level, nothing counts until it takes place on the local level and the only way I can see to do it is to give the Negroes some power through the vote and then I hope like the various racial groups that have gone before that they will in time get integrated into the community.

But the thing I fear is that a feeling of "separatism" will develop and that they will form separate businesses, separate political groups and further increase their separateness. I grant that they need to feel their strength as a group, and to win their own self-confidence and their own pride and that is what has been so wonderful in the Martin Luther King movement. He has given them what they needed so badly, pride, cohesion and so on, but I am not convinced that they will win their objectives with nonviolence and prayer and think votes will be much more powerful. Mr. Nixon thinks so too and so does Mrs. Parks and so does Aubrey [Williams] now. He and Nixon and Jim have just come back from Atlanta from a SCEF meeting and the SCEF agreed to let Nixon have some money to start on. THANK GOD for this. I don't know how much and for what period, but at least enough to get started. I have worked on them just as hard as I have worked on the ECLC as that "respectable money" Palmer talked about is unknown to me . . .

I do not know of any better way to shift the political emphasis of the country than to democratize the South and to do it is a long, hard, tough and slow process but I do think it can be done. I only wish there was some way to work with the Unions as they lag so badly, although they do some good, but so much work is needed there. Of course most of the bombers were Union men and the Defense Committee is working out of Carpenter's Hall and the head of it, Jack Brock is head of a

---

*A leading criminal lawyer and first cousin of Senator Lister Hill.

"Labor" paper and these guys are the "Ace Carter WCCers" which are the real bully boys. They are not the lumpen proletariat either, but smart, fine artisans and mean as Hell when it comes to the Negro.

The White Citizens Council's determined effort to crush white dissent was demonstrated in the case of Virginia's friend Juliette Morgan, a single, 42-year-old librarian and former high school teacher, and one of the handful of whites publicly to support the boycott. Morgan was from a prominent Montgomery family and a devout Episcopalian. Racial segregation and discrimination violated her religious principles and beliefs, and she expressed her opinions openly in letters to the *Montgomery Advertiser*. However, it was a letter Morgan had written to the editor of the *Tuscaloosa News* that drew the wrath of the Citizens Council. Morgan praised the editor for his criticism of the University of Alabama in its treatment of Autherine Lucy, contrasting his bold stand with the cowardly behavior of most white Southern men. The Citizens Council reproduced the letter in a widely distributed flier and launched a relentless campaign to have Morgan fired from her job. A minority of library board members prevented this, arguing that such an action would violate Morgan's First Amendment rights. However, library patrons shunned Morgan, and she was a target of constant harassment.

February 11, 1957
Dearest Clark:

Your letter has just come and I am delighted to have so many "dates" . . .

I know you are remembering my warning about publicity as it is absolutely necessary not to give the *Advertiser* or the WCC another stick to beat us with. It is hard to realize how vindictive they are. Juliette Morgan, a great friend of ours who is in the Library, wrote a letter to the Tuscaloosa *News* praising the Editor and the WCC now has it printed up in a sheet and has distributed it all over the town with invidious comments, and the Mayor and the City Commission are making a demand that she be fired and the poor girl is in a state. No one is too small to escape their venom. People that bomb sleeping children and go after sweet old maid librarians—this is Southern chivalry in all of its glory. She did speak in her letter of "cowardly white southern men" which did not help her popularity. Thank God for the exceptions—but they do have a hard time.

February 15, 1957
Dearest Clark: . . .

There is a blazing row going on down here . . . The MIA although full of brotherly love seems to be going through the same kind of thing that do most organizations composed of mortals. King has captured the imagination and the devotion of the masses of the Negroes here and united them and done a wonderful job—no doubt of it. They adore him and my wash lady tells me every week about how she hears the angels' wings when he speaks . . . There is a great deal of mysticism in him and the Negroes absolutely believe in his "vision" and his "sainthood." I have never been able to feel close to him nor has Aubrey, but I give him all the credit he should have for uniting the Negroes and keeping their morale up and over such a long period and I think his needling Eisenhower is all to the good too and I think he has a genius for the right word and also has a genius for the right act at the right time.

BUT while I think he is terrific as a spiritual leader he knows absolutely nothing about politics and while the MIA calls for registration he wants to keep it nonpartisan and so on . . . Mr. Nixon wants to play politics in the American tradition. He is afraid the Negro vote will be nullified by both parties if it stays strictly nonpartisan. He does not go all out for the nonviolence creed and while he certainly does not want violence he thinks the Negroes should make it clear that they are going to depend on the Courts and on political action to back them as well as God. He is not a churchman, and thinks in political terms and trade union terms and is practical, but he never did manage to unite the Negro community the way King has. Naturally between the two such diverse approaches there was bound to be friction and there is a great deal, to put it mildly. Mr. Nixon has been the Treasurer for all this time and they have . . . asked him to resign but he would not and put up a fight but while he stayed . . . his role is not nearly as important as it used to be . . .

I cannot possibly be in a position to do anything that would contribute to [this divisive situation] by asking specifically for money for the MIA or for Mr. Nixon's group which is still embryonic. When he started to mail out a money-raising letter from the Progressive Democrats a howl went up that he was trying to split the MIA . . . He is coming to New York on Wednesday, February 27th, to see his Union President [A. Philip] Randolph and also Mrs. R. [Roosevelt] if possible. He said he would like to talk to you and Palmer off the record . . . as man to man (southern variety). Cliff and Aubrey like him very much . . . King is so taken up with Glenn Smiley (whom I don't trust) and the Gandhi idea, Cliff and Aubrey simply don't speak his language, although Aubrey knows him best and likes him too, but he is the "new Negro" who seems to feel that his only relationship with the white man has to be on an entirely different basis. He may be right but in this contest of Montgomery, Alabama, when what we are trying to do is to keep people from being killed and to get rid of some of the nastiest public officials known to man, to be told to "pray" for them and "love" them while it might have a public relations angle simply does not ring a bell for us. But how the Negroes love him and look up to him. He has certainly given them pride in themselves . . .

Of course you must understand that he [Nixon] suffers from the same fate of all old leaders that see a younger man come on and take the leadership away from him and do what he has not been able to do which is to unite people around him.

February 1957
Dearest Clark: . . .

I am delighted about the public meeting for John Wesley Dobbs, and think if you could do the same for Mrs. [Mojeska] Simkins that would be wonderful. This to me is the answer we have been seeking for so long, that is to build a countervailing force against the reactionary forces here. The Southern Conference [for Human Welfare] tried and helped but did not succeed, the Progressive Party tried but did not succeed, but these indigenous, local Negro groups which have roots in the communities and which are of long standing and headed by people well known are at least a good beginning and if the ECLC has the political vision to see this and help them it will be doing a wonderful thing . . . I feel so strongly that if the South is not . . . democratized that the . . . the Democratic Party is rendered impotent, and the whole political balance in the country is upset by the Southern wing. There is no doubt in my mind that the Republican Party by and large represents the corporate interests and the Democratic Party represents the Union interests but it is rendered obsolete and absurd and ineffective and ridiculous and also dangerous by the fact that the whole process of democratic rule is blocked by the southern veto power and people who want to use the political system and who want to change things through it are frustrated. As this grows it creates a very dangerous frame of mind which a demagogue like [Richard] Nixon can build on very well.

February 27, 1957
Dearest Clark and Mairi:

I received Mairi's letter and thank you so much, it was wonderful to anticipate such a warm welcome. I am a little nervous as I have for so long been out of any kind of public speaking and really don't know if I have lost the touch or not. Then too there is no doubt that when you live among people so few of whom find you charming, that you begin to doubt if you ever were charming and can ever be again. I have developed durability with the years down here and can do and take what would have destroyed me just a few years ago, but at the same time, I have certainly not developed my lighter side . . .

Clark, I thought after I wrote you that I was really expecting too much of you and I am sorry about so many limitations, but one more public attack on us and I am afraid we could not stay and where we would go I do not know. It is hard for you to imagine the lengths they will go to make your life miserable and make it impossible for you to live here. Our friend at the Library is going through it now and has the whole City Commission trying to abolish her little job at the Library, and just because she wrote a letter to the paper. If I did not feel we do some good here, I would not think the struggle was worth it, but I do really think that we do have some good to offer, for whatever it is worth.

March 4, 1957
Dearest Marge: . . .

For the time being the tensions are somewhat relaxed, the Negroes are back on the buses and there has been no violence for some weeks and actually I do not think many people object to the buses. The bombers are yet to be tried and no one seems to think they will be convicted which is going to be awful, but I hope they are wrong, because if it becomes open season for bombing then no one is safe.*

---

*The first two of the accused bombers were tried in May and acquitted. In the face of that verdict, the state did not pursue the other indictments, and the case was closed.

Virginia wrote about the death of her brother, Sterling Foster.

March, 1957
Dear Clark:

Your letter was waiting for me when I got back from Charlotte where I had gone for my brother's funeral. He died on February 21 and was buried on Monday, February 23. I went up and stayed three days and came home exhausted both from the strain and the ride on the bus. He was only sixty-one which seems young to me now but he had been ill for nearly four years and had had several light strokes and was in fear of being paralyzed and losing his faculties, and while I was so sorry to see him die so young, still I am glad he did not live on to linger in that half dead and half alive state. I am the last one of the family that is left now. I think he had great promise and sweetness and affection and his life was a tragedy as he was, like so many others, twisted and deformed by this environment and never had a clear picture of himself nor of life nor of what he wanted and wanted to do. He knew something was wrong but not what was wrong and he never really believed in himself. How many of these sweet, charming southern men have you and I known, lovable, kind, wanting everyone to love them and really wanting to love everyone else, who simply were thwarted and distorted by this savage and cruel society.

Clark Foreman reported that Virginia's visit to New York was a great success. In addition to "an excellent job of education," she raised $2,000 at the various teas and gatherings arranged by the ECLC. Half of the funds raised went to the Franchise Fund and half supported the work of the ECLC.

As a result of their discussions, Clark worked up a pamphlet on political action directed to a black audience. Virginia thought it was more important to educate white people in the rest of the country about the situation in the South, particularly about how the antidemocratic political system in the South affected them. She feared that she had failed to convince several ECLC board members of the relevance of the Southern fight to their agenda.

April 26, 1957
Dear Clark: . . .

I liked the pamphlet but I am afraid we did not have a clear understanding as we were in a hurry and were so interrupted. I do not think a pamphlet of that kind would do any actual good here except as an educational device and I think the Negroes are getting a good education—wonderful in fact—it is the white people in the rest of the country that need to know the facts of life and my idea was to print a throw away and get the people *up there* to do something about the FILIBUSTER. I think all and every possible pressure should be concentrated on the FILIBUSTER as it is something people can understand, even those of the most limited political experience. The negation, the denial, the whole complete frustration of the whole democratic process and so My idea was to concentrate on the FILIBUSTER AND get the people up there to act on that, so I am changing the format and sending it back to you and then you can see if the ECLC wants to take this on. I don't know of any more basic denial of constitutional rights than a FILIBUSTER . . .

The only thing that worries me about my visit, is that I don't think I really convinced either Corliss or Palmer of the need or necessity for the ECLC to get into the Civil Rights fight. If I did I did not feel it at all. Palmer kept talking about the Preachers and the NAACP and Corliss did not talk at all. At least Dr. Frazier in Washington agreed with my contention completely, he thinks this prayer and pilgrimage* and so on is good public relations but nothing will come of this until it gets into the political field, and it MUST BE gotten there if anything happens at all. I think you agree that the ECLC should make a fight on this too and I think the Board should consider it more carefully and how to do it and where and not just leave it up to you to do the best you can . . .

Lots of love and I hope we are clear on the FILIBUSTER.

May 7, 1957
Dearest Clark: . . .

The MIA began its franchise drive yesterday and long lines of Negroes were at the Courthouse all day and at the Courthouse in We-

---

*Refers to the Prayer Pilgrimage for Freedom organized by King and the Southern Christian Leadership Conference. It was held in Washington on May 17, 1957, and drew an estimated 20,000 participants.

tumpka and also in Tuskegee. In Tuskegee they did not register anyone as they said they had no tables nor chairs! In Montgomery and in Wetumpka there was no outright refusal but no one got registered and were told they "would hear from the Board." Of course whether they do or do not get registered, it will be of great help in the drive to get the Civil Rights Bill passed. I think they will register a few and that will be all, but we will see.

[E. D.] Nixon will concentrate on the South Alabama Counties where there are few and in some cases, no registered voters at all. He is still Treasurer of the MIA but I understand there have been some fairly unpleasant scenes there with personality clashes but I only have this from hearsay . . .

Of course with all the world stirred up, the Civil Rights fight does not seem to be all-important up there, but I am convinced that unless something is done along this line that constitutional government in this country is in for a bad time. The Democratic Committee meeting in Washington was a disgrace, nothing but words and they not very good. The Southern wing has really taken over and rules by fear and filibuster. Never did I think that Lyndon would rule the Congress of the U.S. and the country.* I think if the Southern wing got its wings clipped that some sense might come into the politics of the country but the way it is now, it is absolutely mindless.

Lots of love to you and Mairi and do write and tell me how she is and how the children are and so on.

Devotedly, Va.

PS: As an example of the power of the Negro vote, in Atlanta both the candidates for Mayor said they would not speak on the "race" issue as the Church women had asked them not to! Also four Negroes are running for office there, [T. M.] Alexander, [A. T.] Walden and [Rufus] Clement and some one else whom I cannot remember. I have to hand it to Atlanta.†

---

*Lyndon B. Johnson had become Majority Leader of the Senate in January 1957.
†T. M. Alexander ran for the board of aldermen, the first African American to do so since the nineteenth century, and lost by a narrow margin. Rufus Clement was reelected to his seat on the school board and A.T. Walden won a second term on the City Democratic Executive Committee.

May 14, 1957
Dear Hugo:

Tom Emerson* sent us an English professor and his wife from the University of London and last night I took her to one of the weekly mass meetings that the Negroes hold ever since the boycott began. It was a remarkable occasion and she was very much impressed, particularly with the references to you which were made by the Preacher who gave the "Pep Talk." He was quite a remarkable speaker, a young Preacher named Rev. Lambert . . .

First he told of how a "long, thin man from Kentucky had come and struck the chains of slavery from them . . . and had been acting as a messenger of God." Then after many wanderings he wound up by saying "And now God has spoken to the Supreme Court and they have struck the chains of segregation from us, and WHO DID IT? It was a man from the heart of Dixie, a man from Alabama, and he was THE ONE . . . HE MADE IT UNANIMOUS." And the crowd went wild . . . "Speak it plain, Brother." Having joined both God and Abraham Lincoln, you have become both allegorical and immortal in your own lifetime . . .

As you no doubt know they are coming to Washington on the [Prayer] Pilgrimage and want to see you very much and also want to see the building. I told one of them I know fairly well that I did not know if you would be there or could see them, but I was sure that Spencer† would show them the court which is a shrine to them. These people have never been out of Alabama before, at least most of them. Of course the leaders are very sophisticated. But I told Rufus Lewis to go to the Clerk's Office and ask for Spencer . . . I can assure you that I in no way promised anything and yet I did not feel I could discourage them if the wanted so much to try.

In the aftermath of the *Brown* decision, Southern congressmen challenged the authority of the U.S. Supreme Court with the 1956 "Southern Manifesto" and called for defiance of the Court's ruling by the states. Playing to the charged atmosphere of the Cold War, Senator Eastland and oth-

---

*Tom Emerson was professor of law at Yale University, a leading scholar on the First Amendment, and a close friend of the Durrs.
†Spencer Campbell came from Birmingham, Alabama, and worked as Hugo Black's driver, messenger, and general assistant.

ers continually portrayed the Supreme Court as a weak link in the fight against communism. Fellow Southerner Hugo Black, the leading civil libertarian on the bench, was a major target of their venom. A series of Court rulings during 1956 and 1957 questioning the indiscriminate reach of the House Un-American Activities Committee and other such investigative bodies galvanized right-wing opposition to the Court. Southern segregationists found common ground with virulent anticommunists in the Republican Party, and together they introduced at least one hundred bills aimed at curbing the Court's power.[23]

Cold War realities, family ties, and loyalty to friends intruded upon the planning for Lucy Durr's wedding to Sheldon Hackney. Sensitive to Hugo Black's exposed position, Virginia felt compelled to inform him that Jessica Mitford would be attending the wedding; Black's daughter Josephine ("Jo Jo") was going to be one of Lucy's bridesmaids.

June 5, 1957

Dear Hugo: . . .

I am writing you at this time about a rather embarrassing matter but think you should be informed. I find that Decca is coming to the wedding. She was planning a trip to New York and decided to come by here to take in the wedding. It is too late to stop her and also it would be hard to and painful as she has lost her boy recently* and has already been here once for comfort. She seems to have softened a lot and regards Cliff and me as her best friends and warmest supporters—in her personal life I mean.

The thing that bothers me is this, I know that all the Hounds of Hell are after you, and you are the No. One enemy as far as they are concerned and I wonder if Decca being here with Jo Jo will cause any situation? I mean for you? I do not think there will be any publicity about Decca in the papers and she was very quiet and subdued when she was here but at the same time I do not know AT THIS POINT what her politics are and with the FBI watching you like a hawk and trying to link you with the "communist conspiracy" and all the rest of that business I do think I should let you know she will be here.

You have done a wonderful job and certainly become the Defender of the Faith, but by doing so you have become the Enemy of all the evil forces that are trying to destroy the country and I don't want to do any-

---

*Decca's ten-year-old son Nicholas had been struck and killed by a bus two years earlier.

thing to embarrass you. This may be leaning over backwards, but at the same time I have lost my cheerful faith that all of this is silly and now realize how deep and how cruel and how powerful it all is. I know you are in a position to fight it and we can't do a thing.

Lots of love, Jinksie

Hugo Black responded to Virginia's letter on June 6th and said, "under the circumstances I am sure that it would be most unwise for Josephine to go to Montgomery," but added that she would have to decide for herself. Josephine decided not to attend the wedding.

n.d. [June 1957]

Dear Hugo and Josephine:

I received your letter and also one from Ann and I am so distressed this whole business has arisen. I do feel Jo Jo has priority over Decca and my affection for her is much greater and I started to call Decca and tell her not to come, but the thing is that there are others invited that might prove equally embarrassing IF the papers wanted to get a hold of it and make a scene about it. The whole group of us who were called up before Eastland have been under continuous attack and while it has made us feel very close to each other, it has also served as a lightning rod for all sorts . . . of people and organizations.

There is no way to guarantee that no unpleasant incident will arise. We have had so many that we expect them and see no way to avoid them. As you can see by the enclosed there is some sort of incident every day and since the release of the bombers there has been a general feeling in the community that anything can happen and might. The only deterrent seems to be the fact that John Blue Hill charged each of them $5000 cash on the line and they had a hard time raising the money.

I realize that as a man so much in the public eye and one that is carrying such a heavy load you have to be very discreet and that your public duties and responsibilities have to take precedence over your private life, and this is one of the prices that has to be paid for a public life.

On the other hand, we have never felt that we could disassociate ourselves from old and loyal friends that have stood by us through the years and who to our knowledge have never been guilty of any wrongdoing nor any kind of evil, although I think they have made many and drastic mistakes and I have too.

I think the difference is between a private and a public life and I am so sorry that Jo Jo and Lucy have to be caught up in it. I am glad I wrote to you though so that you could be forewarned and not feel that you were being embarrassed unawares.

We think you are doing a great job on the court and I hope that through what you are doing, the time will come when these sorts of situations will not arise and people will no longer feel they are under continuous threat for innocent actions. If anyone can lick Eastland, I think you can, and I agree that takes precedence over everything else.

Lucy Durr and Sheldon Hackney married on June 15th in St. John's Episcopal Church in Montgomery; Josephine Black did not attend. Still, the local press found an opportunity to link Hugo Black to the Communist Party. A week later, on June 23, the *Montgomery Advertiser* ran a front-page story on Hugo Black, reprinted from London's Communist Party newspaper, the *Daily Worker*, which featured Black as "Profile of the Week."

Cliff's legal work increasingly involved police brutality cases as well as death penalty appeals. The following letter refers to the case of Jeremiah Reeves, who was indicted for rape in 1952 at the age of 15.* The alleged victim, a nineteen-year-old white woman, had waited four months before reporting the rape. Reeves was convicted and sentenced to death by an all-white jury. The NAACP Legal Defense Fund appealed the case to the U.S. Supreme Court, charging that the confession was coerced, and also that blacks were systematically excluded from the jury and that the judge barred the public from the trial. The Supreme Court set aside the conviction. In June 1957, Reeves was convicted a second time and sentenced to death. Fred Gray and Clifford Durr prepared an appeal.

June 21, 1957
Dearest Clark and Mairi: . . .

The wedding was a great success and Lucy did look simply beautiful, the picture does not do her justice at all. It all went off very successfully and she went off in a cloud of joy. I am exhausted and will be for some time, as it was a big production and I tried to do it on a shoestring and failed. . . . I think I was foolish to have tried it, but Lucy did so want to have a real church wedding and I did hate so to deny her when she has been such a wonderful daughter and worked so hard for everything she

---

*There is some question regarding Jeremiah Reeves's age at the time of his arrest. Newspaper accounts vary between 15 and 17; Virginia reported that he was 15.

has gotten. As you know she cooked and cleaned and waited table the two years she was at Radcliffe and in addition for the last six months she waited on table at a restaurant in the Square for her spending money, and she made a good record in the marks too. As you can see I feel guilty about doing something so extravagant as a wedding when we really could not afford it at all.

Josephine Black did not come at the last moment which we regretted very much and I will tell you all about why when I see you.

Decca came and sat up all the way across the country in a coach to get here and had all the proper clothes and looked lovely and all the hostesses were much impressed with her English accent and lovely clothes and so on, she looked like a very young Queen Mary. . . .

We are engaged here in the stark realities all the time, as you are, and here things are really getting very bad. Cliff has two cases with Fred Gray, one of which a young Negro was sent to the Electric chair (he is now in the death house) for rape, with no Negro on the Jury or on the panel (this is Wilcox County) and with no Negro voter in the county and a confession beaten out of him and all the usual brutality. His story is that the girl was extremely willing and made the first advances and after several months of this got frightened she was pregnant and would have a black baby and so accused him of rape to save herself, which is a story that I suppose has been repeated thousands of times. The other case is that of a young Negro in Wilcox County who was killed by the Deputy Sheriff after he got in jail. Then we have a case where the White Union on the Railroad in conjunction with the Railroad are trying to "roll" a whole section of Negroes so they can fill the places with white men. They have met in the office continually and are determined to bring suit. The sad feature of all of these is that there is never any money, the Union men are raising $25.00! and the Negroes have nothing at all. I really don't see how we are going to live from month to month and that is why I feel so guilty about the wedding. Fred has written to the NAACP about the Wilcox County cases but these are so common and they don't have money for all of them that happen in the South and have to concentrate on the really memorable ones. Of course too don't say anything about Cliff's connection with the Wilcox County cases right now. It is the sort of casual brutality that affects him so much, "just a nigger got killed" and that is all there is to it, but you know all of this as well as I do.

In Macon County, the majority black county that was home to Tuskegee Institute and the indefatigable Tuskegee Civic Association, the number of black voters crept steadily upward. There were approximately 23,500 blacks in the county out of a total population of 27,500. By the end of 1955, slightly more than 1,000 blacks had registered to vote in the county, comprising one-third of the electorate. Blacks made up roughly 40 percent of the voters registered in the city of Tuskegee. In an aggressive effort to stem rising black political power, Macon County state representative Sam Engelhardt introduced a bill, which the legislature passed, redrawing the boundaries of Tuskegee to exclude nearly all registered black voters from the city limits.[24]

July 1, 1957
Dearest Clark: . . .

I agree that the Supreme Court decisions are wonderful and that Hugo is a great Judge. Here in Alabama, it all seems a little far away as no one has the slightest intention of obeying them and we have real civil insurrection. The Tuskegee case is the most interesting thing that is happening here and the outcome of that will be one of the most significant things that can happen here. The Alabama Legislature passed a bill introduced by Sam Engelhardt (Senator from Macon County, head of the Ala. WCC etc.) which by redrawing the lines of the town of Tuskegee completely cut out of the town ALL the Negro voters and left only 10 in the town limits, so now the Negroes are boycotting all the white merchants in Tuskegee and the town is drying up. It will be interesting to see whether Jim Folsom signs the bill and if the City Council puts it into effect. This is a real test of strength. Be sure you follow it.

July 8, 1957
Dearest Clark and Mairi: . . .

I agree with you that since the situation here looks so hopeless and seems to be getting worse all the time, that we should look to other fields, but I have now accepted the fact and know that Cliff is not going to leave the South or even Montgomery. If it comes to the point where we will have to move to Elmore County . . . and raise what we eat, we will do that rather than leave. He is simply determined to stay and I think he would hate to leave. The reasons for all of this are too complex to go into, but this is where he wants to stay and this is where he is going to stay. It is not only personal as he feels at home here whatever its ills, it is something else that is too deep for him to ever express. Just the way he sticks by other people when they are in trouble, just the way he stuck by me—he feels he has to stick by the people down here. They are going through trouble and he thinks he can help a little but in any case they are his people and his folks and he is going to stick by them. The fact that they don't seem to particularly care if he does or not and make it almost impossible, does not seem to alter his fundamental desire to stay with them.

One day in mid-July, Virginia visited her friend Juliette Morgan at her mother's home. Morgan, the target of ongoing harassment by the Citizens Council, had taken a leave of absence from her job at the library. She was seeing a psychiatrist in Birmingham and receiving treatment for "acute anxiety." Virginia was keenly aware of the isolation Morgan suffered; none of her family members were sympathetic toward her views. Virginia's efforts to coax her to come out of the house for an afternoon drive failed. Morgan died later that night, apparently from an overdose of sleeping pills.

July 22, 1957
Dearest Clark: . . .

We had such a tragic happening here last week. The girl who was one of the Librarians here, such a lovely, pure kind of girl, with a real flame of righteousness in her and who had written several letters to the paper which had gotten her into trouble and had threatened her with loss of her job etc., well she simply couldn't take it anymore and we think committed suicide. She had a complete nervous breakdown and took sleeping pills and how many or whether too many or what we don't know, but in any case she died. The WCC had given her the full treatment, telephone calls, threats, letters and then the demand that she be fired, which the Mayor agreed to and then he said he would cut off the appropriations for the Library and she got to feeling that she had hurt them too. The thing that made them so furious was that she said in one of her letters that the trouble with the South was the "Cowardly white southern men" and that really made them determined to get her at all costs. Thereby proving her words.

Her funeral was very strange as she was one of the "old families" and there was such a mixture of diehard White Supremacists and the few liberals in town such as the Williams, the Graetzes and us. Then too none of the Negroes could come to the funeral. The young clergyman said he would not forbid it, that after all "God's House was open to all" BUT he had just come here, did not have any influence in the community, and did not think it would be "wise" at this "particular time."

July 29, 1957
Dearest Dec: . . .

I am so glad you enjoyed your visit to New York and long to hear more about who you saw and what you did and if you found everybody still fighting everybody else or if they have finally "jined" together to fight the creeping fascism that is coming upon us. But here in the South it is not creeping and is flagrant and violent. Have the papers out there told about the raids on Tuskegee and how they have treated Dr. Gomillion? I told you how significant that would be and it is becoming so increasingly. Here you have a straight-out fight for the right to vote, and since the Negroes have such an overwhelming majority and such a high percentage of intelligent and highly trained people in the County, there are no ways to get rid of them except by violence and intimidation and this is what they are prepared to do. The raids and hearings they are having are beyond belief and the powers that be are perfectly willing to see the whole town destroyed to keep the Negroes from getting any power in it. This denial of the most elementary democratic right is not only applauded but the other Black Belt counties are planning to follow suit. To say the Federal Government can change this is ridiculous unless they are prepared to use Federal injunctions and Federal force too if it is necessary.

August 27, 1957
Dearest Dec: . . .

We have picked up a little more business with the Negroes the last month or so, but we still are running way behind. There was an article in one of the big magazines about some "Southern Liberal" in which he said it was impossible for any southern liberal to live down here unless they had an outside income, and while I think it is true, still to admit defeat is awful and we don't want to do that. He [Cliff] has been working with Fred Gray on the Tuskegee thing and I think the whole matter there has been handled very simply and wisely and so far without too much disorder, the thing is the Negroes simply won't buy in the town as they say they threw them out as residents and as Voters and so they will not go back in as consumers. Several small businesses have already failed, but the Big Mules don't seem to mind and they have now passed a bill through the Alabama Legislature to simply abolish the whole county and divide it up among five other counties, and this is to be the pattern for all the Black Belt counties, to split and divide them up so that no one county will have a majority of Negroes. I don't know whether it will hold up in Court or not, to simply abolish a county, but in any case that is what they have done, but Folsom has not signed it yet. The point is that by being here he does play a useful role even if not public, and he is determined to stay, but HOW is still the big question . . .

I made a speech at Mrs. Parks's farewell testimonial that was a great success if I do say so myself! Poor woman, she finally had to go to Detroit, she could not make it here after she got sick. She made the most wonderful speech that night, and told them that they could never win unless they fought for the right of everyone to have opportunities, and not just themselves, and also that wherever she had been she had found in varying degrees, the same discrimination and inequality she found here. I do miss her so much as she was such a fine and firm person, not exactly concrete but at least mighty firm asphalt. I feel now that I am paved with pebbles or cobblestones, firm but rough and shaky.

After Arkansas Governor Orval Faubus brought out the National Guard to block the court-ordered integration of Little Rock's Central High School, President Dwight Eisenhower sent the 101st Airborne Division to Little Rock and federalized the Arkansas National Guard. On September 25, 1957, the nine black students assigned to Central High School entered the school with federal military protection.

September 29, 1957
Dearest Dec: . . .
WELL! what do you think about the President? Isn't it wonderful? I never thought he would come out and actually do it. That pretty well

settles for a long time to come where the Negro vote will go, and what scares the living daylights out of me is that it will go to Dick Nixon, who to me is our streamlined version of Hitler and Mussolini etc. If you all can knock him out in California you will save the country . . . If you read Vann Woodward you will see how the Republicans after the Civil War used the Negroes to clamp corporate rule on the country and I am afraid they are now going to use them to clamp fascist rule on the country, but how can you blame the Negroes when the Democrats are so dumb, and spineless and afraid of their shadow? . . .

September 1957
Dearest Clark and Mairi: . . .

I need not tell you how excited the people are here. Aubrey wrote a letter to the President, or rather a telegram and it was printed on the front page of the paper, he congratulated him on taking such firm action. He called up this morning to say that the night had been made hideous with calls and threats and so on and some of them even were long distance calls. His has been the only voice so far that has not condemned the President, that is locally. Well, it is now as though the boil had burst and the question is whether the infection will clear or will . . . infect the whole body politic . . .

We often feel we move in a silent vacuum as people don't say anything at all to us about it. But that does not mean they are not seething. Cliff's Aunt told my neighbor that she would offer her big pecan tree in the back yard if anyone wanted to lynch Aubrey Williams. Last night Cliff called him up several times as he was afraid he might get hurt.

The only amusing thing is to see how shamefaced they all are about having voted with Eisenhower or for him, they are all apologizing for that. They have had a terrible jolt, the thing is they have gotten by with this business of keeping the "niggers in their place" so long, that they expected to keep right on doing it, and this has been like an atomic bomb, and yet I cannot say what the end result will be . . .

The bravery of the Negroes is remarkable I think, they are really marvelous, just think of those children walking to school in the face of that mob, and those men taking all the beating to protect them . . .

As I have said thousands of times before, this fight here must be won by the whole country and if only the Unions could be brought to do something! But they flock to the WCC . . . I wish you could see the rash of Confederate flags, one on every car and particularly teenagers.

October 1957
Dearest Dec:
I meant to get this off yesterday and did not so will fill in the gaps. We had lots of excitement on account of Martin Agronsky of the NBC. He was an old friend of Cliff's and came to town to do a national TV show and was to interview King and there were threats of sabotage and when he came out to our house to dinner on Saturday night, he was worried about them, but Cliff and Aubrey and the Osgoodes* (Arthur was put on the story by the *Advertiser* and covered him the whole time he was here) they all assured him that nothing of the kind would happen and only I, old Gloomy Gus told him I would bet a dollar to a dime they did sabotage the program and then BY GOD they did! It was not sabotaged for the whole country, just for Montgomery and points south, but just as the program went on, the screen went blank and the sound got cut off too, and then just three minutes after the program was over the station came back on and said there had been a power failure, and what it actually was, was someone unknown threw a chain over the power line and short-circuited it, but the strange thing is that there was only one place where it could have been done and it would have taken someone with expert knowledge to do it and so it does sound awfully fishy that the Station here had nothing to do with it. When the screen went dead, we rushed down to the church where the show was broadcast from and such excitement with the police and cameramen and milling hordes and fury in the air as you can imagine. Martin Agronsky was furious as he could be, but at least it went out over the whole country. Never a dull moment here but awfully tiring on the nerves sometimes.

Virginia and Decca both took a great interest in young people who went against the grain of 1950s conformity, though Virginia was con-

---

*Arthur and Virginia Osgoode were neighbors of the Durrs; Arthur worked as a reporter for the *Montgomery Advertiser*.

cerned about the seemingly aimless quality of their rebellion. The following letter describes David Sweet, the son of friends from New Deal days.

November 5, 1957
Dearest Dec:

Who should appear here the other day but Fred and Marilla Sweet's son, David. Do you remember David? He is hitchhiking his way to Berkeley, California to YOUR HOUSE so I thought I would give you a preview so you could make up your mind about it.

Well he is really darling, so handsome and seems very nice and intelligent. He has been going to Oberlin and is going to take the next semester at the U. of Cal. for some reason which I never could fathom, but in any case he is taking this semester to see the world and especially the South. He has a pack, paratroop boots and a slight mustache and $37.00 and on that he is going to go to Georgia, Florida, Louisana, St. Louis, Kansas City, Denver, Los Angeles and San Francisco, with you at the end of the rainbow. He is particularly intrigued with the Dinky Donk and the tales of how pretty she is.

He only stayed with us for one night and we found him quite delightful. We really liked him a lot. Of course he makes you feel awfully old-fashioned and has all the new ideas about Peace and Quakers and Non Violence etc. all of which are fine, but the kind of society which is necessary for those ideas to flower does not seem to be clear, but any change in it must be peaceful. Of course he was thrilled about Sputnik* as I am too, aren't you? I do think it is so wonderfully thrilling to think of a man going out into space and I feel my mind has stretched for eons and infinity too. I really have gotten to be a Sputnik fan and I can't wait for the paper to come to read all about it.

He says he does Market Research when he needs money and that seems to be the least of his worries and also the least of his equipment. I think you would love him briefly but don't think you would forever and ever, as he is too intense and young and full of questions and knows too little to be restful. He really knows a lot but still there is a lot of explain-

---

*The first unmanned space satellite, launched by the Soviet Union on October 4, 1957.

ing to do, which he generally does not agree with, but he has lots of interests and I think will get along.

He is due to get to you about Christmas I should imagine. But he may cut his timetable short. Since he gave us no advance notice I don't imagine he will with you, so I thought I would take my pen in hand and give it to you for him . . .

How is the book going? Any more articles in the mill? Lots of love and do write. Va.

Aubrey Williams signed a book contract to write his memoirs. He shared his advance with Virginia as payment to work as his typist.

n.d. [November 1957]
Dearest Clark and Mairi: . . .

Aubrey's book is quite an undertaking and is running into hundreds of pages, much of which will have to be cut I know but it is better for him to get it out and then try and direct the flow, but since it concerns so much of what I am familiar with and know about and . . . have such strong feelings about, I try not to editorialize and simply let it come out and then hope to prune it later. But the book could be quite significant right now with all the glare on the South, just showing how the situation got this way and how the New Negro came into being. I think the New Deal produced the New Negro, as they could never have gained so much self respect and had so many opportunities for improvement without it. . . . I agree the world situation and the northern Negro has had a lot to do with the present situation, but I do not think you should discount the fact that the New Negro in the South is the one who has made up his mind to fight for his rights and is doing so, and as a Southerner it makes me proud they have so much courage.

February 20, 1958
Dearest Dec: . . .

As for my literary efforts, except for letters they are nil. I simply cannot write with all the interruptions I have and when I get home at night I am too tired. As you can tell from my letters the only kind of writing I can do is to dash it off hot from the griddle.

Thanks for the name of the agent though, I will file it and see if there is any chance of sending him something . . .

To be quite frank with you my dear Decca, living down here makes all the talk about achieving socialism academic to say the least. What we are up against is open and outright and brutal fascism. I noticed in the morning paper that [Louis C.] Wyman the Attorney General of New Hampshire spoke to the Georgia Legislature amid thunderous Confederate cheers, and he made a terrific attack on the President for sending troops into Little Rock. I think the fact that he is a Republican, represents the China Lobby, and is tied in with Styles Bridges, confirms what I have said all along, and that is that the right-wing Republicans and the racists are getting together and their aim is fascism.* I do not see why anyone living in California has any question as to what to do which is to beat Nixon above all and [Senator William F.] Knowland. I think with the lesson of Germany behind us and the choice that was made there, we should certainly have enough sense to avoid . . . this. Nixon is a very dangerous man, he has King and the Negroes as well as the worst Dixiecrats in the state, and that phony Religion of his attracts so many people. He is the No. 1 public enemy in my opinion and Knowland is just as bad, only he is stupid in comparison and a little more honest. So I think the job now for all true believers is to work to beat Nixon, fight against fascism, work for the democratic rights of Negroes and work for the democratic rights of the Unions and try and keep this country from going down the drain into darkness which is much closer than it may seem out in California. Them's my sentiments.

Lots of love dear Decca, and give my love to Marge and Esther.

February 21, 1958
Dearest Clark: . . .

Things here in the South seem to have come to a full stop. I was glad to see that Izzy [Stone] in the last newsletter quoted from our conversation at Christmas. I hope people will begin to wake up and realize that

---

*Louis Wyman, attorney general of New Hampshire, and U.S. Senator Styles Bridges of New Hampshire were both Republicans and staunch anticommunists.

the South thinks it has won the battle and I am not sure it has not. Of course I think the way they have done it, and especially the war on the Negro children in the schools and the way their lives have been made miserable and all the insults and meanness that have been heaped on their heads, is enough to make us Southerners hang our heads in shame, but no one seems to feel it at all, and when Minniejean* gets expelled from Little Rock High School, it is a great victory for white supremacy. I wish I could feel kinder toward my fellow Southerners, I really try to, and I want to forgive them and hope for them and say it is ignorance and so on, but . . . they act so mean, so cruelly, so little and nasty and brutal . . . that I find myself shuddering over them. If it were not for the few lonely exceptions I would really despair.

Black soldiers and military personnel stationed in the South were discriminated against in all the ways that Southern black civilians were as soon as they left their military base. Visiting military and government officials from African nations were given a "passport" by the Montgomery Chamber of Commerce so that they would not be subject to racial restrictions. Such treatment of men serving in the U.S. Armed Forces, Virginia argued, was an abomination and a potential source of violence. Here was an issue, she believed, that lent itself to immediate federal action and could serve as an opening wedge in challenging the segregation system.

March 3, 1958
Dearest Clark and Mairi: . . .
I am convinced that with all of its pains, it is better to be in the South on our own home ground than to be among strangers, although the sad thing is that even so we have to depend mostly on Northerners and on strangers to live. This is to me the crux of the Southern problem. We are dependents and that is why we are so damned mean. I know what it does to me and it is the most galling and degrading thing to know you are good and can do good work and then have to beg to make a living . . .

---

*Minniejean Brown was one of the nine black students who integrated Central High School in Little Rock. Following several altercations with white students, she was suspended by the Board of Education for the remainder of the school year. She transferred to New Lincoln High School in New York.

Yet there is slowly growing here in the South, a body of people who, with the Negroes, are beginning to have some little, very little influence. I think to keep this movement alive, to keep it growing and to keep it here in the South is of the utmost importance and I don't see any help for it but to look to our friends in the North for help until we can get on a self supporting basis . . .

I think the South is either going to be the spearhead of native Fascism or it is going to be the spearhead of a real native progressive movement, but at this point I can't say which . . .

One campaign I wish you would take up is the sending of Negro soldiers and officers South to be Jim Crowed. There is a rising resentment about this which could produce a terrific explosion, as they are sent down to these Southern bases by the thousands, involuntarily, and then they and their families have to put up with Jim Crow. Even the foreign officers that come here, the ones that are dark, get some kind of passports from the Chamber of Commerce to enable them to go to the white restaurants and movies, etc. but the Negro officers don't and this creates bitter and maddening frustration and anger. I think this is an injustice that people could understand and I believe the only way these Southerners are going to come to their senses is when it is demonstrated concretely that Jim Crow is costing them money. Just threaten to move one of these Air Force bases and they would change their ways overnight if not their minds.

March/April 1958
Dearest Dec:

Wonderful news about Simon and Schuster and I can hardly wait to hear if they take the book*. . .

My literary efforts are as usual concerned with the "PROBLEM" and I am afraid people are getting bored with it, at least the fine first fervor is gone and we Southerners feel we have again been abandoned by the rest of the country. The people here say that they have won the war and the rest of the country has come around to their point of view, and they are arrogant and mean as all get out. I can't say I blame

---

*Decca's memoir, *Daughters and Rebels,* which was published in 1960 by Houghton Mifflin.

them as they have all the weight of public opinion, newspapers, radio, State government, City government, County government and THE FEDERAL GOVERNMENT on their side. The Federal courts have ruled and that is all, the federal government itself does nothing to change the climate of opinion, and IN THE OTHER AGENCIES they segregate themselves and the legal advisor at the Base here, a young man and fairly liberal, said the orders were to conform to the local customs off the Base, so the Negro military personnel have no protection if they challenge segregation, and they know they have none, and they themselves are brought up on charges if they do, so how can anyone believe that the Federal government really means it, except to get votes in Chicago?

I hope Mr. Fles is nice to me too, but I am afraid he is more literary than I, I am too much of a propagandist.

As for your book, all I wanted you to remember was that we live in occupied territory and so don't make it impossible for us to remain, as we want to and fully intend to . . .

Cliff is better of his flu which hung on for at least two months and his spirits are better now that Spring has come and he can get up to the Pea Level and start his garden and so on. He sees as clearly as it can be seen, the danger of a general breakdown of law and order and a real fascist threat starting here in the South. He thinks [Richard] Nixon is the real point of danger and hates and fears him very much and gets disgusted with the "liberals" who say he has "changed." I am afraid Nixon is going to get the southern Negro vote though, as he has been so clever with them, such complete hypocrisy, the Administration of which he is a part does nothing to implement the Court decision, the whole Federal government does nothing, Little Rock was forced on them, and I do not think the Negroes feel it helped them very much, and so while his own administration does nothing he goes and deplores it and gets them convinced he is their friend. I think the defeat of Nixon is the most important thing in the country, he has what it takes to be a real fascist leader.

What has Martin Luther King been doing in California so much? I would like to know this. I am afraid he is helping Nixon and I do wish you would try and find out. This is very important if you can.

May 22, 1958
Dearest Clark and Mairi: . . .

After one of the Human Relations meetings of the Southern Regional Council, we resolved to write people about the behavior of Maxwell Field toward the Negro community, [they] won't let speakers come to any Negro or mixed meetings, the Negro officers can't live on the base if they are married, the school has been turned over to the County so it can't be integrated and while the Foreign Officers, no matter how dark, are given passports to Montgomery by the Chamber of Commerce, of course the Negro personnel is strictly Jim Crowed. I think all of this is awful, and has the seeds of terrible potential trouble for all of us and for the country. Think of the effect it has on the Foreign Officers that come here to the Air University by the thousands. So in any case various people wrote letters, and I wrote Mrs. R. [Roosevelt] and the dear sweet lady sends my letter or quotes me to the Army who in turn of course sends it all to the Base and the Chamber of Commerce here and I saw the President of the C. of C. the other day and my name is mud to put it mildly. He took half an hour to tell me of the error of my ways, "We won't have integration for fifty years," he says and after being to the "Nawth" I am inclined to think he is right, it is all a "Sane Nuclear Policy" now and the South and the Negro is forgotten apparently, except I am glad to say by the ECLC. Lots of love and do write.

Attorney General John Patterson soundly defeated Circuit Court Judge George C. Wallace in the runoff primary election for Alabama governor on June 3. Patterson ran with the open support of the Ku Klux Klan, while Wallace had the support of the White Citizens Council. Stunned by his defeat, Wallace vowed that he would never be "outniggered" again.

June 4, 1958
Dearest Dec: . . .

Cliff was quite impressed with Sarah Lawrence and with the girls there. . . . He also gave a lecture at Princeton and enjoyed that so much. I think if he would write around and use his friends, the way I use them to get an education for the girls, he could get a teaching job in some college, but he simply will not do it, because he does not want to leave here, in spite of all the difficulties and the small amount of income which grows less rather than more, and the election of a KKK governor and so on, he still wants to stay here, and I have finally realized that unless some miracle happens we will stay here and that I might as well make the best of it. I know he is useful and his patience and kindness and tolerance are the qualities that are needed in this kind of hate-filled and intolerant atmosphere, but we are so alone and isolated and the rewards are so tiny, that I do get awfully tired of it and long often to flee far far away. I . . . often feel that Cliff is a stage beyond me in development and I can't quite catch up with him, that the stage of revolt and moral indignation and hatred of fascism and fighting against evil, is the one I am in, while he has gone on to some kind of new stage where you forgive people and try to change them and educate them and reform them but not by fighting and by force and by hatred. Maybe this *is* better but it seems to me that tolerance of evil has produced so much worse evil . . . so my mind is ambivalent about it, but no one can say he has not fought evil and tried to do good but he is more hopeful of the Southerners than I am.

June 17, 1958
Dearest Dec: . . .

Our new Governor is KKK in spirit and will be surrounded by such. To think of all the effort I put into extending the franchise in the South and in Alabama it has gone up one half million and they *all voted* either KKK or WCC. There is rejoicing in the air and the Williams old and young are leaving as they think it is hopeless for such a long time and want to go where there is more chance and more hope.

July 1958
Dear Clark: . . .

At the Bar Association meeting last weekend (State) they passed a ruling that no OUTSIDE lawyer can come into Alabama and take part in a case unless he is INTRODUCED by one of the Bar Commission and as they are some of the most reactionary people in the State, the chances of Thurgood Marshall or Robert Carter getting to enter a case here is pretty remote and of course it was aimed at them. I think the thing I really hate worse and am most ashamed of concerning our white southern men is that they don't want to fight this battle with the Negro on a fair basis, they want to render him absolutely helpless, deny him legal aid, money, help from the outside in every way. I have come to the conclusion that there is some psychological need in them to castrate the Negro male in order to feel their own manhood. But not only as they did in Birmingham,* but in every way. Last Saturday night a bunch of the boys over in Elmore County lynched the movie *Island in the Sun* which shows Harry Belafonte making love to a white woman. They came to the Drive-In, cut the power lines, kidnapped the manager and the attendants and held them in an office, blocked the entrance for hours so no one could come in or out and tore the place up. The Sheriff of Elmore County did nothing and only said "I done tole that man not to show that picture, that some of the boys would get mad" . . .

I think the South is a kind of second Algeria. . . . Not that there are not some fine people here but the overwhelming sentiment is so strongly against a free society (if it includes Negroes) that I think they will fight to the death against it, and I think the Northern Republicans are going to use them as a spearhead against Labor. The only hope I can see is that they will need the Negroes as propaganda for the rest of the world, like putting Marian Anderson on the UN.† But they do that and yet in the federal . . . establishments here in the South the Federal government segregates just like anyone else. Hypocrites. I cannot see why our great "Liberals" don't see that the Congress implements integration in the Federal establishment instead of always blaming the States for not integrating the schools. Why don't they show the way? I don't think the Damned Yankees have any idea of doing anything about it but make a big whoop and holler . . .

If we could only have a minimum living here I have now come to the point where I really do want to stay here, I know we are far more useful here than anywhere else and we have gotten used to it now, although I need to get out into the big world every now and then. If the Labor Unions weren't so corrupted we could get business with them, but they

---

*Two Klansman in Birmingham chose a black man at random and castrated him. They confessed to the crime, saying that they wanted "to scare the hell out of them." *Montgomery Advertiser*, Sept. 8, 1957, 6A.

†President Eisenhower named Marian Anderson to the American delegation to the U.N.

are scared of us too and scared to death of the race issue. The Leaders might like to do right if they could, but they know the rank and file is full of KKK and WCC and are scared of their own rank and file. I talked to a woman the other day who had run for the Legislature in Jefferson County and had gotten the endorsement of Labor and she said that meant that the KKK and the WCC put out all kinds of literature against her, but it also meant that the rank and file of Labor voted against her and their own endorsement as they listen to the WCC and KKK more than their own leaders. In other words they vote against themselves. And this was well proven in the last election when the CIO AFL [sic] endorsed [George] Wallace (himself a big Negro baiter of the worst sort and backed by the WCC) but the rank and file of Labor went overwhelmingly for Patterson who was the KKK candidate . . . I am reading W.E.B. Du Bois's *Black Reconstruction* which throws more light on this whole problem than anything else I have ever read. At least he makes sense out of it.

Cliff assisted Fred Gray on a series of death penalty cases during 1958, including the case of Jimmy Wilson, a young black man who was convicted on a robbery charge but was also charged with attempted rape. These cases highlighted the blatant inequity and racism of Alabama's criminal justice system. As Virginia noted elsewhere, "the injustices in the South will continue unless poor oppressed people can get a lawyer to represent them." As it was, they were forced to rely on court-appointed lawyers, "men . . . [who] never make any effort to save them, do nothing to investigate, simply go through the motions."[25] Moreover, black male defendants convicted of raping a white woman were routinely sentenced to death. Often the best Cliff and Fred Gray could do after the accused had been convicted and sentenced to death was to secure clemency from the governor, leaving the defendant facing a life in prison.

n.d. [ca. July/ August 1958]
Dearest Decca: . . .

We are in the midst of the Jimmy Wilson case at the present moment. Of course no pay but telephone calls by the score and lots of people all excited. It looks now as though it was going to be fought through to the Supreme Court and I am so glad. I think simply to beg for Mercy on these horrible sentences and get them commuted to life is no way to really get at the injustice of the original sentences. This is the FOURTH death sentence this summer. One was electrocuted, he was a fifteen-year-old boy accused of rape.* The second was commuted, he was a seventeen-year-old boy accused of rape. In neither instance were the women harmed in any way and both stories were terribly phony. The third was commuted, that was simply murder so no wild emotion over that, and murder of a policeman, and now the Wilson case which is on the face of it a robbery case but in reality is a rape case or attempted rape. I sometimes feel we southern white women are some kind of obscene goddesses that they make these burnt offerings to, "Burn the Nigger, burn the Nigger" is what you hear when one of them comes up and there is something so awful and horrible about it, especially when no white man ever gets the death penalty for rape in any case and of course when it occurs with a Negro woman they never even believe it is rape. A little thirteen-year-old Negro girl who was babysitting got raped by the man of the house when he took her home and the proof was positive and she was terribly torn and harmed and yet nothing was ever done to the white man.

But when these cases come up we do what we can, get letters to the Governor etc. and that in itself is a stupendous job as people are simply scared to death. At least the Wilson case seems to have attracted a lot of attention and that is helpful I hope.

I am so glad about the possibility of a publisher for the book. Of course I have only seen a small part of it, and my oft-repeated suggestion is that you first formulate what you want to prove by it or say in it, not simply an account. That is the awful trouble I am having with Aubrey William's Autobiography which I have been helping him on for the last year. He got paid $1000 in advance for it and had a Publisher but they have not accepted it yet or any part of it, because it does not have any central point that holds it together. His life does have a point and a very important one but when he writes he simply rambles.

I think the point of your life is that you broke out of a prison of family, tradition, etc. just as I broke out of a prison of prejudice, or at least I

---

*Jeremiah Reeves was executed on March 5, 1958.

think I have, and the dramatic quality of your life is the contrast of life "outside" as the prisoners say and life "inside" and after all the point is whether it was worth it or not. I am sure you think it was although what you give up is a lot, because you actually give up your roots and your birthright and sometimes I wonder if after we do that if we will ever again feel fully at home. In any case, I think what you should stress more is not so much what you did as why you did it or what you thought about the results. But I think you write better than I do and if you can ever break down your reticence or even make a crack in it I think you have the makings of a wonderful book.

As a result of Virginia's efforts, Leonard Boudin, counsel to the ECLC, offered to raise money to assist Fred Gray if he decided to appeal Jimmy Wilson's conviction.

n.d. [ca. August 1958]
Dearest Clark: . . .

I was simply thrilled when Leonard [Boudin] called up and said you were going to do something about the Wilson case. I think people thought it was odd we were not more excited about it, but this is the fourth one this summer and we have been interested in all of them and in both the Huff case and then in the Wilson case have tried to get letters and get people interested. Jeremiah Reeves was the first one, and that got to be a real political battle between the WCC and the NAACP and he was electrocuted, he was only fifteen when the alleged "rape" took place and he died for it. The next one, Willie Huff, was saved by commutation of his sentence and we tried to keep that as quiet as possible as the publicity in the Reeves case seemed to have put the Governor on the spot. But I still think for him to rot away his life in the pen on a phony rape charge is awful. The third one was a Negro who had killed a policeman and no rape charge was involved and he was a mental case and the Governor commuted his sentence to life, and now Wilson is the fourth one to be condemned to die. Of course he got the death sentence for the alleged "attempted rape" of the 82-year-old woman rather than the robbery but they did not try him on the rape charge but on the robbery charge, but they condemned him to death really on the rape charge. I hope that we don't have another battle on the political scene by the WCC. . . . I think far more needs to be done than plead for mercy, I think the cases need to be taken up to the Supreme Court and also some of them reopened.

As you know the NAACP cannot do business in Alabama anymore. Actually it was the Jeremiah Reeves case that caused them to be declared verboten and the ACLU does not seem to ever really hire lawyers to do a job, which is what is needed . . .

I do not see any signs of surrender in the Confederacy, in fact they think this time they are going to win the War, and it does look as though they have Eisenhower at least partly on their side.

The choices facing Jimmy Wilson are outlined in the following letter. In the end, Wilson chose not to risk an appeal of his case, which, if lost, would put him at the mercy of incoming Governor John Patterson. Fred Gray represented Jimmy Wilson in a clemency hearing before Governor Jim Folsom, and Folsom commuted his death sentence to life in prison.

n.d. [ca. September 1958]
Dearest Dec: . . .

The news here is something—just the same but more so—breathing defiance and hatred and anger and so on . . . The Jimmy Wilson case has attracted lots of attention throughout the world and he has gotten a stay of execution until the 27th of October and the big question here now is what to do, try and get clemency of which there is a very good chance or to go to the courts with a weak case under Alabama law and there seems no federal question of any significance and take a chance on [John] Patterson coming in and not giving him clemency . . . [He] is simply awful and cruel too. Leonard Boudin has come into the case in the way of trying to help raise money and some legal questions too, but Fred Gray is the lawyer and I think the question of what to do will have to be settled by Wilson himself, whether he wants to take a chance on his life or accept what looks like a good chance for clemency, and life imprisonment! The poor fellow is perfectly ignorant and seems almost in a daze and it is hard to know if he knows what he is saying or if he just says what he thinks the "white folks" want to hear . . .

I am pretty well but feel old and tired and have periods when I don't feel I have a friend in the world—so I thank God for you. Va.

The Fellowship of the Concerned, a women's prayer group, was one of the only interracial groups that functioned in Montgomery—few others were tolerated. By the fall of 1958, however, the prayer group became the target of harassment by militant segregationists.

October 3, 1958
Dearest Marge: . . .

From Virginia and Little Rock and from here, all you hear and see and read is total defiance. No one worries about the education of the children, or at least apparently only a few, just as long as they "keep the niggers out." It is an atmosphere of total irrationality and total ignorance too mostly, and I am afraid it will soon be an atmosphere of total violence. The more the Law goes against them the more the advocates of violence get a hearing. The KKK had a big meeting in the adjoining County last week and the more lawful WCC is losing out to the KKK. The Negroes are magnificent but they too are becoming irrational and are convinced that some white people in Montgomery paid the woman to try and kill King.* They have had so much to put up with and they are now simply convinced that their only chance lies in their own strength alone. They really have no use of "white folks" at all, and while they are glad to get any help you may offer—their distrust is so deep that they really don't trust any "white." Even Aubrey who for so long and so devotedly has fought for their rights, they ignore and pass over. I am friendly with some of the women and we have an interracial church group that meets occasionally and some of us are asked to speak to them in one of their churches from time to time, but they realize the utter impotence of the few white liberals there are.

[A week later:]

Dearest Marge: I always have to write in intervals and that is the reason my letters are so scrappy.

I must tell you about the happenings of the last week. We have a group here called "The Fellowship of the Concerned" and it was started

---

*In a department store in Harlem, while signing copies of his newly published book, *Stride toward Freedom*, Martin Luther King, Jr. was stabbed by a mentally unstable woman.

by Mrs. Tilly of the Southern Regional Council, and is composed of Churchwomen of both races and also it is inter faith and has Protestants, Catholics and Jews in it. So last Saturday a week ago we had a very fine meeting and it was held at the Catholic Crippled Children's Clinic and there were about one hundred women there of both races and Dorothy [Lobman] and [her daughter] Jane were there and Mrs. Henry Weil and Mrs. Ella Swartz and her daughter-in-law. Mrs. Swartz is the sister of Bert Klein and then there were a number of Episcopalians and several Presbyterians and a lot of Methodists and one or two Catholics and the Negro women were well represented too and the wife of the President of Tuskegee* made a speech and all in all it was a very good meeting indeed, and we all felt very much encouraged. There was one strange woman there whom no one knew and when we came out we noticed a group of cars riding around and around and found they were taking flashlight pictures of us and taking down the car numbers. So next week the calls started, people calling up all night long and threatening and abusing and annoying, and Anne Kerns had a visit from two of them with guns on their hips and wanting to know how they felt about integration and their calls were simply awful, "Communist Jew bastard, Nigger loving bitch" etc. and then poor Dorothy got one and would have gotten more but she took the phone off the hook. They called her at one in the morning and said they would be out in fifteen minutes. She was simply terrified, and was so afraid of Bunch [Lobman] finding out about it and she did not wake him up and fortunately being deaf he did not hear the phone, and Jean (her sister) and her husband were visiting and so they all got up and called the police and waited for the visitors to come but they did not get there, but Dorothy had to go back to nitroglycerin [heart medication] as she got so upset. Now practically all the white women that were there have been called and the only ones that escaped were the ones who did not go in their own cars, and since I went with someone else I have escaped so far but of course I have had them before many times.

While it has been awful, and really terrifying in a way (. . . two of them were among the bombers who were freed) . . . at least I feel I have

---

*Vera Foster, wife of Luther Foster.

company now and some of the women are beginning to wake up to what is really going on, and all of us went to our Ministers and for once they showed a little courage and passed a resolution condemning such behavior and asking the Police to do something about it, which of course they won't as they are all part of it. The men and the strange woman all come from the Baptist Laymen's league which has been formed to "root out hidden integrationists." The Rabbi at first warned the Jewish women not to say anything about it, as they were afraid it was only the Jewish women that were being attacked and the whole idea of the Rabbi was not to stir anything up, but when he found all the other women were getting the same treatment and it was coming up at the Ministerial alliance he acted as brave as a lion and perhaps the Jewish Community will wake to the danger a little now. One of the funny side-lights is that several of the women who came without their husbands' approval and who have been praying for their husbands, now are going around shouting Glory Hallelujah as their husbands have finally gotten mad and indignant. But whether their anger will last or not I don't know. The men here are literally scared to death to step out of line, and even the bombings as long as it was the Negroes did not rouse them to any real protest. As Juliette said before she died, "These cowardly southern white men are the cause of it all." But the reaction from that remark helped bring about her death. Thank God for Cliff and your Father [Joe Gelders] and Aubrey and Jim and a handful of others.

Monday, October 20, 1958
Dear Clark: . . .

I told you about Mrs. Tilly and the Fellowship of the Concerned, the interracial meeting we had and the aftermath of all the threatening and abusive telephone calls. For a week they were simply terrible. But the fact that two of the men got drunk and went to see one of the Methodist preachers, we got at least two of their names but when the ladies met together as to what to do, the opinion of all was "Not to go to the Police or the FBI" as they all said that these forces were on the side of the people doing the telephoning. Now it may be that they are afraid of any publicity, but they just assumed that we had no protection from either the local or the federal government and that is the truth.

I do not agree at all that this is a moral question, it is a legal and constitutional question and while preachers and women and so on can perhaps help in public opinion, the big question is to force the Federal government to take some affirmative action. As I have written and written and sent clippings and made all the noise I could about it, the Federal government itself segregates, and until it stops segregating and throws its weight on the side of the Law and stops being so lukewarm, then the battle will not be won. The Congress has got to step in and pass some affirmative legislation too, the Supreme Court cannot do it all, and unless the Congress and the Federal government are forced by strong public opinion to take these steps, then the battle will be lost. But all you read and all you hear is pressure on the States . . .

For God's Sake, don't you of all people begin to talk about the preachers being the key. They can help but this has to have the weight of Law and the Military too.

Established by the 1957 Civil Rights Act, the U.S. Commission on Civil Rights was charged with investigating civil rights violations, particularly in the area of voting. The commission opened its first hearings in Montgomery on December 8, 1958. During the televised hearings, black witnesses from Macon County including professors from the Tuskegee Institute and farmers testified, each recounting their futile efforts to register to vote. Alabama state officials refused to testify.

December 8, 1958
Dear Clark: . . .

I had a note from Corliss about the segregation among the troops business and I am glad he is so interested. No one else seems to get interested at all very much. All are concerned about the Filibuster and the Civil Rights commission. It opened here this morning and there is a tremendous crowd over there—no possibility of getting in. We had a telephone call early this morning, asking if Mr. Durr could tell them all about it, with the inference that of course he was part of it. The woman gave a name and address and when we looked it up found that she worked for our neighborhood druggist, who is a leader in the KKK or WCC but has always been pleasant enough as a druggist. You never know where the calls come from, but this time we found out and know it was inspired by this druggist. The question now is whether to stop trading with him or not or just act as though the fact he set spies upon us means nothing to us. I am all for confronting him with it and asking him if he wants our trade or not. He owes a lot of money to Durr Drug Company and won't pay and maybe that is one reason he is taking out after us.

December 18, 1958
Dearest Clark and Mairi: . . .

Our peaceful little prayer group is completely routed. It only took a few calls to the husbands and there was a panic. Just a bundle of laundry and a few cans of beans were threatened and the men went into complete panic and told the women no more praying, no more meeting. It is wonderful the rationale they use, "We know what you were doing was all right, we do not BLAME you for it, BUT business is business and we cannot compete with . . . Laundry or . . . Insurance Co. or . . . wholesale grocery Co. if they can use this against us. ("This," being that their wives or daughters or sisters-in-law had attended an interracial prayer meeting.)

It is wonderful to see again the old solidarity of the women but in a slightly new field. The same old "Poor, dear, Sweet Olive, isn't it awful what she has to put up with from Earl?" and the closing of the ranks around Olive, or Anne or whoever has been oppressed by the husband. I really believe when you get to the bottom of it that the southern women have more hatred and a deeper resentment against the white southern male than the Negroes do. It is a most unhealthy and really perverted state of mind. I like men and hate to see them held in such low esteem, but I have to admit they do nothing to gain any admiration except a blessed few. Last night they had the regular monthly meeting of the Southern Regional Council and word got around that it would be "covered" as the prayer group was and that all the names would be "exposed" and there was another panic and none of the people were going and so finally it turned out that Cliff and a young Methodist preacher went and Paul Woolley, a typographer and head of COPE.* There were about thirty-five Negroes there and these three men and two white women, both widow ladies. I did not go, as Cliff said if the pictures were taken

---

*Committee on Political Education, an affiliate of the AFL-CIO.

and the exposure did take place he was in better position to take it than I, as the Durr Drug Co. would take his going to a meeting better than my going, particularly after my sister-in-law had come to see me to "warn" me against ever again attending any such interracial meeting. It is all so absurd and ridiculous and seems just writing about it to be utterly crazy and it is, but it is also the actuality and the concrete reality. I honestly think the South has gone crazy and how long it will be before it becomes sane again, I don't know.

Virginia appealed to Lyndon B. Johnson, Majority Leader of the U.S. Senate, to use his political skill and power to end the segregation of black soldiers stationed in the South.

January 9, 1959
Dear Lyndon:

Aubrey came over last night all in a warm glow from the fine reception you gave him and his colored Bishops. He was so delighted and I was so pleased for him and so pleased with you for being so thoughtful and warm to him. He has had a rough time and after being peed on by that polecat Jim Eastland most people think he still stinks. The way he was treated by the "Civil Liberties Clearing House" is beyond belief. "Liberals" especially the ADA [Americans for Democratic Action] type really irritate me, I prefer to put my trust in straight-out politicians. I hope you lick them all as well as that low-down scoundrel [Richard] Nixon.

Aubrey has really worked hard trying to keep the southern Negroes from falling for Nixon which they have done in a big way . . . [Richard] Nixon is playing a devious and underhanded game, on the one hand playing up to the Negroes and on the other working with some of their worst enemies. I can't prove he is behind all of these wild Third Party moves down here, but I know very well that the Republicans are and you see the smooth characters moving behind the scenes and out front . . .

Lyndon you have got to get this matter settled and it seems to me that the best way to do it is to work on the military angle. Certainly to Jim Crow the soldiers, sailors, airmen and so on that come South is a pretty poor way to treat them, and it is a potential source of real violence and trouble. The way the Negro military personnel are treated here as soon as they step off the Base is just awful. The whole Federal establishment is segregated. If these hypocritical Republicans really wanted to end it, all they would have to do is to . . . make it a Federal offense to segregate the Armed Services while on duty. But they only want to keep the Democrats stirred up and divided. They want to use the South as they always have as a club for their own purposes. Now you have broken their power in Texas, can't you free the rest of the South? Hurry because we are not getting any younger and living here is real tough. Give my love to Bird.

January 19, 1959
Dear Lyndon:

Thank you for your nice letter. I appreciated it as Aubrey appreciated your courtesy to him. As I said, after being squirted by that skunk, Jim Eastland, you know lots of people think you smell bad and you begin to detect a faint odor yourself sometimes! . . .

As passionately as I believe in the rights of men and in Civil Rights I think we have to preserve Civil Liberties to get them, and I think the evil forces in this country, like [Richard] Nixon and his gang, are trying to break down the constitutional safeguards on the Negro issue and get absolute control . . . I think the boot lickers of big business like Nixon and his gang are doing what they did after the Civil War, using the Negro to get control and then they will ditch him, as they did after the war, and make their alliance openly with Eastland and his crowd as I am convinced they now have a secret alliance with them.

But just as slavery had to go I think segregation has to go too, and I believe you agree with me. At least I am holding on to that faith. But it seems to me that instead of throwing the issue of the schools into the Congress and dividing the Democrats as the Republicans want to do, that the attack should be on the Republicans for NOT desegregating the Federal Agencies and particularly for NOT protecting the soldiers that come South from segregation. I am enclosing an article which shows the powerful lever the Military has if it wanted to use it, just a whisper of cutting down would make our WCC boys wake up and see the light.* Then

---

*The news clippings included a headline story from the *Montgomery Advertiser* on January 18, 1958, "Air Force Pumps $62.5 Million Dollars into the Economy," which focused on the federal dollars that came to Montgomery through Maxwell and Gunter Air Force bases.

too the fact that the southerners fight for jobs on the BASES and are willing to accept integration in work, eating, restrooms, even recreation ON
THE BASES, shows that they will accept it if they have to to make a living. We southerners are not as dumb as they make us out to be. To see an
officer in the United States Air Force in uniform be Jim Crowed makes
me sick, it is an insult to the U.S. it seems to me. Love, Va. Durr

Late in 1958, Jessica Mitford's daughter Constancia "Dinky" Romilly,
then a freshman at Sarah Lawrence College in New York, traveled by bus to
Montgomery to spend the Christmas holidays with the Durrs. Dinky was
two years old when her family moved from Washington to Oakland, California. She had no memory of the Durrs—but had been hearing stories
about them all of her life. And they lived up to her expectations, particularly
Virginia, who, as she recalled, came sweeping out of the house to greet her,
and teased, "Why Dinky Donk, why aren't you in Cuba fighting with Castro's forces. Why, when your father was your age, he was fighting in Spain."

Dinky remembered being shocked by the segregation signs, and the
stark racial and class divisions in the South. Having grown up in Oakland
as the child of civil rights activists, her experience of racial integration was
exceptional compared to most young people of her age, but the South offered such a dramatic contrast. However, she didn't remember feeling that
her parents' generation had failed as Virginia's letter suggests. She viewed
her mother and stepfather, Bob Treuhaft, as heroes, as the true Democrats,
as champions of the poor and oppressed. Looking back, she remembered
being very unhappy at Sarah Lawrence, an elitist, "ivory tower sort of
place," and probably did seem confused and drifting when she visited the
Durrs. "There was nothing to work for . . . no struggle or activity you
could sink your teeth into." When the sit-ins began in 1960, "It was like I
was born then," she recalled. "That's when my life began." Soon thereafter,
she returned to the South, this time to work in SNCC's office in Atlanta.[26]

January 1959
Dear Clark: . . .

   Tilla . . . was most unhappy at Christmas time and while she seems
to like her family, she hates Montgomery and has no friends here and
just loathes being here. The Dinky Donk came with her and we adored
her, and thought she was a lovely girl and perfectly beautiful although
she and Tilla go in for the sloppy look (the occasion of mine and Tilla's
big quarrel which I don't care for at all) . . . She is not at all a rebel like
Decca or Esmond and is like all of this generation in that they don't

seem to know what to fight for, the hydrogen bomb has made all of our projects look sort of foolish to them and they are looking for something much bigger and more profound and much more important than we had, and the sad thing is that they feel we all failed them, and of course we did fail in a way, but the fight in Spain that Esmond made is a far-off dream to Dinky and the defeat of Hitler is only less a dream, and the facts are that now they are threatened by some awful kind of doomsday which we did not protect them from, and they don't look to the Socialist countries with any real hope and don't think they want that either. In fact they don't know what they want, they just know they don't want what they have. We had a hard time stirring up any young men and the ones we found were pretty sad, and the only one that the Dinky Donk even gave a look at was a typical specimen of the beat generation, he had been to Harvard on a Woodrow Wilson scholarship in biochemistry and had left and come home as it was all so "phony" and all the people there were simply "pseudo" who were on the make and did not really care a damn about anything except as it got them ahead and so he was going to Honduras and pick bananas and the girls thought he was terrific . . .

I hope you all will have her in as I think you would like her very much as we did, we really loved her. She seemed to think we were all "riots" which at least amused her, but her main impression of the South were the "Colored" and "White" signs and her last comment was "How do you stand it?" Well, it is hard, no doubt of that, but I have finally reached the point of thinking that no place else is so much better, it looks as though we were in for a long hard time ahead of us in this country and at least here in the South I am on familiar ground and the good and the bad is so black and white! I am not a subtle person as you know and get confused by all the nuances of liberal life, or radical or progressive or left wing or whatever you call it life, all the schisms and the prisms and prunes and divisions get me upset and angry and from down here it looks so silly that it is unbelievable—when the head of the KKK comes right out and says Blood will flow and we get WCC literature which makes your blood run cold and these poor, God abandoned, oppressed Negroes come in here day after day for help and in the face of this real and critical crisis, it does seem for people to fight each other is too ridiculous. I know you feel that way too. Like you I hate double talk and double-dealing and I am not smart enough to deal with it. When Lister

Hill comes out with an attack on the U. S. Supreme Court, I find it hard to forgive him, but I am sure he would say that to attack his best friend* is simply what he has to do to prevent something worse, but is there anything worse than lying and deceiving and how can people here, these poor ignorant people, ever learn anything when no one speaks the truth to them? It is the poor ignorant misled Southern white people that I feel so sorry for, the Negroes too, but they are coming up, they have leadership but there is none for the poor whites at all.

Virginia had great affection for Hugh "Geno" Foreman, the youngest child of Clark and Mairi Foreman, who was born in 1941. Geno was a rebel, an imaginative and creative young man, "with more energy than he could have time on earth" to expend. He had been in and out of several different schools, one in Berlin where he lived with his sister Joan and finally A. S. Summerhill school. After a few months of college, he dropped out and made his way to visit a friend from Berlin, then a student at Harvard, and joined the folk music scene in Cambridge. Joan Baez met Geno when they were both eighteen, and described him as "a schemer and a dreamer . . . [with] no normal sense of fear . . . six feet tall and beautiful." According to Baez, he "played the guitar and piano . . . both with natural brilliance." Another friend described him as "a white/crazy black blues singer," "a one-man army at war with the Establishment, with Authority, with Squares and with his own tendencies to self-destruct."[89]

Tilla and Geno had been *simpatico* since they were children. After Tilla enrolled in Brandeis in the fall of 1958, they renewed their friendship.

February 9, 1959
Dearest Mairi and Clark: . . .

I thought you would be interested in the excerpts from Tilla's letter about Hugh, who seems to have made a great hit with the students at Brandeis. I wish Pete Seeger would take him on . . . so he could have some vocation to fall back on. Pete, like Hugh, wandered around the countryside and went hungry for several years but in the process he became the living voice of America, in my opinion, and perhaps if Hugh

---

*Lister Hill and Hugo Black had been best friends prior to the 1954 *Brown* decision. Hill and Black both realized that it would be political suicide for Hill even to be seen with Black in the aftermath of the desegregation ruling, so by mutual agreement, they cut all ties. Roger Newman, *Hugo Black: A Biography* (New York: Pantheon Books, 1994), 443–44.

could stay or study with him for a while he might get a more compelling vocation. I do love him as I love all of you and having known him from the time he was conceived, I can sympathize with all of his problems but I think he is essentially a fine and sweet and kind person. But these young people who have parents like us and who find the world so unchanged and so corrupt, they are in a spot. I had been impressed with that with Tilla and the Dinky Donk at Christmas. However hard we have tried, the world is still a mess, their lives are threatened with the hydrogen bomb, we are out of power and out of favor, what we believed in and tried to bring about has not come, and even though I think we fought a fine battle and are still fighting, we have to acknowledge that from their point of view we have not succeeded. So they doubt our aims and ideas, and are looking for something new and different and will have to come to their own decisions and find some new form for their desires and their lives, but the fact that they think the present values and standards are "phony" is some advance, at least they are not gray flannel conformists and boot lickers. . . . I know you do worry about him but essentially you will have to trust him and let him find his own way. And not try to make him feel guilty at all.

ca. February 10, 1959
Dear Marge and Laurent and Esther: . . .

I suppose you saw where Asbury Howard* was beaten up so badly by a group of men AFTER he was arrested and fined for putting up a sign urging Negroes to register and vote. He was arrested and fined $500 and six months in jail for "inciting to riot" (that is putting up the sign) and when he came out of the police court he was set upon by a group of white men and he and his son were badly beaten, ten stitches in his head. Six in his son's head. He announced with his usual courage that he was going right on. He is a remarkable person and so brave.

The courage seems to be all in the Negro group, here everyone is scared to death. Since the church meeting in September and the publishing of the names, all of the church women have been harassed to death and poor Anne Kerns has had not only telephone calls, anony-

---

*A longtime labor and civil rights activist in Bessemer, Alabama.

mous letters, but visits by armed men to threaten them. The reaction of so many people has been, that instead of sympathizing with the Kerns, they have disassociated themselves from them as much as possible. It has left Anne in a very lonely spot and she is showing signs of cracking up under it, so depressed and so lonely and frightened and wants to get out so badly, and I don't blame her. But where to go is the problem. Dorothy [Lobman] is having them and us over to dinner tonight to try and cheer her but she invited another couple who were supposed to be friends of theirs and they said they were sorry they were such cowards but they simply could not afford to associate with them, since the WCC was after them so. So if you get persecuted, you are blamed for being persecuted, rather than the WCC for doing the persecution.

The only comfort I have gotten out of it is that with the persecution now so widespread . . . at least we have a small group that sustains each other and before that I was the only one who had had the "treatment." But now it is spreading widely and the WCC has announced that they are giving the full "treatment" to anyone that steps out of line. They said in an ad in the paper Sunday that they would make a pariah of anyone who did not fervently and whole-heartedly endorse segregation and they would be "ostracized" from the community. So a lot of people are terrified, but *after* they once get the "treatment," they get mad and that is a lot healthier . . .

All the girls are fine and Lulah is just about to be twelve and is having a birthday party on Saturday, I cannot believe she is so old. Cliff is pretty well and has a lot of fun with the Pea Level and is planting more fruit trees and making a spring garden. Aubrey is full of beans as usual, and all sorts of plans and is off now on Adelle Davis's book on eating,* he has stuffed all of us full of vitamins and yogurt and wheat germ and liver and yeast and really I think it has done us all good. He gave us all a copy of the book and I find it interesting to say the least, at least it is better to say you lack vitamins than that you're getting old which is of course the real truth of the matter.

In response to a suit brought by the MIA to desegregate recreational facilities in Montgomery, the city commission voted to close all of the city's

---

*Adelle Davis, *Let's Eat Right to Keep Fit,* published in 1954.

thirteen parks and the zoo, effective on January 1, 1959. The parks remained closed until 1965. At his inauguration on January 20, Governor John Patterson pledged to maintain segregated schools, warning that if a school desegregation suit was brought, the public schools would be shut down. Many black teachers and other members of the black community, trusting that Patterson meant what he said, pressured King and the MIA to suspend its plans to push ahead with a school desegregation suit.[28]

Early 1959
Dearest Dec: ...

I had a long letter from Mary Walton Livingston telling me of the first day of the Negro children coming to school in Fairfax County and no trouble at all and the children took it very well. Isn't that amazing! And wonderful too! The new school is just down the road from where we lived and is a fine new public school.

Here of course, things simply go on getting worse and worse. You think each day that they can't get any worse but they do. They have now taken away (or at least introduced the bill which will pass of course as the Teachers Association say they can't afford to fight it, "someone would think they were integrationists") the Teacher tenure which means they can close the schools and drop all of the Teachers off the payroll without any delay at the first sign of a suit. This is to terrify the Negro teachers and cause them to try and weaken King and the rest of them. The closing of the parks has already produced a rift in the Negro community as so many people lost their jobs then. The terrorization still goes on to anyone that sticks their neck out, telephone calls, anonymous letters but above all, lack of any work, no jobs. Brutal economic pressure and brutal social pressure ... It is hard from down here to know how much the rest of the country really is behind the effort to desegregate. There seem to be so many pious words and so little real action on the part of groups and organizations and even of the Federal government who segregates in its own agencies. Lots of love.

In a runoff election for mayor, the black vote helped to defeat Mayor William "Tacky" Gayle, who had served during the bus boycott, and to elect Earl James, a former city commissioner. The White Citizens Council ran a full-page ad, "Emergency Announcement to White Voters," warning that the black "bloc" vote would decide the election if white voters did not line up behind Gayle.

ca. March 28, 1959
Dearest Mairi and Clark: . . .

I got home to find wild excitement over the fact that Mayor Gayle had been defeated and by the Negro vote in spite of the enclosed ad which was the last and frantic gasp of the WCC. The Negroes had voted for James in the first election and so their vote was NOT the kiss of death after all, and so when the next person asks "What happened to the money? Where did it go," just tell them that some of it went to Montgomery and while I do not think the pressure of [E. D.] Nixon made ALL of the difference, I do think the fact that he was able to exert the pressure made it incumbent upon the MIA to get busy on the voting business, which they did in quite a big way and it has now paid off. I don't mean to say that James is a savior but certainly he could not help but be a big improvement over what we have had, and the Negroes regard it as a great step forward.

Cliff and I had lunch with Dr. Lawrence Reddick* today who is just back from India where he went with Rev. and Mrs. King. He thinks the trip was a great experience for King and made him see that "Love" alone will not cure poverty and degradation and he thinks he is much more likely now to try and make a big pitch for political activity and participation. He said the poverty in India and the lack of any real strong push from the Government to end it in the countryside is very apparent, and that the appeals to love and kindness are not getting too far . . .

Lots of love to you both, and tell Hugh how sorry I am he was not there to join in with Tilla and Danny to give us a view of what life is like among the beatniks! Also give my love to Shelagh and thank you again for a wonderful time.

During the spring of 1959, Congress held hearings on a number of bills to extend civil rights protection in a variety of areas. Senator William Langer, Republican from North Dakota, introduced a bill to prevent discrimination against members of the armed services in places of public accommodation and transportation. Clark Foreman presented a statement in support of this bill in hearings held by the Judiciary Committee's Subcommittee on Constitutional Rights. His statement shows ample evidence of Virginia's collaboration.[29]

---

*Author of *Crusader without Violence* (1954), the first biography of Martin Luther King, Jr., and a professor at Alabama State College.

April 17, 1959
Dearest Clark:

Your letter has just come and I am simply thrilled over the Florida student's letter. If the young people would get behind this it would give it some real steam. They haven't had time to get scared yet and they could really go to town if they get behind it, they need so desperately something that is affirmative rather than negative. I have made copies and am returning the letter.

As for your testimony, I simply think a statement of the facts is the thing to do. Start at Richmond, where the restaurant in the Greyhound Bus is segregated, big "White Restaurant" signs there but the toilets are NOT segregated, then on to Danville where both are and so on through North Carolina and Georgia and Alabama, Mississippi and Arkansas and Texas too. The Greyhound Bus Lines should be able to give you information about the various places if they would. In Montgomery, Ala., the RR station, Bus station and Airport are strictly segregated. I talked to a Negro soldier this morning at the bus station and he said that when he traveled he was segregated all the time in the South, unless he was with his outfit and then they went by troop train which was not. But if he was sent from one camp to the other, traveling on a government order, he was segregated all the way. UNDERSTAND, *not on the train, the plane nor the bus,* but in the stations along the way. Of course any of the military stationed in the South are strictly segregated as to the restaurants, movies, etc. and here the USO is segregated and I understand that is the common practice in the South. The USO is run by the Jewish Welfare Board which you would think would not do it . . .

I would simply ask the Committee if they thought a man should be sent South and segregated when he was drafted into the Armed Services, if that would increase his desire to die for his country? That you did not think it would. . . . Ask the Committee if it is worth the billions in good will we waste by allowing the South to Jim Crow our soldiers and set an example to the allied personnel that come here for training.

Do be sure and send me a copy of your testimony. I know Leonard [Boudin] will do a beautiful job on the constitutionality of it. I only wish you could get some of these Florida students up. I hope you get Alice Dunnigan of the [Chicago] *Defender* to cover it for you.

April 24, 1959

Dearest Clark:

Your letter with the enclosed statement has just come and in general I think it is a fine statement but there are several points which I would change as you can see by the markings on the statement . . .

I read the testimony before the Civil Rights Committee and it all has the aspect of something in a dream, all an elaborate farce. I think the whole thing about politics which we had to learn the very hard way with [Henry] Wallace, is that if you don't have the power to back up what you propose, you might as well stop talking for a time until you can get the power. And in the school desegregation cases, the power is not there. But here in the military, the power is there and running over. Of course keeping on talking might change someone's mind and so you will build up power that way, but the Douglas Bill seems to me to be a pipe dream and until the Negroes have the vote and segregation is ended, the chances of them going to school remain only token, to say the least. The Government has the power to do both if it wanted to, both protect the Negro's right to vote and to end segregation, but I don't think they have the least intention of doing so, simply go through the motions and that is all . . .

But then again, I get to feeling that honest moral indignation over the wrongs of the Negro, of witch hunting or of unemployment is something in the past. People's minds seem to have been simply shattered by TV and movies and radio and they have stopped thinking and really feeling anything, they simply react to what they see and hear and don't have anything but synthetic ideas or emotions. I don't mean all people but the great majority. I don't blame them, I know how they got that way, but at the same time, it is frightening to say the least.

Virginia responded in the following letter to correspondence from Decca, who was visiting with her family in England, just prior to the publication of her memoir, *Daughters and Rebels*.

May 13, 1959

Dearest Dec:

The postcard just came and you had not sent it before and I loved it. All so heathery and misty and blue and just like I would imagine the

Hebrides to be . . . Never heard of Doris Lessing but will read her book with interest. I actually do not see much connection except remotely between the American Negroes and the Africans, they both suffer discrimination on account of color, which is of course a great bond, but I have found that the American Negro is so Americanized and that they regard the African as a "furriner", and are rather disdainful of him. They are really at least most of them, 200% Americans. I spoke to a Negro woman's Club on yesterday afternoon, on the "Need to Vote" and since I have given the same talk ten thousand times it came very easily, and they need it because in spite of the fact that it is true they have great difficulties getting registered, the fact also remains that few of them try very hard. They were just exactly like all Club women, dressed up, devotional, rules, dues, business, chicken salad and cake and also full of the same old "Cold War" attitude and so on. They want to be part of the American society, and except for its discrimination against them, they have few criticisms of it. But of course, because it does discriminate so brutally against them, they have a source of anger that does drive them to action, and they were magnificent in the boycott.

May 1959
Dearest Dec:

Your letter has just come and also the book and also the bedspreads. I have not read the book yet since it only came an hour ago, but the bedspreads are wonderful for the Pea Level, exactly what is needed and thank you so much. I really adore them and they will liven up the place no end and make it look so attractive. Thanks so much for remembering the right colors too, think how nice they will look with all the marigolds and zinnias.

I am glad that Bob is there . . . The thing that makes me gladdest though is that you went back to your youth and your childhood and have recovered so much of the lost affections, which I think is healthy and good and strengthening. Of course you could not have done that unless you have first established yourself as a person, so you can go back and be independent and be yourself, and yet to have captured as much of the affection and devotion as you have is wonderful, as evidently you have come both to love and respect your mother and that is a great thing. Going back to one's childhood and then finding no love left is sad indeed. This has happened to me since I came back South and to Cliff in a way and all of our life here is made strained and bad by the complete concentration of people, including our families and old friends—on the race issue. Their affections have not been as strong as their prejudices, so they simply leave us alone, I mean alone. But then you can come and you leave and I don't know how it would be if you had to stay there all of the time and be involved with them and find yourself on the opposite side of every question, but in any case, you don't have to and you have rediscovered so much of your youth and found it sweet . . .

I suppose you saw all the furor here about the Rabbit Book and this does make you feel you are living in Alice in Wonderland. One of our Black Belt Senators (State Legislature) found that a small child's book (for children 2–5) was in the Library, called *The Rabbits' Wedding* and one rabbit (male) was black and the other rabbit (female) was white and he issued a great blast that this was pro-integration propaganda and would cause miscegenation and cause children to accept integration, and so the poor Librarian said she would put it on the "restricted shelves" and she did! So it can only be gotten now by special request, like *Das Capital*, and the Senator is going to make a study of other books to see which ones need burning. All of this out in the open and no one dares say a word against such insanity . . .

I will have to admit that I cannot see anything right now to give me much pleasure as everyone seems to have succumbed to the same old line, War, War, Segregation, anti-anti and nothing positive at all, and then all laid over with Jesus, God, and the Church. How I do treasure the few brave souls I know.

I am longing to see the final form of the book. It has been rewritten so much that I cannot imagine what its final form will be like. I think for it to end with Esmond going off to War is a fitting ending . . .

Lots of love dearest Dec and do write soon and again thanks for all of the presents.

May 22, 1959
Dearest Clark:

Your letter has just come and I am hastening to answer it at once. . . . Aubrey left today for New York and Washington and had a lot of things he wanted to get out before he left, including the prospectus or outline of a book that Don West wants to write about the Mountain White. You would be interested in it as I was, as it so clearly demonstrates Don's own pride and desire to clear the name of the poor southern white man from the tag of "poor white trash." He is telling of the noble role the poor southern white man played in the abolitionist movement and the underground railroad, all of which is true, but while I do not for a moment doubt his thesis and know that along the mountains there was a long line of hide outs and union men, still the fact remains that the overwhelming majority of the poor southern white men fought for the Confederacy and willingly, and today are the worst and most violent and vicious enemies of the Negro. So I think there has to be another explanation for the poor, southern white man than the fact that he is misunderstood and not treated right in history, as the fact is here today and throughout southern history that the poor southern white man, except at odd times, has hated and resented the Negro. I hate to be old fashioned! But I still think it is economic competition that he fears, and he sees in the Negro and has seen for a long time, the shadow of his own helplessness and poverty and fear and degradation, and it is like a man trying to cut off his own shadow . . .

But it is not just the poor man. Last week the head of the KKK came to town, he is a young fellow named [Robert] Shelton and was the leader of the mob that drove Autherine Lucy off the campus, and was a rubber worker at the B. F. Goodrich plant. His union did not teach him anything nor did it discipline him for his activities, and as he actively supported the present Governor, Patterson, the B. F. Goodrich Co. has now made him a salesman with a big, fine car etc. and he sells tires to the State! So the hopes of those people who look to industry to save the South look a little thin after that. But after Shelton's visit to the Legislature, one of the Black Belt Senators demanded that all the "race" books in the Libraries be burned, and the State Librarian answered and said that to prevent such a happening as that, the libraries had put all of the "Race" books in a separate place and they were not given out to the public and could only be gotten by request! . . .

You give me far more credit than I am due about the bill, as ideas are not worth a damn unless someone puts them into action . . . I don't think any pamphlet is needed on the bill, simply a one-page sheet reprinting the passage from the "To Secure these Rights" . . . Get enough printed so that they can be distributed widely, scattered and given away . . . The idea will either take fire and spread or it won't, but I think it might if the younger people got ahold of it. It is so simple. Put a U.S. Flag at the top of the page and a picture of a Negro man in uniform and ask if the flag is to be dishonored? I have never seen why the damn DAR [Daughters of the American Revolution] had to get the flag all to itself! I am delighted that Thompson of NJ said he would sponsor the bill . . .

The South is like a ring of cattle with all of the horns pointing out of the circle and if you are not in the circle you feel only the sharp points of the horns . . . I am sure [Cliff] never had any idea of how absolutely he would be ostracized, not that people are so unpleasant, they simply leave us alone, the phone never rings, the people never come, and it gets worse all the time instead of better. I have tried joining things, Church groups, League of Women Voters, Human Relations Council, AAUW, Legislative Council, even the Society for the Prevention of Cruelty to Animals, but with the same result in all of the groups, no one is unpleasant but nothing ever comes of any of it, no one calls, no one comes, no one asks me to call, it is simply non-recognition. The Business and Professional Women's Club is the only one that actually blacklisted me, but the others have simply pursued a policy of non-acceptance. But Cliff has had exactly the same experience and Aubrey of course, even worse, but he does get away so often and gets out of it . . .

But you can see how the South has maintained itself so long as it has, it punishes its dissenters so badly that no one dares do it.

June 3, 1959
Dearest Decca:

I have just finished reading Doris Lessing's book and am entirely fascinated with it and with her. You are right, her experiences are so alike, particularly here in the South, and her analysis of the mentality of the white "settler" as she calls it or the white supremacist as we call it is so exact. I recognized myself often. The vague and ever-present self-pity, the explanations and the furies and the wasting of time and the concentration on nothing but clothes, food, and garden clubs, and above all the never-ending and never-ceasing conversation about "Them." I thought it was brilliant . . .

Our latest horror here is the strange death of an old Negro preacher who was found dead by the banks of a fishing pond, and that same day a group of white men beat up terribly some groups of Negroes fishing at the pond and also refused to let some Air Force men (Negroes) fish, although it is a State-owned pond. The Air Force men at least have gotten some publicity but the poor old preacher is dead and all they will say it was "natural causes." We had a case this morning of a man who came in with his head split wide open by a policeman's club and had to take ten stitches in it, and Cliff is going to represent him at the hearing on Friday. They say he was "resisting arrest" which is always what they say when they beat them up. It seems such a long and hopeless way sometimes but I suppose every little bit helps. You just get so tired of the same thing all the time and begin to feel so smothered.

June 25, 1959
Dearest Clark and Mairi: . . .

I have been elected on the National Board of the Women's International League for Peace and Freedom but I don't know whether to accept or not. Mrs. Foster of Tuskegee is elected and a Mrs. Murphy who teaches at Morehouse or Spelman, both lovely women, but with all of the pressures on us here, I simply don't feel I can take on anything else. What do you think? They are such good women but I am not sure how effective and I don't feel I have the time or strength or money to take on any further problems of any kind, Peace included. After living here for nearly ten years, all well-meaning, kindly and good-intentioned people begin to seem silly unless they have something to back it up with and none of them seem to have anything, they look to the South to reform and yet they do nothing to help. I think when Goodrich Rubber promotes the head of the KKK so he can sell tires to the State, you have the perfect picture of what northern industry means toward the rehabilitation of the South, politically and morally at least.

Until people in the rest of the country realize that this southern situation is part of the overall rottenness that infects the country and stop thinking of us as different and do something toward making the Federal government and northern industry stand up and take definite action, all the pious good wishes really don't make any sense.

July 7, 1959
Dearest Clark and Mairi: . . .

I have had several letters from Lyndon [Johnson] and believe that all that is coming out will be some kind of general guarantee of the right to vote or something of that kind.* If it really provided for the Federal guarantee of Federal elections, that would be a big step forward, but I am not sure what form it will take. This is all based on surmise, as Lyndon never *SAYS anything* but generalities but he is polite and answers the letters. I do hope that there will be some group willing to fight for the soldier bill on the floor. In spite of Lyndon's lack of militancy, I think he is so much better than any of the other candidates that I am for him. I can't stand Kennedy nor Humphrey nor Symington and even Stevenson strikes me as weak. Polished and charming but no stamina. I think all these attacks are making Lyndon mad and he might come up fighting. I hope so. What do you think? . . .

Virginia shared Hugo Black's firm belief that free speech was the foundation of American democracy and she admired his role as the leading defender of this principle on the Supreme Court. But Black was often in the minority, as he was in a June 1959 decision, *Barenblatt v. U.S.*, which extended the shadow of McCarthyism. Lloyd Barenblatt, a college professor, refused on first amendment grounds to answer questions posed by the House Un-American Activities Committee about whether or not he was or ever had been a member of the Communist Party. In a 5-4 ruling, the Court upheld Barenblatt's contempt conviction, citing national security in ceding broad power to Congress "which in a different context would certainly have raised constitutional issues of the gravest character." While the Supreme Court indulged anticommunist crusaders, state government along with economic and social pressures conspired to effectively crush dissent in the South. In this climate of fear and repression, Virginia despaired that the power of vehement segregationists remained virtually unchecked.[30]

---

*These discussions culminated with the enactment of the 1960 Civil Rights Act, which provided a few more general provisions regarding voting rights in addition to those included in the 1957 Civil Rights Act. But this bill also lacked strong enforcement power.

July 15, 1959
Dear Hugo: . . .

Mrs. Durr died on last Saturday night at the age of ninety-four. She was buried on Monday afternoon from the First Presbyterian Church, and such an outpouring of people, both to the house and to the Church, and such an outpouring of food, hams, chickens, salads, cakes, such an abundance as I have never seen before. It was an old fashioned "country" funeral, relatives coming from far and near and such a real devotion expressed, that it was very moving. It was a real family gathering of the Clan.

She was as you would have expected scrupulously fair in her division of the estate so each of the children got exactly the same . . . We will have our share which is around $30,000 to $40,000 but all in Durr Drug Co. stock, which is closely held in the family and not sold except in some great emergency, so we will actually have very little more income than we have now, but at least we will have some security for our old age. We have had, as I am sure you have been aware, a real struggle here to get established . . . but we have been able to keep going and things are a little better now, although we are still far from being a prosperous concern, but we have lots of interesting cases and I am sure from the point of view of where we can do the most good . . . it is right here. I think Cliff has done a great deal of good, he feels at home here, his family has been loyal to us and he does not want to leave, and his health has improved and he seems to be much happier here and more cheerful here than any other place. Of course the South will be in turmoil for a long time to come but I do not think any place in the country is free from strife and turmoil. At least here in the South it is more open and at least you know what to expect . . .

I agree with you that John Crommelin, as vicious as he is, should have the right to express his ideas, but the trouble here is that Truth is not free to combat error. That is why I think it is so terrible that a vicious anti-semite like Crommelin is protected by all of the protections of the law and the Constitution, while a gentle saint like Willard Uphaus,* who is the living embodiment of the brotherhood of man and the love of Christian fellowship, should be harassed and persecuted and no doubt will be jailed. I think the Constitution is becoming in-

---

*Founder of the World Fellowship, a peace organization; Uphaus was held in contempt by HUAC for refusing to hand over a guest list for an event sponsored by his organization.

valid as it only works to protect one side and to me the wrong side and the protection it offers or should offer to all citizens is withdrawn from those who are considered a threat in any way to property.

Here in Montgomery, John Crommelin has no difficulty having a public meeting, getting publicity, spreading his vicious ideas—and I think he has this right. BUT what happens when his ideas are not combated and when even our leading citizens are afraid to express any ideas contrary to what he says, and when his followers are growing in numbers and power? I am very much afraid that unless there is some change in the position of some of the members of the Court and one in particular,* whose last opinion shocked me very much, that this movement down here, which is growing rather fast, will become a very dangerous thing. I hope I am wrong but I have never seen people so terrified as they are here to express any dissident opinion. I do not think there is so much hatred or prejudice here, but I do think there is a great deal of fear, and fear keeps people silent, so the Crommelin crowd, who apparently have no fear at all, keep the good people cowed.

It is for exactly this reason that the Communists never attracted me to the point of joining with them, although I am convinced that we will have a socialist society in the future, but it was the principle of having to support by *word* and deed, the policies of the Party whether you agreed with them or not that made it impossible. I think the majority has the right to pass laws and those laws have to be obeyed up to the point that they invade your conscience and then you have to take your chances, but I think the real horror of a police society is the fact that you can't even protest by word, or by writing, or by any kind of expression and must seem to agree with what you don't agree with by any means.

But now I am seeing down here this same kind of deathlike conformity building up, when to speak out, to take any action of any kind, to protest, to write a letter, to hold a meeting, brings down on your head both social and economic ruin and there is no protection in the law. I honor you for the wonderful fight you have put up against this tendency and also Bill Douglas and Justice [Earl] Warren, but unless the ideas that you three have fought for so bravely are upheld and implemented by political action and by Congress, I do not see how you can do it alone.

---

*John Marshall Harlan, who wrote the majority opinion in *Barenblatt v. U.S.*

That is why I am for Lyndon Johnson, although I am sure we would not agree on a great many things, but I do think Lyndon has a respect for a desire to protect the democratic process. I hope I am not wrong . . . I think he is the best prospect we have and of course personally I am fond of him . . . and he certainly has a fine wife. . . . I did not know I was going to write such a long letter but Cliff is over with Lucy and James and I am here alone.

July 17, 1959
Dearest Clark: . . .

I think Aubrey has by now fully decided to leave and the house is on the market with a huge sign in front and Anita is already looking for an apartment in New York. The loneliness and isolation that Aubrey has had to put up with is past belief and I think it has finally become more than he can take any longer. The worst thing of all is that the children don't want to live here or even visit very often as they have no feeling of it being home. We have a few more friends and connections and of course the family connection, but I don't see much prospect of any real base of congenial people here ever, so I will have to depend on my annual visits to New York for that. The only consolation and that is rather a sour one is that the rest of the country also seems to be in pretty bad shape as far as any real communication is concerned and at least here in the South something definite is happening, and it is at least interesting on the public front, and the Negroes are stirring and doing something and so it is not dead and hopeless . . .

The Civil Rights Fight seems to be all bogged down in Washington and what Lyndon is planning is beyond me. I can't figure it out. If he doesn't do something really significant, I think he has absolutely no chance of the nomination. Carl and Anne Braden have just left here and Carl has been in Texas and says that the Negroes there are all against him, and will not touch him with a ten-foot pole. They say he has consistently and for years treated them with absolute lack of courtesy or consideration and they are done with him. So he will need more than kind words to get their vote. The ones here, King and [E. D.] Nixon too I think, are more and more leaning to Stevenson, but I really don't think he has a single chance to get it, do you? At least Lyndon is nice in his letters to us and is courteous and replies but he certainly does not say much. More and more though I am getting the feeling that the Negro issue is about to explode some way or other, their patience is wearing thin finally, and since nothing gets done but investigations and Commissions and so on, the direct actionists are beginning to make a big impression. King is being criticized more and more, and the lack of action has become terribly frustrating to them. Also the African leaders coming over and all of their confidence and authority and power and calls for action and calls for WAR really against the "WHITE MAN" has had its effect very definitely. Of course I think the situation is so different that there is really no comparison as the Negro here is in such a minority and can only succeed by integrating into the community, not overthrowing it.

Well, as usual, I write longer letters than I start out to do and can still think of a thousand things to say but will not bore you any further. Lots of love to each and all.

September 3, 1959
Dearest Marge:

I was so delighted to get another one of your long and very satisfactory letters again and to be in touch with you at last. I have missed hearing from you so much . . .

Since the boycott the Negroes here have done very little militant effort, mostly preaching and talk and now they have written a letter to the School Board asking them when they are going to integrate the schools, which of course is NEVER until they are ordered to by the Courts and then only after every resource has been tried . . .

I will try and get the *Quest for Identity** which you recommended, although I am a little fed up with psychiatry at this point. I think it is a useful tool, and a great step forward and one that will and has helped a lot of people, but we have a Mental Health Clinic here and I am a member of the Mental Health Society and we are picketed every meeting by the KKK as they say this is all part of the "Jewish Communist" Plot . . . But the Mental Health society treats its Negro patients in segregated surroundings and the receptionists call them by their first names and

---

*Authored by Allen Wheels and published in 1958.

while they are trying to repair their broken egos they do all in their power to break them down again. Hell, who wants to be adjusted to this crazy and insane society. I think the "well adjusted" and the "normal" people are often the craziest. A perfectly "normal" and "well adjusted" and even maybe brilliant guy came to talk to the League of Women Voters and calmly told us the strategy of the U.S. Air Force which was to make England a radioactive crystal rock, (all dead of course) and then survive after some fifty million people here had been killed, all in the name of preserving "Freedom." Now can anyone be any crazier than that? Listen Sister, you seem to live among fairly sane people, come to Montgomery for a visit and you will realize that the great proportion of people here are just as mad as hatters. Nigger, Sex, Religion, Violence, Jews, War, why just scratch the surface and these kind sweet pretty women will begin to spew out some of the wildest insanity you ever heard.

I have made a new friend, Anne Braden* who comes from Anniston, Alabama and who is Carl Braden's wife and who sees life in Alabama as I do, but with even deeper insight, much deeper I think. She is a lovely and charming and gentle person with a brilliant mind and is such a comfort to me. I hope you know her or will meet her sometime.

October 27, 1959
Dearest Decca: . . .

There is a curious lull in the South right now. The Negroes have realized that unless the rest of the country helps them they simply cannot win this battle alone. Five years after the [*Brown*] Decision and 76 Negro children in all schools! That is fantastic, as you will admit. If nothing happens in February at the Special session of Congress, then I think we will begin to see some sort of violence erupting, especially from the soldiers who are the bitterest of all, I see them every day getting off the bus and wearing the same uniform and yet the Negroes have to go in the "COLORED" waiting room to wait for their connections. It makes them simply furious and I don't blame them. Often they have

---

*Anne and Carl Braden were organizers for the Southern Conference Education Fund (SCEF).

never been South before and this is where I look to see the real violence break out as it is really intolerable for them.

Dec. 4, 1959
Dear Decca: . . .

Martin Luther King is moving to Atlanta and there have been Paeans of Joy in the papers. They simply will not realize that the Negro movement in the South is not the work of "Agitators," but the work of generations of oppression.

Lots of love dearest Dec. I am looking forward to 1960 so I can read your book. Devotedly, Va.

December 1959
Dearest Clark: . . .

I was not surprised by Harry Golden* backing out on you, but I was terrifically surprised by him agreeing in the first place. I do not share in the general acclamation about him. I think he is a phony, a sincere phony, and I think he presents a totally false picture of the world of today and slides over the really tough issues and makes everything seem all jolly and well-meaning. I think the reason he is so popular is that he presents the picture of "Only in America" that the big guys want spread, the land of unlimited opportunity where boys start out on the East Side and end up on Broadway, where business is benevolent and big business the most benevolent and strikes and segregation are just little pimples on the beautiful whole and so on. Anne Braden and I agree on him entirely. She said in the "kissing case"† he took it up and then dropped it flat when he saw he was offending the powers that be . . . Anne Braden is arriving here on Sunday to stay with me, and Mrs. Martin Luther King is having a big female party for her on Monday night. Thus do we move forward by tentative stages, the females can meet together we hope without harm, but any kind of mixed affair is still a little hazardous . . .

---

*Well-known Jewish liberal based in Charlotte, North Carolina, Golden was publisher of the *Carolina Israelite* and author of several books, including *Only in America*.
†Monroe, North Carolina case involving two young black boys, age 7 and 9, who were tried and sentenced to reform school after one of them kissed or was kissed by a white female playmate. Largely through the efforts of Robert Williams, the case generated protests from around the world, and the boys were soon released.

We had dinner at the Williams last night with the Kings . . . We had a pleasant time . . . and lots of discussion but we were all horrified when King said that the Negroes more and more are turning to Dick Nixon, and he is evidently very strongly tempted. Nixon calls him over long distance for his advice, he invites him to his home, he is making every effort possible to get him on his side, and he says that while he has some doubts of Nixon, still he is the ONLY candidate that does these things, and naturally they do have some effect. I think on the Democratic side, he is very much drawn to Stevenson but apparently Stevenson does not know he exists. As far as Lyndon is concerned he is simply out as far as the Negroes are concerned. I think King is a very bright guy and since I know him better I like him better but also I think he has developed a great deal and gotten rid of a lot of that belief in exhortation alone to do anything.

December 11, 1959
Dearest Dec: . . .

We had planned to get a new old car in place of the old old Jeep, and drive up to Lucy's for Christmas with the grandchildren but have had to forgo it all, which was a terrible disappointment to me as I did so long to go. The Williams are all gone until after January 1st and Mrs. Lobman, my dear friend, is still quite ill and very depressed and I hate vacations in Montgomery as I always want and expect to be gay and I am not one single bit. We are still as unpopular as ever, maybe more so, and since I think we are so attractive I keep fretting over it! I can never understand how far I have strayed from the path I was brought up on, but here the old and dear friends make no pretense of keeping up the old lang syne as they seem to do to you in England. But if you lived there no doubt it would be different. I really shouldn't mind and I am sure I would not if there were any other group for me to affiliate with, but there isn't and while it is easy enough to say "there are the Negroes" in actual fact they too are quite inaccessible as they have millions of clubs and parties and sororities and so on, and in this kind of society it is almost impossible to have a really normal friendship. We can have some friendships with them and do, but none of the normal casual give and take. If I were not such a gregarious person, I would not mind the loneliness so much, but since I am I do mind it very much. Anne Braden has been here recently and she is a perfect darling and I love her and I think she is a very good writer too. After she was gone, the Attorney General came out with a huge warning to all of the people of Alabama to beware of her as she was so dangerous and would bite . . .

February 8, 1960
Dearest Dec: . . .

Old Lyndon Johnson has again appeared on the scene. He is running as hard as can be for President as you know, and while says he is not, I am sure he is. Aubrey Williams is just back from up there and says he overwhelmed him with his cordiality. He needs some liberal support I suppose. I don't think Lyndon is any great tower of strength and principle, but I certainly prefer him to Kennedy. And of course to Nixon. I think he is a scoundrel of the deepest dye. I don't like the kind of phony liberals like Humphrey and even Adlai never appealed to me, perhaps because Ken Galbraith and Little Arthur [Schlesinger] were his brain trust, but in any case, Lyndon is looking for liberal support . . . I can think of others I would prefer but if the choice comes to Lyndon or Nixon, I am for Lyndon 1000 per cent, and I am for Lyndon over Kennedy, as I really dread the powers behind him . . . What do you think of the political scene or do you avoid thinking about it? It was odd to see the Anti-Poll Tax finally sail through as a Constitutional Amendment, but whether it will amount to anything I don't know, but at least it is already just about gone, and that is one thing that I can say I helped get rid of.

The sit-in movement, which began in Greensboro, North Carolina, on February 1, 1960, came to the Deep South on February 25, when 35 black students from Alabama State College tried to get service at the snack bar in the Montgomery County courthouse. The deputy sheriff evicted the protesters and the state board of education expelled nine of the students involved in the sit-in, and placed the rest on probation. Hundreds of blacks gathered at Dexter Avenue Baptist Church, King's former church, to protest the expulsions. When they set out to march on the nearby state capital for a prayer vigil, they were met by an angry mob of five thousand whites, along with hundreds of police. Volunteer deputies on horseback drove the black marchers back to the church. A bloody riot was barely averted.

March 7, 1960
Dearest Clark: . . .

The disturbance on yesterday afternoon was all cooked up. Negroes have held several prayer meetings on the lawn of the Capitol and there was no disturbance, but the Police were determined to make it a big issue, so they deputized hundreds of men, had a big horse brigade and simply drew a cordon around the Capitol, and of course attracted a crowd of white people of some thousands, the worst kind of KKK people who screamed and yelled the most obscene remarks . . . When the Negroes started their march to the Capitol, the police threw them back bodily, and then when the white mob started after them, they did throw them back too, so no one was hurt, but it was a pretty tense situation to say the least. Tilla and her current Air Force beau were there and they said it was awful.

There was a young Italian novelist in town that Carl Marzani* had sent on to us, and he went and was simply horrified and sickened by it. Said he had never seen a mob so full of hate and spite and contempt. And as he had been saying in the most doctrinaire manner the night before, that the Negroes, to win their struggle, had to find allies among the poor whites, and that they were their natural allies, and so on, I was glad for him to find out the truth of the situation and come down off of his cloud. He was very charming, and yet to communicate with him was very difficult, as he had so little real knowledge of the South or of the race problem. He learned fast in the two days he was here.

March 1960
Dearest Clark: . . .

The situation here is still like a powder keg. The "white folks" have showed they are not going to tolerate any foolishness and people are scared to death of these "deputies" who have been sworn in and their big horses. I think the *U.S. News and World Report* gives a pretty good picture of the way the white people are not planning to give an inch and the Negroes realize that if they do continue their demonstrations, it will be

---

*Progressive political activist and partner in Marzani and Munsell, New York–based publisher.

at the risk of their lives. You never saw such unanimity in your life as there seems to be in the white community, although privately some dissent, but not many. I see nothing ahead but violence and more violence, all over the South. Maybe all over the country too. Lots of the students have left the college, but the Negro community is badly split on this demonstration and the College and the Faculty have joined in the denunciations of the students. They want to keep their jobs of course. We had a meeting or at least a tea party of our few white ladies the other afternoon and we were like some little band of early Christians meeting in the catacombs, all of us scared to death. I wish we were as brave as the early Christians and did not mind being thrown to the lions, but we do . . .

This is the craziest town, Tilla went to another one of these Field parties the other night and here in the midst of all the terror and fury and screaming and hollering, here were Negro and white airmen eating and drinking and dancing in the same room. Did you see where the Negro Airman got arrested at the bus station and resisted the officer and told him, "You God-damned sons of bitches think you can do anything to a colored man," and then they had a scuffle and the policeman's gun dropped and the Airman picked it up and fired and the policeman went and got another and now the Airman is in jail on a charge of attempted murder. So far he has not even gotten bail. This has not been played up in the papers but everyone knows about it. The Negro airman was trying to call his Commanding Officer when they arrested him. I will send you any clippings on this that I can find. As I have said all along, this is where I have always thought the real violence was coming from. I hear from one of the Air Force wives that there is some consideration of a plan to take all of the Negro airmen out of the South, and not send any more in . . .

Aubrey will be up the end of the month for a SCEF party at which Hubert Delany* is to be master of ceremonies, I believe, and Mrs. Roosevelt is going to talk. I wish Delany could find out about this Negro airman that is in jail, we haven't been able to find out a thing.

---

*Native North Carolinian and progressive black lawyer, Delany served as a city court judge in New York and was a member of the boards of the ECLC and the NAACP.

March 21, 1960
Dear Clark: . . .

Fred Gray did take the case of the Negro airman and it has gone over to the Grand Jury. I think a direct approach from Delany to Gray is the best. I think Delany has their confidence. I am surprised about the King connection because King is so anti-red and so tied in with [A. J.] Muste and with Bayard Rustin and the pacifists and so on, and since Delany is not only connected with ECLC but also with SCEF, I thought he might have been suspect too. From here I cannot know all of the various fights among the various groups but I do know that the NAACP and the Christian Leadership Conference are not very friendly and in spite of its limitations, I think the [S]CLC is doing more in the South now than the NAACP, probably because of the fact the NAACP is under such handicaps but also because they [SCLC] are closer to the mass of the Negroes through their churches. But the Negro movement down here is a nationalist movement, and they are fighting for a place in the society as it is, and the leadership is in definitely middle-class hands. But by the very nature of their struggle, they are being extremely progressive as they are breaking up the Solid South which has served as a dead weight and anchor for our political system. I have never felt much confidence in Delany's judgment since that awful night at Corliss Lamont's right after [the *Brown* decision] when Delany read me a long lecture over my "defeatist" attitude, when I was just out of the frying pan and knew how hot the fire was. He said at that time that he felt sure the South would "welcome" the decision. Well, let bygones be bygones but he knows differently now.

Virginia met Anne Braden in 1955; their friendship deepened after Anne and her husband, Carl Braden, became field workers for SCEF in 1957. Though Anne was 20 years younger than Virginia, the two women shared much in common. Anne McCarty grew up in Anniston, Alabama, a child of white Southern privilege. After graduating from Randolph-Macon Women's College in Virginia, she worked as a journalist for her hometown paper before moving on to Birmingham and finally Louisville. Anne's experience covering the courthouse in Birmingham for the *Birmingham News* exposed her to the routine racial injustice embedded in the legal system, and this, more than anything else, she recalled, "made a radical of me." Her political transformation culminated in Louisville, where she met

Carl Braden, a labor reporter for the *Louisville Courier Journal* and a long-time labor activist; they married in 1948. The Bradens supported Henry Wallace's campaign for president and worked for labor, civil liberties, and civil rights causes. Increasingly, their activities focused on the desegregation movement. In 1954, they fronted for a black couple to buy a home in an all-white neighborhood in Louisville, an episode that led to Carl Braden's trial and conviction on charges of sedition and a sentence of 15 years in prison. His conviction was overturned in 1956.

Like Cliff and Virginia, Anne endured the pain of alienation from her immediate family, particularly her parents, whom she loved deeply. Their disappointment and disapproval was unyielding. She was drawn to the story of the librarian Juliette Morgan, recognizing aspects of her own life and circumstances in Morgan's struggle to break free, and imagining what her own fate would have been if she had remained in Anniston, Alabama. Anne wrote an article about Morgan that was published in the *Southern Patriot*.[31]

In the following series of letters Virginia responds to Anne's interest in Juliette Morgan and discusses the possibility of writing a larger work on white Southern women. These undated letters were written between March and April 1960. In the first, Virginia writes about the nature of their friendship, worrying that she might have tested their relationship in her efforts to mediate a dispute between Carl Braden and Clark Foreman.

n.d. [spring 1960]
Dearest Anne: . . .

I feel very badly that you don't think I like Carl, when as a matter of fact I love Carl . . .

You know, my darling Anne, I sometimes fear that I will do with you what I have done with other people and regretted it, get too intimate, be too truthful, try too hard to reach an understanding and in so doing tear the fabric of our friendship.

This overpowering need I have to reach a basic understanding and intimacy with someone, to be able to speak the truth as I see it, is perhaps a sign of weakness. But, as you have said to me, all of the natural outlets we might have had, old friends, family, relatives, etc., have been cut off from us, and all that remains to us in the way of female companionship and intimacy must necessarily be with people whom we have come to know later in life, and the friendship is based on a compatibility of views and a common approach.

No matter how much a woman may love her husband . . . I think a woman needs another woman as a close confidant and friend. But there are so few women I can confide in or who would even know what I was talking about and have any sympathy or understanding of it. We do come from very similar backgrounds, we do have very similar outlooks. You are younger . . . but I think we both have a feeling, a deep and passionate compulsion, to help the people of the South and most particularly the white women of the South, whose lives have been so starved and twisted by the kind of life they have had to lead. I know how painful it is to have your own mother so full of fears and . . . terror . . . and frustration, as it was to me to have my mother and my sister in the same situation. Of course this sense of fear and terror and frustration and futility is what I call the despair I have to fight against . . . That is why I have so hoped that you or I or we together could write about Juliette [Morgan], as she is such a perfect example of what I am writing about and tried so hard to free herself and failed, but I think you have succeeded and I have succeeded only partially.

Lots of love, I am going to send this off before I wish I hadn't said it. Va.

n.d. [spring 1960]
Dearest Anne:

I think you did a lovely and graceful account of [Juliette] and . . . I don't think it needs any additions.

As for the fact of her death, or suicide, as I am convinced that was it, I think it would be cruel and awful to mention it, especially in this little piece and if you do you will probably have a suit on your hands . . . No one has ever said openly that Juliette killed herself, it is one of those things in a Southern town that everyone knows and talks about, but I am sure it is not on the death certificate, and I certainly would not go probing around about that. In fact I don't think it is important exactly how she died, she wanted to die, and she would have died some way, by sleeping pills or otherwise because she wanted to die.

I think you have to realize that you have a much deeper task than just Juliette to write about when you write about Southern women. The death wish is strong in many of them and rightly so because they have been so shut off from life. I don't just mean sex frustration, although that is part of it, but I mean just as the Negroes have been barred from life or they have tried to bar them, so have the women been barred from life so often, or the life they have been offered has been nothing but cotton candy. But even women like us who have been saved by events (and our own efforts . . . too) and by having married MEN and not weaklings, still and all we too suffer from a sense of guilt, as we have caused so many people pain and also we have suffered so much hostility from our family and early friends, so we too have problems, although I thank God every night that I was saved from abysmal ignorance and at least I see a glimmer of light amid the encircling gloom . . .

Kind thoughts and warm love for you . . . You are trying to rescue Juliette from oblivion and will probably succeed.

n.d. [spring 1960]
Dear Anne:

Of course you are right, the non-smiling [picture] is . . . the best, but actually neither of them look like her or rather neither of them express her, but then I am not sure I have ever seen a picture that did. Juliette lived two lives, and tried so hard to keep her real self, her deep and feeling self under cover, and had this bright chatty surface . . . I will always remember with such sorrow . . . when she called one morning from a pay station and someone had just come into the Library and announced that they would no longer patronize it because Juliette worked there. She was so distressed and weeping and all I could do was try and encourage her and tell her not to mind so much and so on, but for all of that I should have rushed to her as she was so distressed that she felt she simply could not go back and face it. I often try and think what I would be and do if it were not for Cliff and Aubrey and the fact that I have someone daily to agree with and to stand by me and agree with me. It is hard with just a few people to stand against the tide but it is awful when you are alone in this seething mass of disagreement. She was so cut off from the Negroes too who might have given her some strength as she was too afraid to associate with them.

When we or you write the longer . . . piece it . . . should [emphasize] the fact that the Southern White Woman . . . suffers more or certainly as much under segregation as the Negro . . . I think Lillian Smith did something of this in *Killers of the Dream* but she did not go beyond the Freudian approach, and that is only part of it, but a big part . . .

Lots of love Dear Anne . . . I thank God for you and your insight and sensitivity and I do think if anyone could, you can understand Juliette and in understanding her, you can understand the vast host of silent suffering women who have lived and died in the South and never dared to be themselves or do what they think is right . . .

March 24, 1960
Dearest Dec: . . .

If I could ever understand this society down here, I would have a rational explanation of irrationality, and also I would understand myself. I don't know when I rebelled against the irrationality of my environment and my life, but like you it was early and since then I have had to go back into it and live in it and be worst of all dependent on it and been rejected by it and made miserable by it and so to live and endure it, I have to try and find some really reasonable explanation of it. It is not all economics by any means, it is all kinds of things, prestige and sex and religion and sin and status and ignorance and fear and while economics may be the foundation of the house, the house itself is made up of a million different rooms . . .

I do agree that there is hope among the young. Of course it is hard for me to consider you not among the young yourself but I realize that anyone over 25 they consider old or middle-aged. The student strikes are terrific and I am thrilled over them, but the grim, hard and horrible preparations for fighting down here are horrifying as you can see by the enclosed. We had three young men from Yale the other night for dinner, they represented the *Yale Daily News* and were attractive and smart but they thought it was more of a lark, they did not see the awful implications of violence and a sort of fascist terror that is shaping up here at all.

Do come South and see the wonderful rise of spirit, you would love it. I mean in the Negroes, certainly the white people here are more scared than ever and rightly so.

On March 21, 1960, South African police fired upon a group of demonstrators protesting the pass laws in the black township of Sharpeville. Ten children were among the 69 people killed in the Sharpeville massacre. Virginia feared that the situation in the South, too, could easily dissolve into bloodshed and massive violence.

April 7, 1960
Dear Clark: . . .

I too think this deceptive "Isn't it wonderful about the Negro young people, isn't Martin Luther King marvelous" is simply a lack of wanting to do anything themselves. It is what nearly drove me nuts when I tried to speak in New York.

I think the main thing to concentrate on is the connection between the Southern Racists and the Republicans as here to my mind is the heart of the "conspiracy" and no one has brought it clearly into light but I know it is there. Carey [McWilliams]* told Aubrey that Dan Wakefield was coming down to do a story for the *Nation* and I wish he would concentrate on that. It is the heart of the matter. Not the sit-ins nor the Negroes but the hard cold fact that the Southern racists are supported by the Big Money in spite of what they say up there. That is what makes them so arrogant, they know it down here. They are all for Nixon or Kennedy and they are just about the same. Kennedy got the Republican votes in Wisconsin as well as the Catholic votes. When you get the Catholic Church, the Military and the Big Money all together you really have power, and why people cannot see where we are heading is more than I can imagine.

Things here are going from bad to worse. The feeling is just almost as bad as South Africa and I simply cannot see any peaceful solution of it anymore. The police and the political powers are not going to give an inch and the Negroes are not going to back down and I think it will finally have to come to fighting or some kind of violence although I hope not. We have to live in our ordinary contacts with this worst kind of dead silence and it is like living with a weight on top of you, it is so frustrating but you have heard all of this before.

Jessica Mitford's memoir, *Daughters and Rebels,* was published to enthusiastic reviews, launching her on a highly successful career as a writer

---

*Editor of the *Nation.*

and lecturer. Mitford considered writing her next book on the South, an idea that delighted Virginia.

In the following letter, Virginia reports on a case that would engage Cliff for the next four years. It involved a group of students from MacMurray College in Jacksonville, Illinois, who had come south with their sociology professor, Robert Nesmith, and his wife and daughter to research the non-violent movement. The group was arrested while having lunch with several black members of the Montgomery Improvement Association at the Regal Café, a black-owned restaurant. The city ordinance forbidding blacks and whites from dining together had recently been repealed. They were arrested for disturbing the peace.

n.d. [ca. May 1960]
Dearest Dec:

You did preserve a long silence and I was wondering if anything was happening to you.

The reviews are SIMPLY THRILLING! I really was so delighted and am so proud of you. Of course we thought the book was awfully good . . . and I am so pleased that strangers like it too. I think you have found your true vocation—writing and the book on the South sounds like a wonderful idea. You can say all of the things I don't dare to say, but be sure you read something other than Tennessee Williams and Faulkner before you come. If you are serious about it, I will send you a list to prepare you. Actually, I think you would have a great success, just get some real pretty clothes, and stress the British accent and drop the names of your high connections and you will have no trouble with the "aristocracy," they will simply eat you up. You know how the Southerners love "aristocracy." I can give you introductions galore to "liberals" and to Negroes, but my connections with the "aristocracy" are pretty weak by now, rather tremulous. I think it would be really awfully worthwhile too, as the South has been pawed over so and no one seems to ever get at the real basic facts, like the northern Yankee corporations connections, the fact that most industry in the South is owned in the North, that we are really a colonial country . . .

Cliff's case is one that dropped in our lap out of the Blue. The phone rang and it was a lawyer in Jacksonville, Illinois and he asked Cliff to go and get twelve young white students from MacMurray College (a devout and respectable Methodist College—white) out of jail. So we hot-footed it out to the jail and found these twelve students and a professor and his wife. They were a sociology class that was being taken on a field trip by the professor and the wife came along to chaperone. They all camped out as they were doing the trip on $40.00. The professor and his wife had their 2½-year-old baby with them, and they had taken the baby away from them when they arrested them and put her in the Juvenile Court! They had written to a number of people here for interviews, Negroes and whites and they had no idea of sitting-in or making any demonstration or doing anything out of the way at all. While they were talking to the Negroes at the Montgomery Improvement Association, lunch time came and the Negroes told them that the ordinances against eating together had been repealed and so they all went to a Negro café and one of the police informers saw them all going in, and he called the police and the squad cars came. The highway patrol came, even a fire engine came. (They shut up the café as a public nuisance and a fire hazard after this episode.) Naturally, by the time all of this commotion went on, there was a crowd of people and so then the police arrested them all for "causing a riot." All the time the crowd was gathering to see what was happening, the people were quietly eating inside and never knew anything was happening until they burst in and arrested them all.

Well, Cliff represented them before the Judge the next morning and they were all found guilty and so were the Negroes they were eating with, and so they all (white and Negro) decided to appeal and the case will be heard on May 9th. Cliff has so far gotten $250 out of it and nasty publicity, nasty editorials, ("unorthodox, unrepresentative, not a true son of the South," etc.). Of course I am so pleased he did it and it is wonderful for him to be getting it all, so no one can say I am all to blame. He seemed to enjoy it immensely and never paused to think whether to take it or not, although I am sure the family does not approve, as THEY HAVE NEVER SAID ONE WORD ABOUT IT, NEVER MENTIONED IT IN SPITE OF THE HEADLINES AND THE EDITORIALS. I am sure you know that dead and disapproving silence. Of course the thing about Cliff is that he has never wanted to lose the approval of his family as he loves them dearly, and it pains him terribly when they disapprove of him, but in this case he simply went right ahead and got mad and finally did what he thought he ought to do. I don't know what the result will be. We may lose the family business which has kept us going, although barely, but it certainly saw us through some pretty bad times, and without it I don't know what we would have done. But whatever the results of taking the case, I am delighted he did. . . .

The ACLU is in on the case but they don't pay any lawyer's fees. I can't see what help they are when they wouldn't pay either the bonds or the lawyer's fees and Cliff had to get up cash bonds for them all, and his fee is in doubt to put it mildly as they say they are trying to "beg" around the Campus for it. He hates to be begged for, but the ACLU writes that they never in any circumstances pay lawyers' fees. Just like these DAMyankees, they are so self-righteous but never try to help you live.

May 4, 1960
Dear Lyndon,

Thanks for your two letters. While I sometimes wonder if I am not getting "Bedbug Letter #3" still at the same time, with all you have to do, I think you are sweet to write at all.

I was simply thrilled seeing Bird's picture in *Time* magazine and to know she is speaking out for you. Of course I have always thought . . . that Bird is your secret weapon. She can certainly help you with women . . . Southern womanhood really has something when they are like Bird and my sister was. Of course I am meaner than they are! Not sweet at all, and I am mad now at the way the Yankees are brushing you off simply because you are a "Southerner."

Lyndon, can't you get someone to do some research for you and show how the Republicans and the Yankees have tricked and gulled and used the Negro vote since 1876 to keep themselves in control? Do you know C. Vann Woodward who is the Professor of History at Johns Hopkins University? He is from Arkansas and he is brilliant and he is nice too, and he knows everything about the South . . . The race issue is getting to be the big moral issue of the Campaign and that slimy Nixon calls up Martin Luther King and asks his advice and puts on such a big act when he is a perfect scoundrel as you well know, and would sell them down the river the minute it was to his advantage. We have a dangerous foe. But to break through that blind prejudice against "Southerners." We have got to do it . . .

Well, send along "Bedbug Letter #4" so I will know you got mine. Lots of love to Bird and tell her I am proud of her.

LBJ responded: "If you ever get a 'Bedbug Letter' from me it will only be because somebody has slipped up and hasn't given you the A No. 1 treatment to which you are entitled." He said how much he appreciated her letters and her concern for him and what he was doing, and expressed confidence that "the issue of people living together is far too big to be kept in a political straightjacket indefinitely."[32]

May 25, 1960
Dear Lyndon:

I hope you will have time to read the enclosed clippings about you, one about Aubrey and one about a young man who I think speaks for the rising group of Young Southerners who are tired of always being on the defensive and feeling abused. That is one reason I hope so much you get nominated and elected, I think it would do more than anything to remove this awful Southern inferiority complex.

But I do get worried over the Negro's unbending opposition to your candidacy, but as you can see from the enclosed they are bound to equate the Democratic Party with "White Supremacy" at least here in Alabama certainly, and in most of the South as well. If you have to make some decisive move to convince them you are not their enemy, I hope you will try and remove the disabilities on the Armed Services. I think the bill Powell* introduced . . . to make it a Federal offense to discriminate or segregate any member of the U.S. Armed Forces *in uniform* would make it plain that you do not expect Negroes to die for their country segregated. I simply cannot see how anybody could fight against a bill like that when the very uniform of the United States Armed services is being humiliated

---

*Adam Clayton Powell, Democratic congressman from New York.

as well as its wearer, and I can tell you that the effect on the foreign officers who see it happening does not make friends for us to put it mildly, and God knows we need friends now.

Virginia looked forward to the wedding of Shelagh Foreman, Clark and Mairi's daughter, in New York on June 2.

May 4, 1960
Dearest Dec:

I am thrilled you are coming to the wedding, and I am bending every effort, elbows and fingers in order to come too, and I believe I can make it . . .

Cliff is just back from his circuit riding and found Yale, Princeton, Rutgers, and Sarah Lawrence all very delightful, and he thinks the young people are really waking up, not just the Southern Negroes, but all of the young people he ran into seemed to be on the ball, and he was delighted and very much cheered and heartened.

I can hardly wait to see you in New York. I will write more.

The unpleasant encounter Virginia alludes to in the following letter related to an exchange she had with Joan Baez, a close friend of Hugh "Geno" Foreman, who often stayed with Clark and Mairi when she was in New York. Baez sang at Shelagh Foreman's wedding. The episode was triggered when Virginia asked one of the young men in Geno's group of friends if he would go to the store and get her a pack of cigarettes. Hearing Virginia's Southern accent, Baez asked brusquely if she thought she could order them around just like she ordered black people around in the South. Virginia took offense and in the exchange that followed let Baez know what she thought about her skimpy attire and bare feet.[33]

June 20, 1960
Dearest Mairi and Clark:

We just got home and the first thing I want to do is to write and tell you what a wonderful time I had at the wedding and what a lovely and joyous occasion it was . . .

I am sorry I was so rude to the young, but they got the pent-up hostility of the whole winter which I have tried so hard not to show and was really much deeper than I had even realized. But the fire was certainly misdirected and I am particularly sorry I was so horrid to dear Hugh who has always been my devoted and warm friend as I have been his. I still think these personal rebellions have very little sense in this day of danger and change and it is hard for me to be sympathetic with them when I see the Negro young people risking their jobs and lives and futures to fight for a cause, but certainly it does no good to be so hostile to them and drive them completely away. If they were rebelling for a cause, I would be sympathetic but as it is they only seem to be rebelling, and I never can find out what for.

I had a long visit with Ann and the new baby after I got back to Harrisburg and Lucy and her baby came home with me and we are enjoying her so much. Sheldon will be down the beginning of July.

June 20, 1960
Dear Hugo: . . .

It is funny to get back to Alabama and find all of the violent segregationists for Kennedy and the "moderates" all for Lyndon, whereas in the North all of the "Liberals" were for Kennedy and acted as if Lyndon was Simon Legree himself. I don't think they are very smart up there! Jim Folsom is going out to the convention to work for Lyndon and I hope he can counteract [Jim] Patterson to some degree.

June 27, 1960
Dearest Dec: . . .

The main thing I am not sure you realize about Marge, and perhaps about me, is that we did not have behind us the "remarkable self-confidence" that you and Esmond had. Whatever the sins of your environment, doubt and despair and lack of self-confidence and fear of hostility did not enter into it. We came from the "decadent South" while you came from a society which was still powerful even if anachronistic, and one you could rebel against without pity, while here we have a terrible time rebelling against people whom we both love and feel sorry for, as they are so full of weakness and often despair and are pitiful as well as hateful . . .

The very essence of the Southern attitude [is] this strong desire to be liked and admired, which degenerates into the kind of "Oh! Darling, how lovely you look, what an adorable hat, etc., etc." and which is a mutual defense against self-doubt and despair. I do not think you can understand the South unless you realize it is or was a defeated nation and defeat and despair and poverty and pride (false pride) have been its main characteristics. Do read [Wilbur J.] Cash's *The Mind of the South* before you even think of coming down here to write about it. Actually, the Boers in South Africa have this same kind of deep despair and self-doubt and need for superiority, they too were defeated, so did the Germans and I have often thought that it was the spirit of the triumphant underdog that appealed to Unity,* who must have had a pretty rough time of it actually, so big and awkward and unpopular. This is why I am so fearful of the South, that they will go fascist and whole hog and become the very cesspool of the country, just because there is here that awful self-doubt and weakness and despair. I think Tennessee Williams and Faulkner, with real and true artistic instinct, see and write about the rot here, but never take it beyond the private and the personal. But this same rot is spreading all over the country, or so it seems to me, a real sort of cancer, which is very dangerous. Things may look better out on the Pacific Coast . . . but from here I do not see anything very cheerful in the way of a bright future.

Here again, I am no doubt demonstrating the Southern sense of despair and hopelessness. I do have hope but it is a very long-range affair. I think a book on the South could be good only as a beginning of a book on America and I do think you could do it.

Also try and get *The Making of a Southerner* by Katharine Lumpkin. Old, old book but still very good. Your book will have to be a warning against fascism and a revelation of the already existing rot. The South is not very funny anymore.

June 30, 1960
Dearest Anne:

Dr. Lawrence Reddick got fired for having "Communist" associations and helping the students with their sit-in, and now on the 11th of July, the State Board of Education is meeting again and more of the Faculty

---

*Unity Mitford, Decca's sister, was a Nazi sympathizer in the 1930s.

of Alabama State are expected to be fired. Dr. Trenholm* is meeting all of the demands of the Governor and of the Board, with the rationalization that if he does not, they will close the school down and turn it into a white school and they very well might, but I think he is paying too big a price for keeping it open as he has crawled and crawled and lost the respect of the students and many of the faculty although some of them think he is only trying to keep their jobs for them. But to see the white man's arrogance and his contempt and open desire to humiliate and degrade the Negroes is not a pretty sight. I think what this system has done to most of the white men is more awful than anything else.

I had a fine trip and saw lots of people and spent most of it with grandchildren which was very nice indeed. In my three days in New York, I saw a great variety of people and got both mental and physical indigestion. Except for the race issue, the situation still seems very muddy to me, everyone is for peace but no one seems to have much definite idea about how to go about getting it and everyone is for Civil Liberties but the same thing is true there, no one knows how to get it, although I will give them a thousand per cent for trying. But the whole great mass and horde of people there seem utterly unconcerned about things and the few students picketing Woolworth's was the most encouraging sight I saw up there. Everyone keeps saying it MUST be Stevenson and I don't think he has any chance at all, and I am afraid it will be Kennedy and I much prefer Johnson to him which all north of the Mason-Dixon line think is simply awful but between him and Kennedy I see a great difference.

July 1960
Dear Hugo: . . .

Ed Pepper from Ashland who ran for Public Service Commissioner, got beat on the race issue by Jack Owens and he tried to meet the attack by saying he was going to restore segregation on *interstate carriers* but to no avail and the Black Belters kept on calling him names and the Negroes lost some of their enthusiasm and so he, like so many of the others, fell between two stools and got beat and the real issues which are awfully high rates were all lost in a sea of racism . . .

---

*Dr. H. Councill Trenholm was president of Alabama State College.

Except for the heat, we are well and busy and have pleasant and cool weekends up at the Pea Level. Cliff's fruit trees are coming on nicely and they have decided to plant the whole 365 acres in pine trees as that seems to be the best crop for these parts.

Jim Folsom and Aubrey Williams have gone out to Los Angeles to work for Lyndon and while that is good and it is good that Lyndon wanted them and said he needed their help, at the same time McDonald Gallion, who is the worst racist we have, not even excepting Patterson, is the head of the Johnson for President forces here in Alabama, so it makes a strange and weird combination. I do believe that Lyndon can bring along some of the boys IF he gets nominated and elected but his chances do not look bright from here. If it is Kennedy or Nixon then I think the South will retreat further and further into an iron determination to resist any national influence. Certainly we see no give to speak of as it is now.

The sit-in movement was the first protest since the Montgomery bus boycott to draw sustained media attention South. Nat Hentoff was among the group of journalists who headed to Alabama in 1960 to investigate the racial situation. The article he published in the *New Yorker* on July 16, 1960, was based almost entirely on a conversation he had with Cliff and Virginia. Virginia said she had made it clear to the young reporter that they were speaking to him "off the record" and did not want to be identified in his piece. Hentoff thought he had complied by changing their names to Mr. and Mrs. Winters, but few others in Montgomery fit the description of the couple he described.[34]

July 20, 1960
Dear Mr. Hentoff:

I cannot express strongly enough my surprise and my indignation over your betrayal of our confidence and our privacy. You were received into our home as a friend, you were trusted as a friend and you even call us "friends" in your article, but you have violated every law of friendship and also have behaved journalistically in what seems to me to be a very unethical way.

For the sake of a good story and a good fee, you have left us exposed to the full weight of the wrath of the community. Our telephone has not stopped ringing and we may even be faced with a libel suit. You betrayed personal facts about us that were given to you in confidence and as a background and which we would never in the world have said to anyone other than someone who posed as a trusted friend. You have also attributed remarks to us which you received from other sources.

I am afraid your behavior is rather typical of the Northern hit-and-run liberal who comes South for a few days, interviews those few people who are trying to find some orderly solutions to our problems here, and then goes back to the safety of New York and makes a good story out of them and exposes them to the full blows of their enemies. You have showed no concern whatever for our lives, our livelihood, our friends, our families or our community. You have showed no concern whatever for us as human beings who are vulnerable and who trusted you. I think your total disregard for human consequences is enough to damn any liberalism you may profess.

You also missed entirely the whole point of our story and of why we stay here. We were trying to explain to you the Southern point of view and the pressures on people and the fears they have and the reason why so few speak up and to educate you a little to the realities of life here. But in spite of the difficulties, we told you we stay here because we like the people here, in spite of our disagreements, they are our own people. I will say in all sincerity that we feel in the Southern people some sense of personal loyalty and integrity in personal relations, and we much prefer to trust ourselves to them, rather than to northern "liberals" like yourself who do not hesitate to sacrifice individuals to a "cause" in their own interest. We also prefer to be hit from in front rather than from the rear.

July 22, 1960
Dear Anne:

Your letter has just come and as you know, anytime you can get here, no matter for how short a time, you will be welcome and we do have a crib in case you need one for Beth, but I do hope you can come down for one night at least.

I do envy you the cool breezes and sea air of Little Compton [Rhode Island] as it is simply boiling hot here, humid, heavy and inert. But I am more than boiling over the article in the *New Yorker* of July 16th which has this "interview" with Mr. and Mrs. Winter and daughter of Montgomery. Of course it is us, although the guy came here to see us after he had interviewed lots of other people and said he only wanted to check his information with us. Of course we were absolutely fools to trust him, but actually in the course of the last few years literally dozens and dozens of journalists and writers have come through to see us and he is the first and only one to violate our confidence. He of course promised and swore the conversation was strictly private and he only wanted to get some "background" for his information, and then he goes and writes us up in this completely exposed and shameless way without ever giving us a chance to see it or correct it and of course it has embarrassed us horribly, and the phone has rung and rung and the *Advertiser* was going to do an awful editorial on us and only withdrew it on account of the death of our nephew* (this in itself is what we were trying to tell him about the South and which he missed completely, that there is still some personal responsibility down here if people know you) and even our friends say we were fools and of course in most areas there is that dead and vacuumlike silence, but the thing I hate the most is the picture of us pulling a poor mouth and worried about our or my popularity. Of course lots of the things I said sort of humorously, I thought, and he puts them all down as dead serious. Of course nearly everything he has in there is true, but the whole attitude and writing and point of view is false and we are simply sick over it. I am enclosing the letter I wrote to him which Cliff thought was too violent and which I thought was too restrained. What do you think?

I am sorry your book or our book on Southern Womanhood has to wait as it needs to be done although whether we will ever find time to do it now I don't know. But I really think we need to think hard about it and put into it something more than the background of frustration and helplessness and the few brave and desperate voices that finally break the silence. I think we will have to put into it women like your Mother who took your children to the trial† although she hated everything you were doing, and my mother-in-law, who took us in and gave us bed and board and kept all of us until Cliff was on his feet again, although she too hated everything we did or stood for, particularly me, and she was

---

*Nesbitt Elmore.
†Carl Braden's 1954 trial for sedition in Louisville, Kentucky.

kind to us too. But over and beyond justice and right and ideology and opposing sides, there seems to me is an area of eternal verities which is loyal to people and helps them out in spite of disagreement, and in a world of danger such as we have today, there has to be something to hold on to over and beyond the struggle we are in, something that has eternal value. I am afraid I sound awfully silly and sentimental, but it is a quality you have, that my sister had, and I think Cliff has and one that I want to acquire if I can but I am far from it now. It goes beyond justice to mercy and compassion as the New Testament goes beyond the Old Testament and is the only area large enough to settle the affairs of the world, but they are never settled there or only rarely . . .

Aubrey came back from the Convention tired but not too discouraged. He thinks Johnson may keep Kennedy in line and not let him turn us all over to the Pope, but he seems to have spent most of his time with Frank Wilkinson and Carey McWilliams and also with Bob Kenney and they don't know if who is President is going to decide it all by any means and there is lots of hard work ahead. I think what they do on Linus Pauling is going to be one of the touchstones.* If they send him to jail then we will know that Civil Rights only means equality in a semi-fascist society and I am afraid that is what it is going to mean. There was no mention of CIVIL LIBERTIES in the platform.

ca. August 1, 1960
Dearest Anne:

It was wonderful to hear from you last night and I did appreciate you calling so much. We have been under a severe strain since the *New Yorker* article, as we have had so much criticism and then this editorial last Sunday which I am enclosing. Cliff replied to it and asked them to send a reporter over . . . but so far we have not heard a single word and so I think they will simply ignore it . . . They claim, or at least Hentoff

---

*In June 1960, Linus Pauling, the Nobel Prize-winning chemist, was subpoenaed by the Senate Internal Security Subcommittee to account for a position paper he wrote against nuclear testing and circulated internationally. Pauling refused to cooperate with the committee and risked being jailed for contempt. He was subpoenaed a second time, but was not jailed.

claims, that by using another name he thought he was protecting us, but that is sheer stupidity. The thing I mind most is the SILENCE and I am sure you know what I mean, meeting people who simply say nothing and that is most of them. I really prefer to be cussed out than to deal with the dead shroud of silence. It is hard even for our friends to be sympathetic with us as they think we were so stupid to talk to the man, but actually he is the only one who ever betrayed us this way and we have talked to dozens and dozens . . .

Aubrey and Cliff and I went over to Tuskegee on Monday night to a dinner and Aubrey made a speech. It was Dr. Gomillion's class and they were all graduate students. I never heard Aubrey speak so well or with more feeling. He bore down on the Cold War and the brainwashing of the American people and the lies that were told about Russia and disarmament and the need for people to look behind the news. There was quite a shock in the air at first but I think it went over. Then Cliff made a brief speech on Civil Liberties as opposed to Civil Rights and he too did a magnificent job I thought and ended up with some practical suggestions to political action but on the whole we learned a lot and had a lot of fun. I find most of the Negroes are going to vote for Nixon! They and the worst of the Dixiecrats—a really weird combination, but the same one that put in Eisenhower for two terms. They don't like Nixon especially but they don't like Kennedy at all and they simply hate and can't stand his supporters here like Governor Patterson and Bull Connor. Personally I am in a terrible fix as I know Nixon is a scoundrel and I could not vote for him under any circumstances but I can't stand Kennedy either and don't trust him at all or his family or his brother-in-law or anything about him. Kefauver's election by such a huge majority was good as they broke their backs trying to smear him and used the worst kind of Negro and Jew and Red baiting on him, which he answered by saying he represented ALL of the people and as far as I know never said anything offensive in reply. The fact that he got such a huge vote against such a campaign is very encouraging I think. We must figure out some way to get funds down into the South for the Primary campaigns as that is where it is needed and the reactionaries get lots and lots of money but any fairly good person can't get a dime unless Labor backs them and you know how they have been mostly . . .

Thanks again for calling, it was certainly pleasant to hear a friendly voice on the other end of the line. Give my love to Carl and don't fail to come to see us on the 29th.

On August 6, 1960, Decca wrote to Virginia about several students she had met while collecting information for an article on the students who orchestrated a mass protest against the HUAC hearings that were held in San Francisco the previous May. "As a result of the article we've run across some extremely nice and interesting students, mostly graduates, some English and some from various parts of the U.S. Two of them are going to be in Montgomery some time soon. They are Bob Cassen (English economist) and Tom Hayden, editor of the student paper at the U. of Mich. Tom . . . [is] a very fresh spirit, and I think will be a real doer of deeds. With great trepidation I have given both of them letters to you—trepidation only because of the ghastly *New Yorker* experience."

August 19, 1960
Dear Decca and Bob: . . .

None of the students have appeared so far. I hope they do, as I cannot live thinking some bearded Hentoff is going to betray us to our enemies in everyone who comes, otherwise I would be bored to death . . . Cliff . . . is working hard now on the MacMurray case and I think his brief will be brilliant . . . The case is now headed for the Court of Appeals and we think it will have to go to the U.S. Supreme Court. This "disorderly conduct" charge for "acts tending to provoke a breach of the peace" are the substitutes for the old segregation ordinances and it was under this that the [Fred] Shuttlesworth children were arrested and put in jail when they would not move to the back of the Bus, although it was an *interstate Bus.* Actually Bob, what is happening here is simply this, either the South is brought under the rule of Law and a great and fundamental change takes place here which will affect the whole country, and the political balance of power, or else the South goes on defying the Law and becomes the very core and center of a native fascist movement. I cannot say at this point what the outcome will be, but I know it is people like Cliff and the good Federal Judges and the few people in each community that stand for the law, and of course the power and the thrust of the Negroes, that are the only hope here. If the South fails, if we go into a really lawless state, then I think it will have a very crucial and bad effect on the rest of the country.

The most hopeful thing is Estes Kefauver's victory. He won overwhelmingly over a real stinker, anti-Negro, anti-Semite, anti-human race actually, and when Estes got the goods on him that he was also anti-TVA, he got beat, but at the same time Estes stood for the Civil Rights Bill, for the right of Negroes to vote and did no race baiting and stood on his record which is pretty good and he won a tremendous victory. Of course there is an enormous vote in Tennessee, as they got rid of the Poll Tax a number of years ago (that was our first great victory). But the thing is that the Democratic Party will send in no money in a Democratic Primary contest, so even if a good guy like Estes is running against a perfect stinker who is financed by all of the Texas bad guys (Nixonites), still the Democratic Party does not help him and he has to raise his own campaign funds. This is stupid and silly of course, but it makes it awfully hard for any good guy in the South to win. I think in Estes' case that the Roosevelt, Lehman, faction in New York helped him out, but this is private information. But this is the place for the reform forces to start. In the Democratic primaries in the South.

It is such a joy to write to you . . . as I can say what I really think and that is a rare privilege indeed.

Christopher Bacon and Robert Cassen, young Englishmen sent by Decca, turned up at the Durrs with federal agents on their trail. Both were Harkness Commonwealth Fellows, studying at the University of California at Berkeley. As part of their fellowship, Harkness Fellows were given a car to take a grand tour of the United States. While in San Francisco, Bacon, a political science student, had gone to City Hall to witness the HUAC hearings, and was among the 64 students arrested. He was later released without charge. But as Bacon and Cassen made their way across the South to Alabama, they noticed somewhere around Mobile that they were being followed. They later found out, according to Cassen, that agents from the U.S. Justice Department were following them because of Bacon's arrest in San Francisco. Even though this brought unwelcome police attention, Virginia was grateful for the contact with the young visitors. Bacon and Cassen were the first in a long line of Harkness Fellows to visit Alabama. They passed along the Durrs' name, and soon Montgomery became a routine stop for Harkness Fellows.[35]

The letter refers to the increasingly volatile situation in the South. Four days earlier, after Klansmen and White Citizens Council members wielding axe handles attacked peaceful black demonstrators in Jacksonville, Florida, young black men retaliated.

August 31, 1960
Dearest Dec:

I suppose Chris has left by now and you know all the grim story of the chase. When they called up last Tuesday night from Danny's Diner and said they were being followed, we thought it was one of the usual neuroses of people coming to the South, but when they came in with THREE cars trailing them, we realized it was not a fantasy! It was incredible, these charming, handsome young and bright people, being shadowed and watched as though they were the worst sort of criminals. The hounds that were on their trail never moved, how they ate, slept and went to the bathroom will ever remain a puzzle. The three cars were parked about the house the whole time, and every time anyone went in or out they gunned up and got in position for the chase. There were lots of amusing incidents, but the total score is pretty grim. The Police told one of the newspaper men that it was the Un-American Com. people and another said it was the FBI and another the Immigration so it was probably all three with the CIA thrown in for good measure.

I am sorry it happened of course, it adds one more black mark to our already black reputation. The Police told the newspaper man that they were watching "those people at the Durrs" and since we are already in so bad with the Police as Cliff has had so many cases of police brutality and has fought them so, I am sure they took great delight in having all the support from the Federal agencies. What a state we live in!

But don't feel badly about sending them on to us as we would die of dry rot unless we occasionally came in touch with the hopeful and bright young people, so full of confidence and hope and so determined to bring about a better more peaceful world. I suppose we will survive here as we have survived for these ten years, but it does get harder all the time and sometimes I simply feel I will have to get out or bust! Of course the fact is that things are tightening up terribly here with the sit-ins and so on and now with the rioting in Jacksonville it will get so much worse. But I am positive that the Negroes are not going to turn back, they have had too much success and their spirit is too good, but I am very much afraid that there is going to be a lot of violence. It is shocking to see the spirit that is universal. Last night the renting agency sent two men over to take measurements about papering some rooms in the apartment and both of them were simply fierce and talked about how they had shotguns, pistols and the "first nigger that comes up my walk and asks to marry my daughter will get it just between the eyes" (I think they would have said between the legs except we were "ladies"). I simply could not take it and argued with them and found at bottom they were poor men, paid half of the union wage, frustrated, all their lives they have heard the boss men say, "All right, if you don't like what I am paying you, I can get a nigger to do it for half the money," but instead of realizing it is the boss man who is grinding them down, they turn their hatred toward the Negro . . .

Do tell me all you heard, read and were told by Chris as I am longing to hear the end of the story and of the chase.

September 13, 1960
Dear Dec:

I hope the article is over and you are free to correspond . . .

I am glad you think the kids are going to get "this thing licked." I wished I could share that faith. I admit that the Negro kids here have been magnificent but certainly the white ones have shown no awareness except in the most minute fragments. So many of them have a sort of mindless brutality that frightens me, crew hair cuts, fast cars, and absolutely no regard for anyone on earth except themselves. The way they drive and the way they eat and the mess they make and the completely mindless quality they have is awful . . .

Here we hear nothing but the Baptists and the Methodists roaring against the "Church of Rome." It looks from here as if Lyndon might even get beat as Senator in Texas for joining with the Pope. The Negroes are for Nixon on account of the awful speeches the local Democrats make "Vote for the Democratic Party so our boys will keep on as heads of Committees and can keep the Civil Rights Bills from passing." So you have this crazy combination of the big business men, the poor whites, and middle class

Protestants and the Negroes. The papers are all for Nixon too, so it is hard to see who is for Kennedy and Johnson right now. They are both so bad I can't get very much excited over either although Nixon is such a real scoundrel that I could not vote for him. I suppose I will vote for Kennedy but with no enthusiasm. What are you going to do?

An encounter between a visiting officer from the Ethiopian Air Force and a Montgomery police officer illustrated the insanity of the city's policy that attempted to distinguish between Africans and American blacks, as described in the following letter. Virginia also responds to Decca's plea that she begin working on her autobiography. She wrote on October 6, 1960: "Honestly, Virginia, you must settle down to writing your autobiography, now's the time. I feel you have no idea of the enormous extent of your talent for writing. Just write the whole thing as though it were a letter, it would just be terrific."

October 11, 1960
Dearest Dec: . . .
At Maxwell Field where the Air University is they have all of the Air Officers of the "Free World" come to be trained, and among them was an Ethiopian, who was head of the Air Force and also brother to the Ethiopian Ambassador. He was given the usual "Passport to Montgomery" by the local Chamber of Commerce which is the way to identify the foreign officers and which makes them white even if they are black and admits them to movies and cafes and so on. But of course the American Negro officers do not get these passports. So one night the Ethiopian officer went to town with one of the Negro officers and they got arrested for nothing and were booked on a charge of having concealed weapons in the car which turned out to be a hammer to take tires off the rim. The police arrest the Negroes as a measure of intimidation for anything they can think of. Well the Ethiopian got furious and he was pretty roughly handled but finally they let him [go to] . . . the Field and he got his brother the Ambassador and his brother got the State Department and all Hell broke loose and the policeman was hauled on the carpet and his only defense was, "Hell, how do you expect me to tell an Ethiopian from a nigger?!" Well the upshot of it is that we have sent them a lot of new jet airplanes and the Ethiopian told a man I knew at

Maxwell that he was going to get one of them and come back and bomb Alabama. All of this took place shortly before the UN meeting and of course was all written up in the papers over there and naturally the Africans did not think too well of it and of course it played right into K's [Soviet Premier Nikita Khrushchev's] hands. But the thing that is so unbelievable is that you speak to some of the leading military and they pay no attention to the "episode" and say it has no effect on the Africans and that our economic and military aid is all that counts and that there is too much money invested in the Field here to change the officers to some other part of the country and they go merrily down the slope like the Gadarene swine and you stand aghast at the sheer stupidity but there is apparently nothing that can or will be done about it. But absolutely no connection between cause and effect . . .

As for my writing, I don't think I can ever do it. I could send you some snatches from time to time but there are so many obstacles in the way. Time in the first place, as I work in the office from nine to five usually and the nights are full of domesticity and then I am too tired. You might say that the time I spend writing letters might just as well go toward writing something more permanent, but I really don't think I have the time, energy or discipline to do it. Then I lack what you have in such abundance, and that is the courage to tell the truth about people and my life. I still live among them, I have not escaped them as you have and never will. Hugo and Cliff have done a lot of good in this world and I am still tied to them very, very closely although Hugo is so disapproving. To make a clean break as you have and as Anne Braden has is very rare and takes great courage and a husband that also is either outside the citadel or wants to break too as Esmond did. But these people are Cliff's people, he loves them dearly and does not want to make the break now or ever. He bears the lack of money, the lack of fame (lots of infamy though) and the lack of recognition because he loves them and wants to live among them and actually is more comfortable here than anywhere else. It is something beyond justice and right and wrong and good and evil. It is hard for me to understand but it is a quality of embracing people who are doing evil and trying to change them instead of fighting them. Like dealing with the insane and of course that is what the people down here are, insane on the subject of race. I suppose most evil people are insane and the whole new frontier is to find out why they get that way and how to cure them, rather than punish them for being that way. The only complication comes that unless they are stopped from their evil during the time they are being changed or studied, the innocent suffer so, and it is the suffering of the innocent that hurts so and is so painful and so unjust, so it is a very difficult matter to decide what is wrong and what is right to do, and you have to wait until the given situation comes and decide then, but I do think the FIRST consideration should be to protecting the innocent from the evil doers . . . But to change people instead of punishing them takes the kind of patience and forbearance and love that Cliff has and I wish I had but haven't.

Back to my writing my Auto[biography], actually all my life is in my letters . . . I write good letters because I can write freely but when I get to writing for the public all kinds of inhibitions and barriers and fears and terrors arise and I get stiff and stupid . . . I do think your courage is phenomenal especially when I know how often and how bitterly you have missed your family and sisters and the warmth of the cocoon as much as you wanted to escape and be a butterfly.

October 21, 1960
Dearest Dec: . . .

I disagree completely on "sitting this one out" but can't take time to go into it thoroughly. Actually a non-vote is a vote for Nixon, and I do not think as bad as Kennedy is that he is as big a scoundrel as Nixon, although I certainly don't like him and don't like the Catholic Church in politics at all, but Nixon is the chief one who started the domestic witch hunt, and was the heart and soul of the spy hunt and if he gets to be President, we can see one of the biggest and worst in the world, in my opinion. I think he looks like Torquemada exactly, he terrifies me. I think the actual thinking of the left wingers is that with a Democratic Congress and a Republican President, the country will have a divided leadership and will not be as well able to start a War. But I think they do not take into account the forces behind Nixon which are more powerful than the forces behind Kennedy when it comes to war-making. But the mass of the people, the working people—not the owning class, are *in* the Democratic Party and I think the time has come when we must go to the people, not always wait for them to come to us, which they never do. If we believe in things, we have to fight for them where the people *are*, not where we want them to be. I believed in rights for Negroes, and here I am in the midst of the struggle—and while I have to confess it is much worse than I had thought it could be, still I know that what little good I have ever done is much better done here where the struggle *is*, than somewhere else where it is simply discussed.

November 1, 1960
Dearest Dec: . . .

I have not heard anything about the new revolt of Youth in California and I was very much interested. Send me some clippings . . .

Don't think because I believe in voting for Kennedy that I really like him very much as I don't. I just think "sitting it out" is silly and the whole idea of the left wing people of waiting for people to come to them instead of plunging in where the people are and working with them where they are at, is ridiculous and juvenile in my opinion. Paul Sweezy and Leo [Huberman] make me so mad by being so lofty.* All this thing of simply being sure you are right and then thinking people and history are coming around to you is silly, history has to be struggled and fought for and worked for or it can take some awfully bad twists. But Nixon is really too awful, he is so dishonest, his face simply beams with hypocrisy. But Kennedy can be terribly dangerous with South America in such ferment and the Catholic Church standing so firmly against any change. . . . That is why I think people should make a terrific effort to get into and work in the Democratic Party.

Do send me the name and address of your agent. I have written a play of all things and think it is fairly good and this time I want the opinion of a professional and no kind friends.

I cannot imagine why the movie people have not been at you about the book, as I think it would make a perfectly wonderful movie . . . The movies seem to be the only place where you make any money on books. P. D. East who wrote *The Magnolia Jungle* which I think is splendid says he has only sold 4,000 and of course made nothing. Did you ever get *To Kill a Mockingbird?*† I think it is so good even if a little idealized, but aw-

---

*Editors of the *Monthly Review*.
†Harper Lee's novel of race, class, and justice set in depression-era Alabama, published in 1960.

fully true to much of the South. Also Dan Wakefield has a new paper-back called *Revolt of the South* which is published by Grove Press as an Evergreen Book for 95 cents, most of which consists of tales we told him, so see if you recognize us and them.

The court-ordered desegregation of New Orleans public schools began in mid-November 1960 when four black girls entered the first grade at two previously all-white schools. In what John Steinbeck described as a vivid display of "raw hatred," a "screaming, spitting, hysterical" mob of white mothers gathered outside of the schools and shouted obscenities and threats at the children as they entered and left school each day. By the end of the school year, there was one white student remaining in the William J. Frantz Elementary School, and none at McDonough School No. 19.[36]

December 6, 1960
Dear Clark: . . .

I read the Sunday [*New York Times*] and the *Nation* and the *New Republic* and Izzy [Stone] and the *Guardian* and whatever else comes to hand, and I am continually amazed at the wishful thinking on the part of the rest of the country. They hail with delight when one Negro child among hundreds gets into a school, and do not realize nor seem to care that the screaming women in New Orleans are not just a small minority but represent the majority sentiment. It is really shocking and horrifying to think that we have such deprived and depraved and frustrated people here in the South that they would be so full of hatred and spite that they would take it out on four little babies, but it is true. The thing that frightens me is the fact that the majority of Southern white people have been poor and kicked around and looked down on and still are, and they are as full of bile and meanness as sour old clabber. Of course there are exceptions, but I am speaking of the majority as evidenced by the fact that John Patterson in Alabama (my cousin by the way), [S. Ernest] Vandiver in Georgia, [Ross] Barnett in Mississippi, [Jimmie] Davis in Louisiana, [Orval] Faubus in Arkansas . . . really do represent the overwhelming majority of Southern white people. I think we have raised up a breed of real Nazis down here. I think it is the fault of your people and mine, the slave owners and the "good families" who looked down on and snooted the poor whites almost as much as they looked down on the Negroes, and you know it is true. "Poor white trash" was as much a word of scorn as "Nigger" and almost more so. Perhaps I needed the lesson of being looked down on and snooted and snubbed to realize how bad it is. But at least I had enough self-confidence to believe that I was being snubbed and am being snubbed for my beliefs, not my own person. There is nothing so humiliating as to be snubbed because people feel a revulsion for you as a person, and that is what the Negro and the white have had to put up with down here and while the Negro is beginning to discover himself and rise up out of the darkness, the poor white is still neglected and forlorn, nobody does anything for him, no one cares anything about him except Ross Barnett, Patterson, etc. and so he follows them blindly and with love and loyalty. Then too, like Germany, this is a defeated country, we have the memory and the smell of defeat and despair in our blood, and it makes us mean. We had two men from the south end of the County in this morning on a matter concerning some deeds—both white, blond, complete Anglo-Saxon and neither could read or write. It is hard for us to realize how deprived they have been. It seems to me that these are the people that need to be worked with more than any other group and who are having less attention paid to them except by the demagogues.

On November 8, 1960, in one of the closest presidential elections ever, John F. Kennedy won the presidency by a margin of fewer than 120,000 popular votes. Virginia believed that Nixon's failure to win over a significant number of black voters meant that he would now court the "racist vote" more openly.

December 7, 1960
Dearest Decca:

Your letter has just come and I am glad to see that you are developing housewifely traits late in life. I long to see and hear all about the new house. Do try and send me a picture and also a floor plan of it.

I am glad you had the fight with the PTA as the New Orleans business is so awful that unless the rest of the country is shocked by it then I see no success for us down here. I cannot see why even dull, stupid, apathetic housewives would not get aroused over the anger and hatred in those faces, and directed toward four little babies. It seems to me it is exactly the same spirit that caused the Nazis to gas the Jewish children along with their parents . . . As always, the Republican-Southern Democrat coalition is the stronghold of it as it has been for so long. I think Nixon will now proceed to cultivate the racist vote, as he was actually doing all through the campaign, since he did not get the Negro vote, he will not make an effort to get it any more, and will put his pitch here on the racists and the conservatives. I think Nixon is a very dangerous man, and I am not sure about Kennedy at all. If he really bears down on Civil Rights, he can break up the Unholy Alliance but I am not sure he is going to do it. Certainly with the appointment of [Luther] Hodges* it seems he is not, as Hodges is a very, very conservative businessman and in all of North Carolina there are about six Negro children in white schools, and one of them had to leave as she was the only one in a huge high school and the other children made her life miserable by insults, spitting on her, hitting her, etc. that she finally had to leave . . .

The moving picture on the San Francisco riots† is being shown here by Congressman George Grant, the American Legion and the VFW [Veterans of Foreign Wars]. Today and tomorrow it is being shown to the City and County and State employees at closed showings, but tomorrow night it will be shown in the Armory to the public and we certainly are going. I am enclosing the pamphlet that Aubrey has put out for the kids in SF [San Francisco]. He said he could not get anyone to print it. I think it is good and the article in the *Reporter* magazine of November 24 is also quite good. This kind of thing is what I mean when I say I think we really have a strong Fascist movement in this country. I do not say that they will succeed but I think it is and will continue to be a Hell of a fight.

December 13, 1960
Dear Lyndon:

I only hope this letter reaches you before you get in all the hurley burley and you can really pay some attention to it. I will be brief and to the point.

I go on the premise that you and I agree that the Southern system of segregation has to end. I do not think it can all be left to the U.S. Supreme Court with the accompanying demonstrations and resistance and defiance of the law and that Congress *must* act. Since from long and

---

*Governor of North Carolina, 1954–61.
†*Operation Abolition*, a film about the anti-HUAC protests in San Francisco in May 1960, was released by HUAC and distributed by the American Legion and other groups.

painful experience I know how hard it is to act and how dangerous and rough the resistance is, I am suggesting that you use the same way we used to get rid of the Poll Tax, which as you will or should remember was done by getting rid of it for the Armed Services. That was the opening wedge.

I think the same thing could be done in regard to segregation. If a bill could be passed that would make it a federal offense to discriminate or segregate a member of the Armed Services in uniform the system would soon break down. As you know the South gets millions and maybe billions from the Federal government on account of the Air Bases, etc. and they will not want to stand any risk of losing that money. Here in Montgomery we get over 100 million a year form the Air Force and no one wants to give up any part of it. Besides that when Southern people know it is going to pay off to give up their prejudices, they do it very quickly. Here at Maxwell the white people fight to get the jobs and love them as they pay well and have so many benefits. They accept integration on the Bases without any trouble at all. Never a peep out of them. My daughter is now working at the base and there are Negro WAAFs in the office and she says the white people from Montgomery accept them and don't make any kind of fuss at all.

Besides the justice and right of it, the other fact is that when the Allied officers and soldiers come here for training, many of whom are colored, and are subjected to segregation, we lose an ally right that minute. The Ethiopian head of the Air Force was arrested and put in jail and beat up for nothing, and when there was a protest the police said, "Hell, how do you expect me to tell an Ethiopian from a Nigger?" Of course he can't and they don't and it makes a terrible impression on our allies . . .

Adam Clayton Powell has introduced a Bill of this kind but did not push it much. The President's report "To Secure these Rights" recommends such a Bill and I really do not believe Eastland could filibuster it long. Don't answer, just consider. Actions speak louder than words. Lots of love, Va. Durr

PART 3

The Movement at High Tide
1961–1965

In the spring of 1961, just four months after John F. Kennedy's inauguration, an interracial group of thirteen men and women left Washington, D.C. on two buses headed to the Deep South. Firebombs and white mobs greeted the Freedom Riders when they arrived in Alabama, accelerating the spiral of protests and violence that finally commanded the nation's attention. From the assault on Freedom Riders in 1961 through the mass march from Selma to Montgomery in 1965, Alabama remained a major battleground. There, the growing militancy of Southern blacks and the tentative engagement of the federal government competed with white defiance on the treacherous road to the civil rights legislation of 1964 and 1965.

Fittingly, even before the Freedom Riders came south, the celebration of the Civil War centennial presented the new president with his first civil rights crisis. Shortly after John Kennedy took office, presidential advisor Harris Wofford learned that the Civil War Centennial Commission's inaugural event had been scheduled at a Charleston hotel that barred black participation. Wofford quietly tried to persuade Ulysses S. Grant III, the commission's chairman, to work out a nondiscriminatory arrangement for the April 12 centenary of the firing on Fort Sumter. Grant resisted, claiming that states' rights required deference to South Carolina's segregation policy. Reluctant to intervene publicly and risk offending South Carolina's governor and congressional delegation, an irritated Kennedy finally signed a telegram requesting that the event be moved to desegregated facilities at the Charleston Naval Station or face the loss of federal funds. The commission complied.[1]

The Kennedy administration developed a civil rights policy that attempted to balance fundamental political realities. These included a Congress dominated by powerful Southern Democrats who could easily derail the administration's legislative program, growing pressure exerted by civil rights groups, and news media whose attention was increasingly trained on the violence used to maintain the racial caste system. Consequently, the Kennedy administration advanced a patchwork approach that on the one hand gave some encouragement to civil rights supporters, while on the other undermining the federal government's ability to support the forces of change in the South. This was most clearly seen in the pattern of political appointments made by the president to critical institutions and law enforcement agencies, from the federal courts to U.S. district attorneys. For the most part, Southern senators dictated these choices, filling the posts with staunch opponents of desegregation.

Attorney General Robert Kennedy's first major address promised that the new administration would pursue an aggressive civil rights agenda. Speaking at the University of Georgia on May 6, barely four months after students rioted to bar the court-ordered admission of two black students, Kennedy said that civil rights statutes would be vigorously enforced. His Justice Department had already brought federal court action to reopen the public schools in Prince Edward County, Virginia, and Justice Department officials were poised to prosecute voter registration violations around the South. Kennedy also framed civil rights as a national issue, acknowledging the hypocrisy of Northerners who belonged to private clubs that excluded blacks and Jews and sent their children to all-white private schools, and union officials who criticized the South but practiced discrimination in their unions.[2]

Kennedy's pronouncement was immediately put to the test when the Congress of Racial Equality (CORE) sent two teams of black and white bus riders south to test a recent Supreme Court ruling, *Boynton v. Virginia,* banning segregation in bus terminals servicing interstate carriers. One bus was bombed in Anniston, Alabama, and riders on the second bus were assaulted by a raging mob at the bus terminal in Birmingham, with the police waiting for at least 15 minutes before intervening. The Kennedy administration's efforts to coax Governor John Patterson into providing some protection for the riders elicited a vigorous defense of states' rights and precipitated a near-showdown between state police and federal marshals after a second riot at the Montgomery bus station. Still, the administration's primary concern was to keep the lid on violence in the South, and this, they concluded, was best achieved by finding a way to work with state elected officials—a policy that accommodated Southern defiance. As Virginia wrote to Assistant Attorney General Burke Marshall, "Southerners have no respect for Yankees, they don't think you mean it at all. They think you are simply going through motions for political effect but actually at heart you are with them."

Although Virginia had reservations about John Kennedy, she believed that the national Democratic Party was where the battle for civil rights had to be waged. It was, for her, a continuation of Franklin Roosevelt's effort to democratize the South and liberalize the Democratic Party. With a Democratic administration in the White House, Virginia had greater access and an enhanced sense of possibility. She knew and respected Harris Wofford, head of Kennedy's sub-cabinet group on civil rights. Wofford had visited the Durrs in Montgomery in the early 1950s while he was a law student at Howard University and had participated in the Institute on Nonviolent Social Change held in Montgomery at the end of 1956. She was also confident that her friend Lyndon Johnson, now vice president, was sympathetic to the struggle to end segregation in the South, while also being a supremely pragmatic politician.

Still, the problem was so huge and difficult, Virginia wrote, that it was "like chipping off pieces of an iceberg." She believed that the federal government had to act firmly and decisively to break the back of racial segregation and restore the rule of law in the South; Southerners could not and would not initiate change on their own. At the same time, she regretted the failure of leaders, in the South and nationally, to make any systematic effort to prepare white Southerners for the end of segregation. She trusted that there was a reservoir of decency and reasonableness among Southern whites beneath the surface of rigidly enforced silence and conformity, yet there were few outlets for alternative views to be expressed or discussed. Early in the Kennedy administration, she suggested to Lyndon Johnson that the state advisory committees to the U.S. Civil Rights Commission be reorganized so that they might become forums for Southerners to talk with and debate each other, and not let it become "simply a case of fighting the Gov'mint." She feared the growing resentment toward the government, a deep strain in Southern thinking that was easily exploited by reactionary politicians.

In the aftermath of the sit-ins and freedom rides, organizers with the Student Nonviolent Coordinating Committee (SNCC) helped revive local struggles around the South and created a new dynamic that could not easily be contained. Virginia welcomed the army of young people who took up the cause and was not a little bit surprised. "I never dreamed the younger generation would get so committed and so determined and so brave," she wrote Clark and Mairi Foreman at the end of 1961. "Now I feel I can relax a bit and let them do most of it." Her pace did not slacken, but the influx of young people into the movement boosted her spirits and strengthened her conviction that the balance had shifted in favor of change.

The Durrs always had room for movement people traveling in the South. Their name was passed from one to the next, and their home became a popular stopping place and refuge. It was also a destination for curious Northerners, foreign students, and journalists who came to witness the remarkable events unfolding in the region. After Robert Cassen's visit in 1960, Virginia and Cliff became favorites of Britain's Harkness Fellows. Anthony Lester, who first visited the Durrs in 1961, remembered that their address was part of the information routinely shared among the fellows. Jonathan Steele, a British student who returned to aid voter registration efforts in Mississippi, described their home as "an oasis of normalcy, wisdom, and amazing good humor." For Virginia and Cliff, the company of bright, young, committed people who shared their sentiments was a blessed relief from the isolation that still marked their life in Montgomery.[3]

During the early 1960s, Virginia's letters describe a situation bordering on anarchy. As protest increased, law enforcement agencies, local and state elected officials, and the circuit courts routinely demonstrated their determination to use the power of the state to crush any efforts to breach the wall of segregation. Intervention by the federal government was triggered only by the most desperate circumstances, as when mobs rioted at the Montgomery bus station, or on the campus of the University of Mississippi in 1962 to block James Meredith's enrollment. The hardening of racial attitudes, reliance on police terror, and growing contempt for the federal government permeated the political culture of Alabama; and its most potent expression was in George C. Wallace, who became governor early in 1963. Finally, following the widely televised police assault of young demonstrators in Birmingham that May, President Kennedy introduced a major civil rights bill to the Congress. Three months later, terrorists bombed the Sixteenth Street Baptist Church in Birmingham, killing four children; no arrests were made. The assassination of President Kennedy on November 22 was greeted with cheers in Montgomery.

Virginia's faith and confidence in Lyndon Johnson's commitment to carrying the fight for civil rights forward was richly rewarded. She described his brilliant success in securing passage of the 1964 Civil Rights Act as nothing short of a "political miracle." This comprehensive legislation barred racial segregation and discrimination in all areas of American life. A year later, Johnson engineered the enactment of the Voting Rights Act, which effectively ended the system of disenfranchisement that had been erected throughout the South at the turn of the century. These laws, which stripped away the legal apparatus of Jim Crow, are often viewed as the crowning achievement of the civil rights movement. Yet despite its promise to transform the South, the law's limitations in changing the structures and behavior that had long organized civic life, economic opportunity, and race relations in the South and throughout the nation soon became apparent.

As the edifice of Jim Crow began to crumble, Virginia's attention turned to what was left in its wake. She had long hoped that that there was a significant body of white Southern opinion that would support desegregation once federal law defused the power of the most vehement white resistance. These hopes faded as George Wallace's popularity soared among whites of all classes and backgrounds. There were "absolutely no signs in the white community of any change of heart or mind, simply a furious and rebellious consent to 'token' compliance," Virginia wrote in the aftermath of the Selma to Montgomery march in the spring of 1965. From the vantage point of Alabama, "self pity, race hatred, fear, [and] conformity" were the prevailing sentiments, and Wallace kept them whipped up to fever pitch. The murders of Jimmy Lee Jackson, Rev. James Reeb, and Viola Liuzzo announced that it was still "open season" on civil rights workers in Alabama.

Virginia read the essays of James Baldwin and observed race relations in the North with growing concern. She marveled at the fact that most white Northerners she met thought of the race issue as "something quaint that exists in the deep South," often failing "to realize how it affects their lives." Yet black migration to the North had transformed the nation's racial landscape; by the 1960s, half of all African Americans lived in the North, mostly in urban areas where many were trapped in lives of poverty and hopelessness. In the aftermath of the Civil Rights Act of 1964, she commented that blacks in the South were full of hope, while blacks in the North knew that "the right to vote and go to a movie . . . mean nothing if they have not got the money." She believed that "northern Negroes [were] far more likely to revolt," anticipating the explosion of black frustration and anger that rocked the Watts section of Los Angeles just days after Lyndon Johnson signed the Voting Rights Act, a pattern that would recur in Northern urban areas over the next several years.

In November 1965, Virginia and Cliff visited their friend Studs Terkel in Chicago, where Terkel taped an interview with them about the civil rights movement and the changes that had come to the South. Not content to let the focus remain on the South or on the gains that had been made, Virginia shifted the discussion to persistent economic inequities, starting with Terkel's own backyard:

> Well, now I don't think you've done a very good job in Chicago. I think the South Side of Chicago is as near an approach to hell as I've ever seen . . . Even in Lowndes County, I have never seen such degradation and such garbage and such filth and such crowding and such masses of people living together in such dreadful conditions as I see on the South Side of Chicago. Well, now, what are

you all going to do? . . . We've got our problems in the South. And we may fail, and we may succeed. It may be in the South that we learn to live together. Maybe we'll set a pattern for the country, I don't know. But what are you all going to do? How are you going to deal with your problems? Are you going to let it alone until it breaks out in another Watts, where you, they burn the damned place down. You know they used to burn the Plantation houses down in the South, . . . the slaves did, when they got to the point where they couldn't stand it any longer. . . . Are you going to let it get so bad they're going to burn the damned place down? What are you going to do? It's your problem! . . . You can't come South to solve it. You've got to solve it right here."[4]

While the Southern movement secured far-reaching gains during 1964 and 1965, Virginia watched with dismay as LBJ's bold initiatives on behalf of civil rights were joined by his rapid descent into Vietnam. Her concern turned to shock and despair with the start of the U.S. bombing campaign of North Vietnam shortly after Johnson's inauguration in 1965. His actions in Vietnam, she exclaimed, "put Jim Clark and Bull Connor and George Wallace to shame." She had long worked to link the peace movement and civil rights struggle and was gratified when SNCC activists and Martin Luther King, Jr. joined the vanguard of the growing antiwar movement. At the same time, she observed the resurgence of a familiar pattern as Cold War rhetoric was used to bolster public support for the escalation of America's war and discredit any individual or group who opposed the government's policy. SNCC, the most militant of the civil rights groups, had already become the target of red-baiting by liberals because of its failure to adopt an exclusionary policy barring Communists from the organization and its challenge of the Democratic Party establishment at the 1964 Democratic national convention.

By the end of 1965, Virginia's letters reflect the uncertainty that was shared by many civil rights activists and supporters as they faced the more intractable issues of economic inequality, growing racial polarization, and America's deepening involvement in Vietnam. Looking back over the history she had witnessed and participated in, she concluded that nothing happens just "because its time has come." She took some satisfaction in the realization that social change was the result "of countless acts and thoughts and writings and sacrifice and the present lies in the past and the future lies in the past and the present." But, she conceded, cultural patterns change very slowly and "nothing goes exactly as you wish it would."

On the eve of John F. Kennedy's inauguration, students at the University of Georgia rioted when Charlayne Hunter and Hamilton Holmes arrived on campus to enter the university. The enrollment of the two black students proceeded under the order of Federal District Court Judge Elbert Tuttle. Clark Foreman was a graduate of the University of Georgia, class of 1921.

ca. January 10, 1961
Dearest Clark: . . .

I wonder how you feel about your Alma Mater now? . . . The way the students acted is really horrible. I really did not expect that they would do so badly. I wonder if they ever think of the damage they do us in the world, but I am sure they do not and if they do, they don't care. I suppose Vandiver* turned down the job as Secretary of the Army under pressure and at least the Negroes do have a veto power now over the national appointments and if one of our Southern demagogues wants a national office he has to soften his attacks. One of the Patterson crowd told me quite openly that it was certainly a Hell of a fix to be in, "You have to 'Nigger' some to get elected in Alabama and then if you 'Nigger' too much you can't get a job in the national government." It had no moral significance to him, simply a political problem. The two Senators and Folsom are putting up a C. C. Horton for National Administrator of the Veterans Bureau, and we had a long distance call to ask about him, and we tried to find out, and what a conflicting number of stories we got, he was a racist, he was not, he was anti-Semitic, he was not, and so on and so forth. How hard it is to find out how anyone really stands if you don't know them . . .

Do read *To Kill a Mockingbird*. I think you will like it. It is really Alabama, at least as I knew it, and mostly as I know it now.

Arthur "Tex" Goldschmidt and Elizabeth "Wicki" Wickedon Goldschmidt were old friends of the Durrs from New Deal days. Tex, a native of San Antonio, Texas, and a close associate of Lyndon Johnson, had worked in the Interior Department during the Roosevelt administration and was one of the major contributors to the 1938 *Report on the Economic Conditions of the South*. Wicki, who had worked with Aubrey Williams, went on to become a leading advocate for social security and social welfare programs. The Goldschmidts lived in New York, where Tex worked for the United Nations.

---

*Georgia Governor Ernest Vandiver.

January 20, 1961
Dear Tex and Wicki:

We were so glad to hear from you at Christmas time and only wish we had a fuller report of you . . .

I know you must have had a wonderful time at the [Democratic National] Convention. We were . . . strong for Lyndon and did our best for him, along with Bird's many relatives, but I am afraid the South was a millstone around his neck. We are awfully glad he is in there so close to the seat of power as we are very dubious about young Kennedy. I am afraid we remember Old Joe too vividly . . .

You would have loved to see Lyndon and Bird when the "train" came through. The Democrats lost Montgomery and there was only a small crowd at the station and among them were several with signs calling Lyndon bad names like "The Yellow Rose" of Texas and "Judas Johnson" and a good deal of booing and so on. So all of the local political figures went through their paces, most of them looking like they were taking castor oil, and they were too for I hear Lyndon really bore down on them, and then Bird comes out looking so sweet and pretty and says how glad she is to be home and back in Alabama where she came from and she wants dear Cousin Effie to come up there so she can hug her and so Cousin Effie (an old country woman from Billingsley) comes up and Bird kisses her and then calls on Cousin Cora to come up and up comes Cora (middle-aged cousin from Autaugaville) and so it went until she was surrounded by "kin" from all around and all looking so familiar and sweet and the crowd loved it and it really broke down the wall. So when Lyndon came out . . . she had them all warmed up. Lyndon was good, he bore down on the Catholic issue which of course was the main issue here, and yet I think it was the word he passed in the cars that really kept the boys in line for they were just about to jump the reservation and if they ever run Goldwater* on the Republican side, they will jump as he is their Hero. Can you believe it? Yes, I know you can . . .

Aubrey is embarked as you can see by the papers on his main crusade now, to abolish the Un-American Activities Committee, and is just as

---

*Barry Goldwater, Republican U.S. senator from Arizona.

full of enthusiasm and zeal as if he were seventeen instead of seventy. He really is amazing. He gets brickbats thrown at him all of the time but doesn't seem to mind them too much, although he does get mad at times. He really worked for Lyndon. He got in his old Buick and went all over the South pledging his personal word to the Negro leaders that Lyndon was "all right." I think he did him a lot of good too.

February 14, 1961
Dearest Clark: . . .

I will write to Otto [Nathan]. He sent me his collected writings of Einstein and I wrote to him then but I will again about his mother. I do feel sorry for Otto and I know he is a lonely man and very hard to get along with and quarrels with his friends. But he has had such a hard time. I saw him in Europe where he was at home and saw the honor and the real dignity and place he had in the academic world and he is still a displaced person. No one or only very few know who he is. That is one thing about living in the South and that is that your identity is real. You know who you are because everyone else knows who you are. They may not like you nor did they like your father or mother or grandfather but at least they know you and you have a solid identity . . .

I went to an SOS meeting last night (Save Our Schools) and it was quite good. A young Presbyterian minister became the Chairman and he was wonderful. He knew what he was doing, what kind of a risk he was running but he did it anyway. The few white Southerners who stand up are usually very exceptional indeed. But they are few indeed and the power structure is heavy and hot and breathes down your neck . . .

The whole of Montgomery has gone crazy over the Centennial Commemoration and all of the ladies are in Civil War costumes and the men have long beards and even the children are dressed in pantalets. The funniest thing is that while strict segregation is observed in all of the doings they have a troupe of dancers in black face to represent the happy slaves! Actually! No Negroes allowed but a whole troupe of white people with their faces blackened to represent them. How crazy can people get?

Though Virginia's expectations for the Kennedy administration were not high, she was shocked at his early appointments, which elevated some of the most outspoken defenders of white supremacy, such as Charles

Meriwether, who had managed John Patterson's campaign for governor in 1958. In the following letter, she refers to the case of SCEF field secretary Carl Braden and civil liberties activist Frank Wilkerson. Braden and Wilkerson's defiance before a special HUAC hearing in Atlanta earned them a contempt citation and a year in federal prison.

March 15, 1961
Dearest Clark: . . .

We have just been though a really aggravating time. Kennedy nominated Charlie Meriwether from Alabama to the Export-Import bank. This is the first big local appointment, and he is absolutely the worst, started out Jew-baiting and spreading the fact that Lister's* grandfather was a Jew, (which he was of course) and then went on to perfect the technique of "out-niggering" the whole field of candidates . . . We tried to get some opposition to him and succeeded to a degree but Lister (not minding the insults to his grandfather) supported him and John Sparkman went to town for him, and of all things they used Hugo's 75th Birthday celebrations to plead for mercy on account of his Klan connections and he got in on a wave of "tolerance" on account of Hugo. Have you ever heard of anything more ironical? For Hugo's doctrine of "tolerance" and also Hugo's past Klan connection to be used to get a man confirmed who is as big a scoundrel as they come and who is utterly without principle of any kind. This is reaching the limits of irony. At the same time they send Carl and Frank to jail. All of the "tolerance" is for the right-wing racists.

They have also appointed as District Attorney† the worst "nigger hater" in town. At least John and Lister have recommended him and I suppose he will get it. We tried to organize some resistance to him too, but I am afraid to no avail. The "New Frontier" from here looks even worse than Eisenhower's people, they at least were ineffectual but these guys are the worst . . .

---

*Lister Hill.
†Ben Hardeman, a 57-year-old Montgomery attorney, served as assistant U.S. Attorney, 1951–54. It would be over a year before the Kennedy administration appointed Hardeman to the post. With the civil rights fight looming, there were very few potential candidates who were willing to serve in what was normally a hotly sought position. *Alabama Journal,* March 2, 1961.

I know I was silly to hope for anything from the Kennedy administration. From the ADA liberals who supported him, I should have known it was going to be nothing but a lot of phony talk and no action. But Nixon is so terribly bad, that I did think this man would be better and I admit to some slight hope of improvement, but now I am face to face with the fact that it seems it is going to be even worse.

Cliff won his MacMurray College case and we rejoiced and also rejoiced in the prospect of a fee which would pay off some of the accumulated debts, but then the City announced they were going to try it all over again. This is, of course, like the *New York Times* suit,* simply a harassing operation. They make each of the individual defendants have a completely different record and transcript so the cost is stupendous and they drag it out to worry everyone to death. What you see here is the Law being used to persecute people instead of to protect them.

Virginia was a longtime member of the Women's International League for Peace and Freedom (WILPF) and had recently joined its national board. The group had a narrow base of support, and she was frequently frustrated by the fact that many of the members accepted the premises of the Cold War. Still, it was an important outlet for her, particularly in her efforts to link the peace movement and the civil rights struggle. The following letter refers to a recent WILPF meeting she attended in Atlanta, and also comments on Decca's plans to write a book about the South.

March 24, 1961

Dearest Dec:

I am returning the speech which Anne [Braden] just sent me. I think it is excellent as far as it goes, and I suppose since you are speaking primarily as a writer and an invited guest to other writers and to people interested in books, that it might be wise not to go any further, but of course this is all part of the retreat from reason in this country . . . It is not enough to say the country is going to Hell, you hear that all the time, you have to say why to really educate people. I cannot advise you on the

---

*Montgomery officials sued the *New York Times* along with several of Martin Luther King, Jr.'s associates for libel following the publication of a full-page ad seeking support for King and the Montgomery movement.

proper way to give a short five-minute account of the decline of capitalism and the fear that arouses in capitalists and the rise of fascism and
war as a means of holding on to it, it might take as much as six minutes!
But in some way people have got to know the reason for things . . .

I enjoyed the meeting but felt that most of the women there are still
living in a cloud and really don't feel the hot breath of fascism on their
necks. Some of the Negro women do, like Ella Baker* who is really a
wonder. You should get her out to the West Coast, she is absolutely brilliant and a wonderful speaker and a real "leader" and so attractive too. I
am sure you would simply love her as Anne [Braden] and I do. I know
she would be a terrific hit if you could get her out there to talk about the
student movement, and some of the Bay Area students might could use
her as she can also raise money. But the WILPF is really not a militant
organization . . . They are good on Peace and have a lot of integrity and
are fine women, but since they are mostly upper middle class, they are
not spurred on by stark necessity and do not have the sense of urgency
that I feel at all.

One of our old Seminary Hill neighbors . . . met me in Atlanta . . .
She is head of the Human Relations Council up there and spoke to our
local Human Relations Council last night and did very well indeed. She is
a tall, intelligent rich girl who is a little bleak and has a very fine, rigid,
bleak New England husband who evidently does not provide her with
the warmth and life she hungers for, and which she has found in the
struggle for Negro rights. She has plunged wholeheartedly into it and has
done a fine job, she integrated all the lunch counters in Alexandria practically alone. She tried to commit suicide a few years ago and actually
jumped over the Great Falls in an attempt, but was saved and now seems
to have found a cause to live for and gets on well with the Negroes. She
reminds me of the early New England Abolitionists. Sex, even frustrated,
is a powerful moving force. Of course that is not the whole story by any
means but it is certainly part of it, and I have often thought how many
movements were driven onward by frustrated people who were "subli-

---

*A contemporary of Virginia, Ella Baker was a major force behind the founding of the
Student Nonviolent Coordinating Committee. Baker had worked as a field organizer
for the NAACP in the 1940s, and with King's SCLC in the late 1950s.

mating." I admit it is not nearly as much fun as a lover who is satisfactory but at least it does give rewards and she is getting a lot of them . . .

Actually I think the only difficulty about the Southern book is the line of approach. Just as escaping from the Citadel of the British Upper Class provided you with at least a motivation and the book* with a theme, I think you only need some line to hang the story on. My idea is that the great and amusing and overwhelming thing about the South is the difference between word and deed—the contrast between reality and myth. I think it is tragic and it is also terribly funny as even Dinky Donk could tell. Faulkner and Caldwell and so on have been so grim. P. D. East is funny but tragically so too. But I do think the South can be destroyed more by making fun of it than by anything else . . . I think the rest of the country is really taken in by the "myth" of the Old South and the beautiful women and white pillared mansions and faithful Negro slaves. The whole Civil War Centennial is taken so seriously and people seem to love Civil War books and so on. It is having a bad effect on the thinking of the country, this romantic dream of the South. There are some good things in the South (like Cliff) and some fine people and the struggle of the Negroes is magnificent, but all of this romantic myth is so silly and ridiculous. Miss America has been from Mississippi now for several years and actually people simply love all of the glamour, or fake glamour. But not the fake funniness of Harry Golden who says everything is rosy and segregation can be destroyed by tricks. Perhaps after you come you will find your right line but actually it is the effect of the Old South on the rest of the country that is so bad and needs to be exploded.

Lots of love and do write and do come.

Spring 1961
Dearest Decca:
Wonderful news that you are coming on May 15. I will be furious with you if you only stay for a day or so. You can find lots of material right here in Montgomery and in Tuskegee and Union Springs and in Birmingham. You must stay at least a week to really get caught up . . .

Daughters and Rebels: The Autobiography of Jessica Mitford, published in 1960.

I think it is a wonderful idea to start in New Orleans and interview the awful Banshees that picketed the school and spit on the little children.* I am sure you can get them to talk to you if you put on your best English accent and they think you are from far away. Jim [Dombrowski] of course can be of such great help to you in New Orleans. But to begin with the Banshees and end with Anne [Braden] will be a great beginning and ending. In fact "Southern Womanhood" would be a real field. Think of the contrast between fact and fiction there! You can interview some of the old "Southern Belles" here in Montgomery, or even better do a post mortem on Zelda Sayre Fitzgerald, who is the legend of the Southern Belle . . .

I think the "South" is so complex and varied that you will have to try to get it through some one angle and it may be that the women of the South will be the best angle to see it clearly. Read Lillian Smith's *Killers of the Dream* (very Freudian but quite good) and also *The Mind of the South* by W. J. Cash which I am sure I have recommended before. Lots of love and we are thrilled you are coming but you must stay longer than a "day or so" (day or so indeed!).

While President Kennedy appeared willing to placate Southern conservatives, Attorney General Robert Kennedy indicated that he was prepared to begin enforcing the court's desegregation ruling, and boldly announced his intentions in a speech at the University of Georgia on May 6. Earlier that month, Virginia began corresponding with Burke Marshall, the newly appointed assistant attorney general for civil rights. At Marshall's encouragement, she sent him information about local developments, along with suggestions about what the Justice Department might do to compel Southern compliance with the law.

May 1, 1961
Dear Mr. Marshall:

Dean [Eugene] Rostow of Yale [Law School] told me he had sent my letter to him on to you and I am writing in haste to ask that you regard it as a private letter and not let it get into "channels." I have had a most un-

---

*Refers to the women who mobbed the first-grade girls who desegregated two elementary schools in New Orleans the previous November.

fortunate experience with a letter I wrote to Harris Wofford* that I thought was a private letter, and he sent it over to the Defense Department and it got into "channels" and ended up here in Montgomery at Maxwell Field and as I had mentioned the name of a young Chaplain who was my source of information, it got him into hot water and certainly my name is mud to put it mildly. So I don't want to get both the U.S. Military and the U.S. Department of Justice set against me! I am sure Harris did not intend to do me any harm nor the young Chaplain but the fact remains that the people (Federal officials) here do not obey the Law nor do they have any intention of obeying the Law unless they are forced to, so those of us who are the Law find ourselves at the mercy of the Lawless Law. The present U.S. District Attorney is anything but a believer in the rights of Negroes and the prospective one, Ben Hardeman, is much worse. So since we have the City, County, State and the U.S. law enforcement officers on the side of the lawless, we really have no protection and have to be careful if we want to live here at all.

Judge [Richard] Rives's† young Law Clerk, Gilbert Verbit, has been here for a year, he is one of Rostow's graduates and quite a brilliant boy. He is appalled by the South and I wish you could use him as he has learned all of the stratagems they use. He will certainly back up what I have said about the lawless Law. I am enclosing a sampling from today's paper so you can see how complete and utter is their defiance of the U.S. Law.

I wish you success in your job and will be glad to send you clippings from time to time that illustrate some of the more horrendous aspects of the local lawlessness, if you want me to and will protect me from the wrath of the local Law.

In a short note dated May 4, Marshall assured Virginia that "I am more discreet than you think I am." He wrote that he was "very appreciative of any information of the sort that your letter contains and will also, in the future, appreciate any clippings or other thoughts." Virginia filled up the empty space on his letter with her response.

---

*President Kennedy's advisor on civil rights.
†Judge on U.S. Fifth Circuit Court of Appeals.

n.d.

Dear Mr. Marshall:

I was very pleased to receive the above letter and I am enclosing a clipping which will once again illustrate the thesis that Gene Rostow stated in his speech that the South is openly and defiantly lawless and proud of it. If the U.S. Government cannot bring the "rule of law" to the South, I don't see much chance of bringing it anywhere else in the world. I think the South is once again the testing ground and I hope this time we can settle the matter without open violence.

I am glad you are discreet but how should I know? All I know about you is that you are highly praised by Gene Rostow and his student Gil Verbit, both of whom I admire and like. But I also admire and like and know Harris Wofford and certainly did not expect my private letter to him to end up in the office of the Commanding General of Maxwell Field, and to have one of his aides say to a friend of mine "That Mrs. Durr is a very dangerous woman" because I had pointed out the discrepancy between the President's professions about Federal bases in the Charleston matter and what actually goes on at Maxwell Field. I cannot blame Harris too much as dear Mrs. Roosevelt did exactly the same thing and my letter to her about the Foreign Allied Officers being Jim Crowed ended up on the desk of the Commanding General of the Maxwell Air Force Base, so this seems to be the system. To say I am not popular with the Big Brass is a real understatement.

Actually that is where the U.S. Government has its greatest leverage on account of the huge amount of money these bases bring in, in the case of Montgomery something over 100 million a year as compared with the 16 million which all of the agricultural products . . . bring in . . . To understand the South, you must understand that Southerners have no respect for Yankees, they don't think you mean it at all. They think you are simply going through motions for political effect but actually at heart you are with them. And they have reason to think so as the Commanding Generals, the Big Brass, and the high Officials that come down here do nothing but consort with the worst segregationists because they have the power. Bob Kennedy's speech over at the U. of Georgia is the first time I remember a high Federal official really speaking out plain. *To Secure These Rights*[*] on pages 40–47–82–84–108–146–162–163 has all this business about the Military personnel which was recommended in 1947 but still nothing has been done up to now. I have a copy if you can't get one but I am sure you will find one around. I also wrote to Harris about this but have not heard from him at all. But this is the easiest way and the best and the most realistic way to end segregation in the South and it would.

But to go back to the trouble I've seen. It is nothing compared to the fact that when a poor Godforsaken Negro complains to the Washington FBI they promptly send his complaint back to the local office and there is usually a whitewash except the Negro is in trouble. I have never known a Negro FBI agent but maybe there are some but certainly not here and these [agents] are subjected to the same pressures that anyone living in the South is, social, economic, political and religious. All on the side of segregation. Do keep your eye on the appointment of our local DA, Ben Hardeman and the FBI reports on him, this will be a revealing picture of what goes on down here, he has had three investigations so far but no one seems to think there is any doubt he will get it. I know to have to buck the Senators is pretty tough but after all you might get them off a hot seat if the DA has to actually do anything in the field of Civil Rights. Ed Wadsworth, the Clerk of the 5th Circuit, is the best possibility, a fine person and really brave.

May 9, 1961
Dear Mr. Marshall:

You said you wanted clippings and you will get clippings. I am only afraid you will be swamped as every day there is a new indication of the defiance of the law enforcement agencies of the South, supported by the vast weight of white public opinion.

---

[*] *To Secure These Rights* was issued early in 1947 by a special Committee on Civil Rights appointed by President Harry Truman. It called for the enactment of federal laws to secure civil rights and voting rights, including "legislation providing that no member of the Armed Forces shall be subject to discrimination of any kind by any public authority or place of public accommodation, recreation, transportation, or other service or business." The report went on to say that "the government of a nation has an obligation to protect the dignity of the uniform of its armed services."

As these two clippings show the City Attorney is against integration and fights it tooth and toenail. The State Attorney General, McDonald Gallion, is probably the most extreme in the State and is now forming or trying to form an "Un-Alabama Committee" to look for the Reds among the people who are for integration and from all we can gather our District Attorney will be Ben Hardeman who is known as a "Nigger baiter" so there it is, all of the chief law enforcement officers of the State fiercely on the other side. Judge [Frank] Johnson is fine and of course Judge [Richard] Rives is wonderful but by the time you have appealed that high it is pretty expensive.

Rowland Watts of the ACLU was here on Saturday night and he was complaining that he could not get one single white lawyer in Birmingham to take a Civil Rights case, and here in Montgomery, my husband Cliff Durr was the only one who had taken one, and he was very dissatisfied and said the Negro lawyers had a complete monopoly on the whole business. We pointed out to him that one reason was that for a Negro lawyer to take a case of this kind made him a Hero in his community, and also he was paid large fees or at least very good fees if the NAACP or any of the other Negro agencies came into the picture, while when a white lawyer takes a case of this kind his name is mud and he is punished by the Bar and by the Judges and by the Juries and by all and sundry and he gets NO FEES EITHER from the ACLU, although they do pay some of the court costs . . .

These are the facts of life here in the South and I can imagine no more worthy project than a Legal Peace Corps* to come South and help out. Getting a Negro registered in Lowndes County will provide all the excitement of a tiger hunt.

Marshall wrote to Virginia on May 12, thanking her for her letters and for the clippings. "It is very helpful to continue to get information of this kind, which is otherwise very difficult to find or completely impossible."

The fragile hold of the law was dramatically illustrated several days later when the Freedom Riders arrived in Alabama as part of their challenge to

---

*The Peace Corps, established two months earlier, aimed to help meet the needs of developing countries for trained personnel through a volunteer program that attracted idealistic young Americans who traveled to Africa, Asia, South America, and other parts of the world to lend their skills and expertise.

segregation in interstate travel. On Sunday, May 14, whites bombed a bus carrying the interracial group of riders outside of Anniston, Alabama, and a mob attacked a second group after their bus arrived at the terminal in Birmingham. Governor John Patterson refused to comment on the white mob or on the failure of the police to control the mob, laying all the blame for the violent outbreaks on "the agitators."

Virginia described the crowd waiting for the Freedom Riders to arrive in Montgomery the following day, but the Birmingham group did not travel on to Montgomery on Monday, as originally planned. Later that week, however, a fresh contingent would arrive.

May 15, 1961
Dear Mr. Marshall:

I am taking you at your word and you can see what kind of violence we are dealing with right now. The Greyhound Bus Station is right across the street from our office and it is full of hard faced, slouchy men waiting for them to "come in." I doubt if the police here will give them any protection either.

The thing that makes it so awful is that Bull Connor, the Police Commissioner in Birmingham, is also the Democratic National Committeeman and is being built up by being given patronage to dispense. A Lawyer who wanted to get some FHA business was told he had to go "through" Bull and so he is actually being made stronger all of the time by the Federal government.

Also Sam Engelhardt who is the one who "redistricted" Tuskegee and has taken the lead in the Segregation fight is the Chairman of the Democratic Executive Committee and he too is being given patronage to dispense and building himself up, and of course Governor Patterson by the appointment of Meriwether who was the worst of all, is now riding high and wide and handsome and is considered to be the real "insider" with the Administration.

And now comes the appointment of Ben Hardeman! I heard from a source who is opposed to him, a very high Federal source, that he cannot be stopped. So here we are, dealing with violence, segregation, complete defiance of the Law and the very men who are doing it are the ones whom the Federal Government rewards.

I believe you to be an honest man, I hear you are, and I think Robert Kennedy wants to do a good job, but how can we believe in any speeches when the MEN who are appointed are the worst enemies of integration? I am afraid the patience of the Negroes is coming to an end and it will not be long before they meet violence with violence, they will get killed I know, and it is a suicidal thing to do, but as one of them told me "at least we will take some white men with us."

As you can see if you will read Judge [Walter B.] Jones's column, there is a real philosophy of racialism and . . . it is widely supported and held. The Federal government could stop it if it really meant business but when it plays politics before standing by principle, then there is no hope for us.

I know I sound discouraged, but how would you feel if you believed in the Law of the land and stood up for it and then had all of the City, County, State and FEDERAL officials against you? The Courts are the only recourse we have at all.

Don't feel you have to answer my laments and I will continue to send you clippings and information, and hope that in the vast vortex of Washington, some good may come of it.

The following Saturday, a full-scale riot erupted at the Greyhound bus station in Montgomery when a bus carrying white and black Freedom Riders arrived from Birmingham. Virginia witnessed the scene from Cliff's law office, which overlooked the bus station. She and Jessica Mitford (Decca), who had just arrived in Montgomery on her research tour of the South, had stopped by the office on Saturday morning to pick up the mail. When they saw the crowd gathered, Decca hopped out of the car to see what was going on. Virginia parked the car and went up to the office. Looking down from the second-story window, she watched, horrified, as a howling mob of several hundred men, women, and teenagers beat, clubbed, and stomped the riders and anyone who got in their way.

"I felt absolute stark terror," she recalled. "I'd lived in Montgomery for ten years. We'd gone through the bus boycott and the *Brown* decision and all the things that had happened after [that]. . . . What terrified me so was that the people who were shouting and holding up their babies to 'see the niggers run' were just ordinary Montgomery people who had come downtown on Saturday as they usually do to shop. And they turned into a raving mob. It was a terrifying sight. It destroyed the confidence I'd been building up for ten years. . . . These were the people I was living among and they were really crazy. They were full of hatred and they were full of bigotry and meanness. They were enjoying the sight of these Negroes and these few white students being beat up."[5]

Cliff and Virginia, soon after their marriage. (Courtesy of Ann Durr Lyon)

Virginia with Clifford Judkins Durr, Jr. and Lucy. (Courtesy of Ann Durr Lyon)

Jessica Mitford and daughter Constancia "Dinky" Romilly, December 1941. (Courtesy of Constancia Romilly)

Virginia, Tilla, Cliff, Lucy, and Ann in Washington, 1948. (Courtesy of Ann Durr Lyon)

Clark Foreman, 1948. (Courtesy of Shelagh Foreman)

Virginia at Progressive Party meeting with presidential candidate Henry Wallace and another Wallace supporter, 1948. (Courtesy of John Salmond)

Virginia and her daughters Lucy, Ann, Lulah, and Tilla in Montgomery, 1951. (Courtesy of Ann Durr Lyon)

Virginia and Cliff in Montgomery, early 1950s. (Courtesy of Ann Durr Lyon)

Mass meeting at Martin Luther King, Jr.'s Dexter Avenue Baptist Church, 1958; Virginia is fanning herself, and Tilla is on her right. (Photograph by Charles Moore, courtesy of Black Star)

Virginia and Cliff on the porch at the Pea Level with visitors from England, August 1963: Cliff, Julie Levin, James Cornford, Michael Yudkin, unidentified; Virginia's back is to camera. (Photograph by Andrew Roberts)

Virginia in the early 1960s in a photo from Jessica Mitford's private collection; the two men are unidentified. (Courtesy of Constancia Romilly)

At the Pea Level, 1975. (Courtesy of Ann Durr Lyon)

Cliff and Virginia with grandchildren, James, Paul, and Cliff Lyon. (Courtesy of Ann Durr Lyon)

Following her trip to China, Virginia celebrated her seventy-fifth birthday on Martha's Vineyard with Lulah, Tilla, Lucy, and Ann. (Courtesy of Constancia Romilly)

Virginia and Rosa Parks, 1981. (Courtesy of Ann Durr Lyon)

Virginia with Myles Horton and E. D. Nixon, ca. 1978. (Courtesy of Ann Durr Lyon)

Virginia, Studs Terkel, and John Henry Faulk at a party at the Austin office of the *Texas Observer,* April 1983. (Photograph by Alan Pogue)

At the age of 90, Virginia received an honorary doctorate from the University of Alabama. University official Culpeper Clark called the honor "long overdue." (Photograph by Alvin Benn, courtesy of the *Montgomery Advertiser*)

Despite advance warning of the arrival of the riders and the nightlong vigil kept by groups of whites waiting at the bus station, the police were noticeably absent from the vicinity of the bus station when the melee broke out. It would be nearly a half-hour before law enforcement officials arrived on the scene. By then, more than 20 people had been severely injured. The Kennedy administration immediately ordered several hundred armed federal marshals into Alabama to restore order and prevent further rioting. A defiant Governor Patterson said that the state was enforcing the law and needed no help from the federal government. He charged that the unsolicited dispatching of federal marshals to the state was in violation of the constitution and warned that they might be arrested if they tried to intervene in race riot control. The *Montgomery Advertiser* reminded readers that there had not been such a federal presence in the state since federal troops withdrew in 1872.[6]

Tensions heightened on Sunday as blacks in Montgomery gathered at the Rev. Ralph Abernathy's First Baptist Church to pay homage to the Freedom Riders. Martin Luther King, Jr. arrived that afternoon from Atlanta to address the gathering. Decca was among the handful of whites who attended the meeting at the First Baptist Church. Virginia and Cliff tried to dissuade her. "We knew exactly what it was going to be like and we thought it was dangerous," but she "was hell bent on going to that meeting." Decca and a young friend drove to the meeting in the Durrs' Buick and promised that they would park the car several blocks from the church, to better avoid possible vandalism. When she saw the menacing crowd that had gathered, fear for their own safety convinced them to park close to their destination.[7]

Hundreds of whites gathered outside of the church, shouting epithets at people as they entered. At first, several dozen federal marshals were the only restraining force on hand. Whites began hurling bricks at passing cars and attacking nearby homes. They overturned a car, which happened to be the Durrs' Buick, and set it on fire. When the crowd set its sights on the church, threatening "to clean the niggers out of there," the federal marshals used tear gas to push the mob back. Only then did city police and highway patrolmen join them. More tear gas and aggressive action on the part of the law enforcement officials helped to drive the crowd—by now numbering over a thousand—away from the church, but they regrouped in the surrounding blocks. Finally, the governor called in the National Guard and declared a state of martial law. Hundreds of people remained barricaded in the church until dawn, when National Guardsmen escorted most of them home. Finding that the car had been reduced to a heap of ashes, a groggy Decca returned to the Durrs' home in an army jeep driven by the general of the National Guard troops.[8]

In a case referred to in the following letter, the Justice Department sought and won a temporary restraining order against the Montgomery police department and the Ku Klux Klan from Federal District Court Judge Frank M. Johnson. Johnson barred the Klan from interference with interstate travelers and the Montgomery police from "willfully and deliberately" failing to provide protection in such situations as occurred at the bus terminal. But, to Virginia's dismay, he also issued a restraining order against King, CORE, and others, prohibiting them from continuing the Freedom Rides. King responded by saying that blacks would continue to test segregation laws.

As noted here, Cliff took the case of Frederick and Anna Gach, a young couple whom police arrested and charged with disorderly conduct after they went to the aid of a young black man beaten during the bus station riot.

June 4, 1961
Dear Mr. Marshall:

I wanted to tell you what a terrific job your boys did. In the first place to prepare the case in that time, and a case of such magnitude, was almost unbelievable. But on top of that to try it, this was really stupendous. They were the tiredest looking men I ever saw, especially poor Mr. Doar* who also had to be a witness. Is it really true that you only have twenty-five men in that Department? I think that is scandalous.

Is Dean Rostow really going to send down some of his prize brains to help in the defense? This would be wonderful. He is right about the "respectable" white lawyers being afraid to take any of the cases. Cliff has taken the Gach case and they were simply caught up in the mob and went to the defense of the poor, beaten Negroes, and then were arrested, and of course he is under severe attack, but he is used to it by now. So the burden of the defense rests on these few Negro lawyers, some of whom are very good but some of whom are not and all of whom are young and fairly inexperienced. I do think it would be so wonderful if the American Bar or at least some of it would rise to the occasion and come to the defense of the Law.

We were simply stricken by Judge Johnson's decision. Here again a man reflects, although unconsciously, the desire to live and be accepted by his fellow citizens, he is a brave man and I think a good man, but even

---

*John Doar, chief deputy to Burke Marshall.

he is prejudiced to some extent or fearful of loss of standing. Isolation from your own people is a pretty severe penalty . . .

Sincerely your friend and admirer, Va. Durr

In the following letter to Vice President Lyndon Johnson, Virginia refers to a comment made by Republican Senator Barry Goldwater on ABC's *Issues and Answers*, challenging Johnson to visit the South and lend his support to the integration effort. Goldwater commented that he personally did not think that Johnson "was supportive of civil rights."

June 6, 1961

Dear Lyndon:

I have been reading with great interest your report of your Asian trip and I have also been reading with great interest and fury the nasty attacks on you by Goldwater. He is a fine one, he comes into Alabama and consorts with the worst segregationists and speaks to totally segregated groups and frankly says he is on their side. Get one of your bright boys to go through the *Montgomery Advertiser–Journal* if you want to refute his mean remarks. That is what I hate so about Republicans, they are so terribly hypocritical . . .

Lyndon, we are terribly concerned about the appointment of a man named Ben Hardeman as District Attorney. Lister told somebody that told me that no one wanted it so Ben was the last resort, but he really is awful and has the worst kind of racist reputation. If he is appointed there are lots of people prepared to make a real fight on him, and particularly after the events here in Montgomery. We do not have the City, County or State Law with the U.S. Government and to then have a DA who is also a racist is going to be too bad.

Particularly as there is a fine person who wants it, his name is Ed Wadsworth and he is Clerk of the 5th Circuit Court of Appeals in New Orleans. There is nothing against him and he is really a fine young man . . . Is there any way your famous talent for diplomacy can work this out?

June 16, 1961

Dearest Dec:

Was delighted to get your letter and hear you had gotten home safely. We too adored having you and have missed you terribly but I am glad you got out ahead of the subpoena. They had a huge (2500) White Citizens Council meeting and the main topic was the "international slut" who had come over here and criticized our customs and how they were going to expose her and even if it disrupted international relations. It seems from what we hear that they have gotten you and Ann Pike* all messed up and she is the "slut" and you are the international angle with Winston Churchill as Uncle. So the stupidity and the viciousness compounds itself but until it works itself out, I am glad you are beyond its reach. The meeting at the Coliseum with the WCC was gruesome and all it needed were a few Heil Hitlers to make it a perfect Nazi meeting . . .

Eugene Rostow of Yale is really trying . . . to wake up the American Bar but I doubt if he will have any success but the very fact he is trying is something. As you can see by the Letters in the paper the Alabamians are still unreconstructed and in fact the feeling AGIN THE GOVMINT gets stronger all the time, they are ready for insurrection by now.

I have read Doris Lessing's book *In Pursuit of the English* with great pleasure and profit although it is an awfully grim book and she does not give you much relief from sheer horror. I think the idea and the sort of thing she does is the kind of thing you can do on the Americans but with a much wider scope and not so concentrated which really leaves one with nothing but despair at the sheer . . . horror of the English life and of the kinds of people she describes . . . but I must say that I often feel that is what faces us here in the South. That is why your visit did us so much good as you are so much more hopeful than we are . . .

We have been so busy with all of the work that we sink exhausted into bed at night. I hope the trip to the Farm will be restful. I know how busy you are and will not hope to hear from you for a while but don't wait too long.

Is there any chance of forming a joint group of delegates from various organizations in the Bay Area simply to work on the one problem of segregation in the South? So they will try to work in the South through their own organizations?

---

*Ann Pike, a young Englishwoman, had been attending Huntingdon College in Montgomery, but was expelled after speaking out in favor of the Freedom Riders. The fact that she lived with a young man she was not married to apparently drew wide disapproval as well.

Lots of love dear Dec, we do miss you so much and you were such a joy and such a comfort to us.

In June, Virginia traveled to St. Paul, Minnesota, for the annual meeting of the Women's International League for Peace and Freedom. On her way back to Montgomery she met Supreme Court Justice William O. Douglas, a friend from Washington days, in the Chicago airport. She apparently gave him a vivid account of life in Montgomery. Douglas wrote to Hugo Black about the encounter, saying that he wished there was some way he could help Cliff and Virginia. He was concerned about Virginia, reporting that she "said Alabama was in a dreadful state of mind and that she was going to get her six shooter out. I hope she was kidding." Black reassured Douglas that the remark was facetious but added, "some of the treatment accorded her would greatly arouse many people."[9]

Virginia reports on the WILPF meeting to Decca and also refers to Decca's new book project, a study of the funeral industry, which culminated with *The American Way of Death*, published in 1963.

July 7, 1961

Dearest Dec:

I just got home and found your letter here and also the ashtrays. Thank you so much for both. The ashtrays were more needed but I enjoyed the letter more of course and I am so amused and pleased too at your burial society popularity . . .

I heard from some of the women at the WILPF meeting in St. Paul that you had been both on the radio and in the paper with a report of your Southern tour and they thought it was awfully good . . . I was rather shocked over the fact that these fine women are so good on Peace and Civil Rights and so very poor on Civil Liberties. They simply take all of the premises of the Cold War for granted. I made a big hit the first day with my speech on Civil Rights but my new-found popularity was soon lost or at least badly diminished by my attack on the premises of the Cold War. If the half of the world that is socialist is to be called "part of the worldwide 'Communist conspiracy'" then how in the world are they going to make peace with a conspiracy? They were for excluding Communists from SANE and so on and I had a real nasty row with the guy from ACLU who took all of the same tripe for granted and said the Supreme Court had to be "practical" or the Congress would abolish it entirely. I know some of the Court will appreciate that, that they are

mere tools of the Congress to be abolished if necessary. Mrs. Pauling*
was there . . . I really adored her and so would you. She has a little of the
Girl Guide manner about her, very controlled and sane but so nice and
so full of good sense and humor too. I do hope you meet her . . .

Cliff is simply swamped with work. The Gach case comes up on
Monday and also the Caesar Davis case† Then he is literally swamped
with the mass of paper work on the MacMurray College case.

These are all in essence the same cases. The segregation statutes are no
longer valid and the Southerners know that so all of these arrests take
place under the "Disorderly Conduct" statutes which say that "conduct
calculated to provoke a breach of the peace" is unlawful and so the burden is not on the one who does the violence or commits the arrest but on
the one who provoked it, even if he or she is complying with the law.

In the MacMurray case, Cliff won this one in the Court of Appeals of
Alabama. They sent it back on the grounds that the complaint did not
spell out what they had done to breach the peace, which was of course, the
fact they ate lunch in a Negro restaurant with Negroes, but since this is
legal there was really nothing specific they had done, so he won this one.

Now he is suing the Police and the City of Montgomery in the Federal Court for false arrest and malicious prosecution, for $500.00 or
thereabouts.

He hopes to stop them from acting as they have done under this ordinance, which is the same one they are using in Jackson, and sees it as the
only way to make the Police obey the law.

The Civil Rights Commission, established by the 1957 Civil Rights Act,
provided for the establishment of state advisory committees to advise the
commission and report on developments in their respective states. When
the Civil Rights Commission came up for reauthorization in 1961, a fairly
routine matter that did not attract much attention, Virginia saw an opportunity for making the advisory committees forums for promoting discussion and debate among Southerners—something she believed was
desperately needed.

---

*Ava Helen Pauling, a peace activist and wife of scientist Linus Pauling.
†Caesar Davis, a 22-year-old black man, was arrested and beaten by the police after a
white woman charged that he had called her several times trying to arrange for a sexual
encounter. He was found guilty in police court and sentenced to 60 days hard labor.
Cliff appealed the case.

July 19, 1961

Dear Bird:

Will you please pass the enclosed on to Lyndon or either read it your-self and tell him the substance of it. I know how busy he is and yet I think this is real important.

Dear Lyndon:

I see the Civil Rights Commission Bill is coming up and I hope it passes . . .

But can't you do something about these STATE ADVISORY COM-MITTEES? Is there any way you could combine your idea of the local committees with this Committee, which frankly I don't like. It is responsi-ble only to the U.S. Government and is supposed to report only to them, and in effect is rather like a reporting or really sort of spying organization and I don't like it, secret reports etc. I think it makes it impossible for any-one to serve unless they are ready to commit suicide and certainly neither Cliff nor I were willing. I really think this whole idea of State Committees reporting to the U.S. Government and especially having secret reports to a government organization is not right, I don't like it. The only way to solve this problem is to get the people down here taking part in it, fighting about it between themselves and not let it become simply a case of fight-ing the "Govmint." Lyndon you must see what I mean. Is there no way you could have a national meeting of national organizations and then get them to appoint someone to represent the organizations in each State. I am enclosing Gene Rostow's statement from Yale and he is working on the Bar Association with Whitney North Seymour and trying to get the Bar to set up Committees in each State of local lawyers. I don't think any-thing will come of this but the idea is good but has to be broader . . .

Lyndon, the feeling down here is getting simply awful and the Mili-tary are really making it much worse as they are all on the side of the rabid segregationists, so far as I am able to observe. They resent bitterly the President's order to desegregate and are talking darkly all the time about "Communists" and "Plots" and so on. I can give you names, dates, times and places but there again I hate to seem to be "informing" on specific people and I don't think that is the way things get settled. We really need desperately to get the big national organizations in on this. I think these State Committees should be entirely revised in line with your suggestions if you can figure it out some way.

The city of Montgomery charged Frederick and Anna Gach, who came to the aid of one of the Freedom Riders, with disorderly conduct for using profanity and refusing a police escort from the scene. Immediately following their arrest, Anna Gach was fired from her job as a typesetter at a local newspaper. Cliff represented them.

July 24, 1961
Dearest Dec:

Your letter was received and I am sure you read all about the Gach trial in the *Advertiser*. While it was a victory of sorts to get the fine reduced from $300 to $75.00 and for them not to get any time which the Judge was dying to give them, still it was a sickening demonstration of the lack of justice and the lack of law. About twenty of the Police Force simply lied and the Sheriff told Cliff the morning of the trial that he had not been able to "find" any of our witnesses—not one! So we finally had only the one newspaperman, Don Martin. This was really a disgrace for the Sheriff to do this but it shows how the law agencies all work together and particularly when it is a matter of their prestige. He knew he would not win in the Alabama Supreme Court and did not see how to get it on to the U.S. Supreme Court without lots of money and time and then there was always the fact of the weight of evidence, that she did say these words. I think it was a terrible thing and it made me sick and Cliff too, although he did not think he could do any better by appealing. Anna was so nervous and so terrified of having to go to jail and really made a very poor witness as she was so outraged by the treatment she was getting that she "lectured" the jury and the Judge and the witnesses and gave an interview to the papers about how she would never live in Montgomery and what a stinking place it was and so on. Her very honesty is what makes her so fine but also a poor witness. In any case she made Cliff feel that if she got "time" she would lose her mind and she might have and it made him feel he simply could not take a chance.

You will have to realize that the whole business of the "Riders" has now become a "Communist Plot" and the morning papers say that it happened when "Khrushchev pushed the button" and people believe this nonsense and even believe that Bobby Kennedy was a part to it. In the face of such hysteria it seems that Cliff did the best he could do under the circumstances, but it was a dreadful disappointment and shock to me and I hated it. I am writing to Ben Smith myself as I don't believe Cliff could go through a long trial without any help as he collapsed after two days of the Gach trial. The whole atmosphere of hostility, of bias and prejudice, and the whole weight of the Police Department, the Sheriff's Office and the Judge and the newspapers (they were not too good on this) and the numbers of lawyers on the other side, all of this makes trying one of the cases a real grind and Cliff simply does not have the physical strength to stand up to it day after day.

I am delighted and amused about the Burial Societies being such a huge success and think you have evidently hit on something that people feel very deeply about as they should. It is a real racket.

As for not being able to write about the South, I think the trouble is that it is not funny, not funny at all, except in spots, and I don't see how you could do a light and humorous piece about it. I think the thing you could do is the thing that made your book so interesting, and that is the contrast between the magnolias and roses and whipped cream and the violence and brutality and horror that breaks out. But you will have to digest it for a while . . .

Anne Braden has been here and looks awful, simply sick. I do hope you will write and persuade her to take a vacation. She said she could not while "Carl was in jail." Now that is silly, she needs to get strong to fight for him.

July 1961
Dearest Dec: . . .

I hope we can get up to the country and away from the office next week. Cliff is so tired and it is so hot and now that Lulah is gone too, we are just the two and while the household is nothing, still it is the heat that is so awful coming and going and at night. It is always cool at night up at the Pea Level and I do hope we can get up there soon. I think Cliff is going to have a total collapse unless we do. He has been working hard all week on the Bessie Mae Prince case, another police brutality case and it is so discouraging as it is like trying to sweep the sea back with a broom. The trouble is the people of Montgomery, at least the great majority of the white people want the police to be brutal and approve of it. I am reading a book now by a Peter Evans of England about Kenya and the parallels are so striking, the same exact turn of phrase and the same line of thinking and the same kind of behavior, except worse there of course. They had awful violence on both sides.

Virginia finally succeeded in getting some aid for Cliff in his efforts to get justice in the Alabama courts. Ben Smith, a New Orleans-based lawyer, agreed to work with Cliff on the MacMurray case. Smith, who was in his thirties, had been a student leader of Henry Wallace's Louisiana Progressive Party in 1948, and represented Jim Dombrowksi before the Eastland committee in 1954.

July 26, 1961
Dearest Clark and Mairi: . . .

It certainly was a shame that I missed you, Clark, but I hope the trip . . . was worthwhile. I am so glad Leonard* came through on his promise to speak with Ben Smith. Ben called up and volunteered to help Cliff in October on the MacMurray case and I am so relieved as I don't think he has the physical strength to stand it . . . Cliff is feeling very badly and I am worried about him. He is tired and discouraged and feels all of his efforts are in vain, that the South and the Southerners are not going to reform themselves and can only be driven to it step by step and protesting all the way. It really has gotten so that living here becomes increasingly unpleasant, you never know when someone will take the most normal occasion to be insulting. I called up a real estate agent whose name I had seen outside a house for rent and asked about the rent and he seemed all right and polite enough and said he would have to make an inquiry and then he called up and said he could not handle the deal as he would not be responsible for renting a house to us as he was sure the neighbors would protest at having such people among them on account of our aiding and abetting the integration effort and he personally would not touch us with a ten foot pole. This was an entire stranger, a man I had never met or never even knew existed before and the occasion was simply to ask the rent of a vacant house. So it is like living among land mines, you never know when they are going to blow up in your face. I come increasingly to dislike the place and the people and although there are a few I like, I simply hate it most of the time, and want to get out. It gets worse instead of better and I am afraid it is going to continue to get worse all the time. All of my worst side is brought out here, and living as I do among people who both dislike and

---

*Leonard Boudin, partner in Rabinowitz and Boudin and leading civil liberties lawyer who served as counsel to the Emergency Civil Liberties Committee.

disapprove of me I become less attractive all of the time, and bitchier and more unhappy. But there seems no other place to go where we can even survive so perhaps I will get used to it by necessity. I think the awful August and July heat makes this time of the year particularly bad. But the Southerners have sacrificed all of the qualities they used to pride themselves upon, good manners, loyalty to old friends, kindness and benevolence and . . . in their determination to preserve segregation . . .

Lyndon Johnson responded to Virginia's letter of July 19, which she sent care of Lady Bird, urging him to revise and broaden the function of the state advisory committees to the Civil Rights Commission. "As always I am happy to have your thinking," Johnson wrote. "However I don't think any important changes can be made in the Civil Rights Commission legislation this year. It is difficult to secure Congressional action on any aspect of this problem. We have to do the best we can with what is available. But I do hope someday we can go forward in a sensible manner."[10]

September 14, 1961
Dear Lyndon:

Bird was so sweet to show you my letter but then she always has been and still is, and I think is a terrific asset to the Democratic Party. I only wish she could come South and meet more people in the "hard core" South. I don't like to use her friendship to get to you as I know you may resent it as Hugo used to do so heartily, but actually I don't have a home address for you and I get panicky when I think of all the ranks of people who defend you against intrusion, but if it finally gets to you I will write to the office.

My whole idea of the Citizens Advisory Committees of the Civil Rights Commission is to expand them and let the Government appoint some people and let the Governors appoint some people and let the big national organizations appoint some people and let some argument and controversy get started down here, rather than the hardening of the white population against the "Government." I think it is very dangerous indeed and may lead to the South going Republican next time. The Committees might be useful if they were reorganized along the lines you first suggested but now they are too small and weak to be effective in changing opinion down here and are resented very much by most of the white population so far as I can determine . . .

Give my love to Bird and love to you too, Va. Durr

Virginia comments on a draft of an article Decca wrote based on her tour through the South the previous spring. The article was published in *Esquire* in May 1962.

September 18, 1961
Dearest Dec:

I laughed until I cried over the Southern piece. I really thought it was a scream. I had no changes to make, I think it is terrific.

Of course it will make lots of people mad but that won't worry you. When you say the educated Negroes are more careful of their diction than the educated whites, that will really burn people up . . .

The one really glaring oversight and weak point and the danger of harm is what you say about the mob being so badly dressed, which of course they were, although the Saturday morning mob was not and I did not see the Sunday evening one, but all of the news accounts said they were.

But of course this poverty is the crux of the problem and while you could hardly bring in the reasons for it in a short piece still by entirely ignoring it you ignore the people in the South who determine its future. I did not introduce you to any of the "poor whites" because they are so hard to know. We used to have some clients but when Negroes started coming to us they stopped. Of course some of the people in the apartment are in that category but you never talked to them. But to totally ignore the overwhelming majority of the people does show both the weakness of our position and the weakness of the entire liberal cause in the South. Your only reference to them is when you make the screaming funny remark about Kissin' Jim but there again you don't get any information.

This is the weakness of the entire liberal cause but you could not be expected to find people we don't know either, but the middle class and few "upper class" . . . people and the Negroes are not going to really settle the issue and I think it is going to be settled by the great majority of the white people who were represented in the mobs we saw and why they act the way they do is what we have to find out.

But the piece is not intended to be a deep sociological study and it really is as funny as can be. I think you got off the Southern "ladies" wonderfully well and did justice by the Negroes too, and certainly gave the Country Clubbers their due!

Rev. William Sloane Coffin, Yale University chaplain, had been arrested the previous May along with a group of other Freedom Riders when they tried to integrate the lunch counter at the bus station, and was released on bail. Virginia comments on the use of the "balancing doctrine," in the context of both civil rights and civil liberties cases, which weighed the government's need to protect societal interests against the exercise of individual rights.

October 5, 1961
Dearest Clark and Mairi: . . .

Not one word about the HUAC hearings. I have not seen the *Guardian* so I am completely in the dark about it. I must renew my subscription. I hope you were not subpoenaed. It does seem so topsy turvy for all of the radicals to be standing up for the Constitution and legal processes and all of the "liberals" going for the "balancing doctrine." It was curious to see it in full flower at the trial of the Yale Chaplain. There the Judge and the Prosecutor decided that they were acting in a way "calculated to provoke a breach of the peace" as two white hoodlums did not like them to have integrated coffee and poured coffee on the stools. The white hoodlums were not arrested but the freedom riders were and given fines and sentences for "provoking" the white hoodlums. This is certainly a dangerous doctrine and Frankfurter* has really given us into the hands of our enemies with it unless it is reversed. If I do something which is perfectly legal but it makes you mad, then you do something completely illegal in retaliation, I am to blame for making you mad! . . .

I really have no news. I had a pleasant trip to Atlanta and stayed with Mrs. Mays† and found all of Atlanta really very proud of themselves. Of course you know that Mr. [John Wesley] Dobbs died, had a huge funeral. Ivan Allen‡ is a Chamber of Commerce character and the whole idea is that violence is bad for business so the "upper

---

*Felix Frankfurter, U.S. Supreme Court Justice.
†Sadie Mays, social worker and teacher, and wife of Benjamin Mays, president of Morehouse College.
‡Ivan Allen, in a runoff with arch-segregationist Lester Maddox, won the Democratic primary for mayor. The black vote secured his margin of victory.

classes" and the business men have come out in favor of token integration and opening up some of the lunch counters but the "lower classes" (white) all went for [Lester] Maddox who is a real KKK character and now there is a real class division in the white community as well as a racial division. Do you know Margaret Long?* She seems very good and she wrote how pitiful it was for these ten or twelve young Negroes to be taken into the white schools with so little welcome or grace and with the clear understanding that they were only there on sufferance, but of course I think when a breach is finally made in the walls, it is worth it. Mrs. Paschall† is being very active and seems very nice too. In fact there are some wonderful people in Atlanta. I like them very much indeed.

In the following letter, Virginia refers to Bob Zellner, who was a close friend of the Durrs and "like a member of the family." The son of a Methodist minister from Mobile, Alabama, he was attending Huntingdon College in Montgomery when he became involved in the civil rights movement. He had been moved by the sit-ins in 1960 and attended several mass meetings in Montgomery as part of a research assignment. Zellner, along with a dozen other white students at Huntingdon, sent a small contribution along with a letter of support to the Rev. Ralph Abernathy after Abernathy and the MIA were name named in a libel suit brought by Montgomery officials for an ad they published in the *New York Times*. Abernathy told Anne Braden about the students, and by the summer of 1961 Anne had recruited Bob Zellner to join the staff of SCEF. SCEF provided a subsidy for Zellner to coordinate his work with SNCC while working to organize students on white Southern campuses. In the incident referred to here, Zellner was beaten and then arrested following a march led by high school students in McComb, Mississippi.[11]

October 9, 1961
Dearest Dec:
Are you still on the funeral pyre? I am longing to hear how your piece on the South was received by *Esquire*. . . .

---

*Staff member of the Southern Regional Council and editor of its journal, *New South*.
†Eliza Paschall, director of the Atlanta Council on Human Relations.

I am . . . sending you a book Carl Marzani sent me by a man named Sachs* from South Africa, not Solly but his brother, and I am amazed at the tremendous alikeness of the "Poor White" of South Africa and the "Poor White" of the U.S. South. This is the problem that is so hard. Everything you said about them is true, they are ugly, mean, full of hatred, self-righteous and ignorant and also POOR. But while all of this is true and true indeed, it does no good to simply say so unless we realize that it is a disease that has to be cured, not just an ugly manifestation of poor-spiritedness. I think this is the thing that Cliff has taught me above all others, that it does no good to just call names. Certainly everything you say and everything everyone else has said about the South is absolutely true—worse if anything could be, and certainly the poor whites are the most obnoxious and unattractive group in the South, BUT they represent just exactly the same kind of people you have everywhere, this is what oppression and poverty and false religion and despair does to people. It does not make them any nobler and so the thing is not to exclaim over how awful they are but to try to find out why they are so awful and what to do about it, and stressing their awfulness does no good at all as I think fundamentally they are aware of that and that is what makes them so mean to the Negroes. I really do think you should come South again and study the POOR WHITE and do it fairly thoroughly as this is the group that is going to be the "Strom" (Thurmond) troopers . . .

Life continues to be interesting but for us it is rather quiet. Bob Zellner got in jail over in Mississippi last week and that caused some excitement as he called up all scared to death, but he stuck it out and did well and will be tried on the 23rd. He is accused both of inciting to riot and damaging the morals of a juvenile. This last sounds awful but the whole thing is that some Negro High School students marched in support of a group who was sitting-in in McComb Mississippi . . .

Lots of love and do come and visit and tell me how the funeral book is doing.

---

*Bernard Sachs, *The Road from Sharpeville* (New York: Marzani & Munsell, Inc., 1961).

Tom Hayden, Southern representative of the Students for a Democratic Society, and Herb Mills, a labor organizer from the San Francisco area, stayed with the Durrs while en route from Albany, Georgia, to Mississippi. They were working with the Student Nonviolent Coordinating Committee (SNCC), which Virginia incorrectly identifies as "King's student group."

November 30, 1961
Dear Mairi and Clark: . . .

Cliff and Ben Smith and the Plaintiffs are now in Court, Federal Court this time, Thank God! It is the MacMurray case where the arrested Professor and the students (two of them) are suing the local police for false arrest and malicious prosecution. We don't look to win the case but hope it scares the Hell out of them as it is a case of man bites dog certainly. They got in on Monday and have been here all week, and such a confusion and stir, as they are all staying with us, four of them and in addition we had two of the young white men who are working in Mississippi with King's Student group. They called from Albany, Georgia and said they were just about being run out of town there and wanted to get to Jackson and could we put them up. Cliff explained we had every bed full and one cot up and had no place to put them and finally when they seemed to be so anxious to come he got me to speak to them and I said I was so sorry but we only had the floor for them to sleep on and they immediately said that was wonderful! Just keep the heat on. So in the middle of the night they arrived and I found them huddled on the floor with cushions from the couch and sound asleep the next morning covered by all the overcoats they could find. Evidently they thought the accommodations were splendid and certainly enjoyed the breakfast and then left for Mississippi. One is named Tom Hayden and the other is named Herb Mills, one from Michigan and the other from California and both now "Deep Southerners" and so brave. I don't know how they have courage to go to Mississippi but they say the Negro community protects them and like "fish swimming in the sea" they are all right as long as they stay in the Negro community and what they are doing is training people to become voters. They are as dedicated and as brave and as good as they can be, and so casual about it all.

December 8, 1961
Dearest Mairi and Clark: . . .

At this moment our plans are to get to New York on the afternoon of Wednesday, December 27th! . . . We will call on arrival and would love to come to dinner if it is not too much trouble, which of course it is, but it does give us a longer time to see you both . . . As for after-dinner guests, actually the same old friends who have stood by us so long and you too are the ones we would like to see the most, if they can come and are in NY. You know them as well as I do. Carey McWilliams if possible but I am sure he is hard to pin down. But Leonard [Boudin], Corliss [Lamont], Palmer [Weber], Otto [Nathan] if possible (if he is not *impossible*) and the same old faithfuls that we love so well. It seems as if I always favor the men but I certainly meant wives too as you well know. Hubert Delany if he can come but don't have too many. As you know I love a large audience but Cliff hates too many people and withdraws and wants to go home so keep it small whoever comes . . .

Please don't worry over us too much as we will simply want to have a visit with you, that is the main thing and we are so looking forward to it. The last visit we had or rather I had, was Cliff's life saver in that it produced Ben to help him in the MacMurray case. I must write Leonard and tell him how wonderful it was for Cliff to have some help. Of course the jury decided against them but they have good grounds for appeal and are going to appeal. If you can get a copy of Judge Richard Rives (our great friend here) of the Fifth Circuit Court of Appeals in New Orleans in the *Bailey v. Patterson* case which came up from Mississippi you will see what the essence of the whole matter is. It is a wonderful dissent. It was a well-tried case and Ben Smith was splendid, and he is so gay and clever and charming as well as being so brave and smart. They had three of the biggest law firms in Montgomery against them and of all the Southern oratory, "blood will flow in the streets" "riot, revolution and mongrelization" same old strings they pluck on, but they sounded awfully phony to us. But if Cliff had had to have two days alone against that whole battery of lawyers it would have been really gruesome, as it was he was *so tired* but seems to have recovered by now. Of course they all slept and ate at our house and that was a big chore to keep them all fed and in the midst of it two boys arrived who had just been chased out of Albany, Georgia and were on their way to Jackson, Miss. Tom Hayden and Herb Mills, one from Minnesota and the other from California and both very nice indeed, and they seemed to appreciate sleeping on the floor so much. . . . I often feel I am running a station on the underground railroad but I love doing it. I never dreamed the younger generation would get so committed and so determined and be so brave. It makes me feel so restful now that they are so wonderful, I feel I can relax and let them do most of it.

In the fall of 1962, Sheldon and Lucy Hackney moved to New Haven, Connecticut, where Sheldon enrolled in the doctoral program in history at Yale to study with C. Vann Woodward. Woodward, who had recently been appointed the Sterling Professor of History, took a year's leave and arrived at Yale the following fall.

January 9, 1962
Dearest Clark and Mairi:

Thanks once again for the hundredth time at least for the lovely party and hospitality. I did it enjoy it very much, and particularly seeing you both. . . . The news of the children sounded cheerful in spite of Clark's disapproval of Hugh's being a wandering troubadour. Whatever his magic is he certainly has the power to attract young people, and they all seem to adore him and say he is not a "fake" and that seems to be the highest compliment they can pay him or anyone else. I suppose in a world ruled as it is by TV and radio and movies and lies that really is the highest compliment they can pay anyone or anything, that it is not "fake."

We had a delightful time in New Haven, although I almost froze to death as Lucy and Sheldon try to save money by keeping the temperature just above freezing or so it seemed to me, but they say it is healthy and British . . .

On Saturday night, Tom Emerson came over with his new wife. Tom rock-like and silent as usual and Ruth very chatty and also extremely nice we thought. Also the Fowler Harpers. Fowler as usual being shocking and contrary and making me mad by asking Cliff why he stayed in the South and "made a martyr of himself." Now that is fine encouragement to a man who is putting up a fight, isn't it? I told him Cliff would not have to be a martyr if the Yale Law School turned out some graduates with a few guts or a little courage instead of always seeking the almighty dollar so we had a lively time . . . All in all the stay was gay and very pleasant indeed and we thought Lucy and Sheldon both seemed to like New Haven very much although Lucy works too hard, and the life of a graduate student's wife is just as hard or harder than his in my opinion. We came back through terrible snowstorms and were delighted to finally get back to the Sunny South to be greeted with the news that they were going to lock the toilets, plug the fountains and tear up the seats in the Airport to keep it from being integrated. Now they say they will only do it if the Negroes come "crowding" in. What a mad world we do live in. Lots of love to both of you and many thanks for the wonderful dinner and wonderful party of friends . . .

On March 10, Circuit Court Judge George C. Wallace launched his campaign for governor with a pledge to maintain school segregation in Alabama "even to the point of standing at the schoolhouse door."

ca. March 1962
Dear Vann and Glenn:

If I sound a "little" depressed I really think I am justified as the Governor's race has started and the "niggering" is getting pretty bad. It not only distresses me but it shames me so. These are my people, there is no way I can disassociate myself from them. Nor would I want to as nothing is as awful as a man or woman with no roots to hold them to their native soil, but what shames me so is the sheer cowardliness of it all. After all the Negroes are a minority, the white people have all the power, place, position, money and even numbers, and yet they rave and rant about the "Negroes taking over" and "Miscegenation and intermarriage" and it reveals a kind of inferiority complex and fear and Freudian sort of illness that is so deep it frightens me, as it seems to be so utterly beyond the reach of reason. Of course they get no other diet. From *Lifeline* in the morning (H. L. Hunt) to Cash Stanley in the afternoon paper, they get nothing else but. . . . Here the Unholy Alliance is in full flower with the Military going along and lending their support to it all, no one is as popular with the Military as the leading John Birchers. "Time may erode all things" as St. John says, but it also erodes us and I am feeling very eroded.

I got your *Reunion and Reaction** yesterday in a new paperback, and read it again last night. The last chapter is a masterpiece. I think it is

---

*Reunion and Reaction: The Compromise of 1877 and the End of Reconstruction, second edition, published in 1956.

even more timely now than ever. I am afraid the same pattern is going to repeat itself, but this time it will not be reaction but fascism. . . .

March 23, 1962
To Mairi and Clark: . . .

I am going into the hospital on the 2nd of April for an operation on my foot, which has bothered me for years, no doubt the result of trying to be a Southern Belle and wear shoes three sizes too small, and dance all night in silver slippers with no ventilation . . .

Life in the Confederacy is still lively, we are having a boy* come today just out of jail in Baton Rouge, he spent eleven days in the "hole" and lost eleven pounds, and I have stocked up for him with everything I could think of to eat. One student sends on another student and so we never know who will appear. But it is lucky for us that we do have such interesting visitors for we are far from being favorites here in Montgomery, although we do have now a few staunch friends we can count on. But Montgomery goes on its merry way to Hell. This last week the Concert series was called off and the drama series as the artists and actors guilds will not play to segregated audiences. Then too the Library is threatening to be closed on account of a suit which is being brought and above all the State Democratic Committee announced this morning that to keep some Negroes in Birmingham from running in the Primary, they might call off the elections and hand pick the candidates! We have given up the parks, we have given up the drama and music, we have given up parades, bands, and now it looks as if we are going to give up elections and libraries and of course the schools if they are integrated. When they sold the Zoo and closed it up and sold all the monkeys on account of the order to integrate it, I really wondered who the monkeys were . . .

Of course we pay a terrible price for this, juvenile delinquency has gone up tremendously, and many of the worst ones comes from some of the "best homes." But to answer this they put on more police and make heavier penalties and advocate "getting tough" with the young people. It is really absolutely crazy.

---

*Bob Zellner.

March 28, 1962
Dear Vann and Glenn:...

The Cradle is still rocking, we had a sit-in at the Library and when the Police came the students spoke Spanish which really threw them off, but they were not arrested as they left, but a suit is being brought. Bob Zellner is out of jail for the third time, this time it was Baton Rouge and they got him for criminal anarchy, don't ask me how. He was visiting another prisoner and was arrested himself. He was put in the "hole" and sweated so that he lost eleven pounds in eleven days, he said it was real torture. He did not laugh over this one. He is mad. We are in the full flight of the Governor's election and only Jim Folsom is making any sense at all, and he is talking really very well, but whether he can do anything is the mystery. Except for him they are all "niggering" at a great rate.... How it will end I simply could not say. I really see no signs of sanity coming so far. Have you read James Baldwin's *Nobody Knows My Name?* It is a powerful and disturbing book. Lots of love to both of you, in which Cliff of course joins.

Virginia developed a friendship with Ava Helen Pauling through her work with the Women's International League for Peace and Freedom (WILPF). They worked together to increase the participation of black women in the organization.

May, 1962
Dear Ava Helen:...

I do not agree with you all the way on the WILPF . . . There is nothing I hate so much as the kind of peace people who spread hate and fear by protecting themselves by red baiting. But I think there are many fine women in it and what they have done here in the South has been unique—they were the first National women's group that came South and did not segregate. All of the others, no matter what pious professions they make in Convention, come South and segregate themselves but the WILPF did not. Thus they won the confidence of the Negro Women and through them the idea of the necessity to have Peace in order to get any Civil Rights is slowly leaking into the rising Negro movement here which I think is extremely important . . .

Just as I think the Negro movement must join the Peace movement to have any hope of success so do I think the Peace movement must be more aware of the Negro movement for the seat of the Fire Eaters is here, and the Administration plays its double game by promising the Negroes some things and doing a little but never enough to dislodge the men like [Richard] Russell and [Carl] Vinson and those who head the Military Committees—as well as all of the other Southerners who are so Militaristic. The Administration as you know is far more interested in Military appropriations than in Civil Rights and will do nothing to really hurt the powerful Southerners, who are their main support for Militarism, but they can be shaken if the Negroes and the poor whites ever get to vote—even the poor whites do not vote very much. I hope you will read *The Mind of the South* by W. J. Cash (now in paperback) before you come [South] again.

Virginia refers in the following letter to C. Vann Woodward's recent appointment to Yale and vents her disapproval of Mississippi journalist Hodding Carter, one of the "go slow" Southern moderates, who had been enlisted to represent the voice of the liberal South with occasional articles in the *New York Times Magazine*. She also takes note of George Wallace's sweep of the Democratic primary for governor in a runoff election. This ensured that he would be the next governor of Alabama.

June 1, 1962
Dear Vann and Glenn:

It looks as if the *Times* has taken on Hodding Carter rather than you. Hodding does make me so furious, saying just to let the South alone and the Freedom riders do more harm than good and so on—typically Hodding. And for the Yale Law School to have him up to speak. I do hope you will get the Yale Law School all straightened out when you get there . . .

I saw "Judgment at Nuremburg" last night and I am struck with the similarity of the self-pity and also unreality . . .

But with our new Governor I am feeling blue, "Nigger, Nigger" and now the Federal Judges. And people go wild over him, and not just the uneducated people either. This deep feeling of persecution runs through all of the population. Did you see Decca's article in the May *Esquire*? It really made everyone furious and of course I caught it. It never occurred to them that she might be somewhat jaundiced by having been caught in two riots—they just say it was her bad manners and English snootiness. It really wasn't very funny either but she was not feeling funny after the treatment she got.

Big Jim [Folsom] was drunk I am afraid but no drunker than usual, but what he said was what did it.* "The Civil War is over, we are living in the space age now—I like what Bobby Kennedy did, I believe in Law and Order—the image of Alabama is awful etc. etc." He spoke the truth and his following repudiated him. The white ones all swarmed to Wallace who preached riot and insurrection and made them all mad, and proud.

Through their joint efforts, Virginia and Ava Helen Pauling tried to make sure that a Southern delegate, preferably African American, would attend the national meeting of the WILPF. Pauling provided funds to cover the travel expenses of Vera Foster, wife of Luther Foster, the president of Tuskegee Institute.

July 9, 1962
Dear Ava Helen:

I am sorry to be so long in reporting about the delegate from the South. It turned out that Anne Braden could not go, and then I turned to Atlanta, as I felt that they had done so much to keep the WILPF going in the South, particularly Josephine Murphy, but she had a sick husband. Coretta King had engagements and Mrs. Mays, of course, is not well enough to come . . .

On the advice of Mrs. [Irene] West, I called Mrs. [Vera] Foster at Tuskegee. She is an official delegate and I had thought of course her way would be paid, but it turns out the national has not been able to send her anything for her trip and she had decided she could not come at all, but with the receipt of this amount she said she could come, so the last I know is that she *is* coming . . .

Mrs. Foster, whom you have no doubt met, is extremely intelligent and very capable. She lives in the kind of ivory tower that most of these Negro colleges down South are, but when she once gets off the campus,

---

*Refers to Jim Folsom's televised campaign appearance the night before the primary election.

the full force of segregation and discrimination hits her . . . she is not able to come to Montgomery for instance to shop, and get anything to eat, to drink or any rest room to go to, unless she goes down into the Negro ghetto here. She is in the . . . position most of these academic Negroes are in, they are dependent for their money either on the State, which is violently reactionary or (as is the case of Tuskegee) dependent on the beneficence of the biggest and most reactionary capitalists in the country, Aldrich, Rockefellers and so on, so they are caught in a curious position and are divided people, but basically the ever-present, dreadful and vile fact of segregation is what stares them in the face and that is what they have usually spent their time fighting. As Vera Foster said, I think so well, "When there is a hand on your throat, it is hard to think about anything but getting it off." But she has become through the WILPF very much interested in Peace and as she is so intelligent, she can grasp its significance in the fight for freedom. I hope you will look her up and speak to her as she says she will wait for you to make the first advance as I told her you did not want to be thanked . . .

I was glad to see the Peace Conference that was held in Ghana. I think the whole African, Asian and South American world are potential allies of the most important kind. I also think the Negroes in the United States are, and in spite of the ones who parrot the State Department line, there are many others whom I believe can be brought into support of the whole struggle for Peace. But Peace and Freedom for them must go hand in hand. They cannot feel Peace means much when they are still so bound.

July 10, 1962
Dear Vann and Glenn:
Thanks very much for the invitation to visit in August but we will not take you up on it this time. We will try and get by for a drink with you at least but will postpone our visit to another time, as I know getting settled is a big job and we will be encumbered with daughters and grandchildren and it will be a real task force . . . We are going to try and find a school for Lulah who . . . has finally come to the same point Tilla did, she simply will not go to school any longer, says the others are so mean to her, call her Daddy (he is the one who gets in the paper) a Nigger Lover and a Communist and they talk about her Uncle Hugo . . . and she has

had all she can take. The young people here do have some ways that are hardly edifying, such as throwing lye on the Negro women waiting for the Bus. The Bus lines here after great pressure agreed to take on a Negro bus driver, this was all part of the "Equal Job Opportunity" deal that Lyndon is head of, and it took countless trips all over and the strongest kind of pressure to get the Negro the job. While he was in training the KKK burned crosses at the bus terminals, then the Bus Company put him on the worst run they could have, the one where all the KKK live out in Highland Gardens. The bus is rocked every day, and lye is now being thrown on the buses and on the Negroes waiting for the buses, and the Police have refused any sort of protection, and the City Commission has raised the tax rate on the bus franchise and the bus company now says it has had it and they will get out, which they probably will. The white folks say let the niggers walk, they walked for a year so let them walk all the time, so they are doing their best to drive the bus company out and the rocks and the lye are part of it. Pleasant isn't it and no word in the paper except little glimpses here and there which make no sense unless you know what is going on. But the kids are the ones who are riding around throwing the lye and doing most of the rocking. And there is absolutely no protection, the Police are part of it, the Sheriff says it is all in the City limits so he can't do anything and the Federal government after making all the promises and getting the Negro hired has no one to turn to as they did appoint Hardeman as DA and so we, who are on the side of the Negro in this, are left absolutely with no protection . . .

P.S. As for the prayer opinion* which is causing so much furor here—sermon after sermon about it and the politicians say "They have put the niggers in the schools and taken God out of them," I think that it is simply a red light that no tax money can go to Catholic schools and it is better to get people stirred up over this than to split the country over the Catholic issue, what do you think? Did you see where the Governor of Georgia† had taken on our new Governor elect? Isn't that wonderful. If we can only get Southerner to fighting Southerner we may be saved.

Engel v. Vitale, decided on June 25, 1962, ruled that state-sponsored or state-mandated prayer in public schools violated the First Amendment. Hugo Black wrote the majority opinion.
†Ernest Vandiver.

Virginia began corresponding with Maxwell Geismar, a noted literary critic, in the late 1950s. In the following letter, she comments on Robert Williams, a former president of the NAACP branch in Monroe, North Carolina, a hotbed of Klan activity. Williams advocated that blacks take up arms and be prepared to defend themselves and their families. While there was a long tradition of self-defense among African Americans, Williams's bold pronouncements at a time of heightened racial tensions drew much attention. He and his wife started a newsletter, *The Crusader*, in 1961. Later that year, after being indicted for kidnapping, Williams and his family fled to Cuba. Williams wrote about his experience in *Negroes with Guns*, published in 1962.

September 4, 1962
Dear Max: . . .

I have not read *Black Like Me** but since you recommend it I will although I doubt if I can get it here. We have integrated our Library here finally but on a vertical basis, taken out the chairs! Can you believe people could be so silly? I have read reviews of it and I have heard P. D. East speak of him and he thinks he is terrific . . .

I am interested in your connection with the North Carolina group of Negroes that was headed by [Robert] Williams. I used to get his paper but I do not or did not agree with his tactics. While I can understand his desperation, I do not think he realized (or perhaps he did and decided to fight it all the way) the weakness of his position. The white supremacists in the South are simply longing to put the label of violence and illegality on the Negro. They themselves are breaking the law, but they want to put the label on the Negro and have succeeded to some extent in Albany [Georgia]. I think the Negroes have to proceed through the Courts and the political channels and *with the Law behind them and a court order in their hand*, then sit down for their rights. Their support in both parties is very precarious indeed and they simply have to win a larger number of white Americans over to their side and they will not do it by illegal tactics. I live with contacts on both sides and unless the Negroes get the U.S. government and the U.S. people behind them they will not win anything much but a token. I think their battle is far from won, be-

---

*John Howard Griffin's account of his travels in the Deep South in 1959 after using a skin-darkening procedure that changed his skin color from "white" to "black."

cause it is involved in the whole battle of Labor in this country and that is certainly far from won . . .

I do hope you are feeling well. Good luck and warm regards and thanks for all of the enlightenment and pleasure you have given to us.

On September 11, 1962, President Kennedy and Lyndon Johnson visited the space program facilities at Huntsville, Alabama.

September 12, 1962
Dear Lyndon:

I thought it was sad to see you and the President treated with such discourtesy on yesterday and only Bob Jones there to even greet you.

Of course Kennedy is very unpopular here now on account of the racial issue, but the main thing in my opinion is that he is not regarded with any respect or fear. All of the Dixiecrats or even the Democrats (so-called) think he is impotent to do anything to them and generally impotent. I suppose you have heard the wedding night joke a million times as I have, but this pretty well summarizes the feeling about him here at least, that he simply is impotent to deliver any of his promises, or to do anyone any harm if they don't go along.

With the power of the Federal Government at stake and the immense power it has, it does seem to me that at least through the Military he could get something done. I really think that if it was made a Federal offense to discriminate against the military personnel of the Armed Services, that these Southern defiers would collapse in short order, as most of these towns live off of the bases. Look at Montgomery alone, we get 110 million dollars a year from Gunter and Maxwell but they simply flaunt their defiance.

It really seems ridiculous to think we can export our "way of life" when we cannot even get the Federal government obeyed in our own country and the fact of our failure seems to me to be a terrible handicap to the respect other countries would have for us.

Lyndon, you and I are both Southerners and we know the boys are not going to give an inch. I think there would be general relief if the issue was finally resolved. I do not see anyone refusing to work at Maxwell even if it is integrated, they all clamor for those jobs and work and eat and even go swimming with Negroes on the Base and then come home and holler about white supremacy because they are afraid of their neighbors.

I also think there should be more wooing of the Southern people. Send Lady Bird down, she can charm the other birds off the branches and you can too when you try, also you can lay it on the line when you have to, I have seen you do it.

Hope this reaches you through the maze of protocol.

In the fall of 1962, the desegregation of the University of Mississippi loomed as the next major test of federal will and Southern resistance. President Kennedy sent federal troops to restore order and oversee James Meredith's enrollment after riots rocked the campus and claimed two lives.

Lulah enrolled at the Windsor Mountain School in Lenox, Massachusetts, and would complete high school there. "It turned out to be a wonderful experience," Lulah later recalled. "It was amazing to have your parents considered such demons and [then] go to a place where they're considered such heroes. It was so liberating to be able to embrace all of that after having a childhood where so much of it had to be quiet."[12]

September 27, 1962
Dearest Clark: . . .

We are absolutely on pins and needles and waiting with the most intense interest to see what comes off in Mississippi. Of course it will be a preview of what is going to come off here, as our new Governor has pledged himself to do just exactly the same thing. If the Federal Government does not stand up now, we are lost, but I think they will. As much as I don't like the Kennedys and particularly their foreign and military policy, I can never forget the feeling of relief and joy I had when the Federal Marshals came to Montgomery and once more you had a feeling of physical safety. To know that the mob is ruling is really and truly terrifying and I will never get over the trauma it caused my soul . . .

Actually both Cliff and I are feeling very well. While we miss Lulah a lot, we are so delighted that she is having such a good time and likes the school so much. Did I tell you she is rooming with Harry Belafonte's daughter? (But breathe it not in the Land of Cotton) and we are, after thirty-five years, enjoying suiting ourselves in time, food, quiet and lack of worry except for ourselves and the world.

Virginia commented on the election results, including Lister Hill's slim margin over Republican challenger Jim Martin, and Richard Nixon's defeat in the gubernatorial race in California. She also expressed her continuing concern about Kennedy's foreign policy, particularly in the aftermath of the Cuban missile crisis.

November 13, 1962
Dearest Mairi and Clark: . . .

Were you surprised at Lister's close squeeze? In spite of going over so to the conservative side and sending [Ross] Barnett* a telegram and thanking him for defending "our way of life" still he nearly got beat by his opponent blaming him for "Kennedyism and for Mississippi and for Federal troops and so on." He lost Mobile, Montgomery and Birmingham . . .

I was so delighted to see Nixon get beat and I do hope it is for good. Sunday night on the Howard Smith show (we now have a television, inherited) he and [Murray] Chotiner† were like a couple of old-fashioned gangsters, they really looked horrible. I thought that Alger [Hiss] looked fine in spite of losing so much of his beautiful hair. He was so beautiful in his Brooks Brothers suits, do you remember? And his gloves always turned back? Poor Alger, it makes me sick to think of what he has gone through and I am convinced he is not guilty . . .

Decca writes her new book will be out in the Spring, all about funerals. She says the Dink is there in New York and is having a love affair . . . with a young Negro named Chuck McDew‡ who is one of the heroes of the "Movement" and works for SNCC . . .

I hear you were picketing the UN on Cuba during the crisis. This came via Arthur Lobman to Dorothy. I really was terribly upset. I thought this was it and we were all going to be incinerated, so that whether we were segregated or integrated made very little difference. I think it was an awfully brazen thing to do, and if Khrushchev and the Russians had not backed off, I don't know what would have happened. I

---

*Governor of Mississippi.
†Murray Chotiner had been one of Richard Nixon's closest advisors since his 1946 Congressional campaign. He devised the Red-baiting strategy that helped Nixon defeat incumbent Jerry Voorhis and win his first race for Congress.
‡Charles "Chuck" McDew was director of the Student Nonviolent Coordinating Committee (1961–63).

hope they got a quid pro quo but down here the papers have been full of nothing but crowing as to how we made them eat crow. I really have no confidence in Kennedy in his foreign policy at all, do you?

Outside of Mississippi and Cuba, Life goes in a calm manner with very little excitement. We have a pretty rigid schedule which takes us through the week and then on Saturday Cliff goes to the country and comes back and gets me on Sunday and we spend Sunday up there in the country, usually planting or hoeing or building or something equally rustic. He can't hardly wait to live up there but my enthusiasm is cool to put it mildly but of course if we ever get a decent house I might like it better, but I do love the comforts of life, the nice warm bath and electric blanket. Bathing in the Creek and going to the privy is simply not my idea of a good life. I don't want to go back to Nature.

On December 14, 1962, a bomb exploded in Bethel Baptist Church in Birmingham, the former pulpit of civil rights leader Fred Shuttlesworth, while children were in the basement of the church rehearsing for a Christmas pageant. Two of the children suffered facial injuries.

December 20, 1962
Dearest Marge: . . .

I suppose you saw where they bombed the church in Birmingham last week and hurt two little Negro girls. What heroes we produce.

We are well, stay busy, work hard and make little money but at least we live comfortably . . . I still think Montgomery by and large is an awful place, full of sin and corruption and hypocrisy but what place is not? . . . I used to want to get out so badly that I almost went crazy with longing to leave, but after this long a time I am used to it now and at least it is interesting. It is like having front seats at some dreadfully involved and horrible tragedy with some comedy overtones and knowing most of the characters too and also being caught up in it occasionally.

Cliff is the one who has come into his own. He has really been wonderful. The Negroes all say his cases against the Police have meant that they have stopped beating Negroes up as a routine measure, they still do it sometimes but not as a routine. He has also helped a lot in the loan shark and insurance rackets that bleed the Negroes to death. He has really been awfully useful and if he gets no money or fame or honor or anything but criticism and ostracism out of it, he usually takes it very well indeed, although he sometimes gets angry but by and large he seems to have more tolerance for people here than I do, he thinks they have never had a chance to be or know anything else, but I do not forgive them so easily. Those hate-filled faces during the bus riot and which you saw on the TV during the Oxford riots, I cannot see much difference between them and the Nazis, if any. The thing is what to do about them? I do not believe in waiting on a change of heart, I think the U.S. Government has to really crack down on them. They have gotten by with standing on the Negro for 300 years and think they still can, but I hope the U.S. Government and the people of the U.S. will finally help put a stop to it. We can't do it all down here, we have to have the help of the Government and the people of the rest of the country.

December 21, 1962
Dear Max:

I do think the Stokeleys are lovely people . . . their sweet optimism did get on my nerves and I hope now that Oxford has really waked them up, but you say she is waked up already. I was fascinated to see that Faulkner's nephew* led the Mississippi Guardsmen on campus and really saved the day. Hurrah! Finally one Faulkner (he calls himself Falkner) acted and redeemed some of the white South I hope.

Heaven's Yes, I am still a Marxist. I do not think his economic analysis can possibly be denied or the world understood unless one accepts his analysis of the struggle between capitalism and socialism, but at the same time Socialism has not produced the new man I had hoped for at one time and believed in. Under socialism men seem to have all of the same old qualities that are so human, and while they are better fed, better housed, have better education and better health, they still fight, get jealous, compete, lie, and so on. I think Socialism gives men a better chance to have a good life by giving them at least a minimum chance to eat and live and have an education but so far it has

---

*Murray "Chooky" Falkner was captain of the Mississippi National Guard unit that helped to put down the riot.

certainly not produced a new man who loves his neighbor as himself and recognizes all men as brothers under God or under Nature or under the sun or whatever name people want to call Eternity and Universality.

Freud has also explored the dark recesses of man and while I am not a total Freudian, still I do think he pushes back the dark a lot. You can't understand these white southern racists purely on the basis that they need cheap Negro labor, it is the long generations of guilt when they took the black women in the face of the total helplessness of the black men that must haunt them and turn them into savages, or the fact that they are denying their own children, or their blood brothers and sisters. In a Southern town like Montgomery there is enough scandal and knowledge under the sweet surface of tea and cocktails and fancy dress balls to upset the whole town, but it is never spoken except in whispers and while all of the old settlers know it, it has never become public knowledge, but it is here. There could be a dozen novels written here, and all of the dark in Faulkner is true but he so completely lacked any economic base of interpretation.

December 1962
Dearest Clark and Mairi:

I am sorry to write on such ugly paper but as usual I have more to do than I can get done and I do want to say MERRY CHRISTMAS AND HAPPY NEW YEAR and have to do it in between the various chores, which keep us going. Thank God for them . . .

I wish I could send you a million dollars, a trip to Europe, a new car or an old car or a good job in the South, so we could spend our declining years together, but since I can do none of these things I do send you my love and good wishes.

In an earlier letter to Marge Frantz, Virginia complained about the persistent red-baiting among liberal groups like the Southern Regional Council, directed particularly at SCEF and the efforts of people like Anne and Carl Braden, Jim Dombrowski, and Aubrey Williams. That letter apparently drew a response from Marge that Virginia took strong exception to. Frantz had left the Communist Party in the mid-1950s.

January 7, 1963
Dearest Marge: . . .

I was amazed at the part of your letter about red-baiting. You must not read your husband's articles, especially the one in the Yale Law Review, which both Cliff and I consider the best statement of the First Amendment position we have ever read. Back in the SCHW days I was opposed to red-baiting, not only because of you and your father and some others whom I loved, but because I thought then as I do now that you cannot bar any political group and keep political freedom. And if private organizations bar them, as the ACLU did or SANE does today, it only leads to bolstering the case of the Government barring them. I have seen this kind of red-baiting weaken and I think ruin the Labor Unions and I certainly do not want to see it ruin the Negro movement and here too my principles and my affections are one as I adore Jim and Anne and Carl and Aubrey too, and they are the main victims . . .

I have heard your revulsion against the Communist Party over and over again [and] from others who feel just as you do. You are only stating the objections I had back in the thirties and forties but it is like the case of a woman who never married a man and one who is divorced from him, you have all the bitterness which I do not share. Certainly I have never thought the Communists were or are the Enemy and I see the Enemy which is Fascism at work every day. If you don't like to hear that word, then what other word do you use in its place? What do you think we have here in Alabama, Democracy? Have we ever had it? You know we have not. How absurd to quote two cheers for Democracy to anyone living here in Alabama—when my house has two young Methodist preachers now just out of jail for trying to get Negroes registered in Mississippi. You talk about me calming down and losing my righteous indignation. I am only sorry you have lost yours. We need a Damned Sight more, not less, of righteous indignation, self-righteous too if it comes to that, when we are trying here to bring about the most elementary democracy, the right to vote, and have been at it all these years and still don't have it. You are a fine one to talk, I must say, about calming me down. You and your father woke me up and now that I am awake I hope to God I will never get calmed down so I can accept such a society as we have here. I don't see how you can accept California when all you do out there is make weapons of death. Why aren't you in Strike for Peace or the WILPF, what are you doing to save the lives of your children? I do think you are preaching Heresy when you say to calm down in the face of the evils of the world and I will delight in an opportunity of having several arguments with you if not a hair pulling in the bargain. I will never accept you as a pacifier and as an appeaser. Lots of love, Va.

P.S. So how do you like James Baldwin, he makes my indignation seem like a mild Summer breeze.

February 18, 1963
Dear Ava Helen: . . .

With the breakdown of law, the Negroes are afraid and Vera Foster was quite frank with me last week when I saw her in Tuskegee. She said "Race is all we can fight right now, Peace on top of Race is too much." She expressed herself as being fond of you, delighted with you, admiring of you, would be glad to see you at the College, but publicly she simply says she can do nothing for "Peace" as with our new Governor the struggle for race equality is all they can do . . . I still think a private visit to Tuskegee on your part would do a great deal of good. I am more and more convinced that the Peace movement and the struggle here in the South for Civil Liberties and Civil Rights must be one if we are to ever get anywhere. Actually they are the same fight, both minorities seeking to be heard and not persecuted.

Lots of love and do let me know what goes on. Cliff is so busy right now on the Zellner case that he does not have time to think of anything else, and if the invitation is not to be, or not to be until next Fall or whatever time, let us know that too.

On the occasion of the centennial of the Emancipation Proclamation, the U.S. Commission on Civil Rights issued a report on the civil rights progress of the pervious hundred years. The report, *Freedom to Be Free*, was released on Lincoln's Birthday and presented to President Kennedy at a reception for civil rights leaders at the White House. According to an Associated Press story, published in the *Montgomery Advertiser*, the report emphasized "more forces are working for the realization of civil rights for all Americans than ever before in history," and allowed that while progress is "slow and often painful," it "is steady and appears to be inevitable." Virginia took strong exception to this rosy view, and registered her dissent in the following letter to C. Vann Woodward, who was listed as one of the consultants for the historical account upon which the report was based.[13]

The commission's report, however, barely reflected the study originally submitted by John Hope Franklin. Franklin, the preeminent historian and author of *From Slavery to Freedom*, was hired by the Commission to write a history of civil rights in the United States since Emancipation; he in turn recruited Rayford Logan, C. Vann Woodword, and Allen Nevins to work with him as consultants on the project. The three consultants aided with different sections, read and commented on Franklin's draft, and enthusiastically endorsed the final manuscript. The commission, however, was, Franklin recalled, "sorely disappointed" with the text he submitted, contending that it lacked sufficient emphasis on the progress that had been made over the decades. The commission members equated progress made by African Americans with progress in civil rights, even though, as Franklin attempted to explain, black advancement often proceeded in spite of the denial of basic citizenship rights. In the end, the commission hired several individuals to anonymously rewrite and revise the report and bring it into line with their perspective.[14]

From where Virginia sat in Montgomery, Alabama, progress, even in 1963, was certainly not steady and hardly seemed inevitable. Barely a month earlier, on the occasion of his gubernatorial inauguration, a defiant George Wallace pledged "segregation now, segregation tomorrow, segregation forever." Even before he was inaugurated, Wallace defied Floyd Mann, who was still commissioner of public safety, and had Bob Zellner arrested on the grounds that he was planning to organize a demonstration on Inauguration Day.

February 25, 1963

Dear Vann:

On February 13 as I recall, the *Montgomery Advertiser* had a front page story saying the President had entertained Civil Rights Leaders at the White House and you and John Hope had produced an historical account of what had happened in the field of Civil Rights and what was going to happen, both accounts according to the paper being very glowing indeed, and prophesying continued progress and advance.

This is what I disagree with, we may make progress inch by inch but the prospects are certainly not glowing from the viewpoint of Montgomery, Alabama and until the Damned Yankees wake up and see that the Southern struggle affects them too and they have to do a whole lot more than they are doing, then we are in for a bad time for a long time to come with tokenism here and there. You know how mean we Southerners can be and often are. Especially on this issue. And now they are getting allies in the Military and in the Birchers and in the Goldwater Republicans and in the Nixon and Chotiner Republicans and it looks to me as if 1964 was going to be a repeat of 1876 about which you have written so eloquently. Of course I see things from a worm's view position, I know that, but remember my love, and be humble, you did prophesy wrong in the Jim Crow book* and all Hell has broken loose since then.

We are right in the midst of Bob Zellner's case so I am feeling bitter. He was spending the night with us with another young Methodist and went over to Huntingdon [College] to see some of his friends and eat dinner in the new dining Hall and was arrested as he was walking from the dining room to his car. First they told him it was "conspiracy" and then later changed it to "vagrancy." He was arrested on the express orders of Governor Wallace and by his Director of Public Safety, although neither had been sworn into office [yet]. They said they were acting on notice given by a "confidential informant" that he was in town to organize demonstrations on Inauguration Day which was a complete and utter lie. Anyway Cliff amid great publicity (which is going to mean I am afraid that he will lose the Durr Drug Co. business) got him off on the vagrancy charge and immediately they rearrested him on a "false pretense charge" on the grounds he gave a check and then covered it after he had given it. If the check had gone through it would have been covered but the exact minute he

---

*The Strange Career of Jim Crow (New York: Oxford University Press, 1955).

gave it he did not have enough to cover it, and so he is being tried on Wednesday on a felonious count of "false pretense" which carries from one to ten years in the Pen. He has been indicted by the Grand Jury and Cliff is out now trying to get witnesses . . . It is a clear frame-up, even the Solicitor says so in private but he is going right ahead trying to send him to the Pen, and he has very little chance of being cleared by a Montgomery County Jury, so it is going to mean appeal after appeal and this is what they mean when they say we "believe in Law and Order and not Violence." So it is hard to see a glowing future, nothing but inch by inch progress at a terrible price. But I do want to see the full report so send it to me if you have it. I would adore to stay with you and Glenn and will look forward to it. Lots of love to both of you, I may disagree with you but never cease to love you both.

March 7, 1963
Dearest Mairi and Clark:

I was delighted to get your fine letter and I too have missed our exchanges. We had a wonderful Christmas with Lucy and her family and Lulah here and then on the 8th of January Bob Zellner was spending the night with us and got arrested and from then on we have lived in the middle of a vortex of excitement . . .

Bob stayed with us most of the time and his father and mother and girl friends and other Methodist preachers from time to time. Nearly twenty-five of the Preachers were willing to testify for him which was good and I think his arrest has really waked up some of the Methodists, especially as he got arrested on the campus of the Methodist College here doing absolutely nothing but walking along . . .

The only sour note which entered was that the other lawyer* who was supposed to come into the case to help Cliff, simply came in and took it over and as Cliff needed help so badly there was nothing we could do.

---

*Charles "Chuck" Morgan, a Birmingham-based lawyer. The case ended in a hung jury.

He demanded and got a $2000 fee before he would touch it, and only came in a few days before the trial as he would not have anything to do with it until he got his fee. This starving Student organization agreed to pay him that much, as he is the only white lawyer other than Cliff in Alabama they could get and he is a good lawyer and very belligerent and aggressive, but after we had worked six weeks on the case and never have received one penny, it is a little hard to accept the fact that he gets all of the fee and all of the credit for winning the case, but Cliff says that is my femaleness, but I don't think so, I think it is a sense of fairness but Cliff was simply unwilling to take on the whole trial as he gets so tired, and in this case we had all of the entire machinery of the State lined up against us. But Cliff says he is so glad for another white lawyer to be willing to take on some of these cases and Morgan is a good lawyer and not a bad guy, he simply thinks Cliff is an idiot for not demanding and getting big fees. As he says it keeps you from getting other cases which we know fairly well!

But the fact any white lawyer other than Cliff would come into the case is a good indication that some stir is going on, and there is some opposition to Alabama being another Mississippi. The "good guys" all say they are definitely opposed to integration but want "law and order" and the bad guys say the same but their ideas of law and order are different.

In May 1963, the SCLC's campaign to desegregate Birmingham led to a violent confrontation with Public Safety Commissioner Bull Connor. Connor's police unleashed dogs and turned firehouses on young demonstrators while he patrolled the area in a tank. Images of this police assault on the peaceful protest flashed across the country and around the world, and sparked spontaneous mass protests throughout the United States. As Virginia notes, a biracial committee finally worked out a fragile agreement providing for the desegregation of lunch counters in downtown stores and the hiring of an unspecified number of black clerks.

While the demonstrations were going on in Birmingham, Bob Zellner and other civil rights activists were arrested in Attalla, Alabama as they tried to continue William Moore's freedom walk. Moore, a white postman from Baltimore, was murdered as he staged a one-man march for integration, starting in Chattanooga, Tennessee, and heading towards Mississippi with a placard that read "Eat at Joe's Both Black and White."

May 20, 1963
Dearest Clark and Mairi: . . .

Aubrey has left for good. He left last week and seemed glad to go. After living here nearly twenty years he said there were three people he hated to leave, which is rather sad, isn't it? Anita is packing up and will leave by the end of the month. They want to settle near Washington, so he can be near his grandchildren, I don't think he expects to live long and he wants to be closer to them, and then too, he has gotten so fed up with Alabama, lost his hope of it. After the Birmingham business I think he thought it was best he got out. I must say to see the cynical settlement, with the white people on it all of the worst reactionaries and worst conservatives, not a single man or woman who ever had taken a stand. It was simply a case of the Big Mules having their northern drivers call them up and say they had to do something and they did, but whether anything will come of it or not I don't know. Even this limited agreement is being fought by the Governor and Bull Connor and they are deliberately trying to stir up riots and make the Negroes break it. Nasty business all around . . .

Bob [Zellner] and Sam [Shirah] are here at Kilby in jail and Cliff has been to see them. Says one boy from New York is on a hunger strike and is in bad shape, although they seem to be in pretty good shape Cliff says. I can't get to see them as only members of the family and lawyers can see them. They are both segregated and isolated from the other prisoners. The whole theory is that the white prisoners would be so infuriated by their presence they would rend them limb to limb. This is the basis of the whole arrests, to protect them from the hatred and violence of the white population. Of course [William] Moore's death gave credence to it after he was murdered . . .

June 3, 1963
Dearest Clark and Mairi: . . .

We are rejoicing over winning the MacMurray case in the 5th Circuit Court of Appeals. Judge Brown wrote a magnificent decision saying that to arrest people to prevent other, threatening people [from] harming them was a denial of the most basic rights of Americans and turning justice upside down. Of course we won't get any damages although the Court sent it back for the determination of the AMOUNT of damages (probably one cent) but at least we won and it is thrilling to sometimes come off the victor against these dark and evil forces of backwardness and brutality . . .

On June 11, 1963, in a nationally televised speech, President Kennedy announced that he would introduce a major civil rights bill to end racial discrimination in public accommodations and in public education.

June 13, 1963
Dearest Otto:

I received the notice that you had subscribed for me again to the *New Statesman and Nation* and I do appreciate it very much . . .

The hope I now have is that the race issue has now become a national issue and is to be fought out on a national basis. I am sure when Kennedy introduces the Civil Rights Bills that the Southerners will filibuster them, and we might have a chance to win IF THE REPUBLICANS DO NOT SUPPLY THE NEEDED VOTES AS THEY HAVE ALWAYS DONE. As they did in 1879 [sic] at the time of the Hayes Tilden deal, they are trying to play a double game and Wallace and Barnett are surrounded by Republicans who are trying to encourage them to have independent electors and a third party and throw the election to the Republicans. It may work but I doubt if this time it will. At least I hope not, but unless the country can be really aroused I think the South will win and if it does, there is going to be a real outbreak of violence. The Negroes have lost their patience finally after all of these years. It just goes to show that when people live without hope, they accept the worse, but when they are given hope they refuse and fight, and it is thrilling to me to have seen the change in the Negroes from hopelessness to hope and to fighting for themselves . . .

Thank you again, dear Otto, you are so kind and so loving and sweet to me and I do appreciate it.

July 10, 1963
Dear Ava Helen: . . .

I don't excuse Vera Foster, I just try and understand her. They have just fired Howard Zinn* at the Spelman College in Atlanta, a splendid white sociologist who did the brilliant piece on Albany, and our dear, sweet Mrs. Manly of WILPF's husband did it. The sad thing is that the Negroes share in the same prejudices the white people do, except about themselves. Of course there are exceptions, but not many. I am afraid neither race, sex, color nor nationality make any difference in the outlook of people who have been exposed so long to lies . . .

Virginia discussed plans for her fall visit to the west coast in the following letter. She also reveals that Cliff continued to be under the cloud of FBI suspicion, which made him, in effect, ineligible for any government appointment.

July 23, 1963
Dear Ava Helen:

Your letter has just come and I was delighted, as always to hear from you. I think the idea of driving up to San Francisco is wonderful, if you can spare the time. I would love to see Carmel and the Big Sur, which I have read so much about and it sounds as though it were a really wildly and grandly beautiful part of the earth . . .

I have written to Decca that we will not arrive until Thursday night if we do drive up or maybe Friday, but that if she can arrange any kind of meeting through Emma Gelders Stern (old friend from Birmingham, Alabama and who is active in WILPF and WSP [Women's Strike for Peace], wonderful old suffragette type) I would be absolutely delighted to speak to them if they want to hear me. Would there be any chance of you staying over for that and also speaking if it can be arranged? Perhaps the two of us together can shake them up a bit. Of course I make

---

*Howard Zinn was an active supporter of the student protests. His account on the movement in Albany, Georgia, *Albany: A Study in National Responsibility*, was published by the Southern Regional Council.

the same speech all the time, I start off with the race issue since that is the one I know about the most and is the one most people want to hear me speak about since I come from the center of it, but then I go on to say that the struggle is not just a struggle by or for the Negroes but a struggle to make this country the kind of country we promised it would be, and if we fail, we simply fail as citizens and the country fails and we are in danger of slipping down the slippery slope into violence, police terror and a form of the corporate state. The main thing I stress is positive action and positive values and positive thought too. I find most people think the race issue is something quaint that exists in the deep South or a political issue only, they do not often seem to realize how it affects their lives, so I give them a little background of the political history and how it has affected them . . .

I appreciate your thinking of us, and we do live in the midst of change and also sometimes of violence, but we never feel ourselves personally in danger, so far we don't at all, although things may get much worse, the kind of danger we live in is the same kind you do, such as today a friend sent us a letter from the head of the Alabama Commission of Civil Rights, in which he said Cliff could not be considered as a member of the Advisory Committee as he COULD NEVER BE CLEARED BY THE FBI. This kind of derogation, this kind of smear, . . . this kind of dirty business has followed us now for twenty years, ever since Cliff took on Hoover and refused to pay any attention to those secret dossiers where T 17 reports that so and so is such and such, or T 28 reports and Miss so and so went to see so and so, ad infinitum. Cliff simply refused to look at them and made a big fight on Hoover for sending them around, and refused to enforce the loyalty order which was based on these same faceless informer charges, and we have been pursued and harassed and smeared ever since, it is like a fog. And how do you fight it? You have fought it and won and if it was open and in the papers maybe we could but it is always behind closed doors and spread by word of mouth. It is stupid to say to you how false it is, as I am sure you know it. We are great believers in free speech, free thought and free assembly and do not feel any group can be outlawed, as the Communists have been, without bringing all of our constitutional safeguards into danger, but as for ourselves we have never, could never, and would never give our conscience into the keeping of any church, any party or any state. We are protestants and always have been. We agree with our brother-in-law, Hugo Black, one hundred per cent and think his opinions express better than anything else we know the principles we have always lived by.

It is like being followed by a ghost, who rises to haunt you when you least expect it, and when people say McCarthyism is dead, we know its ghost is still very much alive and is built into the very system we live in. I hope the mad and wild attacks of Barnett and Wallace will perhaps wake Washington up, but so far I see they only say "You can't prove that by the FBI" and Hoover still remains the Grand Panjandrum of who is respectable and who is not. I think this is the most rotten thing in our country today.

During the late 1950s and early 1960s, the Nation of Islam, also known as the Black Muslims, gained national visibility through the charismatic leadership of Malcolm X, the Nation's national representative. The Nation emphasized independent black economic development and the cultivation of a strong black identity, while offering a scathing critique of white society. Whites, according to the teachings of the Nation, were "the devil by nature." Mike Wallace, who introduced white America to the Nation of Islam with his 1959 television documentary, "The Hate That Hate Produced," expressed dismay at "Negro extremists speaking against whites simply because of whiteness."

By 1963, Malcolm X's call for black separatism, racial pride, and self-defense "by any means necessary" stood as a potent alternative to the leadership of Martin Luther King, Jr. for growing numbers of African Americans. Virginia was a strong critic of this approach, in which Clark Foreman apparently found merit.

July 30, 1963
Dearest Clark and Mairi: . . .

Cliff was very full of his conversation with you and with Paul when he returned, and I am anxious to see the other side of it. He feels the Black Muslim approach is so terribly wrong, that there are so many forces here in the South who are simply looking for some way to "get at" the Negroes, the violence of their feeling is terrible, and if they have a chance to mow them down they will. On the other hand, there is as you know, so many intimate and warm associations among Negro and white and I don't think we Southerners can bear the thought of the Negroes hating us. I am enclosing these two letters from Gomillion, WHICH I VERY MUCH WANT BACK, but there is sometimes often an intimacy and a connection and a working basis between white and black here or white and colored or white and Negro or whatever term you want to use. I really think that the Southerner's soul is in the keeping of the Negroes in so many cases and if it ever comes to open hatred and violence and fighting, it will kill the soul of many and many a white person here.

In our case, while I do not in any way denigrate the very great help you were in our time of trouble, and Corliss and Gene Cotton and many, many others, right here on the ground, it was the Negroes who restored our faith in ourselves and made us feel we could once again be useful and have sustained us with their friendship and help ever since. It is literally unbearable for us to think of being at war with the Negroes. I may sound like an old sentimental "Missis" and they may think I am, but I do feel when I was at my lowest point, when I literally felt I could not bear life itself, "they restoreth my soul." After we got home from New Orleans and had to move and Cliff was sick and we had no money and (again here you and Corliss came to the rescue) it was the Negroes who came around and welcomed us home and made us feel we were Heroes rather than heels, because they knew that whoever Eastland was after was their friend. I don't know how widespread our feeling is, but I do know that if we were divided now we would be ruined entirely . . .

From here the chances of the Civil Rights Bill passing are slim to say the least . . .

August 5, 1963
Dear Clark:

I have just read your letter and it bothered me as I hate to think we are so far apart in our thinking. I am not sure just where, except you keep referring to the Black Muslims as though they were a good organization and to me, they are simply one of the worst and most liable to do the cause of the Negro harm . . .

Of course I don't think the Negroes should love or trust the "Whites" but I do think that more and more there is going to be a community of interests between the Negroes and a great many white people and that community has to grow to get anything done and to simply preach hatred of the white man is not going to help it to grow. Just as I found that to get rid of the Poll Tax I had to get the help of the Negro, just as the merchants in Birmingham found to keep the businesses going they had to make concessions, just as civil rights and civil liberties are both in jeopardy, I think the goals of the white and Negro communities are going to come closer and must come closer to get anywhere. I don't love "Negroes" but there are certain ones of them whom I love and admire very much and I am sure that is the case with Cliff and they have certainly been good friends to us and we know we represent only a token but we feel that there are lots more people all the time joining in.

Slavery was ended when the white people began to find that the slave system was hurting them, and I am sure that more and more white people are going to find that keeping the Negro down is going to hurt them. What bothers me more than anything else is that I am afraid that while the K's [Kennedys] go for the rights of Negroes, they are going to get worse and worse over the Reds. As awful as they are, I cannot help but get a kick out of the Barnett and Bennett and Wallace charges that it is all a communist plot by the Kennedys, they are being hoist on their own petard . . .

Well, sixty does seem a lot older than 59 somehow. I hope I won't feel it so when I pass it, which will be tomorrow. By the way we NEVER DID GET OUR *RIGHTS** and I do wish you would send it to us.

Joan Baez and Bob Dylan refused to appear on ABC's new folk program, *Hootenanny*, because Pete Seeger was blacklisted from the show, causing Virginia to revise her initial impression of Baez.

September 3, 1963
Dearest Mairi and Clark: . . .
You do have a lot of company and I am sure you enjoy it as I do. I have forgiven Joannie Baez everything, long hair, short shorts, bare feet

---

*Quarterly publication of the Emergency Civil Liberties Committee.

and all for taking such a principled stand on Pete Seeger whom I adore as you know. I do think it was so wonderful of her to be willing to jeopardize her own career for him, and it is the kind of standing up for the life of others that I admire more than anything else in the world, so while I am sure what I think of her makes no matter one way or the other, do tell her how much I do admire the stand she took.

As for Clark's and my disagreement about the Black Muslims, I am not yet convinced that they have anything good to offer. I also think as the slaves precipitated the last Revolution (Civil War) in this country, the Negro struggle will be the precipitating agent in the revolution ahead of us, but I do not think they can make it without white allies and I am not sure they will lead it alone. What I meant by the white people giving up slavery was that the Northern industrialists and Yankees gave it up because it was not economic, and down here the big industrialists are willing to do away with segregation because that is not to their advantage, but I do not think the great majority of the Southern whites are in that position at all, and in fact seem to be going in the other direction. Vide Wallace. It is wonderful that the white Tuskegee School Board is now disagreeing with him and violently talking about the "rights of cities" as opposed to "States' Rights." He really thinks he is going to lead the counter-revolution and when you see the effect he has on an audience, he might to a degree.

While Virginia worried about black separatism, she acknowledged in the following letter that the real problem was that Southern whites would not accept anything more than "the merest and barest token of integration."

The letter describes their recent trip to California, which included a visit with Linus and Ava Helen Pauling. This was the first time Virginia and Cliff met Linus Pauling, a sponsor of the infamous peace petition that Virginia signed in 1951. During their visit, Pauling received word that he had been awarded the Nobel Prize for Peace. They also visited with Bob Treuhaft and Jessica "Decca" Mitford, who had recently published *The American Way of Death*.

November 5, 1963
Dearest Mairi and Clark: . . .
We had a wonderful trip to California and enjoyed it very much indeed. We met some lovely people and adored the Paulings with whom

we stayed. We were with them at their remote ranch in the Big Sur when he got word of the Nobel Peace Prize and that was really thrilling. He is such a lovely man and he was so entirely delighted and thrilled and so pleased at his vindication. He has had a struggle as you know. We liked her so much too, I had met her once before but only briefly but we got to be fast friends . . . It was exciting at Decca's too when we got there as her book, as you know, has been a terrific best seller much to her surprise and to mine too. She sold the paperback rights while we were there for $105,000, imagine! I had read it in galley last Spring when I was staying with you all, remember, and I did not think it would be a best seller at all, but apparently there is and has been a deep well of resentment against the way the undertakers have behaved. I know when our boy died I had a horror of them taking over and still do, as I think they make death a sorry kind of parade and corrupt it, but then of course I think advertising and commercialization corrupts most things in America. She is having a nationwide tour under the auspices of her publisher and will be in Atlanta this week, but I am not going over as it is too frantic. The Dinky Donk is there, working for SNCC. I was over in Atlanta at Mrs. Tilly's to do last week and saw her both evenings I was there and she seems happy and Chuck [McDew] is married to her best friend and she seems not to mind. SNCC is down on Raymond Street in the Negro section and it is . . . full of young people ranging from Sarah Lawrence to the cotton fields and all so full of zeal. Very inspiring. I like Jim Forman* very much and think he is going a good job . . .

Cliff spoke a number of times in California and I did too, in fact I spoke nine times and came back with no voice. I found a great deal of interest in the South but very little actual knowledge and many, many questions. I hate to be a prophet of doom, but all of the things I have prophesied have come to pass and I only hope they do not continue to go so badly, as they now seem to be going. The fact is that except for the merest and barest token integration, the South has not given in an inch and does not intend to do so and I see no power in the country that is prepared to make them give in and is able to. All of the professions of the President, the military and so on, seem to have no effect at all on the

---

*James Forman was executive secretary of SNCC.

local scene. Montgomery is just as segregated as it was when we came here except for the busses (on which practically no whites ride) and for the Library (which practically no Negroes use) and for the Airport the same is true there (practically no Negroes use it) and so still a Negro Airman in the uniform of his country cannot get a lousy Coca-Cola when he comes to town or a decent meal or even in the bus stations there are separate waiting rooms and lunch counters although not marked, but rarely do you see a Negro in the white waiting room or at the white lunch counter and the same is true in Atlanta. In fact in Atlanta, they say there is re-segregation. I saw the Bonds and he is just back from Africa and Julia (wife and perfectly lovely) says she is now willing to go to Africa and be safe in a Black Country. It was shocking to hear her say that as she is beautiful and very fair and such a lady, but she hates her life here and I can't blame her. Our Governor Wallace seems to speak what the North likes to hear too, "lazy, dirty, laughing Africans." I simply wonder how long the Negroes can take it and not retaliate. I am afraid nonviolence is not going to last long.

Do write and tell me the news in the Foreman family. I suppose you saw where Jim [Dombrowksi] and Ben [Smith] were arrested for seditious conspiracy and criminal anarchy; did you ever hear of anything so absurd? They are not indicted but all of the files are now in Eastland's hands and what is coming of that I don't know.* Lots of love and do write.

P.S. Wallace "named me" before the Committee when he testified against the Civil Rights Bill as a member of the "Conspiracy" which is behind the whole Negro movement. Very flattering in a way but I am not sure I appreciate it. He has got his Un-Alabama Committee going but they do not have subpoena powers, the Legislature is too fearful he may use them against the Legislators. He is very vindictive. He thinks he is a Little Caesar and acts like one. I used to think he was a clown but not any more.

In 1963, SNCC activists moved into Selma, in the heart of Alabama's Black Belt, and revived a flagging voter registration movement. That fall, hundreds of blacks turned out to register to vote and engaged in mass

---

*Louisiana's Joint Legislative Committee on Un-American Activities, working in concert with the counsel to Senator Eastland's Senate Internal Security Subcommittee, authorized a raid on the homes and offices of Jim Dombrowski and Ben Smith. They seized all of SCEF's records, including contributor lists and mailing lists.

protests against segregation. Sheriff Jim Clark and his police attacked peaceful demonstrators with electric cattle prods and clubs, and arrested around four hundred people.

November 6, 1963
Dear Tex and Wicki: . . .

The news from Alabama is bad. Wallace seems to be the HERO and all of the dreadful injustice is in full flower still and apparently not much hope of change. Only tokens here and there which are something but not much. It is odd to live in and yet out of a society, where we represent such a tiny and powerless minority of white people and while we do what we can and I know Cliff does a great deal, still the problem is so huge and so difficult, that it is like chipping pieces off an iceberg. I am afraid it will take a hydrogen bomb to break it up or something. I don't know how long nonviolence is going to last in the face of all the horrors that go on, the way the police have acted in Selma is beyond belief. Thanks again and lots of love and we look forward to seeing you in January.

November 13, 1963
Dearest Otto: . . .

Life in Montgomery continues to be interesting and tiring. Selma is now the place where the fight is hottest, only forty miles from here. We have a stream of visitors coming and going, we sort of run a refuge for wandering visitors who are working for the cause of the Negro and of course we believe for the cause of America as well. We feel that we are now at the point where the fight is simply to preserve or to maintain or to extend the law to the South, and if we do not do so, anarchy and violence will result.

John F. Kennedy's assassination on November 22, 1963, was greeted with cheers in Montgomery, a response that was not uncommon in the South.

November 26, 1963
Dear Hugo:

Your letter came on Friday morning and we went home to hear the dreadful news. We still feel a state of shock over it. It seems unbelievable that such a thing could happen in this country. I think the worse thing was the cheering that broke out at Lanier High School (you know it is just across the street from us) and the kids began to holler "Hurrah for Dallas" and began blaring their horns and REJOICING. Something is terrible wrong here when high school kids REJOICE over the assassination of the President and I think it is due largely to the message of hatred that Wallace has been preaching day in and day out . . . The bars had people in them drinking to the DEATH OF THE PRESIDENT. Of course there was mourning too, but there was also this attitude of rejoicing which I think is very bad indeed. I do hope Lyndon is able to bring some harmony and some peace to the country without giving up the principles Kennedy stood for. The people down here accept things when they have to, they have completely accepted integration on the military bases and on the buses, airplanes and trains, now at the Library, but still the parks are all closed and the fever is now directed toward motels and hot dog stands. It is a kind of hysteria that Wallace keeps whipped up to white hot pitch all the time. I hope Lyndon can quiet down the fire eaters without giving up the principle of Law and Order and obedience to Law . . .

We feel Lyndon has some fine qualities, he has certainly been faithful to us in friendship and been loyal which is a fine quality and a *rare* quality we have found. I think he really has a love for the political process of the country and I HOPE he will stick by the Civil Rights Bill, but I am not sure of him on this so we have to take him on faith which we do.

Virginia referred in the following letter to the bombing of the Sixteenth Street Baptist Church in Birmingham, which took place on September 15th and claimed the lives of Addie Mae Collins, Denise McNair, Carole Robertson, and Cynthia Wesley.

November 29, 1963
Dear Max: . . .

The last week has been so shocking and tragic that I am still in a state of unbelieving. I simply cannot realize that anything so horrible can happen—that when four little girls in Sunday school are killed and NOTHING IS DONE TO FIND THEIR KILLERS the depths of hatred are so vast that I should really be surprised by nothing at all, but I was not only surprised but terribly shocked. I was not an admirer of

Kennedy's but I did think he was intelligent and did not want to blow the world up and while I know Lyndon well and have know him for thirty years and know he is awfully "smart," I still am not really convinced of his intelligent knowledge of the world. I hope he will grow with the job.

January 10, 1964
Dear Hugo: . . .

We do not expect any offer of a job from Lyndon as I know Lyndon is not going to hurt his political chances and quite rightly. We are still suspect and Wallace called me a Communist or a member of the Communist conspiracy before a Committee of Congress and Jim Eastland now has all of the files of the Southern Conference which he shanghaied and no doubt will continue to feed them into the Alabama Sovereignty Committee, which does not as yet have subpoena powers but they are trying to get them. The Louisiana Committee has again attacked Aubrey and issued a report based on the seized files. While my conscience is clear, I feel I live in an Alice in Wonderland world down here and you never know what to expect. I wrote a letter to the paper about the re-opening of the parks at the request of the Mayor and when we got home the porch, lawn and front of the house was littered with the vilest kind of smear sheet. But on the other hand the friends we have here pay no attention at all to such matters as they get the same thing. We have made some wonderful friends and actually I do not think we want to leave for good, although we certainly do like to get out every now and then.

Sensitive to the Durrs' isolation in Montgomery, Anthony Lester, who had visited the Durrs in 1961, arranged for Cliff to deliver a series of lectures in London early in 1964, and raised money to cover Cliff's and Virginia's expenses. The Durrs spent several weeks in London, an experience Virginia described as "a perfect dream of joy."

They cut their trip to England short so they could attend a celebration in Washington in honor of Aubrey Williams, who was dying of cancer. While in Washington, they made their first visit to the White House since Lyndon Johnson had become president. Virginia expressed confidence in Johnson's support of the Civil Rights bill, but voiced concern about the early direction of his foreign policy, and her fears regarding the overwhelming influence of the military.

March 25, 1964
Dearest Mairi and Clark:

I am so sorry that the virus bug got me and I was not able to come and see you . . . But I managed to get to the White House to Tea. Bird invited the Williams and us over on Tuesday and Ann and Walter and she called by telephone and could not have been sweeter or kinder and we had a fine time. We first had a tour of the White House and then had tea with her. She is just the same, hasn't changed one bit. She is very much interested in the South and is trying to do something to bring up its morale and says she wants to honor those Southerners who have contributed so much to the good of the world IF SHE KNEW WHO THEY WERE, so if you have any suggestions, send them in . . . The two girls got in from school, each with a roommate and one with her hair in curlers and so Bird does her best to create a homelike atmosphere and succeeds I think although living in the White House among all the pomp and ceremony is difficult. I may not always agree with Lyndon but certainly I have never had any cause to disagree with Bird, she has always been the same and never changed at all. She is a perfect marvel of discretion and tact and never says anything which could be repeated or could do any harm and she does not take any position even faintly contrary to Lyndon's, unlike Mrs. Roosevelt . . .

Lyndon came in while we were at tea and was pleasant and nice and abstracted and looked terribly worried which I am sure he is. He then rushed off to New York in his whirlybird which we saw take off amid much roar and uproar.

The trip to England already seems a perfect dream of joy. I never felt so civilized as I did while I was there. I love the British amenities, tea in the afternoon, but above all the marvelous and wonderful freedom of speech, the arguments, the outspoken points of view, the ability to have people of all persuasions in the same room and all of them listened to and argued with, I became intoxicated with freedom . . .

We certainly saw a variety of people, mostly academic of course, and mostly the students and their friends whom we had entertained, but we really had a gay time and I simply loved being popular again and having the telephone ring and being asked out all the time. Same old Southern desire to be loved by all! But Montgomery will take all of my conceit out of me in short order, it has already started, the phone does not ring here much and we have not been missed except by a handful of people. But in London we were the rage for the six weeks we were there. All kinds of people entertained us and we were still being asked when we had to leave, I am glad we left while we were still so popular.

In cities like Jacksonsville, Florida, where the mayor refused even to meet with black leaders, black protest and white defiance pushed racial tensions to the breaking point. On March 23, 1964, clashes between black protesters and white police erupted into two days of street violence. Black youths targeted the downtown business district, vandalizing property and fire-bombing several buildings. On the first night, a young white man driving around with three friends randomly gunned down a black mother of six children.[15] Virginia reported on how these developments were being viewed among people she saw in Washington, and expressed fear that young blacks had completely lost faith in the political process. Hugo Black was undoubtedly among the people Virginia was referring to here. Black viewed direct action protests as a threat to the social order and in some cases a violation of property rights. This was reflected in his opinions in two major cases, *Bell v. Maryland* (1964) and *Cox v. Louisiana* (1965).

April 10, 1964
Dear Jim:

It seems ages since I have been in touch with you. With Aubrey gone we don't see you but I hope you know if you can ever get up here we would love to have you stay with us and we always have plenty of room for you.

We saw the Williams both going and coming and when we left we did not ever expect to see Aubrey alive again, he looked so terribly sick. So when we got word in England that they were having this big celebration for him, we came home a week or ten days early so we could see him again. Cliff got to the luncheon and made a fine speech so I hear, but I was sick with a virus I picked up in England and had fever of 103 degrees, so I could not make it. But I got well enough to go to the White House with Anita and Cliff and Ann and Walter . . . We had a pleasant, private visit with Bird in the private part of the White House and Lyndon came up for a while . . . at least I can say for Lyndon he is really COMMITTED to the Civil Rights Bill. His political fortunes are tied up with it and he feels very strongly about it indeed. Of course all the years we were fighting on it, or on the Poll Tax Bill, he opposed us openly and supported the Filibuster but even then he said he was for it when it was politically possible. I suppose that is the point of a practical politician, but I think he has made his first great mistake in supporting the expulsion of the Brazilian President by the Military, he will suffer the same fate if he is not careful, I think the Military in this country are entirely too strong and too rich. I see them and hear them here in Montgomery and I have yet to meet one who is a democratic person, I don't mean party, I mean principle. But the fact they had us to tea and had the Williams is at least a sign that they don't desert their old friends, at least privately . . .

Jim, when we were in Washington, we saw lots of people, some very high up (this does not include the President and Bird as the conversation there was purely personal) and we found that there is a very STRONG AND GROWING FEELING AGAINST THE KINDS OF DEMONSTRATIONS THAT HAVE OCCURRED LATELY, such as the ones in Jacksonville and people lying down in front of trucks, sitting in State Houses and so on. This is considered to be ILLEGAL . . . and we were told in no uncertain terms that the feeling was the Courts were going to be much stricter and harder on such kinds of demonstrations. I wrote Ella [Baker] this as I thought the kids should know the feeling but I am sure they will not change as I think they have totally lost faith in both legal and political processes, but I have not, and I think when they get the Law on their side they are in a much stronger position. But in any case I wanted you to know what we found to be the sentiment.

April 15, 1964
Dear Wicki:

Your letter has just come and was so satisfactory . . .

Personally I think Wallace is doing Lyndon a real service as he is making it clear he is not a "Southerner." Lyndon told us when we were at the White House that "no colored man in Jackson, Mississippi, ever took as much abuse as a President of the United States who comes from the South" and it is true that the Negroes still have their fingers crossed about him, very little enthusiasm for him, and it is in the big cities and in the minority groups where he is weakest and Wallace really draws the line for him which he needs to have drawn. He is very strong with the Democratic Party people, the pros, very strong with small business and a good section of the big business, *and with the rank and file of people*, but the "liberals" still are skeptical of him in view of his past record on Civil Rights and think Robert Kennedy is the only one who really had guts to do something. Kennedy and his crowd (and I meet them very often down here, those who come down from the North) certainly do not trust Lyndon's liberalism in my opinion, and if he can't get the Civil Rights Bill through he will get the blame. I don't think John Kennedy could have possibly gotten it through and I hope Lyndon can, but I am not sure of that. I have come to the conclusion that the "demonstrations" of the wilder kind such as blocking traffic and doing the kind of frightening things like occupying State Houses and Mayor's offices are doing the Negroes great harm and hurting the chances of the Bill, but I went over to Tuskegee Institute last weekend to a "Conference on the Disadvantaged" and found the conservative, college type Negroes simply wild with frustration, they feel that political and legal pressures have failed and here it is ten years after the Brown decision and they are STILL segregated . . .

May Risher . . . asked us to visit her in Mississippi but I have never managed to get over there. It is not a State I would like to visit . . . I heard from the Woodwards that the Yale Chaplain (Bill Coffin) had recruited thousands of white students to go to Mississippi this Summer. I don't know what is going to happen, but I really rather dread the Summer. Lucy and her family will be here and Lulah, and I know that will be pleasant but the political situation is *so awful* that I dread to see the long, hot Summer come.

From Virginia's perspective, as bad as things were, they could clearly get worse. The Fifth Circuit Court of Appeals, which comprised the Deep South states of Alabama, Florida, Georgia, Louisiana, Mississippi, and Texas, had ruled consistently in favor of civil rights. With one vacancy on the Fifth Circuit, Senator Eastland had an opportunity to shift the balance on that court by securing the appointment of a segregationist, which would have serious consequences for any civil rights legislation that was passed.

At the same time, George Wallace had launched a run for the presidency and found that his appeal extended beyond the Deep South. On April 7 he took more than one-third of the ballots cast in the Democratic primary in Wisconsin, followed by a 30 percent tally of votes in the Indiana primary.

In the following letter, Virginia referred to a new edition of Lewis H. Blair, *A Southern Prophecy: The Prosperity of the South Is Dependant upon the Elevation of the Negro,* originally published in 1889. The 1964 edition included an introduction by C. Vann Woodward. She gave a copy of the book to Lyndon Johnson when she visited the White House in March.

April 21, 1964
Dear Vann: . . .

I don't know if Lyndon read the book or not, but I do think he is doing everything humanly possible to get the Civil Rights Bill passed but I am not sure about it yet at all. Are you?

The thing that has gotten us worried even more is the state of the Judiciary. [Benjamin] Cameron of Mississippi died, who was on the 5th Circuit Court of Appeals and now there is a vacancy . . . If they put on another segregationist Judge we are sunk, no matter what bill comes out. Eastland is also trying to split up the 5th Circuit and split [Richard] Rives and [Elbert] Tuttle off from [John Minor] Wisdom and [John Robert] Brown, and if he gets his way and has the veto power over the Judges on the new Circuit and the old one too, we might as well concede defeat. From a historical point of view, this is very interesting, to see their defenses in depth, while everyone is watching the Senate fight, Eastland and his crowd are consolidating or trying to consolidate themselves on the Judiciary. They never give up.

Here in Alabama we are watching Wallace, but I don't feel as badly as you do, after all Wisconsin was Joe McCarthy's state and at least half of the Republicans crossed over, the McCarthy Republicans. I think it does prove that there are bigoted people in the north as well as the south, but also I think it proves that the Republican party is willing to go along with the most violent racism if they think it serves their purpose. Wallace is riding high down here now, and it looks as if he is going to elect his slate of unpledged Electors on the 5th of May. We won't even be able to vote for Johnson. It really is a madhouse here. After the rationality of the British and their cold-blooded realism, it is like coming back into an insane asylum.

We are certainly looking forward to the Summer with Lucy and Sheldon and their family. It is going to be a long, hot Summer, you should come South and observe it historically. Mississippi is going to be the focus but Alabama will provide some excitement too. Lots of love.

George Wallace trounced the Democratic Loyalists in Alabama's primary election, tapping into "Dixiecrat" sentiments, and previewing the party realignment that would transform the political landscape in the South.

May 7, 1964
Dearest Clark and Mairi,

As always we were delighted to hear from you . . .

Well, I am sure you saw where Wallace simply swept the board on Tuesday, won five to one over the Loyalists who spent most of their time clearing their own skirts of any doubt that they were not true, blue white supremacists, and talking about how awful the Civil Rights Bill was and how "evil and iniquitous" and then ending up saying we should stick by the Democratic Party and vote for the Electors pledged to Lyndon. The reply of the Alabama Electorate was well put by a letter in the *Advertiser*, "What do they think we are, a bunch of Nuts?" So the Alabama Electorate having been made fully aware of the horrors of the Civil Rights Bill voted for the man who went all the way and said DON'T VOTE FOR THE DEMOCRATIC PARTY AND LYNDON JOHNSON and won five to one. It is a total collapse of leadership of the old Democratic forces, John Sparkman and Lister Hill and all the rest and Wallace now reigns supreme . . . He is really dangerous, he is like a little bantam rooster and he expresses so perfectly the small, ignorant, frustrated white man of Alabama. Evidently he also expresses them in the North too, although of course there he is always getting the right wing Republican vote but he gets it here too. I think we have a real demagogue on our hands, bad as Joe McCarthy and really more plausible, Anglo-Saxon, Protestant, Democrat (his sort) and he is bearing down on Christ vs. Communism. He has already accused me of being a "Communist" . . . and of course he was protected by immunity then, but I don't know when he will take after us again. That is one reason Aubrey left, he said he was too sick and too weak to stand up to him and he did not want to make a spectacle of himself by not doing it.

We have no idea of leaving, although we are planning to go to England next fall again. Cliff . . . says he is going to wind up his cases and then close the office, that practicing law here has become too frustrating. It is like running a free legal aid bureau and then he never wins before a Montgomery County jury, although he has a 99 percent record in the appeals courts, but the expense of the office and the total frustration of trying to stand up for the Law in the face of the Judges, juries, and State government is really too much, after so long a time . . . He may change his mind and I hope he does, but for the time being he has had it. He feels the young Negro lawyers here can now take care of the Negroes and are very good, and he has no more influence than they when it comes to juries. I wish he could get some part time teaching jobs and lectures, as I do not think the bucolic life is going to suit him in the long run and I know it will not suit me. I like nature just so long . . .

Dinky Donk is coming this weekend. She is arranging Dick Gregory's tour.* I don't know what she will do here. Wasn't it wonderful Dr. Gomillion got elected to the School Board in Macon County, he really is terrific.

Anthony Lester returned to the South in the summer of 1964 to investigate the justice system for a small, newly established organization called Amnesty International. Lester spent most of his time in Mississippi and Amnesty published his report.[16] Lester was delighted at the opportunity to see the Durrs again, but later recalled that they seemed even more isolated in 1964 than when he had first visited with them in 1961.

The following letters highlight major developments during the summer of 1964, including the passage of the Civil Rights Act, which Lyndon Johnson signed on July 2, and the 1964 presidential campaign which found George Wallace competing with the likely Republican nominee, Barry Goldwater, to represent the disaffected voice of white Southerners. The influx of students to the Deep South during what later became known as "Freedom Summer," and the courage of people like Fannie Lou Hamer, who led the Mississippi Freedom Party delegation to the Democratic convention in August, boosted Virginia's spirits, yet white Southern defiance was unyielding. The initiation of the summer project in Mississippi was marked by the disappearance of three civil rights workers, James Chaney, Andrew Goodman, and Michael Schwerner, who, it was later learned, had been turned over to a mob of Klansmen by a deputy sheriff. They were executed and buried in a remote part of Neshoba County.

---

*Comedian Dick Gregory went on tour to raise money for SNCC.

June 15, 1964
Dearest Clark and Mairi:

Anthony Lester is the young barrister who was responsible for our trip to England and any help you can give him will certainly be very much appreciated by us as he was the soul of kindness to us and went to infinite trouble . . . He is coming over for some international organization called AMNESTY to look into the administration of justice in the South. What he is looking for are specific cases and I thought you might know of some that are going to be tried this Summer . . .

We will have lots of visitors this Summer from the advance bookings, as so many people are coming South on the Great Crusade. I am thrilled that Lyndon got cloture and think it was a work of political genius, and I am sure the Bill will do a lot of good, although no one here has any intention of obeying it until they are made to do so. The editorials all say it will be like Prohibition, simply a gesture on the books. We have a full house but with the place in the country we have lots of room for people with sleeping bags which they all say they have.

It is hotter than the hinges of Hell and it looks as if it were to be a very hot Summer in all ways. But at least we are used to it and we have England to look forward to in the Fall.

July 6, 1964
Dear Anne:

I was so glad to get a direct word from you. I am sure Ella [Baker] will try and get us but we are up in the country so much and are moving up there for good next year . . .

We are having a lot of visitors. A group came up to the Pea Level yesterday from Tuskegee where they have a Summer program. There are also some delightful ones there. Young, bright, handsome, learned, dedicated and amusing, they are really charming as well as nice and good and earnest. I don't know where all of them came from, I don't mean geographically but spiritually and mentally, they come from such disparate backgrounds.

I am delighted and surprised to hear about the progress in Louisville, as here there is nothing yet but a few tentative probings which so far have been successful and no violence which has surprised us. All of the movies and several of the restaurants have obeyed the Law without any kind of fuss at all. Wallace of course is still fuming and threatening and fussing and making speeches, and he seems carried away by his success and the reaction he has met with and it looks as if he is seriously running for President, I think he thinks he can be "The Leader." He certainly has a great appeal to the Alabamians, of all kinds and conditions, educated and uneducated and even, off as it may seem, to some of the Negroes, this is something beyond my comprehension, and while it is a small group, they do seem to admire him.

July 13, 1964
Dearest Aubrey and Anita:

We were delighted to hear from you this morning . . . We certainly are enjoying Lucy and her family and in spite of it being such a "long, hot Summer" we are having a very pleasant time on account of them being here . . . We have, of course, numerous visitors. There is a large concentration of northern students over at Tuskegee for the Summer and we have seen a lot of them, one of them is from Troy, Alabama, named John Rosenberg and he is very nice indeed. He is already in bad trouble with his family. Two English boys have been here and left yesterday. They went to Selma on Friday and promptly got picked up for "questioning" although they were doing nothing at all but taking pictures, but their films were snatched and torn out of the camera and all of the rolls of film were confiscated. The Sheriff's office questioned them, both the Sheriff and some of his deputies and then they were also questioned by the FBI, mainly if they were "Communists" and when they told them they were staying with us, one of the deputies said "Don't you know they are SELF-CONFESSED COMMUNISTS?" Certified! So all of the agents that come in seem to still be hunting for "Communists" instead of the people who killed the young boys. I am sure the body they found is one of them, feet tied together! It really makes me sick . . .

Ray Jenkins* is having a wonderful time needling the Wallace crowd. He thinks Wallace is going to hurt Goldwater and all of the Goldwater

---

*Editor of the *Montgomery Journal*.

people want him to get out of the race and leave it all to Goldwater. But so far Wallace is determined to stay in. He still wants to be a Democrat, although I think if the Democratic Party still accepts him they are crazy. He is running against Lyndon on third party tickets all over the place. He said openly he will hurt Lyndon more than Goldwater and that is why he wants to stay in the race, so he has just about admitted he is doing it to hurt Lyndon and help Goldwater, but the Goldwater people are afraid he will hurt them worse. But there is no one around for Lyndon that I hear about. Some of the young men here . . . got all steamed up about getting Lyndon on the ballot by some suit but they get no advice or help out of Washington, the Democratic National Committee said this was a White House matter and evidently Lyndon has not made up his mind how to deal with Wallace. I only hope he boots him out of the Democratic Party and makes him run as something else . . .

While you have time to think, you ought to put your mind on what makes some of these white Southerners so mean. Why are they so brutally cruel? Why do they need a scapegoat, why do they need to kill, maim, shoot, drown, torture and demean others to make themselves feel big? There is something horribly pitiful in a way there, that would make a man feel big only in making others suffer. It is like the Germans were, a total lack of self-respect . . . I don't believe the Southern problem can be solved without helping the white men too to gain their self-respect, something has been done to them that is awful, some kind of deep self-hatred or self-despising. I wish I could understand it. Do you? Lots of love to both of you.

Virginia took great satisfaction in Lyndon Johnson's brilliant success in shepherding a strong civil rights bill through Congress, although she saw little hope for actual enforcement of the law in the Deep South. And she worried about the direction of Johnson's foreign policy. He had recently made a series of statements warning that the United States was prepared to "risk war" to oppose the threat of "dominion or conquest" by Communist China in Southeast Asia. Election-year concerns guided the Johnson administration's deepening involvement in Vietnam. After U.S. forces provoked an encounter with the North Vietnamese in the Gulf of Tonkin early in August, North Vietnamese gunboats fired on American destroyers. The United States responded with a retaliatory air strike, and Johnson used the occasion to secure a Congressional resolution authorizing him to take "all necessary measures to repel any armed attacks against the forces of the United States and to prevent further aggression." His strong but measured response helped to neutralize his Republican challenger, Barry Goldwater, who urged a massive bombing campaign in North Vietnam. Johnson pledged that while he was determined to defend America's interest, he would limit American involvement in Southeast Asia if possible.[17]

July 13, 1964
Dearest Mairi:

It was such a joy to get your letter and to find out about the Foreman family . . . Summer visitors have started, two young Englishmen left on yesterday and Anthony [Lester] is coming the first of August. I am sure you will like him, or at least I think you will, as he is so charming and interested and interesting. We are devoted to him, of course. He was responsible for our trip and it was one of the nicest things that ever happened to us.

Cliff has been asked back [to England] in November and is planning to go and I am hoping to go . . . I simply hate to be left here as without him, it is lonely and frightening too. I feel still after fourteen years that I am surrounded by hostility and disapproval, and while we do have now a few friends and the Negroes are extremely friendly, still I never know when the telephone will ring, or some lethal voice come out of the night, and it does not make one feel comfortable. I should be braver but I am not. I get scared and lie awake and wonder who in the world hates us so much as that . . .

The passage of the Civil Rights Bill so far has made little difference. There is no sign of giving in and Wallace has said he will not enforce it . . . Law in most of Alabama simply does not exist at all, it is the lawbreakers who are in charge of enforcing the law and the FBI is as bad as the others. I hope Lyndon comes to realize that when he sends in the FBI, he is only adding to the lawbreakers usually. I am sick over the kids in Mississippi being killed and the body they found this morning seems to me to be bound to be one of them. Feet tied together, typically representative of the spirit of attacking and tormenting the helpless. They don't believe in giving anyone a chance, cowards all . . .

It still seems a political miracle that Lyndon got the Civil Rights Bill through. He has certainly come a long way from the gangling young

Congressman we knew with his sweet wife. She is still sweet I think and unspoiled and I think is a fine influence on him. He does scare me though with the speeches he makes on Viet Nam and foreign policy, and with the Republicans pushing him all the time, I am so afraid he will follow along in Truman's tracks and try to out do them in fire eating, and land us in another great mess or even worse, another great war. I do not have the same confidence in him on foreign affairs that I do in domestic affairs, and while I think he is basically a conservative in both, I do think he knows the score in domestic affairs. But Lyndon is really in the center and the Republicans are now on the far right, and there is so little pressure (except for the Civil Rights movement) on the left, that I don't know what will happen . . . Isn't it inconceivable to think of Goldwater being a possible President? To think there are so many people in this country who are for him. But to think of all the people here who are for him and Wallace too.

On August 30, Tilla married Frank Parker, a young civil rights activist and Harvard Law School student. Virginia described the wedding, which was held at Ann and Walter's home in Harrisburg, Pennsylvania, in the following letter. She also shared some gossip about Dinky's romance with James Forman, executive secretary of SNCC.

September 1, 1964
Dearest Dec:
You have been such a bad correspondent that you have missed out on all the excitement of the Summer. Tilla is now married. Married last Sunday or rather day before yesterday, August 30 in Harrisburg, Pa. . . . She married a SNCC kid named Frank Parker whom she met last March when we were at Oxford and who is a student at the Harvard Law School, very bright boy, brilliant in fact, but very, very opinionated, dedicated to the "movement" beyond all things and thinks Tilla is terribly lacking in political dedication but they do seem very much in love . . .
We went up and all of his family came over from Ohio and it was a very gay and joyful occasion, lots of Rhine wine and jollity and she did look absolutely beautiful and they went off this time very happy and married . . . He wore his SNCC button to pin on his white carnation. He is only twenty-four and has a lot of seasoning to get before he becomes

really mature, but he is bright, dedicated and lots of fun. Jim Forman sent him over to us last Summer when he was doing volunteer work for them and we kept him for about two weeks and became quite fond of him, although we thought he was terribly amusing, as he considered us the remnants of the "Old South" and frequently addressed us as "You white folks" and then enumerated our sins. He got a scholarship to University College at Oxford and we saw him again and that is where Tilla met him and then he went over to see her in the Spring in Strasbourg . . .

Too bad you did not see the Freedom fight* on the TV, terribly exciting.

I have seen the Dink several times. She is right in the midst of it, absolutely lives it and breathes it and nothing else right now. I did see the HT† article on her which I thought must be Judy Viorst it was so good. The gossip in SNCC circles is that she and Jim Forman are having an affair . . . He is a fine person I think; I like him very much. He is 36 years old and from Chicago . . . but this is all gossip and rumor. She refuses to discuss her love life with me, both because she thinks I gossip too much and she KNOWS I will write it all to you which I am of course doing as I think you are as interested as I am (possibly a little more so!) in her life. I simply adore her. I really think she is marvelous and whoever she takes on is all right with me and if you could only come and simply visit, it would be wonderful.

While the Civil Rights Act promised to end legalized segregation in the South, Virginia became increasingly concerned about the economic inequality and exploitation that plagued large numbers of blacks in the North as well as the South, predicting that Northern blacks were most likely to rebel against these conditions.

September 1964
Dearest Clark: . . .

As I get older I am getting more radical all the time. I don't believe Civil Liberties or Civil Rights will do much as long as economic control continues to stay in such a few hands and we are all prisoners of money, owned by someone else. And race, religion, sex, and all other controver-

---

*Refers to the Mississippi Freedom Democratic Party's challenge at the Democratic national convention.
†*New York Herald Tribune.*

sial subjects can be discussed but get on money and who controls it and how it can be distributed, and then you are a gone goose. When I see those filthy slums in New York, with the garbage rotting in the streets and the people rotting in the buildings, and they have civil rights and to some extent civil liberties, but they can't do much with either because their lives are controlled entirely by the ones who control the money and their jobs.

I hope and think Lyndon is going to win but I don't know how he is going to keep his various forces together if unemployment grows and I think the Negroes here in the South are full of hope now but the ones in the North know the right to vote and go to a movie and so on mean nothing if they have not got the money. I think the northern Negroes are far more likely to revolt than the ones in the South, although you have a sort of Civil War going on in Mississippi, but nonviolent on one side and extremely violent on the other.

Barbara and John Beecher* are coming up next week and live in our house up at the Pea Level for a month or so. He is now in NO [New Orleans] doing work for the *San Francisco Chronicle* and wants to do some things on the Black Belt. He and I grew up together in Birmingham, and I like him and think she is very nice, although I think he is best taken in small doses as he stays so wrought up all the time and is so serious but he can express some sense of humor some time, but in any case I am delighted to have them. Cliff will be in England about three weeks and the "British Universities Durr Association" cabled me to be sure and come with him, they would send me a round trip air ticket, but I simply cannot pick up and go right now so quickly, and really am not too anxious to do it, as I am anxious to get organized after the long, hot Summer and all the visits and the wedding and all of the excitement that went on before it.

October 19, 1964
Dearest Anne:

I am thrilled you are coming! And call me on Friday night or Saturday from NO and let me know exactly what time you are coming . . .

---

*Poet and journalist.

I hope you can find out about Montgomery, as far as anyone can tell it is quiet as a mill pond, no stirrings at all, in spite of George Wallace's wild spoutings. The Negroes say the integration that has taken place has caused no difficulty at all, but it is mighty little although they go to the movies, cafeterias, some restaurants and so on. But I am afraid, as have the Negroes in the North, they will discover that token integration does not mean much, although the joy of Mr. Nixon and Fred Gray and Bernice and Mrs. West at actually GOING to Morrisons and to the hotels was beyond belief. I never saw such exultation as when Mr. Nixon called up to tell me about his first dinner at the Albert Pick and how he had tipped the white waitress $1.50. The insults they have suffered are beyond our imagining and I wonder if they ever will actually forgive the white people of the South . . .

I really am delighted you are coming as there are so many things to talk over and it seems to me it has been an awfully long time. Lots of love, Va.

Lyndon Johnson won the 1964 presidential election by one of the largest margins in history, but the Republican Party made inroads in the South, with Barry Goldwater taking Alabama, Georgia, South Carolina, Louisiana, and Mississippi. In the end, Virginia thought this shakeout of staunch segregationists might pave the way for building a "real" Democratic Party in Alabama.

Friday, [November] the 13th, 1964
Dearest Dec: . . .

I have been busy here ever since the Election working on trying to start a new Democratic group. All sorts of people are trying to pick up the pieces—and all of the old crowd are singing the "unity" plea, take back Wallace and Bull Connor, forgive all the ones who voted for Goldwater and let's all love each other and start again, but I refuse, so a few of us are trying to start a real bona fide Democratic Party, but I do not know with what success. I only hope Lyndon will not cross us up by taking back all the SOBs and letting them ruin things again . . .

As you probably saw by the papers, the Goldwater landslide simply swept all of the local County officers out of office, who have been there for ages, and consternation reigns supreme. I am so glad they had such a jolt, for so long they have been wolves in sheep's clothing or Democrats in Republican clothing and I am simply delighted that they all got beat—they deserved it. We now have five Republican Congressmen, all fierce racists who ran on Goldwater's coattails. I do hope the good Republicans have nothing to do with them. We are terribly concerned to see that the same old crowd does not get back in. I have been on the phone all morning trying to get up support, but I still find people awfully queasy about an integrated Democratic Party. Still scared to death . . .

I cannot find your letter and feel I am being rather repetitive and random. The phone keeps ringing about this Democratic meeting tonight, and I am afraid few will be present, all are waiting to see which way the cat jumps—where the power, patronage and politicians are going, there it goes again. I am continually surprised to find how few people have any principles, simply waiting to jump on the bandwagon. But they did beat Goldwater in the country, if not here. I don't know when anything has given me more satisfaction and while Lyndon is no lily, still I cannot believe he won't be a lot better. I hope so anyway. Lots of love, and let me know if we can meet up anywhere.

Virginia attended Lyndon Johnson's inauguration and was treated like a member of the family. While in Washington, she heard Hugo Black read his opinion in *Cox v. Louisiana*. The majority on the Court voted to reverse a conviction for protesting near a courthouse, and Black dissented. He urged reliance on "the temperate process of the law," warning that it was not a "far step from what to many seems the earnest, honest, patriotic, kind-spirited multitude of today to the fanatical, threatening, lawless mob of tomorrow."[18]

February 10, 1965
Dear Glenn and Vann:

Certainly the most restful part of my visit was my visit to you and I look back on the lovely quiet and rest and delicious food and loving care with longing and nostalgia. Thank you once again . . .

I finally made it to Washington and was able to go to all the festivities. When I got there I found that Bird had put me down as a "guest of the family" so I got the best tickets to everything and enjoyed it all. When I went to get them, I found I had been put in the same group with her cousins from Alabama, all fine, country people, everyone of which HAD VOTED FOR WALLACE AND OPPOSED LYNDON [in the

Democratic primary] of course on grounds of the race issue. But they were all for Bird and she did not let it interfere with her affection for them, real Southern tribalism, and rather comforting I thought . . . Our Governor Wallace was there acting as though he were the original Democrat and passing out the word, or at least his henchmen were, that he might get the support of the White House in his race with John Sparkman. Can you image such nerve? John is going to have a hard race with him if he runs and it seems now as if he will. He and the Yankee business interests seem to have made a deal and he has gotten lots of big concerns to come to Alabama. Of course we do have great advantages in the way of water, climate and so on, but "cheap labor" and no unions seem to be his biggest selling points. They don't seem to mind his segregationist policies at all, in fact I think they rather like them . . .

I can't think of anyone I met whom you might know. There were . . . thousands of people and such diverse ones. Country kin, and so many of those sort of bleached blonde women dripping in furs who look like overripe peaches about to burst. They never seem to change their expression from early twenties to old sixties and when they do get old they look awful. Of course the place was full of Texans, but rather subdued, as they were under strict orders not to shoot the place up or make any noise. The whole thing did have a kind of barbecue flavor to it, but I liked it, I thought it had an authentic Southern flavor of friendliness and good time.

Hugo and Elizabeth* had me up to lunch at the Court and I heard Hugo read his dissent in the Cox case, where he so STRONGLY condemned the Negroes for taking their struggle to the streets and urged them to "trust the Courts." I agree that these long-continued street struggles might stir up a real resentment which will react badly against them, but I do not see how he can expect them to trust the State Courts here which are so set against them, and so prejudiced and unfair. But he is really upset about the lack of law and order and thinks it is very demoralizing.

Utterly and completely and wholly a change to get back to Alabama. There is integration, certainly as far as public accommodations goes there seems to be no trouble at all, BUT AMONG the white people I see no change of attitude at all, except the same precious few. All on the defensive, all critical of Washington, [Hubert] Horatio Humphrey now

---

*Hugo Black married the former Elizabeth DeMeritte in 1957.

seems their main target, all determined not to give an inch until they have to. It is so cruel and hard for the Negroes to realize that it was not "just the law" that was keeping them apart, that now that the law is changed, the white people have NOT changed, I really think they thought they would . . .

Thanks again for your warm and affectionate hospitality . . . Lots of love and let me know what kinds of clippings you want. Devotedly, Va.

Late in January, presidential advisors McGeorge Bundy and Robert Mc-Namara told Lyndon Johnson that the United States must take more aggressive action in Vietnam or face "disastrous defeat." On February 6, Johnson ordered a retaliatory strike against several army barracks in North Vietnam following a Viet Cong attack on an American base at Pleiku. On February 13, the United States initiated an eight-week-long bombing campaign against selected targets in North Vietnam. As biographer Robert Dallek notes, Johnson's refusal to make a public statement about the expanded air war reflected his ambivalence about deepening involvement in Vietnam as well as his desire not to distract attention from his domestic reform agenda. The day after the bombing campaign, named "Rolling Thunder," began, a *New York Times* columnist reported that the United States had entered "an undeclared and unexplained war in Vietnam."[19]

February 12, 1965
Dearest Clark and Mairi: . . .

In spite of my cold, I enjoyed the Inauguration and went to lots of the parties . . . it really was lots of fun, but I did not have any desire to STAY in Washington now. It is too big, too rich and too money minded and actually I am not in agreement with it, domestically perhaps, but on foreign affairs, No. I am really shocked and surprised and dismayed and horrified over the recent bombings [in Viet Nam]. I really did not think Lyndon would do such a thing and I don't think Izzy did either, I saw him in Washington and for the first time he was VERY OPTIMISTIC. Helen Lamb* seems to have known more and seen more clearly the dangers than anyone else . . .

---

*Helen Boyden Lamb, economist and author, was an early leader in the anti-Vietnam war protest. Her 1964 pamphlet, "The Tragedy of Vietnam: Where Do We Go From Here?" urged immediate withdrawal of American forces, which numbered 18,000 in 1964. Lamb married Corliss Lamont in 1962.

The reason I was so strong for Lyndon was I thought he would keep us out of a War, and I cannot understand his recent actions. Do you think he is doing it to screen our getting out? It is really so surprising and shocking to me. Do you suppose we are going to keep on and on making the same awful mistakes and doing the same awful damage? . . .

Lots of love and thanks again. Do write when you can as I love so to hear from you.

In March 1965 thousands of people from around the country responded to Martin Luther King, Jr.'s call to join in a march from Selma to Montgomery. King's appeal followed the attack by state police on the original group of marchers, who had set out on Sunday, March 7 for the state capital to demand that the state legislature reform voter registration procedures. The march was organized after Jimmy Lee Jackson was killed by police during a protest. State troopers and police on horseback waited for the marchers on the Edmund Pettis Bridge and enveloped them in a cloud of tear gas before charging into the crowd and beating them back with clubs and cattle prods. The violent assault was broadcast nationally and aroused a wave of indignation. The next week, Lyndon Johnson addressed the nation, proclaiming, "It is wrong—deadly wrong to deny any of your fellow Americans the right to vote in this country." He promised to introduce a comprehensive voting rights bill, and ended his speech with the words of the movement's anthem, "and we shall overcome."

The Durrs' home was a major destination for friends and strangers who flocked to Alabama to participate in the historic march that began on March 21. She reported that they had over a hundred visitors. While all of them did not stay overnight at the Durrs, "they had all their meals and coffee and bathed and dressed and dropped in at all hours of the day and night." It was thrilling, she later wrote Marge Frantz, and "it made me feel that all of our efforts were bearing fruit . . . When I remember the tiny beginning in Birmingham [in 1938] and now see what a great flood it has become, I do get the feeling that no effort is ever wasted if you can just live long enough."[20]

March 18, 1965
Dearest Clark and Mairi: . . .

The trouble here of course has kept us all occupied and we have had a constant stream of visitors, I never saw so many people as have come down here. Clergy of all sorts, and also students and professors and so on. So many call or come by who knew us or knew of us or knew some one who knew us . . . People finally seem really aroused. It is funny when you think that we were working on this thirty years ago or longer, and now Lyndon is the great champion of the vote when he used to filibuster along with the rest. We always seem to be right too soon.

Our latest visitor . . . got beat up in the riot Tuesday afternoon and called and asked if he could come out, and arrived pretty stunned and in rather a state of shock. He is not at all the usual type, no blue jeans or beard, and seems to be well-mannered and is a worker for CORE . . . He finally quieted down, we gave him a drink and a tranquilizer and he is still here but I think he will leave today to get back with the crowd—they all hate to be separate from the crowd. He marched yesterday and got sopping wet and I thought would be sick, but seems all right today. Never a dull moment in Montgomery I must say, but often rather exhausting indeed. I will be glad to get some peace and quiet. The trouble is that they all leave, no one ever stays, they all come and then go and leave us here and leave the Negroes here. I do wish that sometimes some one would stay and battle here. We are like New York, they like to visit but don't want to live here . . .

The Rev. James Reeb of Boston was among the hundreds who responded to King's appeal and went to Selma. On March 9, a group of whites attacked him and two other ministers after they left a black-owned restaurant. He died two days later from his injuries.

March 18, 1965
To Elizabeth and Hugo: . . .
We have really been in the midst of wild excitement, people have been streaming through here . . . There have been hundreds of people coming to Selma and to Montgomery, hundreds and hundreds of clergymen. It seems like an old-fashioned revival. We went to the memorial service for the Rev. Reeb which was very moving and I never saw such a tremendous outpouring of clergy in my life, all kinds. We thought Lyndon's speeches have been splendid, and he has finally made it a moral issue and I think will meet with more response down here, although it is still painfully slow and painfully defensive and the people feel so mistreated and misunderstood and sorry for themselves, they would not even pass a resolution of sympathy in the Legislature for Mrs. Reeb, said it would seem to cast [a bad] reflection on Dallas County! To go any further toward madness seems difficult. George Wallace expresses their

feelings of persecution and gets stronger all the time, and I do not see any signs of repentance on his part or on the part of the white population at all so far, although a few of the Ministers are beginning to speak out and that is a beginning perhaps.

Tension between SNCC and Martin Luther King, Jr. and the SCLC became pronounced during the time of the Selma-to-Montgomery march. King's failure to consult with SNCC leaders about key decisions concerning the march infuriated James Forman. Frustrated with King's approach, he moved SNCC's base of operation from Selma to Montgomery and began organizing students from Tuskegee in protests at the state capital. In the aftermath of a brutal police assault on the student demonstrators, Forman, while sharing a platform with King at a mass meeting in Montgomery, warned: "If we can't sit at the table of democracy then we'll knock the fucking legs off." While Virginia was sympathetic to Forman, she thought that SNCC's growing militancy would work to King's advantage.[21]

Virginia regretted these growing divisions within the movement, especially when white defiance and violence was rampant. The following letter refers to the murder of two of the volunteers who came South to participate in the march—Rev. James Reeb and Viola Liuzzo, a white woman who was shot while driving marchers from Montgomery back to Selma.

March 29, 1965
Dearest Dec: . . .

There is a concerted effort to kill off SNCC and Jim too. Poor fellow is so tired and sick too, and I cannot help but think he made a mistake to give King such a perfect opportunity to emerge as the all-wise Father and Savior with the whole world watching, while he emerges as the wild, irresponsible, violent one. I think he did a lot of good in getting the local kids out but nationally I think King won the public relations contest hands down—he has now become deified. Of course with the kinds of devils we have to fight against, Wallace, Clark, Connor and Lingo and the cowardly snakes who strike in the night and who killed Reeb and Mrs. Liuzzo, I think it is awful that the Civil Rights Movement has to split, but this seems to be the nature of all Movements, . . . they always seem to be ruined and killed off from within, by splitting and killing each other off, we saw that plainly enough in the Labor movement. But one thing I know is that the kids are not going to listen to anyone at all, and I might as well quit worrying as it is not anything I can do anything about. It is odd that out of middle-class America these kinds of kids should come, all willing to die for a cause. I don't mean "all," but lots of them in any case. The ones we had here were daughters and sons of professors, industrialists, ministers, doctors, all middle-class and perfectly willing to go to jail, get beaten up, go on hunger strikes, and endure all kinds of cold, hunger and general misery for the cause. The cause is human freedom on the part of the SNCC kids, pretty vague, not just Negro freedom, or not just doing away with segregation—they want something much bigger but since they do not define it, it is pretty vague. But they all want Peace in Viet Nam as well as a stop to Southern oppression and that at least is definite. I adore them and admire them but at the same time I cannot help but think their political tactics are bad, as they don't seem to make any effort to win people over, and in fact seem to take delight in offending their most deeply felt standards. The only thing they do that does not seem to me in line with their efforts is their total contempt for the Southern White. I admit there is reason for it, but the Negro cannot really win without at least some friends here and they seem to be racists in reverse when it comes to the Southern White. I think they antagonize them unnecessarily, but I am sure they think they are perfectly hopeless.

I am enclosing some clippings which I thought might throw some light on the situation . . . Lots of love and do write and tell me what the reaction abroad was to all of this. Devotedly, Va.

Aubrey Williams died in Washington, D.C., on March 5, 1965.

April 1, 1965
Dearest Wicki: . . .

Yes, we did go up to Aubrey's funeral and Cliff spoke at the Memorial Service along with Frank Bane and Jim Dombrowski. Lyndon and Lady Bird called, sent a telegram and beautiful White House flowers but neither came to the service which was a great disappointment to all of his friends. Oscar Chapman was there and Ben Cohen but they were about all of the officials whom he had known that came. You and Tex were missed very much and I am sorry you were sick and could not come, it was a beautiful service and Anita had all of the out-of-town people over afterward for lunch and it was really a very happy occasion, full of fond memories and laughter. There were a lot of people from New York and from Chicago . . . and Marie Lane came from California and in all there were about two hundred people there. I thought the obituaries in the [*New York Times*] and the *Washington Post* were beautiful and Alan Barth did a lovely little editorial on him. We miss him terribly but after seeing him at Christmas we can only be thankful he is free from his suffering . . .

We too are worried and sickened by our foreign policy and I am really astonished at Lyndon being taken in so by the military policy of force. He has been magnificent on the Klan and on the Southern situation but he does not seem to realize that his actions in Viet Nam put Jim Clark and Bull Connor and George Wallace to shame, I never heard of such horrors as we are perpetrating. I am afraid we are going to lose the world entirely and no country will ever want us to help them militarily if it means the country and the people are exterminated . . .

Since we got home from Washington we have lived in turmoil. Literally hundreds of people have come by or called, we had people sleeping on the floor during the March, such an assortment you never saw. Vann Woodward the historian from Yale who is as you know an old, old friend, came and Lou Pollak who has just been made Dean of the Yale Law School came with him, and Tom Emerson's son was here in jail for demonstrating so he came when he got out, and then a poet friend of my old days in Birmingham came and slept on the sofa and there was an Episcopal Rector on the floor and several others and of course all had to be fed and then people who were sleeping on the pews of Negro churches came by to bathe and wash and feed. It was lots of fun but really terribly hectic. A terribly nice Dane . . . who is head of the Cultural Section of the Danish TV arrived as well and he was a lovely, cultured and charming man . . . The State Department sends us these foreign visitors, we are official hosts for them, and I am afraid we are part of a gigantic hoax to make them believe that there are not so many Southern segregationists as they have been led to believe. Some of them are very nice, some quite dull, but in the desert of Montgomery society (at least for us) all very welcome. I think the March was magnificent and the day left us feeling so good, only to be ruined by the awful murder of Mrs. Liuzzo, and now Montgomery has become so defensive and brought out all the old charges which show the real terror and irrationality of their fears. They accuse all the Marchers of immorality, public fornication, Negro mixing, and even accuse her and say she was having sex relations with the Negro boy on the front seat when she was shot, and going at least seventy miles an hour as the car went off the road and went hundreds of feet before it stopped . . . It reveals the real cesspool that lies below the surface here and is the cause of the horrible brutality, fierce resistance and irrational behavior. It would take a trained Freudian to discover the roots of the behavior of these men who have slept with Negro women all their lives, had children by them, still do, and then get up and scream white supremacy and deny their own children. It certainly produces brutes. Lots of love and do write and tell me how you are.

Devotedly, Va.

April 5, 1965
Dearest Mairi and Clark:

Joan Baez was simply magnificent here. I will have to take back any unkind remarks I ever made about her manners, she was really superb, both in voice and in courage and in "MANNER" the grand manner. I think she won more converts than King among the young people. Lots of love, Va.

April 19, 1965
Dearest Carl and Anne: . . .

The aftermath of the March here has really been awful, at least locally. I think it had a great effect nationally and the March or the threat of the Boycott caused the State Chamber of Commerce to come out with a big AD calling for "Law and Order" but that is the only result it has had that I can see locally. The whole town has united in self defense, and all you hear are tales of sexual orgies, nuns who were really prostitutes, churches turned into whorehouses, and beatniks, bums, communists, scum and so on. I went to a woman doctor the other day, nice woman and a good doctor and she said "How could you have had such scum, beatniks, prostitutes, etc." in your house? Since I was helpless at the time I only asked her if she had ever heard what the local people said about the Union Army when it came here, as she had said her Grandfather came here with the Union Army, and she did pause at that, but I must say the Yankees who come here soon become the worst Confederates of all.

The great and continuing excitement here has been the picketing of the churches. Two Methodist and one Presbyterian have let them in but the Presbyterian Church put them in the balcony. Judge Rives, our local Federal Judge on the Fifth Circuit, got up and walked out of his church (Trinity Presbyterian) when they refused to seat the Negroes . . . But while he acted according to his conscience, he is so upset as he simply loved "The Church," his son had been buried there and his daughter married there, and as for us, we not only have the Church to contend with but Cliff's brother and his ancestors who started the Church and have sat in the same pew for five generations. So far we simply stay away, which is not a very brave thing to do, but the choice is to stay away or walk out and irretrievably end all connection with Cliff's family. Sad situation. I do not think anyone has ever known the anguish people here go through with their families, it really is very cruel and sad and painful. The SNCC kids are picketing the Dime Stores as they say voting and church and so on do not help unless you have a job and of course they are right.

Jim Forman came to see us the other afternoon, and brought the whole SNCC staff with him, causing as you can imagine great excitement in the neighborhood and Terry (pretty dark girl who helped me so much) has been forbidden [in] my house on account of it, but she still comes but in defiance of her in-laws. I did not have any chance to talk to Jim as the other eight were there, but he did say the time had come to make the distinction plain between . . . SNCC and SCLC and that peace talk and "do not rock the boat" had gone on too long, that SCLC and SNCC had totally different aims, and he thought the alliance of big business and Negro leaders was entirely false as in Atlanta, which I think is true, but the question is whether SNCC has the strength to stand alone and the money to do it with, and will this break not give added strength to King and leave them out in the cold to take all the red baiting, which is fierce as you know. The thousands of people who came here during the March were not reactionaries, but good people in my opinion and I think the public "break" gave King a perfect platform to draw the distinction between his "responsible" organization and SNCC. But I do not see how he is ever going to get 2,000 College kids to come South this Summer without

SNCC. I think he needs them as much as they need him, and I do think they need him. But apparently they don't think so, and of course there is nothing anyone can do about it, at least anyone old as we are. Jim looks at you with those amber colored eyes of his, and you know he will die to end being called a "Nigger" or being treated as one . . .

I have seen the country, or at least Alabama and that is the vantage point I have, take on the same attitudes that Germany did, self-pity, race hatred, fear, conformity, "blood brotherhood" and I really cannot see at this point where it is going to end, as I see absolutely no signs in the white community of any change of heart or mind, simply a furious and rebellious consent to making a "token" compliance. I hope my vantage point is so bad that things are better in other places. What do you think? I see great changes in the Negro community and in the Negroes and that is all to the good, but the white handful here is still so small and so surrounded by hostility. One by one they leave or retire into silence.

I should be rejoicing today, as it is Easter and Christ is risen and the countryside is so beautiful. I have never seen such azaleas, such roses, such blue phlox and flowering trees as we have had this Spring, it has been marvelous, but when I come up against the human element it is like running into barbed wire and I get to feeling that I live surrounded by barbed wire and if I move I will get stuck. I hope this, like most of my moods, will pass and I will get a more cheerful view of life.

April 28, 1965
Dearest Dec:

I was delighted to get your letter from Le Havre, and know you were still in the land of the living. I was afraid you had succumbed to the dolce fa niente (think this is right but doubt it) of Italy and had been seduced by Italy and the Italians whom I consider the most charming people and the most beautiful country in Europe . . .

More and more I see this Society as really crazy, they have lost all sense of reality. Dickinson's* crazy speeches about sexual orgies are quoted and BELIEVED all over town. I heard the story about the rapes

---

*Alabama Congressman William Dickinson gave a speech on the floor of the House, describing the invasion of Selma by assorted "adventurers, beatniks, [and] prostitutes," and scenes of sexual orgies.

so much that I called St. Margaret's Hospital and they said not a word of truth. The only sensible remark I have heard is one old lady who was told the story of the white girl that got raped 47 times in the Ben Moore Hotel (where SNCC had headquarters when they first came) and she said in a mild way "I wonder why she didn't holler instead of counting?" But no one laughed except me. All of the cesspool of sickness connected with sex guilt comes out in these stories and poor Mrs. Liuzzo has now been turned into some kind of sex fiend as well as a dope fiend. I really get both sick and frightened by them. I cling to the small circle we have and we do have visitors but the great majority of the people frighten me, they are so insane and prejudiced and I do not see how we can avoid wholesale violence . . .

Collie Leroy Williams, Jr., William Orville Eaton, and Eugene Thomas were charged with murdering Viola Liuzzo. All three were members of the Ku Klux Klan's Eastview klavern in Bessemer, Alabama, as was Gary Thomas Rowe, the FBI informant whose testimony led to their indictment. Rowe was in the car with the three men when Liuzzo was gunned down. Collins accused Rowe of killing Liuzzo; Rowe admitted to aiming a gun at the victim, but said he did not fire it. Virginia attended the trial, which was held in the courthouse in Hayneville. For the duration of the trial, voter registration was temporarily moved from the courthouse to the old jailhouse. Matt Murphy, the 51-year-old defense counsel, was from Birmingham. Virginia had known him as a young child. Murphy was a descendent of the Percys of Mississippi and the deBardeleben family, owners of the Tennessee Coal and Iron Company and Birmingham's founding family; for her, he epitomized the rot and decay of Southern society.[22]

May 6, 1965
Dearest Anne and Carl:
The three days at the trial made me sick literally, the poor dead woman was on trial and the Counsel for the KKK (whom I had known as a baby in Birmingham) asked the most vile and obscene questions about the state of her underwear and her dead body, trying to influence the Jury to think she had been having sex relations with the young Negro boy. Then too, he asked repeatedly about dope needle punctures. The Doctor who performed the autopsy said there was not one vestige of proof that she had had sex intercourse or taken hypodermic shots,

but the Jury heard all of the vile insinuations. The FBI witness (not a pleasant character to say the least) said that her shooting was pure chance, she drew up beside them at a red light and she was sitting on the front seat by a "nigger" so they said "Let's take that car" and pursued them up the highway and when they got to the car shot her full in the face, twelve bullets, it was purely impersonal, but the depths of horror it invokes is past belief . . . I do not think there will be any conviction. The Jury is still out . . .

The tiny little village, the old Courthouse, the primroses and purple vetch really made a beautiful picture and the spectators in the Courtroom and the ones in the town, all looked just like nice country people in for a show, but the feeling was so strongly on the side of the KKK and the hate and hostility shown to the newsmen and me because I was identified with them was really awful. What has possessed these people, there seems to be some kind of devil that has perverted them all and yet so often in personal relationships they are very nice and kind.

Like the man that shot Medgar Evers,* this Counsel, Matt Murphy, was the last decaying branch of an old, aristocratic family tree, the Percys from Mississippi, who used to own great plantations around Greenville, and one of them wrote *Lanterns on the Levee* and one wrote *The Moviegoer* so there was some talent in the family too. His grandfather and Uncle had both been General Counsel for the Tenn. Coal, Iron and RR Co. in Bessemer . . . Two of the defendants were unemployed steelworkers who had been brutalized by the TCI and certainly not saved by the Steel Workers Union. And here was the descendant and scion of Southern aristocracy and the unemployed steel workers all combined in this horrible brew of savagery and brutality and indecency too. The only hopeful note in Hayneville were three SNCC kids (bearded, sandaled and dirty too), Negro and white together who were helping register Negroes at the old jail. There were almost a hundred around the old jail. How brave they are, I think they are the bravest people in the whole country. I will never even say again they should shave off their beards or wash. Lots of love, Va.

---

*NAACP field secretary for Mississippi, murdered by Byron De La Beckwith on June 11, 1963.

May 10, 1965
Dearest Vann:

Thank you so much for Warren's* book which I find intensely interesting, history as it is made.

I am enclosing a few items for you to add to your collection. I collected these over at Mrs. Liuzzo's trial, which had a fascination for me and I went in spite of the pain it caused me . . . No one would go with me, and I had to go alone and No. 80 is scary, so lonesome, and then when I got there the place was full of fearsome people, huge, menacing State troopers with guns on their hips, and huge menacing Sheriffs and Deputy Sheriffs with guns on their hips, and huge menacing KKK's with guns no doubt in their pockets. Then the KKK and the States Righters were out in full force with their literature which I am enclosing. The Prosecutor looked huge and menacing too, and the Defense Counsel likewise, but I knew him when he was a baby so he was not so fearsome, just crazy. You know his mother was a Percy, Mississippi Percy, at least her father was one of the original but the Snopes strain got in through the DeBardelebens who were big coal operators in Birmingham and who shot their miners down with machine guns in a sort of enfilade in the Thirties, killed numbers of them too, totally unarmed men, who were simply marching through a defile to the mine to present their demands . . . He really was simply incredible, trying to find out if Mrs. Liuzzo had had sexual intercourse with the Negro boy . . . and he asked the Doctor who performed the autopsy all about the state of her underwear, her body and the fact she only had on a girdle and not any underpants was the main topic of his questioning for some time. He also tried to prove she was a dope addict. It was a real degradation of her body and of her and disgusting and vile. All mixed with this were accusations generally of "communism" and "Castro spies." The world Press covered it and there were over forty newsmen there, but they do not expect White Southerners to be anything but barbarians, an attitude I find very hard to take, and even if they kindly make an exception of you, it really does not help your pride much.

---

*Robert Penn Warren, *Who Speaks for the Negro?* (New York: Random House, 1965).

Actually it turned out better than I had thought with ten for conviction and the people in the courtroom and the men on the Jury all said or rather some of them said, that they resented Matt Murphy's violent racism. "He must have thought we were awful ignorant" one said and "That fellow really tried to stir things up." Actually the two who held out were said to have done so because they would not believe the informer since he had lied so much before, and the fact of an informer who takes money for lying or telling on his friends is still considered bad conduct and he was awfully close to the men he told on, had a gun in his hand, too, although he said he never fired it.

Hayneville is the tiniest, sleepiest little place you ever saw, in the middle of "Bloody Lowndes" (so called on account of the fact more Negroes AND WHITE MEN have gotten killed there than in any place in Alabama) and the people in the Courtroom and the jury all look country, red, sunburned, but I did not think they looked "mean" with the kind of special meanness that the head of the Klan (Robert Shelton) shows so plainly. The Klan last night had a big Rally and the three defendants were treated to a Hero's reception and honored for killing the woman and getting off too.

There is some kind of grim justice in all this, for the men were unemployed steel workers and came from Bessemer, and Bessemer is as you probably know, one if the dirtiest, grimmest, most awful places in the world, dominated by the TCI. Used to feed men into the mills like they did the ore and burned them up, worked twelve hours per day and twenty-four on the swing shift. Bull Connor was head of the Steel Police and so was Crack Hanna who tried to kill Joe Gelders. The men now have a Union but a racist, kind of Company Union, and they are still threatened with unemployment, and take out their hatred and helplessness on the "niggers." I believe the Negro is a shadow of the white man, and he hates him and tries to kill him and is afraid of him because he sees himself in him, and his own helplessness and impotence. What do you think? Lots of love, Va.

May 27, 1965
Dearest Anne: . . .

King was in town on Monday but it only got a couple of lines in the paper and that on the back pages. A delegation went up to the Capitol to see their legislators but he did not go with them, as that was one of the requirements of the visit, that they only be "Alabama Negroes." Mrs. West just called, simply furious, she always calls me when she gets furious with the "white people" to say that the one Negro student who was about to graduate at the High School, the others failed, has been refused graduation on the basis she asked for help during an examination, which Mrs. West says is an absolute lie and all a plot on the part of the white folks to keep her from graduating. And of course it may be, one can never tell. The overwhelmingly sad thing is that the kids got treated just awful all year by both students and teachers. Between George Wallace and Lyndon Johnson, I am getting sick and tired of being an unwilling accomplice to deeds I despise. Napalm, bombs, bullets abroad and down here hatred, bigotry and unfairness and injustice. But the SNCC kids don't give up and neither do the older Negroes give up, and I won't either but I would like some peace and quiet, but it is nowhere. Love, Va.

Decca wrote Virginia in an earlier letter that she was working on a profile for *Esquire* of Ronald Reagan, whom she described as "an aging movy actor who is being touted for Governor of California by the far right wing."[23] In the end, the magazine decided not to publish the article. Reagan was elected governor of California in 1966.

May 31, 1965
Dearest Dec:

I never heard you say you were tired before, I hope you are not sick. I always think of you having more energy than anyone I ever knew, no doubt the whole wheat bread you ate as a child! It very likely is the fact you are bored writing to order and I am sure it is dull. Too bad about the Ronald Reagan thing, perhaps now that he is being built up so in California by that PR firm, they are afraid he might get elected and of course he might. I'll believe anything now. When I think of my faith in Lyndon and actually *believing* he would not do what he is doing, *but he did say he would not*, and now he is doing just what he said he would not do, all in the name of "Freedom," and "Peace" . . . Now he is being praised quite often by the blood-thirsty Southerners and of course by the Goldwater people and I think he will no doubt sell the Negro movement down the river if he needs the Southern votes for his Wars. Really he

makes me sick. I don't believe one word he says nor Adlai Stevenson.*
Of all the liars, Adlai is the worse, he is really disgusting. I do think the
TV people have been good and so have the big papers, except the Wash.
Post has been sort of wishy washy.

Yesterday a great, big, handsome Harvard lad† appeared at the Pea
Level with an English boy we knew, and announced that he was the fore-
runner of a lot of Harvard boys who are coming to Montgomery to start
a paper for the Negroes in Alabama. All of them have been or are on the
Harvard Crimson and one of them is going to be Kay Meyer's‡ son, Don-
nie. They are all rich, come from rather famous families and HAVE
NEVER BEEN SOUTH BEFORE, except to Mississippi for a time. There
is not to be a Negro on the Staff as far as I can discover. They said they
were going to "consult" with SNICK [SNCC] and I would certainly like
to see that. I told him I thought they were a little overly ambitious to
think they could find out in two months what the Negroes in Alabama
wanted to read and to establish a paper for them, but all passed over his
head like a cloud. This will be something to watch, they have lots of
money too, and the poor SNICK kids have none and can't even pay their
parking tickets. He said his mother started the "Wednesday in Mississippi" group, whom I met in Boston, all very rich and fashionable with
beautiful tweed suits, who fly to Mississippi each Wednesday (not all,
just one at a time) and stay ONE WHOLE DAY and fly back and report
on the horrendous happenings there. I think I rather got off on the
wrong foot with him or he with me, but his suitcase is still here and he
will return. Why don't they work in the white community? It seems to
me that it is like going to Germany and working with the Jews when it is
the Nazis that need working on. But that bores them, they simply think
the Southern whites are hopeless (and I am often inclined to agree with
them) but how do they think they are going to change the society here
by utterly ignoring the white people, and such a lot as these rich, fashionable Harvard boys could readily get accepted—at least for a time. I
really think there has been a great deterioration in the attitude of the

---

*U.S. Ambassador to the U.N.
†Geoffrey Cowan.
‡Katharine Graham, publisher of the *Washington Post*.

Southern white people since the March. Their feeling of self-pity, their feeling of being oppressed, of being a hated minority, of having everyone against them. . . . I really am beginning to think the Southern whites are hopeless and yet I don't know how to escape them.

But after all everything has a beginning and everything any of us do has some effect. I agree that the students have been a force for reviving the whole American concept of protest, but I think the student revival started after the Negro students in the South began to protest and they did not do that until the Montgomery Bus Boycott and that did not start until Mrs. Park protested and Mrs. Park did not protest until Claudette Colvin protested . . . Now that the faculties are doing the "teach-in" that is something too, and so many of the newspaper and TV men have been good. I have to try hard to hold on to hope here in the face of the attitudes I run into all the time.

I am certainly looking forward to getting out of it next Winter. If I did not get out of it occasionally I am sure I could not stand it, it is so wearing . . . I think since Rev. Reeb's murder and Mrs. Liuzzo's murder, I have really been rather frightened, as they were so cowardly and so cold-blooded and neither of them were doing anything but giving some sympathy to the Negroes and yet their murderers will never be convicted or punished, it is murder without penalty or murder without pain and the victims get no sympathy at all, even from the "nice people." "They ought to have stayed home where they belong and not come messing in our business." How can you deal with such total irrationality? I can't. I simply have to survive it, if I can.

June 21, 1965
Dearest Dec: . . .

The rich Harvard boys and the rich Wednesday in Mississippi ladies do annoy me, and while I am glad for any fresh streams that come into the South and disturb the stagnation, still I do get mad at their missionary attitude, when they own us and control us and are also responsible for the situation here. I feel that the South and the Negro has become rather a fashionable cause, as you can still be "in" and live on Park Avenue and make a big splash by spending a few weeks in the South, when the people in Harlem also need help very badly, but the South is more glamorous, but as you say a few years ago no one would help at all, and I am glad of all the help we get although it is often given by the very exploiters of the South and that is hard to take . . .

I think I told you that Angus Cameron of Knopf . . . wants me to write a book—he thinks I have a wonderful story to tell, but I know I do not have your grim determination, I was not raised in such a hard school, and simply lack the kind of absolute ruthlessness you have to have to be a writer I believe—there are too many disturbing elements in the world, . . . as Esmond said I was "too soft" but actually I think I am too lazy. Such a chance though. I do hate to miss it. I wish I had you to drive me to it. Lots of love, Va.

Following advance work by Geoffrey Cowan, a small group of Harvard students settled in an apartment upstairs from the Durrs and began publishing a newspaper, the *Southern Courier,* out of a small office in downtown Montgomery. Most of them had worked on the *Harvard Crimson,* and, "instead of protesting and marching," they wanted to use their skills to contribute to the movement. Their plan was to become part of the community and publish a newspaper in the Deep South that would appeal to blacks and whites. The Durrs provided support and introductions to local people in Montgomery who might be sympathetic and helpful. The paper was a notable success; it was published for more than four years.[24]

June 30, 1965
Dearest Clark and Mairi: . . .

Aren't you simply astonished at Lyndon? I am, as I thought he was cautious above all. For a long time I tried to think he was doing what he is doing to show the 26 million Goldwaterities what they were asking for and was choosing a little War to avoid a big War, and I wish I could still think he was that wise and Machiavellian, but now it seems to me he is heading straight for disaster and ruin and atomic War. I don't see how he is going to get out of it. The Peace movement does not, in my opinion, seem strong enough to even slow him up, and judging by W. S. White who is one of our local columnists, and who seems to speak for him, the Peace movement serves to do nothing but irritate him.

Our Summer visitors have started and we now have two groups staying in the House. I made them rent the upstairs apartments as I could not manage them, and so on one side we have a lot of Law School students . . . There are about ten of them, from various Law Schools . . . I cannot help but feel that most of them are visiting the aborigines with the most kindly feelings BUT really do not feel we white Southerners belong to the human race. I try to educate them and think I shake them up a little but not much. On the other side, there are a lot of Harvard Crimson boys who are going to start a newspaper, they are financed by various rich people like the Rockefellers and the Hochschilds . . . but I cannot figure them out—why they want to start a Civil Rights paper in Alabama right now of all places, but I wish them well. In addition to the permanent visitors (who feed themselves except occasionally) we have had several from the Commonwealth Fund, Englishmen, Frenchmen and Danes. I like the visitors, they keep me interested and amused but they ALWAYS LEAVE and when they leave the same old waters close over their heads. I get far more thrill out of Julian Bond getting elected in Georgia*. . .

Lots of love to you and Mairi. Do write and tell me all the news. Devotedly, Va.

On July 2, while addressing a rally in Petersburg, Virginia, Martin Luther King, Jr. declared that the war in Vietnam must be stopped and called for a negotiated settlement. It was his most forceful public statement on the war to date and was prominently reported in the press around the country.[25]

July 8, 1965
Dearest Dec: . . .

I was delighted that King came out against the War . . . More and more I am beginning to think (as Joe Alsop apparently does) that Lyndon has gone off his rocker, he is acting so entirely out of character as far as I knew him, but maybe my judgment of him was clouded by my fondness for him and for Bird and having known them so long. After you have known someone for thirty years, it is hard to think of them

---

*On June 16, 1965, Julian Bond, former public relations director for SNCC, was elected to the Georgia legislature from a district in Atlanta.

willing to press the trigger for nuclear war—and Lyndon was always above everything the cautious type. I know it all terrifies you with Benjy the right age, it terrifies me too, and I have read with passionate interest everything that is written about it and spoken about it, and welcome any sign of protest. Staughton Lynd who is a great friend is becoming apparently the real leader of the protest . . . I really adore Staughton, he is absolutely pure in heart and so full of moral courage. We saw him a lot at Yale as he is a friend of Lucy's and Sheldon's and then I saw quite a lot of him when he was over at Atlanta University, where he became disillusioned as I knew he would. This happens over and over, and always to me reveals the unrealistic attitude so many people seem to have toward the struggle the Negroes are putting up. They come to one of these Negro colleges all full of zeal and desire to right wrongs, and passionate champions of human equality, and thinking "The Negroes" are leading the fight for human freedom (with which I agree) and then they get so overcome with disappointment when they find that they are just human beings after all and often the colleges are small Cranfords, with tea drinking, ambitions, social snubs, competition, and exactly like, in fact, the white colleges except the Negroes are working toward integration into the white society. There are some wonderful people in the Negro colleges, but the middle-class Negro is just exactly like the middle-class Southern white, has the same standards, the same food, and the same ambitions and even admires the same thing. I was invited to speak at a "Woman's Day" at one of the Negro churches and thought of course it was due to my work against the poll tax, or Cliff's civil rights cases, or our stand for integration, but not at all, I was introduced as "belonging to one of the old and aristocratic families in Montgomery!" And actually the pleasure they got out of my coming was the fact the Durrs lived here a long time and have been well known, isn't that fantastic . . . People are so fascinating, and so hard to understand . . . and when you think you do understand them, you are surprised over again.

Douglass Cater, a native of Montgomery and a highly respected journalist, had served as Washington editor and then national affairs editor of the *Reporter* magazine before joining the Johnson White House as a special assistant to the president in 1964.

July 29, 1965
Dear Doug:

I am enclosing the latest appeal from the Alabama Republican Party which is rather absurd as you can see. But at least it is active whereas the Democratic Party at this point seems nonexistent—nothing but the Wallace Party and the Republican Party which seem very much the same. Carl Elliott* is making some noises and John Sparkman gets around and Richmond Flowers† has been very brave and outspoken but there is no organization, no enthusiasm, and it is still Wallace, Wallace all the way. My cousin John Patterson seems to be the next Governor as of this point, and he told me the other day that he was not going to have to "seg" as much as he had before, but of course he will "seg" as much as he thinks necessary. He is still trying to live down his support of Kennedy.

You ask me in the last paragraph "I hope you will keep faith that the President is doing his best . . . " I wish I could reply that my faith has not been shaken, but I cannot. I think domestically he has been marvelous, and what he has done here in the South is the answer to a long-held dream, and I do not know of anyone who could have done it but him, BUT I am simply appalled at the easy assurance of the officers at Maxwell (some of course, not all, for I only know some) that we are on our way to a War with China and they are of course, exultant. I think the escalation of the War is dangerous and I cannot see why we have to turn it now into an American War and do the very thing Lyndon said HE WOULD NOT DO WHEN HE WAS RUNNING. He seems to be out-Goldwatering Goldwater, and none of his explanations on the TV really seem to me to come to grips with the essence of the situation at all. In fact the government statements to anyone who has followed the War have been so conflicting and so at odds with what they have said before, and are so often contradicted by the news which comes on at the same time, that I am confused and concerned and worried and really

---

*Liberal ex-congressman from northern Alabama who was defeated in the 1964 Goldwater sweep; he was considering a run for governor.
†Richmond Flowers, the attorney general of Alabama, had begun to challenge Governor Wallace's defiant behavior in the aftermath of the Birmingham church bombing in September 1963 that killed four girls.

upset . . . [If he] is going to commit us to an endless land War in Asia, I think he has really ceased to be the Lyndon I knew and become someone else I do not know and cannot have faith in. So far I have not signed the Petitions that come pouring in, nor have I written nasty letters or signed them, and I am desperately trying to hold on to my faith in him—for when he was filibustering the worst against the Civil Rights Bills—I still believed in him in spite of what he was doing because then I KNEW he did not mean it, but now I do not know anything and I lie awake at night worrying, not only [about] the fate of my country but of his fate too, for I think he could be one of our greatest Presidents but he could also lead us into such disaster that his name will go down in history as one of our worst. I only wish I KNEW. Sincerely your friend, Va. Durr

August 16, 1965
Dearest Dec: . . .

Angus Cameron wrote me and is serious about my book but I doubt if I will ever do it. I seem to be full of inhibitions, scared really I suppose. But I now have a bona fide offer and so if I don't do it it will be my own fault. Angus thinks I write wonderful letters but letters are not inhibited as they are not going to be published, but when it comes to the printed page! Goodness, I can imagine everyone's fury if I told the truth. Lots of love, Va. Will write again soon and if I do write anything I will send it on. Jonah and the Whale will be the first chapter. IF I WRITE IT.

The entire July-August issue of the *Monthly Review* was devoted to a 93-page essay by Anne Braden on "The Southern Freedom Movement in Perspective," a concise and informative history. While Braden focused primarily on the 1955–65 period, she did mention formative developments during the preceding decades. Still, Virginia took strong exception to Braden's approach and to her failure to mention leading figures from the earlier era, particularly the late Aubrey Williams.

September 10, 1965
Dearest Jim:

I have wracked, by day and night, my brains to think of people who have money and are interested in the work of the SCEF or sympathetic and who were friends of Aubrey's. I think you know all of them that I do, I do not know any of Aubrey's friends that you don't and you probably know more . . .

You know Aubrey had almost no friends here, that is at the last. He became increasingly isolated. He suffered more here than anyone ever knew, or than he ever let on. After his children left he really was desperately lonely. He would come to town, looking for someone to have a cup of coffee with, he was such a convivial and congenial person, he loved to gossip and discuss baseball and politics and was not a stern crusader by any means, he really took people as they were and while he made judgments about them, he did not expect very much, but he would usually end up at our office, having seen no one in all of downtown that he felt friendly enough with to ask to go have a cup of coffee with him. You have seen so much cruelty and have forgiven it but I am afraid I do not have your forgiving spirit. It is hard for me to forgive the treatment Aubrey received here, and Cliff too. That is why I am still quite furious with Anne Braden of all people, for neglecting even to mention them [in the *Monthly Review* article]. I am going to have to write a book myself to give people credit for what they have done. Of course it is a difference in generations, one generation's heroes are not the next generation's, but I really do think to date the beginning of the "Movement" in the South from 1954 or 1960 is so unfair and historically so inaccurate. I am going to write Anne and ask her "why?" but I want to do it when I am calm and not mad and angry as I love Anne too much to risk a break with her, and in this case the flame of anger still burns after re-reading the article again. That is your great asset, you can chastise without getting mad yourself or at least not showing it. Of course I have never thought you were as cool and collected as you usually appear.

September 21, 1965
Dearest Dec: . . .

The two books came, the *Letters from Mississippi*, and the one by Sally Belfrage.* The girl can really WRITE, it is the most vivid and moving kind of book and holds your interest every minute. Some of the kids

---

Letters from Mississippi, edited by Elizabeth Sutherland (1965); and *Freedom Summer*, Sally Belfrage's account of her experiences as a volunteer in Mississippi.

that wrote some of the letters live here and are very nice, very dedicated and good people. I think I told you they are putting out a paper called the *Southern Courier* . . . I admire them and I like them, but . . . I do expect these kinds of kids to have more sophistication than they seem to me to have. They are exactly like the kind of missionaries who came South after the Civil War to help the poor "Freedmen and women" and they did help them, and they started schools for them, and many of the Negroes came out of those schools who are leading the struggle today, but at the same time these wonderful, kind and good missionaries came South to save the "poor Freedmen" their relatives and associates were fastening on the South the kind of economic chains which they fastened on every Colonial economy and made most of the South slaves, rather than just the Negroes and only benefited the kind of sub-managers whom they used to do their dirty work, and at the same time they were doing the dirty work, they were giving money for the poor freedmen. When you try to point out the economic facts of life they say, "You sound like the clichés of the Thirties" and they seem to think they are going to have some kind of Second Coming at which all things will be made pure, and it will be a Negro Jesus this time (not MLK JR.) but maybe Bob Moses,* in any case they are dedicated and idealistic but either they do not know, or will not discuss the economic facts of life, which do you think it is?

I lent Doris Lessing's book to them that you gave me, *Going Home,* and tried to get them to see the analogy, but they look at you as if in a trance and either don't hear you or maybe simply pay you no mind. Of course I think to change the economic system you are going to have to get political power for those whom it oppresses but I do think you have to show the people whom it oppresses the nature of the "system" under which they are oppressed, but they say they have to "go to the people" and learn from them, and now how in the Hell do they expect a Negro sharecropper who cannot read and write to tell them how to understand and change the most intricate and complicated economic system on earth. I feel I am living in a community of Saints and I am not a Saint myself.

---

*SNCC field secretary, Mississippi, 1961–1965.

All they can see is that those of us who fought Fascism and Hitler and were New Dealers live in the past and they are living in the future. They are sweet and kind and nice to us, but [treat us] as if we were living relics. There is one young Negro boy who works with them (literally he is a boy, they all are) and he seems just like them. They come from either middle-class or upper-class parents, they have all been to the best colleges, they live on little and they work hard and consort almost entirely with Negroes, (of course they have not had a very cordial reception in the white community) but they concentrate entirely on the Negro community so far, and if they don't change that—working only with Negroes—I cannot see how they are going to accomplish much change at all, I think it puts too much burden on the Negroes to think they can do it all by themselves.

Of course I live under George Wallace and I am an old anti-fascist and live in the past and speak in the "clichés of the Thirties" (this made me mad) but what I see is a new form of Fascism with the same old battle cries "Crusade against Communism"—"Freedom" (for free enterprise) and Patriotism and Loyalty and so forth and so on, and of course more and more the vituperation against the Negro and now after the Watts riots,* more and more of "I told you so." The papers are full of muggings and crime . . . against whites by Negroes and rather than see any lightening of the prejudice it seems to me it is being strengthened . . . I don't think politically they see the forces that are building up against the Negroes and themselves all over the country. I think they are so much weaker than they imagine they are, and are only being "allowed" to do this as long as they stick only to voting and political rights, and when in the North they move to jobs and housing, the roof falls in. I mean they are no longer "allowed" by the powers that be to do anything or very much. I am sure I need to get out into more hopeful territory, but here I see so little change or improvement and such ill grace along with what small gains are made, but at least there are small gains, a few more children in school, a few more voters on the lists, and public accommodations have not been so much of a problem, but still the Ne-

---

*In August 1965, five days of rioting in Watts, a section of Los Angeles, left thirty-four people dead and millions of dollars in property damage.

groes can't get jobs, and that is the curse of the system and the crux of the matter . . .

They are wonderful kids and I am sure that they learn a lot by being in the South. I think the worst thing about them is that they always leave, they never stay, I don't blame them, but at the same time you have to stick with things to do much about them. Or to do anything.

Lots of love and sorry I sound discouraged. I suppose it hurts to be put on the shelf but it also puzzles me as to what these kinds of kids are looking toward. They seem to think all of History started with the Movement in 1960 and their involvement in it, and I do not think we should be so blamed for failing when we tried so hard and after all we did beat Hitler but as they say "Who was Hitler?" The only terms they understand is to say Hitler was Jim Clarke and Bull Connor and Al Lingo rolled into one and the most powerful man on earth but we beat him. But God knows he did not stay beat.

October 12, 1965
Dearest Dec:

I hasten to answer your last letter which arrived this morning, as I am so anxious to get back on a single track, I cannot keep up with two crossings of letters and get confused . . .

As to my being hard on the young, perhaps I am, but I have to protect myself. I live surrounded by them, and fresh inundations come daily, and they sleep, eat, live, and talk, continuously and unceasingly in our living room . . .

I know I should not expect such young people to know history but I think they should try and learn from history. I think most of them are wonderful, Negro and white alike, and they are the best thing that has happened to this country since 1930, but I do not want to see them killed and destroyed as were so many of the people from the 1930s . . . who were killed and destroyed both physically and morally (turned into informers and so on) and these kids seem to be quite often very unrealistic. The Negro kids are more realistic but they too are often totally romantic. Of course if they did not have this courage and did not have the valor they do, they would never be in it. But they seem to me to want two things at the same time, to wage a "Revolution" as they call it and at the same time call on the U.S. Government to protect them while they are waging it. I hate to tell them that the U.S. Government is not going to do it, but they are not and have said so plainly and also showed they will not. These kids are in great danger all the time, and they should learn what happened to the people in the 30s and understand how far they are willing to go, and not expect to be bailed out. I think they have a right to do what they think they have to do, but not to expect to be protected by the U.S. Government, and of course down here there is no rule of law and they are subject to being murdered and with no recourse.

Most of them, even the Negro kids from the North, are fairly well off, at least their parents are, they have a safe refuge from which they came and one to which they can return, and while they are here they are missionaries in the South. I suppose as a native Southerner I get irritated that the South needs missionaries but we do, but I do think their main aim should be to cultivate and leave behind a body of native Southern kids who would go on about the work. This is their main aim they say but so often they don't do it, and there are some white kids they could work with, I admit few and far between but some, but they really are scornful of the ones they meet or most of them.

I sound terribly defensive and perhaps I am hard on them, but if so, I certainly take a lot of trouble over them and really like them very much, or most of them. The ones who were here this Summer have invited us to Amherst and to Yale, and they were two of the ones I argued with the most, but I think they really rather liked it. I think the great fear of most people is to be ignored, and I certainly do not ignore them, I take them very seriously indeed. But I do not excuse them when I think they do wrong.

In any case, they certainly keep us interested. Bob and Dottie [Zellner] are due to arrive this month. I don't know what Bob will do, but I hope he will find a job.

Lots of love, dearest Dec . . . I don't mind your lecturing me at all, if I dish it out, I have to take it, isn't that right?

PS: I agree wholeheartedly about LBJ, but I still cannot condemn Bird, I simply think she can't help herself, and does the best she can.

October 21, 1965
Dearest Clark and Mairi: . . .

I still feel a little hard toward Anne on account of her article, which I do not think was historically true, and then too I naturally feel hurt when she leaves out the SCHW and the Progressive Party and Cliff and me and you and Aubrey and Palmer and Louis [Burnham] . . . and Joe Gelders and so many others who bore the heat and burden of the day and laid the predicate to the present "Movement." I too had a nice letter from her and I hope we can get it all straightened out, but perhaps it is the fact she is twenty years younger than we are, and really does not feel that anything did happen until 1961.

I got the first volume of Curtis MacDougall's book* which is really wonderful, so good, splendid in fact, well written, concise and fair and balanced I think. You come out very well indeed and as one of the most active and dedicated and successful workers in it. The first volume is only $5.00 from Carl Marzani's firm, Liberty Books, and it is certainly well worth it, I had no idea it would be so good. When he sent me some of the manuscript it was all great detail about that awful [Frank] Kingdon whom I could never stand anyway, and his common dyed hair, bitchy wife, and I simply did not see the point of writing in such detail about somebody who to me meant so little, but he works it in very well and also works him over pretty well. I do think he was such a phony, always did. It almost makes you weep when you read it to think of all the people who have gone bad, died, or been ruined. We survivors are lucky to be alive and still have some spirit left. It makes it so plain how absolutely unrelenting the U.S. government or the forces behind the U.S. government are in destroying any group or movement that they consider has any power to change their plans of domination. I can see the same pattern repeating itself in the fight on the Peace movement and it is now extending to the Civil Rights movement if they take a stand on Peace. Staughton Lynd is already called a "TRAITOR" and "TREASON" is once again the watchword. They seem to think that young men who do not want to die in Vietnam are traitors—when I think they are great patriots . . .

Yes, we are all going into old age, and while I don't like it, I do think one of the best things about it is the few friends who have survived the years, and of course you know we think of you and Mairi as the ones who have stayed the course the longest with us.

Devotedly, Va.

Gideon's Army (New York: Marzani & Munsell, 1965), a 3-volume history of Henry Wallace's 1948 Progressive Party campaign.

October 26, 1965

Dearest Anne:

I am glad you believe in nonviolence and return a soft answer to my angry one, as I am like you in hating to quarrel with you. I hope you will take time though to write to me and if you do not have time to say why you left out the work of the SCHW or the Progressive Party, why you left out the work Aubrey did here in Montgomery? I am enclosing Mrs. Parks' piece which she sent me in which I have marked what she said, and I think she is the best witness I know of, and both she and Mr. Nixon will admit that the Montgomery bus boycott did not just "come about" but was the result of years and years of work and preparation. I do not believe things just "happen" because their time has come, I think everything that happens is the result of countless acts and thoughts and writings and sacrifices and the present lies in the past and the future lies both in the past and the present. I feel the Montgomery bus boycott was the crown and result of Aubrey's life and sacrifice and I do want him to have the credit for it, as I think he deserves it. The very fact that he was able to win the trust of Mr. Nixon and Mrs. Parks and some of the other people here, was the beginning of the feeling that they had some allies and were not utterly alone.

There seems to me to be some kind of strange and, to me, totally incomprehensible attitude toward the people who fought in the Thirties. Dr. Gomillion is a case in point, he was a pioneer, he did great work, he really more than anyone got the whole movement for the right to vote moving and yet he is not only not held in esteem but he is regarded and is spoken of as an "Uncle Tom" and it really makes me furious as I simply cannot understand why the young people who are in a position to make a fight because of his pioneer[ing] work, would now revile him . . . and speak of him with contempt.

It seems to me the difference comes in the fact that those of us who began to fight in the Thirties wanted an integrated society, we did not see the fight as a "Negro Revolution" but as a fight to bring about an integrated society where everyone would have a chance. I cannot swallow the kind of "white baiting" that goes on, as if every "white" had to be guilty and bite the dust. I thought Isabel Cerney's letter in the last *Patriot* when she spoke of "500 years of WHITE MISRULE" was utterly absurd. She simply wipes out the Bill of Rights, the French, American and Russian Revolutions—all of the efforts and trials and successes of the past 500 years. I do not intend to bite the dust and beat my breast because I am white any more than I intend to hold a person in contempt because they are Negro. I am sorry we have to write rather than talk, but I am afraid there is a difference between our outlook and since I think you do love me, as I know I do love you, I am very anxious to get it out and get it straight if we can, as even if I disagree with you, I do not want to feel hurt or angry with you, as I did over Aubrey.

Lots of love and write me when you can. Or better still come to see me. We will be gone from Nov. 2 to Nov. 10.

Late in October, nationwide demonstrations protested the United States' war in Vietnam as troop levels reached 200,000. On October 18, 1965, the FBI arrested the first person charged under a new federal law that banned the burning of draft cards. Opinion polls registered strong public support for Johnson's policy in Vietnam.

October 27, 1965
Dearest Dec: . . .

The KKK passed a Resolution upholding our actions in Viet Nam and condemning the actions of the "so-called students." I am used to police brutality and mass marches and unequal justice and after the freeing of the murderers in Hayneville* I expect anything to happen, as it seems to be open season on Civil Rights workers and nothing will be done. I am glad in a way that the students are having to realize that if they act WITHOUT THE PERMITTED BOUNDARIES they will get slugged as it will make them stop expecting a revolution by permission . . .

You should see the change that has come over the attitude toward King since he spoke up about the Viet Nam War—all of the welcome has gone out and he is now being attacked viciously. Even my old fondness for Ladybird is going, as I see her smiling and planting flowers and beautifying the Highways and then the next picture on TV is of towns and villages and people being blown up, hardly beautified. I wonder if

---

*Leroy Collins was acquitted.

she knows how it looks or if she cares or if other people feel the same sense of horrified shock at the cold callousness of our behavior, all to save the peasants of Viet Nam from "communism." Evidently we prefer Viet Nam dead than red. This last is the brilliant phrase of an Andrew Kopkind who writes from Berkeley for the NS&N* . . .

I will send on the article† as soon as it comes out . . . I think the protection of "pure, white Southern womanhood" reached its apogee in the murder of a "pure, white Southern woman," you know she‡ came from Chattanooga. You should have heard the arguments in the Jonathan Daniels's§ case about "protecting our womenfolks"—and Lowndes County simply full of mulattoes and all of the prominent men known to have two families if not more. Of course the British aristocracy repudiated its bastards (unless it made them Dukes as some of the Kings did) but at least they did not refuse to let their own children go to school or ride the bus or be human, or did they? I am convinced that this long history of repudiation of their own children is one thing that has made the white Southern men (or many of them) so utterly crazy and insane.

We are going to St. Louis on Tuesday and I feel like shouting Hallelujah—I am so glad to get away, even for a week. Lots of love, Va.

---

*The *New Statesman and Nation.*
†Virginia published an article on the Viola Liuzzo trial under the pen name Eliza Heard, "Economics and a Murder Trial," *New South,* October 1965.
‡Viola Liuzzo.
§Jonathan Daniels, an Episcopal seminary student from New Hampshire, was shot and killed by Tom Coleman, a white highway department worker, in Hayneville, Alabama. Coleman was tried for murder and acquitted.

PART 4
"A Big Change Has Come"
1966–1968

The end of segregation and the arrival of federal registrars to oversee enforcement of the Voting Rights Act were, for Virginia, "the fulfillment of a dream" that began with the founding of the Southern Conference for Human Welfare nearly 30 years earlier. Yet as Jim Crow laws fell, the way in which race defined attitudes and structured opportunity became more apparent. Many white Southerners were unmoved and unchanged by the civil rights movement; George Wallace stood as a stark reminder of that. When Martin Luther King, Jr. turned his attention to housing discrimination and black poverty in the urban North, liberal support for the civil rights leader faded. "Law and order" became the dominant refrain, ignoring the harsh realities of urban life, as black rage and frustration exploded into violence in cities across the nation.

Although Virginia resisted all appeals to racial separatism, she acknowledged the limits of integration as a tool for social change in light of what it had become—a simple mixing of blacks, often just the token few, into the existing structures of American society. In a conversation with Studs Terkel at the end of 1965, she tried to articulate a vision for a revolution in social attitudes and relations that transcended race:

> I wish I could say that I thought integration was the answer, but I don't . . . I think the only possibility that the world has of surviving, really . . . is that we've got to get to the point where we recognize the fact that our own safety and our own life lies in the hands of other people. I mean, we've got to understand the fact that we're all interconnected and that nothing we do doesn't have

a result or an influence. We've got to get to the point where we realize that we are literally one people . . . made of one blood. And this is not only true for this country, but for the whole world. And I don't know how many generations it is going to take to get there, but until we get to that point, we're none of us safe, we're just, you know, we're all subject to disaster and destruction."[1]

Uncertainty about the future yielded to the immediate challenges of life in Alabama. The first major statewide election after the enactment of the Voting Rights Act announced that the changes promised by the civil rights movement would be vigorously contested in the coming years. While the number of black voters soared in 1966, white Alabama voters also went to the polls in record numbers in response to a targeted voter registration drive sponsored by George Wallace and his supporters. Prohibited by law from seeking a second term, Wallace engineered the election of his wife, Lurleen, in a racially charged campaign; "Stand up for Alabama" was the campaign's rallying cry. "Four more years of Wallace," Virginia moaned, "and then probably more Wallace after that, unless he gets to be President, which he truly thinks he will."

The election results were disappointing, but the battle was just beginning. Virginia remained confident that the transformation in black attitudes and aspirations bore the promise of a new South. She took historian C. Vann Woodward to task when he suggested, in an article published in January 1967, that that the civil rights movement had run its course. The movement was hardly over, she insisted, and not even weaker; its gains and achievements were just beginning to be realized. Most important was the "new spirit and new determination" evident among blacks "to get their due as Americans." She observed that "when people change their feelings about themselves" and their possibilities "then . . . a big change has come." What it all meant for Alabama and for the South would be worked out in the years ahead, as blacks became more involved in politics, won elected office, and struggled to define and secure their full rights as promised by the civil rights legislation of 1964 and 1965.

While George Wallace continued to exert iron control over state government as well as Alabama's Democratic Party, federal antipoverty programs provided a critical opening for community action and political participation at the local level. Funding for Head Start, the preschool program that was a cornerstone of Lyndon Johnson's "War on Poverty," became available for summer-long projects in 1965. Four different groups of black women in Montgomery obtained grants to initiate the city's first Head Start programs that summer. Afterward, they combined to form the Montgomery Child Development Agency (CDA), and in September 1966 Virginia was elected to the CDA's board, one of the few whites to serve.

Early in 1966, the Montgomery Community Action Commission was established to oversee local poverty programs and distribute grant money. It was dominated by local businessmen, Republican politicians, and Wallace supporters, and tension quickly grew between the board of the Community Action Commission and the women who had established the Head Start programs over issues of control, funding, and staffing. Virginia wrote to presidential advisor Douglass Cater about the problem, urging that there be a federal investigation. Her letters to Cater describe a situation that was repeated throughout the South as the poverty programs pitted local people against entrenched political forces. This struggle, she warned, tested the will and capacity of the federal government to support the stated intention of the most ambitious domestic program since the New Deal— to provide for "maximum feasible participation" of poor people in the planning and implementation of programs designed to aid them.

Virginia viewed black political empowerment as essential to representing the aspirations and interests of the formerly disenfranchised, and critical to the transformation of Southern politics. But she argued that there was an important distinction to be made between Black Power and black separatism—one that, in her view, got lost in Stokely Carmichael's strident rhetoric. Carmichael led in forming the Lowndes County Freedom Organization, a black political party in a neighboring county, and captured national attention in 1966 after becoming chairman of SNCC. A brilliant and charismatic figure, the 24-year-old Carmichael helped shape a resurgent black consciousness that thrived in response both to the gains of the movement and to its failure to bring significant change to the lives of many blacks.

There were aspects of Carmichael's program that Virginia herself had advocated, such as his urging of white activists to work on changing white attitudes. But the news media seized upon his call for black separatism and his occasional appeals to anti-white sentiment, and Virginia took strong exception to this approach. Weary of the long struggle against the politics of white supremacy, she looked toward a politics that reached beyond race. She was sensitive to the depth of black grievances against whites, but her experience in the movement had raised her expectations about the capacity of black Southerners to act upon the democratic ideal and create a political environment free from the stigma of race prejudice. This, she believed, was one of the great contributions of the movement: black Southerners led in establishing the foundation for the kind of interracial political coalition essential to effecting change in the South and countering the reactionary politics that continued to dominate Alabama.

Virginia's criticism of Stokely Carmichael was part of an ongoing conversation with Northern friends about race and politics in the later 1960s, and also about "white guilt," which she viewed as a form of liberal paternalism. However, while taking strong exception to his rhetoric, she was bewildered by the media's near-obsession with Carmichael and the country's extreme reaction to Black Power. In essence, here was a young black man working in one of the poorest counties in the nation, advocating power through the ballot, "a simple and . . . lawful doctrine," yet the media portrayed him as a symbol "of riot and revolution." At the same time, George Wallace, "a real counter-revolutionary" was fighting and defying the federal government and "acting like a two-bit Hitler," but few outside Alabama evidenced much concern about him. This was, she wrote, a sobering example of "the madness" that seemed to possess the country in the late 1960s, as the politics of white resentment gained national appeal and Lyndon Johnson's presidency unraveled amid the horrors of Vietnam.

Now in her mid-sixties, Virginia reflected more on the passage of time, marked by the death of friends, the ailments of advancing years, and growing historical interest in the New Deal era. This was particularly evident in her correspondence with Clark Foreman, one of her oldest friends and the one whose political odyssey most closely mirrored her own. Clark suffered a series of heart attacks late in 1966, and he and Mairi retired to Puerto Rico the following year. Writing to Clark, Virginia looked back to their New Deal days with a hint of nostalgia. "We are lucky to have lived through the 30s and 40s," she wrote, "when we did feel our country was on the right track, we were fighting the good fight . . . and we did and do have the satisfaction of it." She was pleased that they were starting to become the subjects of historical inquiry as historians and archivists began to collect their memories and papers; in 1967, a full-length history of the Southern Conference for Human Welfare appeared. While present challenges continued to be of much greater moment to Virginia than past battles, she believed that an understanding of history was important to the ongoing freedom struggle. In remembering the Southern Conference, she confided to Clark that she thought it important for the world to know "that there were some white people in the South who worked and cared and worried and tried and did something . . . to begin a joint Negro and white cooperation."

To Virginia's delight, Cliff's role in the Roosevelt administration had begun attracting the interest of book publishers and historians. She reported on a visit made by two young men from the Institute of Policy Studies in Washington who "think they have discovered the prime, original New Dealer in all of his . . . coloring." Cliff spent six weeks in residence at the Institute for Policy Studies and this was followed by a second lecture tour of England late in the fall of 1967. It was, once again, organized by the former students who had visited with the Durrs during the 1960s and who were now professors, journalists, lawyers, and young leaders in Britain's

Labor Party. Virginia and Cliff savored these visits abroad with their younger friends, and the intellectual stimulation and rich social life that they afforded. As Cliff put it, "our cornbread really has returned upon the water."

Cliff closed his law office in 1965, and spent more time at the Pea Level adding rooms to the house there and making it suitable to live in year round. The Pea Level, described by Tilla as "an ever-expanding lean-to shelter with many porches and folding cots," was an inviting retreat for the many visitors who passed through. It was the place where Cliff and Virginia most enjoyed entertaining their growing brood of grandchildren, wading and fishing in the creek. As Cliff settled into retirement, he felt hopeful about the future. Her father, Lulah recalled, "was convinced that my generation . . . and the people slightly older than me were going to change the world." In the spring of 1967, he delivered the graduation address to her class; he talked about the role young people played in changing the South and their leadership of the growing movement to end the war in Vietnam. The future was in their hands, he told them, and they had the power to do great things for the country and the world. It was a fantastic speech, Lulah recalled—one that conveyed her father's faith in them and filled her and her classmates with a sense of possibility.[2]

While Cliff prepared for their move to the Pea Level, Virginia embarked on a new political adventure. In December 1967, she was a founding member of the National Democratic Party of Alabama (NPDA), headed by John Cashin, a black dentist from Huntsville, Alabama. Modeled on the Mississippi Freedom Democratic Party, the NPDA offered itself as an alternative to the state Democratic Party, which was controlled and dominated by George Wallace. With Wallace planning a run for president again on an independent ticket, the NPDA would help ensure that the candidate of the national party appeared on the ballot in Alabama. But the biracial party had larger ambitions: by nominating a full slate of candidates for local, state, and national office, it aimed to mobilize the black electorate throughout Alabama, especially in the Black Belt, and to begin the process of building a new Democratic Party from the ground up.[3]

Virginia attended the 1968 Democratic convention as a delegate of the NDPA on a slate pledged to antiwar candidate Eugene McCarthy. Her letters offer a fascinating account of that pivotal episode in American political history. She barely mentions the mayhem that enveloped the convention, with Chicago's Mayor Richard Daley trumping Bull Connor as field marshal of a massive police assault on antiwar demonstrators and bystanders. This televised state of siege remains one of the most potent images of the era, but such blatant and violent abuse of power was not particularly shocking to Virginia. The coming together of opposition both to the war and to the old-line Democratic Party structures in the South was, for her, a most hopeful development. "I have lived as a small minority for so long . . . in Alabama," she wrote Otto Nathan, "that to have so many other people to agree with may have gone to my head."[4] Following in the path blazed by the Mississippi Freedom Democratic Party in 1964, interracial challenge delegations represented all of the Deep South states at the 1968 convention. Former SNCC leader and Georgia state legislator Julian Bond emerged as the symbol of New South politics. The Solid South was breaking up, new coalitions were forming, and the face of the Democratic Party was changing. "Coming out of Alabama it seemed glorious to me," she wrote.

Virginia returned to Alabama and plunged into the campaign for local and state candidates running on the ticket of the National Democratic Party of Alabama. She was one of the party's regular speakers and visited black churches and similar venues in Montgomery and surrounding rural areas. It was as if she were picking up where she left off in 1948, the last time she had actively participated in a political campaign. She took great satisfaction in "feeling useful again" and being "once again back in the battle."

In the first general election in Georgia following the Voting Rights Act, SNCC activist Julian Bond was one of seven black representatives elected to the Georgia legislature. On January 10, the Georgia legislature voted to deny him his seat after he refused to retract his endorsement of a SNCC statement opposing the war in Vietnam, issued several days earlier. SNCC urged young men to refuse the draft and seek alternative service by working in the civil rights movement or with other human relations groups.

January 17, 1966

Dearest Clark and Mairi:

I cannot remember if I wrote to you or not to thank you for the lovely party . . . It was such a joy to see you both and see you looking so well, and also to see so many old friends again. I do adore them, really I think there is no one quite as nice as the "Foreman friends" or the friends I see at the Foremans.

When I got home, I found a letter from Julia Bond (Mrs. Horace Mann Bond) asking me over to Julian's "seating" and so I went but as you know it turned out to be more of a lynching bee than a "seating." I was so proud of Julian, he both looked beautiful and acted beautifully. He never lost his poise, never got off base, never apologized, never backed down a minute and really made a wonderful impression I thought, but ONLY FOUR WHITE MEN voted to seat him, all of the Negroes did, but ONLY FOUR WHITE MEN and they were all from DeKalb or Fulton county. The background, according to gossip, is that Governor [Carl] Sanders is planning to run against "Hummon"* and the Talmadge and Roy Harris people wanted to put him between a rock and a hard place, where he would seem to be "soft on communism" or would lose the Negro vote, and Sanders took a chance on losing the Negro vote, and I hope he does. He went whole hog over to the side of the racists, and Denmark Groover and Jones Lane are about the worst I ever heard in my life, all cloaked in the mantle of extreme patriotism. More and more the racists are turning black into red, and the old tried and true "communist" smear is being used. With the murder in Tuskegee† and the unseating or non-seating of Julian Bond, there is a sea change down here, much, much more bitterness on both sides, much, much more militancy and black nationalism.

Dr. Bond is such a cynic and never expects anything good of any white people anyway, although he does make a few exceptions, so he said he expected it. Chuck Morgan put up a wonderful defense I thought and so he will take the case on up. Bob Zellner was right there by his side the whole time, so he did have two white men standing by him, but both from Alabama. It was a disgraceful performance and it made you realize how thin the layer is over the racism and hatred and prejudice that lies just underneath, even in Atlanta.

I hope Lyndon is getting us out of this war, if he keeps on at it, I don't know what is going to happen. I never heard such horrible tales as they tell on him now, I have lost faith in him, but I cannot believe he is as callous and cruel as they make him out to be, certainly no one believes him much anymore, at least no one I see believes him, do you see anyone that does? . . . I keep wondering if Lyndon has changed or were we utterly wrong about him which do you think?

---

*U.S. Senator Herman Talmadge.
†Sammy Younge, Jr., a 21-year-old Navy veteran and student at Tuskegee Institute, was murdered on January 3, 1966, by a white gas station attendant when he tried to use the "white" restroom.

In the winter of 1966, Virginia and Cliff spent several weeks in Los Angeles while Cliff was a visiting lecture at the University of California, Los Angeles.

March 4, 1966
The Guest House
UCLA
Los Angeles, California
Dear Max: . . .

California is simply lovely, warm, full of flowers and we have had the most wonderful and warmest reception. But I keep feeling . . . it is like a mirage. If those conduits that come 500 miles across the desert ever were cut, the place would dry up and blow away. At night with all the lights on, it is lovely, and the enduring sea and the enduring mountains are magnificent, but there is still a quality of impermanence about it. The people seem rather rootless, the food has not got much taste, I don't know why, it looks lovely, but seems tasteless, so we cook here in this little place as much as we can. There is a tinsel quality about it, and when it is all lit up it looks like some marvelous Christmas Tree promising all sorts of delights, but somehow they are not quite up to the promise. I did meet one simply marvelous man, named Abby Mann, and he wrote the script for *Judgment at Nuremburg*, and he is against the war and really a very straightforward and fine person. I adored him. Also I met Stanley Kramer* . . . and tonight I am going to hear him at the Jewish Temple just down the street, where he will conduct the service and then speak on the "Moral Responsibility of Movie Makers." It should be interesting. The very fact that he even thinks they have a moral responsibility is good. I wish the TV people had more. I think the coverage of the war has been pretty good, at least we have had some honest reporting, but then it gets all fogged up trying to please everybody and sell soap. I think the most horrible thing they do is the juxtaposition of a burned child, covered with jellied gasoline and a human torch, and then the very next minute—a silly ad for Aqua Velva to help the burning of after shave. The total lack of feeling is so horrible, after shave burning and a

---

*Film director and producer; produced *Judgment at Nuremburg*.

child turned into a torch, just the same, and I think finally . . . the outraged populace will turn on them, if their minds have not been turned
into jelly and into dull vacuous caves and sometimes I am afraid our
civilization has done just that . . . simply dehumanized our population.
Or lots of them. Thank God! you still get mad, I am so thankful for
righteous indignation. Lots of love, Va. Durr

On February 22, 1966, Cliff was awarded the Florina Lasker Award by
the New York American Civil Liberties Union at a dinner at the Waldorf
Astoria. Cliff and Virginia flew back from California to accept the award,
and Virginia was delighted that the "Popular Front" turned out for the
event—old friends on the left who were still viewed with suspicion by the
ACLU.

In the following letter describing the dinner, Virginia refers to Julian
Bond's case, challenging his exclusion from the Georgia legislature. Bond
retained Leonard Boudin and Victor Rabinowitz to join Howard Moore in
appealing his case to the U.S. Supreme Court. The Atlanta press made
much of the fact that Rabinowitz and Boudin's firm represented the Cuban
government. Chuck Morgan and the ACLU withdrew from the case.

March 5, 1966

Dearest Clark and Mairi:

Strange to go to New York and find you both gone, it did not seem
like the same place, in spite of a huge room at the Waldorf, I much prefer
the confines of Hugh's room at 250 [Riverside Drive].

The luncheon was a lovely occasion and only marred by the Julian
Bond incident that we read about on our way there. We were distressed
at the withdrawal, I asked Leonard about it, who did not come as he
thought it might be rather embarrassing, and he said they refused to put
his name on the amicus curiae brief and then withdrew when he got in.
Cliff thinks it is a terribly important case, one of the most important we
have ever had, as he thinks it can lay a precedent of keeping Negroes out
of the legislative bodies.

But lots of other people came, and I am sure the ACLU was surprised
to find such a broad representation, Alger Hiss, John Abt, Nat Witt,
Corliss and Helen (I was so glad to see them and delighted they came,
but Corliss looked awfully badly I thought, so gray and thin, is he all
right?) and Helen looked wonderful and happy and I was so glad to see

them. Considering all the past, I thought they were nice to come. There were about 400 people there, the biggest lunch they ever had, or so they told us. Charles Siepmann got so sentimental over Cliff that he nearly wept, but I was not crazy about his speech, as he made Cliff out to be a simple saint which he is not, he is a tough and courageous man who knows what he is doing, and decided that since we were in for such a long and hard fight he had rather fight on familiar territory rather than among strangers, he has always said after his McCarthy experience in Washington that he wanted to live where he knew who the sons of bitches were, and certainly they are plain in Alabama. But Charles really meant all of it, and we had dinner that night and he was still euphoric over the event.

California still continues to dazzle us, but I still feel it may vanish any minute, too beautiful and artificial to last . . .

We go to San Francisco next week and will stay with Decca and then to Boulder where we will stay with the Condons and then home. It was or has been a fascinating visit and I feel like Cinderella at the Ball, I am having a wonderful time but I know it will soon be over and the coach will turn again into a pumpkin. Lots of love, Va.

Barred by the Alabama state constitution from seeking a consecutive term as governor, George Wallace promoted his wife for governor. In the Democratic primary election on May 3, Lurleen Wallace won a sweeping victory in a field of ten candidates.[5]

May 31, 1966
Dear Wicki: . . .

We had a wonderful time in California and tell Tex that his brother Walter was very nice to us indeed . . .

To think of all the work, worry, time, energy, struggle, fights, insults, pinches, kisses, hugs (all from disgusting old Senators) and effort over a space of years and years to get the VOTE for the South and particularly for Alabama, so we got it, and John Doar, whom I adore, came down to see everyone got it, and Poll Watchers came and nearly a million people turned out, and finally after all this time WE GOT THE VOTE AND GOT LURLEEN. You can imagine how disappointed I was. I suppose people have to learn by their mistakes, but in this case it was a clear and overwhelming vote for race hatred, no matter how dressed up with sweet talk. Four more years of Wallace, and then probably more Wallace after that, unless he gets to be president which he truly thinks he will.

I cannot see that Alabama has changed one iota as far as any change of mind, and they will not change until they are made to, and it does not look as if that is going to happen very fast, certainly not as far as the schools are concerned. Don't even have integrated cemeteries . . . a "Green Beret" [back dead fromVietnam] was refused burial in the white cemetery . . . and the military made no protest and took him over to Georgia and buried him there. I went to the funeral and it was so sad, so much resentment and hatred combined with so much religion.

July 11, 1966
Dearest Clark:

I was shocked and horrified when I got Mairi's letter about your coronary attack, but much cheered up and encouraged when I spoke to her last night on the telephone. She sounded as though you would be up and about in no time at all, but I hope you take care of yourself. You and Lyndon, so unlike in everything else but alike in that you both wear yourselves out both physically and emotionally . . . But he seems to have recovered his health if not his heart.* I think he has lost both his heart and his mind, and is taking us down the road to ruin as fast as it is possible to go. I simply shudder when he comes on the screen, and he literally makes me sick—I do not believe one word he says, and in fact I don't think he does, more and more he reminds me of the mindless Texan in *Dr. Strangelove* who rode the bomb to destruction both of himself and the world . . .

Do take care of yourself, and read *The Last Gentlemen* by Walker Percy if you can get it. Also *The One-Eyed Man* which is not very good but interesting—all Southern. The Southern scene, if hot, is interesting to say the least, although I now find myself classified as being on the extreme right as I resent being called "white" as a form of insult and think it is absurd and self-defeating to find the Negroes using the same stupid

---

*Lyndon Johnson suffered a heart attack in June 1955 at the age of 46.

abuse they have had, and it is so blinding to the real causes. Also I believe in integration all along the way, although I do not mind at all "Black Power" which I think is only majority rule by another name, but I do mind this anti-white business as I think it is wrong, rude and very self-defeating. Joanne Grant* agreed with me when she was here which pleased me. She and Ella Baker stayed with me and I thought we had a wonderful time, both smart women and I like them very much indeed. Apparently she and Vic now have it made and she seems very happy and satisfied indeed. Lots of love and I will write again for amusement if now news. Devotedly, Va.

July 15, 1966
Dearest Otto: . . .

I am enclosing an item from the morning paper that I thought might interest you, as it shows so clearly that the corporate interests find George Wallace very much to their liking, they are coming here in droves to get away from Unions and taxes and getting cheap labor, tax benefits and also the State puts in roads and bridges and as one of them very naively told me "they can control the place where they are." The separation between white and black is all to their liking as it keeps labor in competition and they can get it cheap. Cheap labor seems to have been the curse of the South, and it is going to hurt the rest of the country if it continues, which I do not doubt it will, as I think the corporations have no morals or principles and are backing Wallace to the limit down here, and will continue to do so, he is just the kind of demagogue they like, appeals to the worse instincts of men, and works them up into simply irrelevant rages against the Negroes as Hitler did against the Jews.

I think it is such a good indication of the chaotic and stupid fears of our society, that Wallace is a truly dangerous man, backed by the Big Money, the Big Corporations, and who is an outlaw, who is defying the Courts, who is known for brutality, defiance of law, the utmost bigotry and hatred of Negroes, who is building up hatred against the government in every way—he is passed over as some kind of Southern dema-

---

*Joanne Grant, New York-based civil rights activist, journalist, and filmmaker, visited Virginia with Ella Baker while filming *Fundi*, a documentary on Baker. Grant married Victor Rabinowitz, civil liberties and civil rights lawyer.

gogue of no importance and Stokely Carmichael (whom I do not know, and have never met) is made out to be either another "Castro" by the rightists or the last, great hope of the revolution by the leftists, when he has some 2,000 Negro voters registered in the most backward County in the State, with no means of livelihood except through the white men, most of whom are illiterate and yet by some miracle he is expected to start or begin the revolution with these same few troops, how are they going to live? They own very little land, they are living on welfare and are steadily being driven off the land and out of the County. Ninety people own almost 100 percent of the land. Over in Macon County, since there the Negroes do have some economic base with Tuskegee Institute and the Veterans Hospital, they have built up some "black power" and do have a good number of Negro officials, but the Black Panther people look on them with scorn and hatred and say they are the bourgeoisie. If Carmichael can bring off a revolution in Lowndes County he will indeed by a genius, but there is so much talk BEFORE the voting, and who knows how it will turn out in November, and furthermore if they elect, say a tax assessor, and the Negro tax assessor raises taxes on the big plantations, at that point don't they know the plantation owners will go to Court and it will be years and years in the Court. In fact the landowners in Wilcox County have already gone into Court and they have a white tax assessor. The only chance the Negroes have to gain anything is by protection of the Federal government and the Federal courts and in coalition with white people who have the same problems. This is supposed to be very reactionary and rightist now.

Lots of love and do write. Va.

August 2, 1966
Dearest Clark:

I keep hoping to hear from Mairi that you are home again, and I do hope that everything is going well and that you are mending fast and will soon be out again. I am sure it has been boring, but perhaps it gave you some time to think and meditate too, which you have certainly lacked the last few years . . .

I will not spend another Alabama Summer in Montgomery. The heat is so cruel, so unrelenting . . . that I live in a perpetual sweat and also in a perpetual feeling of smothering. This may be due to the psychological atmosphere, but I think most of it is due to the terrible heat that goes on day after day with no break. I feel I am doing penance for some sins by having to endure such dreadful and long drawn out heat . . . I always thought that people got used to things in time, such as the Summer heat and George Wallace and even Lyndon Johnson, but I seem to have a fresh ground for grievance against both of them each new day and certainly even if I am going to be sixty-three on Saturday, I have never gotten used to the Alabama heat. The longer I live in Alabama, the less I like it. It seems to me that it has the most dreadful combination of provincialism and sort of a smart alec pretension to being as good as anyone else, based on nothing, but the fact that George Wallace continually tells them that they are as good or better and more cultured and more gifted and more intelligent than the rest of the people in the country, but I get so tired of living in an atmosphere of hostility, knowing that of the white people there are not more than a dozen who have any sympathy for our point of view, and of course now that the Negroes are withdrawing so, there is no kind of joint enterprise that one can work in. I do not doubt that they are disappointed in the reaction of the white people after the civil rights laws were passed, but I think to turn the movement into a continual denunciation of "white folks" and "whitey" is not only evading the issue but is bound to weaken their friends as well . . .

I read your piece in the *Monthly Review** and thought it was excellent. I think that the fact we had so many Negro friends and co-workers in those days, makes it hard to accept the division now, which I think is wrong. The Southern Conference was built on mutual aid and help and we did think we were building a New Jerusalem together, but now it seems to me that the division gets worse and worse and there is really no joint movement at all. I do not see why you did not mention in your article the meeting in Norfolk, when you stood up and demanded that the meeting go on, and we sang "The Star-Spangled Banner" until Henry came or prayed or something to fill in the time, at least we did not get

*Commenting on Anne Braden's "otherwise fine account" of the Southern Freedom Movement, Clark Foreman observed that it gave scant attention to black participation in Henry Wallace's 1948 campaign—the first time in the twentieth century that blacks were thoroughly integrated into a national political campaign. "Negroes in the Wallace Campaign," *Monthly Review,* June 1966, 41–43.

arrested after all of the threats. At least it gives me great joy to see that horror old [Howard W.] Smith defeated in Virginia and [Pat] Robertson, and Young Harry [Byrd] came mighty close to getting beat, and so I feel that everything we did there was worth it.

The reason I get so put out with Anne Braden (which I think is due to the fact that she is so much younger than we are) is that although she works for SCEF, she apparently has no regard for nor any knowledge of or any appreciation of the fact that we were the first southwide group that worked with the Negroes and we did pioneer in these fields that are just now bearing fruit, and [thinks] that nothing really happened until 1961 when SNCC was formed.[†] I think the white South needs some knowledge of the fact that there were native Southern whites who did work all through the New Deal with the Negroes, and that we did succeed in what we were trying to do, although I admit it takes strange forms. But the fight for the right to vote and against the Poll Tax, the work here with the Boycott, the long struggle against segregation, the fight for government help, all of the things we did are now bearing fruit and yet it is as if we had never done them at all, that nothing got done at all by any Southern Whites. I suppose I am like any old veteran of the wars, I feel that we won the battles, or at least some of them, and that we deserve some stars in our crown.

But it is like the fact we defeated Hitler, all the young people can see is that we are now almost taking his place. At least Lyndon is and he moves from horror to horror. I really do believe he is mad. I even feel Bird has lost her feeling for people, how they can say and believe such lies as they give out, and continue day after day to burn and kill and destroy and preach "beautification" at the same time—it is really too much.

Goodness what a gloomy letter when I meant to cheer you up and I am sure I did not. Now is it better to send a gloomy letter or to send none, as I have no more time to write. We have a house full and it really is as hot as Hell. I think I have said that before.

Well, this is such a poor letter I am not going to read it over. It is sort of a stream of consciousness letter, but fortunately my stream often changes and goes over dams and meanders through meadows, and even

---

†SNCC was founded in April 1960.

sometimes gets cool and shady, so I know however I feel at the moment, I will feel differently later on. Lots and lots of love, I think of you often and wish I could help you pass the time. Devotedly, Va.

Virginia despaired over deepening racial polarization which eclipsed the interracial vision of the civil rights movement. In Alabama, George and Lurleen Wallace kept white anger and resistance to integration stirred to a feverish pitch. After Stokely Carmichael became chairman of SNCC in May 1966, the vanguard organization of the southern movement directed its appeal almost exclusively to African Americans, promoting a program that emphasized racial pride and black power. Virginia had no personal connection with SNCC's new younger leadership. John Lewis, who had served as chairman of SNCC from 1963 to 1966, left the organization in June 1966 and Julian Bond left later that summer. Bob Zellner, however, remained in SNCC until December 1966, when the organization voted to expel its white members.

October 25, 1966
Dearest Mairi and Clark:
I did love your wonderful letter, Mairi, and I have meant to answer it every day, but somehow I stay busy with a million little details . . .
Alabama is so incredible really, it is beyond belief how the people follow George and Lurleen, there is no doubt in anyone's mind that the election is already won, and the people adore them, turn out in huge crowds and worship them, "STAND UP FOR ALABAMA" does not mean one single, damn thing except to prevent integration all they can, but it seems to set people on fire, and the kids are the worse, they pursue you downtown with Wallace stickers and it is all your life is worth to refuse one, as they look at you and go screaming on "STAND UP FOR ALABAMA." I think it is very frightening . . . [Lester] Maddox in Georgia was the final blow, to think of the great state of Georgia electing a man like Maddox, but I think Jim Johnson will win in Arkansas too, so we will have four states in a row with crazy men as Governors. The only alternative [in Alabama] is a segregationist, reactionary Republican, but we will have to vote for him I am afraid. I sound low spirited . . . but really the madness of Alabama is enough to get anyone down who is not mad too.
And I don't go for the hate Whitey bit either. I have not spent the best part of my life fighting racial hatred to forgive it when it is turned

against me. Whatever Stokely Carmichael says in explanation, the bare fact is that he is building or trying to build a Negro movement based on hatred of "whites" and he is succeeding to a great degree . . .

The older Negroes are still friendly but the young ones are just as hostile as they can be, and they are also hostile to the older and more conservative Negroes. Imagine Dr. Gomillion being insulted and called an "Uncle Tom" by them . . . My friends in SNCC are all gone, Julian Bond and John Lewis and Bob Zellner, and Jim Forman has become just like Stokely . . .

Of course the hatred may have been there all the time and is just coming out, but it is certainly coming out now in a very bitter way. I don't know what is going to happen in Lowndes County but I think the failure of the juries to indict or convict, in spite of a Negro majority is a pretty good sign. "A necessitous man is not a free man," and God knows the people over in Lowndes County are necessitous . . .

Lots of love and do write.

November 18, 1966
Dearest Clark and Mairi:

I am so distressed to hear that Clark is still in the Hospital, and I wish he would have told me more in detail about his condition. How could he have a heart attack if the cardiogram did not pick it up? Please write again and be more specific. I am so glad you are going to Puerto Rico, and wish you could settle down there as I think New York is enough to give anyone heart attacks, and you have lived under such pressure. I don't know how you have survived as long as you have . . . [despite] such warm and devoted friends and supporters, I still think it has been an awfully hard job, to keep together such a diverse group and such a warring group of individualists . . .

I wish there was some way we could get to Puerto Rico but we have already spent far more than we should have on Cliff's illness and so far have not been reimbursed by any of our insurance or Medicare but still hope for it. Perhaps after you get there you can promote some kind of teaching job for him at the University or anywhere, but I am sure you would like one too, perhaps you can promote one for both of you, and tell all about the New Deal and the Revolution that took place then as well as the Negro Revolution we have lived through. I do hope Leonard [Boudin] is right about Julian Bond, we had dinner with his mother and father when we were in Atlanta last weekend, the one before last, and I know they are simply thrilled to have him re-elected with such a majority*. . . Sorry to write in haste, I always seem to and make a million mistakes, we just got back and found your letter and I am writing you so the postman will get it before I even unpack our bags or get settled again.

I am not glad that my predictions about the Black Panthers† turned out to be correct, it is simply that I think the situation here in the South is so bad, we are faced with such danger and such terrible people like Maddox and Wallace, [John] McKeithen and [Claude] Kirk now in Florida,‡ that there is absolutely no way to survive, either black or white, unless we work together and in spite of what Stokely's friends say he says, from what I read and hear him say, he certainly does whip up hatred of "whitey" all the time and makes the issue black against white, which I think is clouding the issue. I agree that to be politically effective Negroes have to vote in block, stick together and help each other out, but I do not think he is helping the Southern scene by stirring people up to such passions of hatred and making it all on color. They were defeated in Lowndes County both by pressure but more on account of the fact that about 500 Negroes over there believed that there was no future in a separate movement and stuck to the Democratic candidates, but this margin of 500 Negroes was the deciding factor in every race. What to me is the most incredible thing about Stokely Carmichael is that one young twenty-year-old man, operating in one small, backward, feudalistic Alabama County, and preaching still that the way to win was through the ballot, not even preaching violent revolution, but preaching "Black Power" through the ballot, and I admit flailing the white folks all the

---

*On December 5, 1966, the U.S. Supreme Court unanimously ruled that the Georgia legislature's refusal to seat Bond due to statements he had made violated his rights under the First Amendment.
†Refers to the Lowndes County Freedom Organization; its symbol was the black panther.
‡John McKeithan, Democrat, was elected governor of Louisiana in 1964, running as a 100 percent segregationist; and Republican Claude Kirk, a staunch segregationist, won the governor's race in Florida in 1966.

time, but when you think of the situation and the result and the whole matter, the fact that he terrified the country as he did, got people all stirred up, writing reams about him, became a symbol of riot and bloodshed and revolution, all of this to me is a clear indication of how completely crazy this country is, it is really made to go into such a tailspin over a young Negro boy preaching such a simple and really lawful doctrine. And all the time we have George Wallace, fighting and defying the U.S. Government, accusing all of the members of the Administration of being traitors and beatniks, communists, socialists, do-gooders and pinks, abusing the President in the most unmeasured terms, announcing his hatred and defiance of the Democratic and Republican Party, saying he is going to run and really stir up the country . . . in short acting like a two-bit Hitler and NOBODY gets very excited about him except those of us who have to live here. I think George is a real counter-revolutionary and when you see the absolute adoration people have for him and for Lurleen it is frightening. He has something that makes them feel good (same old Southern sweet talk I used to use!) based on the premise that every man or woman is a fool, full of self-doubt, inferiority complex and looking for reassurance which he gives to them by telling them they are as cultured and educated and refined as anybody and of course always, always insidiously demeaning the Negroes and preaching segregation . . . Of course as in Georgia, Jim Martin the Republican tried to out-seg him and it was the same thing of a rich racist and one who pretends to be for the poor folks, and so many, many Negro boxes went for the Wallaces but they would have won without any as the mass of the white people adore them. The "nice people" as our mothers used to say, or the "establishment" as they say now, all voted for the Republican, racist as he was, and look down on George as being very common and refer to his wife as "that girl he married out of the ten cent store" but in spite of this snobbery, they are eager not to get in bad with him, and I do not think that when it came to any real conflict they would stand against him, I think it would only be the Negroes and a handful of white people like us, who see him as a really dangerous person.

I used to say to Cliff when we came here that if I could just find out what the people of Alabama liked and wanted, perhaps something could be done, and after fifteen years I have found out, and that is that the white people want segregation, they want something to lift their self-esteem, they want religion (segregated), football (segregated), and the biggest crowd I ever saw at one time was a syrup sopping contest (both free and segregated) which shows that I am a snob because I find them so utterly uncultivated and unrefined and lacking in the first elements of culture or knowledge of any sort. It is hard to feel sorry for them as they are so full of certainty that they are God's Chosen right now or Wallace's chosen, and the only thing I can do is to try and understand how they got the way they are and still keep trying with a tiny handful that stands against him to keep him from making the State into a total police state. I used to have such faith that the Federal government would bring the South into line and it has helped, but I have lost faith in Lyndon totally, I think he is a syrup sopper too. Showing his belly the way he does* seems to be unrefined to put it mildly. But more than his grossness is the horrible fact of his total inhumanity in which we are all implicated, did you ever think Lyndon would turn out to be this way? I think he has become almost a kind of monster.

Hugh "Geno" Foreman left the United States in March 1965. He was deeply affected by the murder of Malcolm X and bitterly opposed to America's war in Vietnam. As his sister Shelagh Foreman recalled, "he had no hope for this country. It was not a place where he wanted to live." He and his wife Marcy settled briefly in Rome, where their daughter Haydee was born, and Geno struggled to get work as a musician. Finding it hard to make a living in Rome, they moved to London. That was not destined to bring good fortune. Geno's neck was fractured in an accident, and he died within weeks on November 15, 1966, after suffering medical complications. He was 26 years old.

November 21, 1966
Dearest Mairi and Clark:
I still cannot believe it and I sit here thinking of Hugh as a baby and growing up and I do hope that in Marci [sic] and the baby he found some happiness and fulfillment before he died. All of his life he was looking for something and I do not know if he ever found it. I hope so.

---

*Refers to a famous news photo of President Johnson displaying a recent surgical scar.

Like so many of the young men today, particularly the best ones, they cannot find in our society what they need and want, and become rebels and defiant ones and actually become destroyers and often get destroyed themselves in the process, but they literally cannot stand the kind of society they are offered and as so many of the wild ones told us in California, "All we want to do is to tear it down and start all over, it is rotten through and through." Of course the young and militant Negroes say exactly the same. If you try and point out that it does have some good features, that there are some good people, they simply look at you in pity and I am afraid contempt and freeze up, they have rejected it in toto.

We were lucky to have lived through the 30s and 40s when we did feel our country was on the right track, we were fighting a good fight for good things and we did and do have the satisfaction of it, but after 1945 and especially after 1948, it all seemed to go bad, and even Kennedy never aroused me to any enthusiasm. I could not reconcile his intelligence with his policy toward Cuba and his cold opportunism toward the South, when he preached equality and then appointed judges and officers who were absolutely determined that none of it should come true. The best I can hope for now is some kind of moderate Republican victory, which will end the war and give us a few years of peace and I hope time to start again to change things. Above all get rid of Lyndon . . . All I can hold on to is hope that the American people are not as corrupted as he is . . .

The trouble is that our children find our society so repugnant that they do not feel our efforts, either in the past or present are really significant, but of course I think they are, and I think they were, and I think both of you, Clark and Mairi, are and have been magnificently brave in the face of the worst kind of opposition and destructive tactics. And I think you have done a lot of good, if Julian Bond does get into the Georgia Legislature I think it will be a great victory and I think all of the fights you have put up have been of great importance and import. Your life has been of so much help and comfort to so many people and especially to me and I wish I could come up and try and bring you some comfort in this time of sorrow and grief, which I know is immense. Lots of love and I will write again. Va.

November 30, 1966
Dearest Mairi and Clark:

I think about you so much and so often and would love so much to come and see you, but we think it best not to go North this Winter. Cliff seems to be doing quite well, and I don't want to take any chances on his catching cold or flu.

Clark, as you are recovering, do you think you would have time to see if you had any papers or letters of any interest concerning the SCHW? As you may know the University of Tennessee has opened an Estes Kefauver Civil Rights Collection in the Estes Kefauver Memorial Library, and they want every scrap we have, any of us, concerning the early days middle days or late days of the SCHW. We have become of historical interest. I do not think I have much to contribute but I am looking through what I have . . . If you have time and strength to put down any of your recollections, please do so and send them on to the University . . . I think it is very important for the world to know that there were some white people in the South who worked and cared and worried and tried and did something and tried to begin a joint Negro and white co-operation. I don't mind Black Power—I think it is nothing more than majority rule, but I do mind the whole issue getting down to color, this time anti-whitism. No matter how much it is explained away, when you hear them speak you know their anger and hatred is directed toward "whites" and it is easier to arouse a Negro audience to hatred of "whites" than to explain to them so they can understand the kind of unjust society they live in. To have these reservations about Black Power makes me a square and also Miss Ann, but I do not like being called white one single bit.

Every night I long to call you up, but then this is something I have to control, as each month when the telephone bill comes in, Cliff thinks I have got telephonitis beyond control. Perhaps I have. But when you love people so much and cannot reach them, it is very frustrating . . .

Lots of love to all and write if you can. Devotedly, Va.

December 5, 1966
Dearest Clark and Mairi:

I received your letter this morning and after it and after talking to you on yesterday, I feel better about you. I have had you in my mind and heart day after day, and I am so sorry we are not coming North, so I can be with you . . .

As for the SCHW papers, some are in AU* and some in Tuskegee and now the University of Tennessee is trying to get all they can lay hands on, as the historical importance of what we did way back there is beginning to be realized . . .

Of course I think this anti-whitey business is both wrong and does no good. I think Negroes have good reason to hate whites, I think Irishmen have good reason to hate the English, I think the Vietnamese have good reason to hate the Americans and do, but my point is that nothing comes of putting the struggle into such limited terms. The forces of exploitation and oppression have been white, black, yellow, red and brown at times, and they vary from time to time and country to country, but to put it simply in terms of color is both deceiving and does not get to the root of the trouble. Lyndon has done more for the Negroes than anyone else I know in terms of concrete gain, but I think he is the worst and most dangerous President we have ever had.

What I cannot understand is the way some radicals and liberals continue to insist that Stokely Carmichael and the SNCC kids are not anti-white, when week after week I read what they say, I hear them say it, and whatever the esoteric and unknown meaning of what they say means beyond its actual content, its actual content is hatred of whites as whites. Stokely said on Tuesday at his trial in Selma, "Their color is showing as we say in my community—WHITE" and he is building up a whole cult of people who make it their business to show whites how much contempt they have for them. Fortunately we have friends here, Negro friends, who do not share his views, and only yesterday we were invited to the Celebration of the 11th Anniversary of the Montgomery Bus Boycott where Coretta King spoke and although we were the only white people there, we could not have been welcomed in a kinder manner by the people there. Of course the SNCC kids say that the Boycott did not mean anything (but I think it did), and nothing that was ever done meant anything till they came along.

I think that he is trying to express his total contempt for Western civilization from the standpoint of the colored world, and while his cri-

---

*Atlanta University.

tique might be valid from the standpoint of Trinidad or even Lowndes County (although there he got beat and by Negroes, not whites) where there is an overwhelming majority of Negroes, I think for the United States, or even for Alabama it is not valid, and we simply have to have a multi-racial society if we are going to exist at all. In any case I refuse to join in the kind of self-flagellation of guilt that so many white people seem to enjoy under his lashing. I was absolutely shocked last Christmas at Helen and John Gray's when all of these Cambridge intellectuals let this Negro woman insult them in every way possible and seemed to not only cringe under it but to feel it was deserved, but it made me mad as could be and she and I had a lively row as you can image. In fact I think to excuse Negroes or young people for extreme, personal rudeness under the excuse that they have had such a hard time and need some outlet, is being terribly benign and patronizing . . .

Lot of love to both of you, I am sure I repeat myself in my letters but the same things happen over and over and we live in the midst of the same problems. That is why I like so much to get out of the South for a season, it gets so tiresome sometimes, the same thing over and over. Lots of love again. Devotedly, Va.

December 18, 1966
Dearest Otto:

I do not much feel like a MERRY CHRISTMAS this year, but it is a great joy to hear from our friends, and your note came on yesterday and also one from Ava Helen and Linus who are leaving for India in January, they are just back from England and France where they have been speaking, of course on the necessity for Peace. I am sure you did the same thing in Japan and in India. But there seems to be no Peace, and I am very much afraid that the escalation will grow and grow and we will end up by fighting China . . .

As for the South, things are better in some ways and worse in others. For a Negro who has money, things are definitely better, they can go to movies, theatres, hotels, motels, restaurants, and ride when and where they please and are usually treated quite well. Jobs have opened up in stores, hospitals, and some in manufacturing, although the Unions are the strongest in opposition (another theory that went wrong) but for the poor Negro without money, things are just about the same. The integration in the schools is only token and the children have a hard time, and they and their parents become very bitter. The churches are still closed tight as a drum except in very rare instances. There is a growing and increasing bitterness among the Negroes, which is expressed in many different ways, and the increasing use of insults against "whitey" and the increasing use of racism against the white people, which they may deserve, but which I think obscures the issue so that the real issues are not insisted upon nor understood. There is still dreadful brutality and injustice and the KKK is growing and there is a pronounced rise in anti-Semitism, Wallace is one of the leaders in this, and he is being very clever, trying to win the Negroes over to his side by giving them (not promising them) schools, jobs, and lots of opportunities IF THEY WILL STAY SEGREGATED. He recently refused to let a Negro Catholic nun come to the Governor's Mansion with a group of white Catholic women, and said no "social mixing allowed" and this is his line, stay in your place and you will be rewarded.

I am convinced though, that it is too late, that the Negroes will never go back in their "place" and more and more they are becoming more militant, but I still cannot see that open violence will win them anything, although I think they certainly should practice self-defense, but they are so outnumbered, even here in Alabama, except in a few counties, and all of the instruments of force and violence are on the other side. I do not see how any revolution succeeds without the support of the people who live in the area and here in Alabama there are only a few counties that have a black majority and in those counties the land and the commercial enterprises and the jobs are all controlled by white people.

I suppose you know Clark Foreman has been very ill, two heart attacks and his wife has been terribly worried over him, and just in the midst of it his son died suddenly over in England. So much trouble people have.

Lots of love, dearest Otto, and I hope we will see you in this year . . . Sincerely and devotedly, Va.

December 1966
Dear Tex and Wicki:
    Sorry we are not getting up "North" this Christmas but Cliff has been sick since July and is just getting well . . . I would love to see you both and share our opinions of LBJ. I think he has gone mad and we will be at

war with China unless somebody or something stops him. Of course down here they hate him for all of the wrong reasons, and in the field of race relations he has done very well and there has been progress.

I suppose you heard about Hugh Foreman's death, so sad and so unnecessary. Clark has had two heart attacks and is just out of the hospital . . . I hear from Kittie Mae Wirtz sometimes and of course the Strauss's, but our days in Washington are not only long ago and far away but seem to have been in a different age. Life in Alabama is not dull, but it is "Wallace All the Way" and when you find one white person who condemns murder as a means of "keeping them in their place" you feel you have found a real ally. But things will never be as bad as they were when we came. Lots of love to both of you.

In "What Happened to the Civil Rights Movement," published in the January 1967 issue of *Harper's* magazine, C. Vann Woodward reviewed the dramatic changes that had swept the South and the nation in the preceding decade. Drawing parallels with the post–Civil War Reconstruction era, Woodward speculated on the future course of change now that the wave had crested and political reaction had gathered force.

January 17, 1967
Dear Vann:

Thanks for sending on the *Harper's* article which we read with great interest. I agree with you that Civil Rights has now become déjà vu but I do not agree with you that it is over or even weaker. I think the great mass demonstrations are over, the visiting firemen, the floods of sympathizers, and the excitement, BUT all of this has left in its wake a new spirit and a new determination on the part of the Negroes to get their due as Americans.

It has come down to the nitty gritty, and on a local level there are fights going on all the time. I am engaged in a fight now over Head Start as I am one of the few white people on the Board, and we are trying to keep community participation, rather than have it turned over to white and some Negro social workers to be run on a mass scale from the top. Sad to say whatever comes of the fight, I am very much afraid that all of these poverty programs are going to be slashed. But they have so far done a lot of good. They have given people hope and aroused their responsibility and made them feel their government has some concern for them, as did [the] WPA etc. back in the old days, but I think the Republican–Pole Cat combination will ruin them if it can, and it probably can. Also in the voting field there is great activity. We were invited last night to a big celebration for the first Negro Sheriff over in Macon County* but did not go, simply because after a whole day of Wallace watching we did not have the energy to go eighty-five miles to a celebration. But in the Negro community this is a great event. Also the Justice Department is down here on the Motley killing, a really horrible cold blooded killing of a young man who was literally beat to death by the police, and there were witnesses, both white and Negro who saw it, but now the coroner and the Grand Jury say he fell out of bed.

The thing that has changed is the Negro. I hate to say there is a "New Negro" because that is absurd, but the old Negro no longer feels so hopeless or beat down or pathetic or apathetic, and when people change their feelings about themselves, then I think a big change has come. And you find it everywhere, which is evident in listening to any private conversation of any white Southerner, one way or another, who may be integrationist or most of course, segregationists, but they realize the Negro is not what he used to be.

As for SNCC, I agree that for the country to get all excited over Stokely Carmichael and Lowndes County is an expression of the madness that possesses us and makes us think that South Vietnam is our ally and that North Vietnam is our enemy and we have to destroy the enemy and save our ally. It is all a hoax as you well know, but such a terrible one that I am afraid the whole country is going to Hell. What we are doing to those poor people is so awful that it literally makes me sick, but what it is doing to us is so awful that it makes me even sicker. I am so thrilled to find another man from Arkansas, beside you, that I can be proud of. I am simply enchanted with Fulbright.† I do hope he sticks and I think he will, after all you Arkansas people are rather like razorbacks, won't be civilized, and even if you pretend to be there is always that wildness there. At least you fight back and I think he is doing a brilliant job.

---

*Lucius Amerson, 32-year-old Korean war veteran and employee of the Veteran Hospital in Tuskegee, was likely the first black since the Reconstruction era to be elected sheriff of a Southern county.
†U.S. Senator William Fulbright, Democrat from Arkansas, head of the Senate Foreign Relations Committee and leading critic of the war in Vietnam.

In spite of his sins and in spite of myself I feel sorry for poor Lyndon. I think the whole Kennedy attack on him was ridiculous, I think that time he acted magnificently and to accuse him of taking over the Presidency is absurd, and then all of the nasty comments on his table manners, his nose picking and scratching, this is sheer unadulterated snobbishness and venom. But why, when he is insulted by this crew all the time, does he then go along and do their bidding and take their advice on Vietnam? This is what is beyond me.

We got an invitation yesterday to the White House for January 31 for the unveiling of a portrait of President Roosevelt. I would love to go but Cliff would not love to go and then too, I think he feels it would be wrong to accept the invitation, feeling as we do, and expressing ourselves as we do, about Lyndon. As you know he is more of a gentleman than I am a lady. Cliff joined in with Bob Hutchins and a lot of others and wrote Lyndon a letter—did you see it? I thought it was very good.

Lots of love to you and to Glenn. When is your son getting married? How is the book coming? I really think the article was splendid. I agree the wave has receded but it left a lot of residue and I do not believe that will be swept away. Still hopeful.

Devotedly, Va. Durr

Clark and Mairi Foreman bought land in Puerto Rico on a remote hilltop in Adjuntas, overlooking the Carribbean Sea, and made plans to build a house and retire there.

January 23, 1967
Dearest Mairi and Clark:

I was delighted to get your card from Puerto Rico. I had no idea where you were, as you said you were not going there until February, and when I called the apartment several times, no one answered and I was concerned. I kept thinking maybe Clark was sick again and had to go back to the Hospital so it was a great relief to get your postcard.

The place does look beautiful and I am glad it is hot in the day but cool at night. When your house is built, we will certainly come to visit and perhaps by that time Cliff can get some lectures, in any case we will try. We still have Lulah to put through college . . .

I am actually getting to be rather fond of Montgomery in an odd way. I am in several integrated groups now, the Head Start program, and the Human Relations Council, and the United Churchwomen of all things, and it is a real pioneering event. Now we get integrated, what next? And what next is a new adventure, we both have to learn each other and how to act. Just now a woman who is a supervisor in the public schools here (Negro) called me and said "This is Forte" (not Mrs. Forte) and I was so surprised at her saying just her last name and then I realized this was her way of refusing to say "This is Maggie" which she would still think was required and not daring to say "Mrs." Now isn't that strange—to think there is still this awful hangover? It is almost impossible for them to call me by my first name, so we have to stay indefinitely on the "Mrs." Basis, which is ridiculous isn't it? But when I called Mr. Nixon "Ed" once, he told me in his usual flat-out manner, "Don't ever call me 'Ed' because I would be lynched if I called you 'Virginia' and until I can call you by your first name, don't call me by mine." Good advice. So while life is difficult and under the Wallaces may get more so, at least there is some opposition and a few white people who are opposed and the situation changes from day to day.

We do not plan to go anywhere until May, when we plan to go up to see Lulah graduate, and Cliff has been asked to make the Graduation Address. Lulah writes that Alger Hiss was up with his beautiful girl friend (name unknown) and she thought he was simply marvelous, really great. I wonder who this girl friend is? Of course there was a terrible Red–baiting attack on him and on the school* for having him there, but Lulah said the students thought he was simply great. I am sure that no man in the days of the Inquisition ever had to go through as much torture as he had to go through and I am sure still does, and I think he has borne it wonderfully, what do you think sustains him, innocence or courage or principle or what, how can a man know his very name is a symbol of hatred and treason and guilt and yet be so calm and so controlled? I often wonder if that mystery will ever be solved, I have always rather thought he was protecting Priscilla but I of course am not sure. I simply do not believe he betrayed anything to anybody.

---

*Windsor Mountain School in Lenox, Massachusetts.

Will you be back in New York by May? I do hope so, it seems so long since we have seen you, and we really miss it terribly.

In September 1966, Virginia was elected to the Montgomery Head Start Children's Development Agency, organized by black women who had initiated the city's Head Start programs in the summer of 1965. By the time Virginia joined the board, the relationship between the Children's Development Agency and the Community Action Commission, the agency charged with oversight of Head Start and other poverty programs, had deteriorated almost beyond repair. Charged with dispensing federal funds, Montgomery's Community Action Committee was run by local white business and professional people, some with close ties to the local Republican Party. In the following letter to presidential advisor Douglass Cater, who was also a native of Montgomery, Virginia explained some of the problems and sought a federal investigation.

February 11, 1967
Dear Douglass:

I saw your mother yesterday at the United Churchwomen and she said . . . that you were overworked and tired out . . . So I am sorry to add to your burdens and if you can tell me one other person in Washington, D.C. who is interested in Montgomery, Alabama, I will be glad to transfer my attention and worries to them, but aside from you I do not know of anyone with any power who seems to care one single bit.

I will state my case briefly and give my reasons on another page so you can show them to someone if you think they will read it, but as *this is a personal letter* I will say that to see a Democratic program which I think is a splendid program and is doing a lot of good being ruined and making enemies by being administered by retired Air Force Officers and whose chairman is Joe Stewart, D.D.S., who is Bill Dickinson's campaign manager and who while serving as chairman of the Poverty Program is sending out letters begging people to join the Bill Dickinson campaign club . . . really this is going too far from the original concept of the Poverty Program as being nonpolitical and community centered . . .

This Administration has done more for the South, has done more for the Negro people and for the poor white people of the whole South than any Administration in history . . . The very people who are opposed to what [the president] has done are administering the program. I don't have to tell you about Bill Dickinson and I hope you have read his masterpiece . . . about the Selma March . . . "Sex and Selma" . . . which the First National Bank and most other business establishments displayed when it first came out. It is still a best seller here . . .

I think Federal programs should be administered by people responsible to the Federal government. To turn over one-half million dollars to its enemies seems to me to be committing suicide. Sincerely your friend (I hope), Virginia Durr.

The official letter provides Virginia's assessment of the problems surrounding the Head Start program.

February 11, 1967
Dear Douglass:

You asked me to set forth my reasons for dissatisfaction with the way the Community Action Committee of the Poverty program is acting in regard to the Head Start program. I will do my best based on my personal experience which is all I know.

1. In 1965, when the Head Start program funds became available no white group in Montgomery, Alabama made any request, but four Negro groups did, one of them the AKA sorority which ran a program at the Y on Cleveland Avenue. My daughter* served the summer of 1965 and I thought it was very well run indeed and did a great deal of good. This was run entirely by the Negro women of the community and my daughter and one of her friends "integrated" it.

2. The Negro groups came together and formed the Montgomery Head Start Child Development Agency and applied for another grant for the summer of 1966, but by this time the Community Action Committee had been formed and they were informed their application had to go through this Committee and there was much delay and confusion and finally there was only a follow-up program from the year before in which my daughter also worked, and while this was a small program I thought it did well.

---

*Lulah Durr worked in the program at the YMCA during the summer of 1965; she was actually the only white person on the staff. It was, she recalled, an exciting program, staffed by talented and dedicated young women.

3. The same Negro groups, now added by some white Board members, such as Colonel Page who is Administrator of St. Jude's [Hospital], then applied for a full year program and this was processed after long delays and finally granted and began in November 1966. The Montgomery Head Start Child Development Agency was the delegate Agency and the Community Action Committee was supposed to be the coordinating Agency who handled the money, hired the personnel on *our* recommendation (that is, the Montgomery Child Development Agency) did the bookkeeping and was to help the delegate agency in all ways.

4. I was elected to the Board of the delegate agency, Montgomery Child Development Agency, in September after it had been funded and the program was getting underway. I soon saw that the Community Action Committee was rapidly acquiring all the power as they had the power of the purse and bad feeling was growing between the two groups. I think the whole tangle of accusation and counter-accusation could only be straightened out by an impartial investigation form Washington, but the fact remains that the two groups are now at loggerheads and have no trust in each other and there is very bitter feeling.

5. My experience and observations lead me to believe that the Community Action Agency is determined to do away with the local Montgomery Child Development Agency. Their attitude has been anything but cooperative and while the coordinator has been smiling on the surface he has sent the most derogatory reports to Atlanta and a Mr. Lavoy who came over here to investigate did nothing but yell and shake his finger and say he was a "hatchet man." Mr. Jim May with whom I talked was extremely rude and accusatory. They seem to have [not the] faintest idea that this program was set up to help the people of the community and give them some responsibility and give them some pride in doing for themselves. They keep saying that they have to "save money" and the best way is to close down the local Head Start centers in the Negro churches and communities and channel all of the children to the two Catholic schools and bus them back and forth.

6. The Chairman of the local Community Action Committee is a Dr. Joe Stewart who is campaign manager for William Dickinson, our local Republican Congressman, and who while serving as chairman is send-

ing out letters forming a Bill Dickinson Campaign Committee or Congressional Club and asking for money to pay his expenses for TV, Radio and other expenses. I think this is a clear violation of the intent of the program to stay out of politics although that does not seem possible, as most of the people in the Community Action Committee seem to be Republican or Wallace Democrats, which is hardly favorable to a Federal program.

7. I would suggest and request that an impartial investigator come down here from Washington and see if there is any way this mess can be straightened out. I would also suggest and request that he be a man who sees the program as I think it was conceived, to help a community help itself, even if they do not always do it in the most efficient manner, rather than having it a program administered by trained social workers and run in an authoritarian manner. To see the pride the Negro community has taken in these centers, the pride they have taken in their participation and the fact that they originally conceived the whole program, to see all of this turned into suspicion, dislike and even, I may go so far as to say resentment and in some cases hatred is a sorry sight. I think the Community Action Committee, whatever its ends may have been, have served to bring this condition of affairs about. There is no trust on either side and a rapidly growing bitterness. I hope very much that something can be done, both to save the program and to save the bad situation that has developed.

February 13, 1967
Dear Douglass:

Thanks for coming through, thanks a lot, lot more too. A Mr. Dean called from Atlanta this morning and said that he had received a call from Mr. [Sargent] Shriver and that he himself would investigate the mess that has been made here. Thank Goodness!

And it is not just here in Montgomery. Earl Pippin who used to be Vice President of the AFL-CIO . . . and Barney Weeks, the President of the CIO-AFL and Dr. Charles Gomillion of Tuskegee who is the father and founder and beginner of the whole Negro movement on the right to vote, these men went to Washington and got no satisfaction—and they are full of complaints.

They spoke to a man named Ted Henshaw of the Democratic National Committee and he told them that there was *no* hope of any help politically from Washington, that a decision had been made to let Alabama stew in her own Wallace juices, that time, money, and power was needed for more important states and we could expect NOTHING from Washington.

I know Lyndon has felt a great loyalty to John [Sparkman] and Lister [Hill] and I am sure they have advised him to leave Alabama alone as it would only hurt them, but now John has been elected for six years and Lister certainly cannot and should not run again. I don't know if you have seen or talked to him lately, but the general talk is that he is showing his age to put it mildly, but in any case I think Lyndon has paid off his debts to them . . .

Well I put *my* faith in our local boy and thanks again for your help—at least now we have a chance. Sincerely and thankfully, Va. Durr

February 27, 1967
Dear Douglass:
You may be interested in knowing how the struggle over the Head Start program came out. As you know, all we asked for was an impartial investigation. So Mr. Dean came over backed up by Mr. Jones (both of them Negroes) and he did not see *one member* of the Child Development Agency which was originally responsible for Head Start and still is legally, but saw only the CAC [Community Action Committee] people and took part in cutting off the ties between the two groups and announced that the CAC would now have entire control of the program.

So Joe Stewart, Bill Dickinson's campaign manager, and Charlie Jaeger of the First National Bank . . . are now in full control with their assorted followers. A Democratic program which I think is splendid, is now in the hands of some of the worst enemies of the Democratic Party, and the money and power that goes with it.

I simply do not understand this kind of politics, but the real issue seems to me to be the fact that tax money is being spent and administered by a Board that is not responsible to any elected agency. These are the old Community Chest people. The very people Lyndon and Aubrey fought to establish the NYA and the WPA, who would have ruined those programs too if they had gotten hold of them. I evidently belong to a past age when the Federal government was supposed to administer its own programs.

The situation in Birmingham is just the same, whole Poverty Program in the hands of its enemies, and the people it is supposed to help getting madder and madder all the time. It is a real mess.

Sincerely and for the last time, and thanks too, V. Durr

April 4, 1967
Dearest Wicki:

I received your note with the attached speech from the *Congressional Record*, and after living in the South for sixteen years, I was really surprised that anyone still paid any attention to that kind of raving and ranting. I don't know Rarick,* but I do know the usual type of Congressmen from Louisiana as I know the usual type from Alabama, and since they have now found that outright racism is not so popular they are covering up their outright racism with cries of "communism," "socialism," "States Rights, etc." If you heard Lurleen Wallace on the TV the other night when she called for total defiance of the Federal Government, you would have had the line in all of its absurdity and all of its arrogance. Of course this was schools, not the poverty program.

The Poverty Program is of course now the burning grievance as it actually pays money to these "no count niggers" so they do not want to chop cotton for $3.00 a day and if you have seen the latest denunciations of the vegetable co-operative in Dallas, Marengo, etc. funded by the poverty program or the OEO, you will realize that they learn nothing nor do they ever give up. The attack is headed by Joe Smitherman who is the Mayor of Selma . . . The Co-operative was started by Lewis Black, [who] works for the Southern Regional Council and is considered by the Carmichael militants to be a perfect Uncle Tom. But what bothers me far more than the attacks on the poverty program is that the OEO, especially in Atlanta, and especially in my experience with them in the Head Start program, are so frightened of attack by the right wingers that they let them take over the program. I told you Joe Stewart who is campaign manager for Bill Dickinson of "Sex and Selma" fame, is the Chairman of the CAP here in Montgomery and it is loaded with junior

---

*Congressman John R. Rarick, Klan-backed candidate elected from Louisiana in 1966.

executive types and a few "representatives of the poor" and run by an ex-Air Force Officer, Mr. [Charles] Sheldon who is the biggest liar I have ever come across and who had made most of the Negro community furious. The whole fight you and Aubrey waged and I thought Lyndon too, to save the WPA from the Community Chest and the Red Cross and the social agencies, has now been lost and the whole poverty program is turned over to the conservative forces who are interposed between the Federal officials and the poor. I think it is a perfect mess and a total failure in helping the poor folks make their own decisions and run their own program, and yet to fight it as it should be puts you in with the worst enemies of any kind of help for the poor. But for Federal money to be in the control of a private group and run by private associations such as the Community Chest groups simply makes a mockery of what I thought the poverty program was intended to be. The Negroes hate the CAC and all over are trying to get out from under it. I think a Federal program should be run by Federal officials. Phil Landrum is starting a big attack on the poverty program and all of the Southern men are joining in, including Lister Hill. Since they are all hot warriors for Viet Nam, I doubt if Lyndon will do anything to curb them as he evidently feels that the Communists in Viet Nam are more danger than the possibilities of disaffection in the South. Our only recourse is Joe Clark who has put up a Committee to investigate and Bobby Kennedy who is on the Committee . . . but I simply still cannot go over to Bobby Kennedy, but perhaps I will have to if Lyndon does not stop being so blind to what is going on in this country and do something about it, and not turn the poor over to their worst enemies. It makes me mad every time I think about what we have been through with the Head Start program. We have been treated with total contempt.

Lots of love and hope to see you in May in New York. Va.

April 24, 1967
Dearest Dec:

I was as always delighted to hear from you and wish you had told me about your success as an advertising representative for *Ramparts** I read

---

*Ramparts started as a liberal Catholic quarterly in 1962. By the mid-1960s, it had become a major New Left publication and voice of the antiwar movement.

it and think it is incredible, but it is like psychedelic art, so smashing that it exhausts me after a few minutes, I wish I had the strength to bear it for a long period of time, but it is so screaming. Perhaps in this day of pop and bombs, nothing gets over but loud noises, but for me it really is exhausting and I can only take it in small doses.

Bob Zellner stopped by with a friend on Friday night, he and Dottie and baby are going to settle in New Orleans and he is going to work for something called "GROW" (Grass Roots Organizing Work) and he plans to work among the benighted white Southerners if possible. I only hope it will be possible, as I know he is a marked man already as when we got home after he had spent the night, we were told a police car had spent the evening parked here, no doubt waiting for him to appear. George Wallace has a very personal grudge against him. Bob looks wonderful, big, strong, and almost fat and full of joy and delight in life and the world. He told us all about the fights in SNCC and says Jim is working on a long, detailed piece for *Ramparts* which he thinks is great, but too detailed and too long, but he shows the CIA influence and traces it, so my feeling or hunch that so much of "Hate Whitey" came from outside influences, was or is true, although there is of course a lot of genuine hate Whitey feeling . . . We spent the weekend in Tuscaloosa with a young man named Bruce Payne who teaches in a Negro college over there, and who came from Berkeley originally and he was quite a Free Speecher he says, in any case he knew Bob quite well, and seemed to be part of the Berkeley movement, and he is finding so much of his work blocked by this blind anti-white feeling. So he is leaving and so are the best of the white teachers at Tuskegee, as they feel that there is nothing more they can do, so they leave these Negro kids in the hands of the old fuddy duddies, Hungarian refugees, Cuban refugees, etc. and some say it is because they think Stokely is right, there should be no white teachers, so all the good ones go and the rest are there for the salaries and to teach them fascism, it really makes me boil. In any case Bob thinks Jim's article is great. He says he thinks Jim is going to get out of the "Movement" and get a writing job, and he says Dinky looks simply marvelous more beautiful than ever, radiant he put it, and whatever the legality of the situation, it is a very cozy, domestic set-up. Among the young crowd, this goes on all the time, and no one thinks it odd even, and when I point out that it puts all the burden on the woman, they think I am being rather old-fashioned and still protesting women's rights. Apparently the idea is that the women make the living, have the babies, arrange for their care and the men enjoy all the joys of married life, home, children, but none of the worries, none of the responsibilities, and come and go as they please engaged in greater things, so perhaps the men have finally gotten to the state of affairs they really have wanted all the time, when they can have their cake and eat it too.

In any case the young will inherit the earth and so they have to learn to live with it. Also they do seem to have devoted friendships, they actually love one another or seem to, and since I love them too, I have to take them as they are and realize they are simply different in their ideas. Certainly I was raised to think that marriage was the end and be-all of a woman's life, and chiefly to get a meal ticket for life, like the Heroines in Jane Austen, I was raised to do nothing but get a husband and was lucky I got a good one, that I did actually "marry well" as the saying went . . .

We will be in New York the end of May so let me know if there is any chance you will be there too. Devotedly, Va.

Clark Foreman retired as director of the Emergency Civil Liberties Committee at the end of 1967, and he and Mairi moved to Adjuntas, Puerto Rico. The first history of the Southern Conference for Human Welfare was published that year. Entitled *And Promises to Keep: The Southern Conference for Human Welfare, 1938–1948*, it was written by Thomas Krueger, an assistant professor of history at the University of Illinois.

June 16, 1967
Dearest Clark and Mairi:

It was, as always, a great joy to see you and be with you and to know there are two people and one place where I can say what I think and be myself and feel I am loved "in spite of myself"—that is warts and all and I know I have many. I thought Clark looked fairly well in spite of his illness although I am not an advocate of the mustache and beard as I like his face and the more I can see the better! I am glad you are going to be out of the rat race in New York and all of the hatchet men there, how you have stood it for so long I do not know.

Clark, a book has just come out called *The Southern Conference For Human Welfare—1938–1948* by someone named Krueger and it is published by the Vanderbilt University Press, Nashville, Tenn. and is $6.50. I read it when we were at Vann Woodward's and while it is dull I think it is accurate and really a very fair, objective and good job, and it certainly gives you all the credit you deserve for your work in it and keeping it alive. I hope you get it as I think it will be used quite a lot when History is written and I did not note any errors in it, but you might. I remember the man coming to interview us, and we thought he was very nice indeed, and honest and well-meaning and he did a thorough and honest job I think. Of course I don't think he was right about Joe Gelders. I think Joe was a Communist, even if he did not carry a card and in fact a dedicated one, but I never thought it mattered whether he did or not, although it might have been more honest if he had, but then if he had he never would have been able to do anything, what is your opinion? It all seems so long ago and far away but at the same time, it is nice to know we will have a place in History, however small it may be, and of course I don't think it is small what we did, I think it began something and did something that is bearing lots of fruit, some good and some bad, but good on the whole.

We got home and moved up in the country where we are now, and are going to stay there for the Summer. I don't want Cliff to spend any more money up there until I see whether I like it enough to live up there all the time. It is fine in the Summer but I am not sure how I would like it in the Winter. It is rather isolated and remote as Elmore County is one of the worst counties in the State, full of KKK and WCC and just plain hoodlums and ignorant devils—with a very bad Sheriff and deputies. But we are still holding on to the apartment so we will not give it up until I have made a good try at it.

Lots of love and do tell me how the house gets on and how Joannie is doing. I do wish you could stop by here on your way North, you have never once been to see us and we would love it so much. Devotedly, Va.

June 19, 1967
Dear Glenn and Vann:
As usual your house was the nicest and most comfortable and your dinners (as well as breakfasts) were the best and we had the best conversation and the most fun there—I really have come to the con-

clusions that reconstructed Southerners are the most attractive people there are, they are not self righteous like so many of our Yankee friends, they know from experience the ease of evil ways, and the difficulty breaking away from them, all of us have had to pay for our convictions so they are not held lightly, and I am of the opinion, which of course is very conceited that we emancipated Southerners are really prizes! . . .

I wish you would come with us on some of our journeyings and see how uncomfortably people live, not only physically but spiritually and intellectually. I really do find the most comfort and joy in being with Southerners—which may make me a hopeless provincial but then I am one.

I was so forcibly reminded of the above in Boston and Cambridge, where we visited old, old friends who are bred in the womb of Back Bay and Cambridge and who come from long lines of Abolitionists and who still think they are paying you a compliment by saying although all white Southerners are [the] devil's disciples, "still in spite of the fact she comes from Alabama, really Mrs. Durr is not so bad." It makes me grind my teeth. I do not want to be a heroine in foreign lands, I want to keep my pride as a Southerner, although I must confess it is often hard here in Alabama living under the rule of George and Lurleen. I take so much personal pride in any Southerner that can sustain my pride in being Southern . . .

What did you think of the Krueger book after reading it? I thought it was . . . honest and factual . . . he did get most all the facts straight, even though he got none of the agony and blood and turmoil and tears and fights and struggles into it, simply bloodless. Only novelists can write the history of the South with any degree of accuracy—no solid historian could write the truth and be believed.

We got home to ninety degree weather and everything dry and parched but hope for relief soon. Did you know Vann that the Legislature of Arkansas passed a RESOLUTION AGAINST THE VIET NAM WAR? Isn't that wonderful? I hope it means that Fulbright won't have such a hard time. There is something about these razorbacks, they know it is root hog or die, and so they root. More power to them and more power to you as well, both of you, and lots of love. Va. Durr

July 5, 1967

Dearest Dec:

We will be in Washington from the first of September to the middle of October while Cliff is being "Oral Professor" at the Institute for Policy Studies. They seem to be simply mad about him, are sending down TWO young men next week to help him with his files and to get his lectures organized . . . They think they have discovered the prime, original New Dealer in all of his original coloring and indeed they have, and are pumping him dry of all of his experiences and all of his correspondence and all of his Defense Plant stuff, it is the most fascinating bit to them, how he and the others practically sneaked through the arming of the country in the face of the isolationists, you must well remember that, the meetings in the cherry tree when we were trying to get the U.S. armed and went to the parties where you broke the picture of Willkie. So they are paying him quite well to stay in Washington for six weeks and get it all down and so that is where we will be from the 1st of September until the 15th of October, then if all works out we will go to both England and France . . . What I am afraid of is that the Civil Rights Movement or our part of it is rather déjà vu and we have fallen between the Black Power group and the student group who are now preaching a rather naive form of revolution, as does Black Power, but I simply cannot take Revolution seriously when they are at one and the same time calling on the Police to protect them and also the Justice Department to protect their right of free speech, I do think it is being *really* naive to think that any government is going to protect real revolutionaries, so I think it is more a form of verbal exercise. But more than that, all of these sweet [English] boys whom we like so much are very much bound up in the Labor Party and while they are opposed to the Viet Nam War, they don't want to really stick their necks out and oppose the leadership, sort of like the loyal Democrats here, and I have told them I simply will not and cannot stop speaking against the War. I am afraid that while the Civil Rights fight had the backing and even approval of the powers that be, that the fight against Viet Nam does not have, and all of the young men who have their futures to make don't want to get caught too far off base, but I hope I am wrong . . .

I am so glad you met Studs Terkel whom I adore, and I really do think he likes me and Cliff. I know you are perfectly right about the book, no one will subsidize conversation about a book, and exactly right too, I wonder how many people talk good books? Must be millions. But the fact remains that unless some one or some way I can buy some time (a quiet time as they say) my chances of writing one are rather slim, but probably the real reason is I don't know exactly what I am going to write about! I think my life has been fascinating but how to write it so anyone else will think so. That is the question . . .

Lots of love, write again, Va.

During the summer of 1967, race riots erupted in more than 60 cities across the nation. In Newark, New Jersey, where black unemployment and housing shortages were among the worst in the nation, 25 people lost their lives during four days of rioting in mid-July. The worst disturbance occurred in Detroit a week later; 43 people were killed and property damage exceeded that in Watts. The governor called in federal troops to restore order, and Army tanks patrolled the streets.

July 18, 1967
Dearest Dec:

Your letter was joyfully received and I know you are glad to be at home once more and in your own bed and not wandering around . . .

The Summer visitors have come and some have gone and more are expected. They come through like flotsam and jetsam, one never knows who to expect or what they will turn out to be, we are looking for two young Englishmen next week, who are Nicholas Bosanquet's friends, who was in Mississippi and stayed with us several times. Since our young friends in England have arranged for Cliff's lectures, I think we had better leave ourselves in their hands and not strike out on our own . . .

The riots have certainly stirred up bad feelings here and also a certain amount of smug satisfaction among the "I Told You So" people. I wonder if the attention they draw to the horrible conditions are worth the price that is paid in death and destruction, what do you think? What I am afraid of is a much worse police state and oppression—but it might have come anyway. From this point in time and space, I see no advantage to the "Movement" from such disorganized, violent and destructive happenings, especially when the Negroes themselves seem to pay the price and bear the burden and have to live among the ruins. Perhaps it makes some people think constructively but not among most of the people I see, I think it is hardening their attitudes but perhaps they were already hard enough. I am really puzzled over whether they do good or not, but I suppose the main thing is that people finally break out into violence after so much being hemmed in, and pay the price and accept the consequences, no matter how bad they are.

Lots of love and do reply soon. Devotedly, Va.

August 14, 1967
Dearest Dec:

We have had streams of visitors this Summer, it seems to me more than ever, and the last was the Labour Party Research Director . . . He was sent by the State Department, you know it really is one of the ironies of life that we are hosts for the State Department. I thought he was simply awful, like a barrel of eels, never could get a good grip on him all evening, he seemed to be great and then he totally contradicted himself. He was one of these self-conscious proletarians, and always was telling great tales of how he told off the British Ambassador and what he said to the Lord so and so, and how he despised Oxford and Cambridge and how old George Brown was one of the greatest and his wife Sophie was snubbed by the snobs, and he really was so awful that I began to feel that Dickens had invented him and he could not be real . . . I almost hate to go to England and find such servility, but of course he was terribly servile really to America and to money and to power and to all the rich and great.

We are going to have a beautiful house in Washington for September, very large and handsome, some friends of ours lent it to us, so do come and see us there. I know you won't—you are so hard to catch up with. I am rather looking forward to being in Washington for six weeks or so. I had a long letter from the Chief Archivist of the United States plus one from Bird, saying that as one of the "oldest, best, most devoted and most loyal" of the friends of the Johnsons, I was being asked to donate to the Johnson Library all my letters, pictures, memories, thoughts and so on for the future historians. Goodness I did feel a fraud. Shall I simply say what I think of him now for the future historians? I really think he is off his rocker . . .

All the girls seem well and busy. All ardent supporters of anti-Viet Nam programs one way or another.

August 31, 1967
Dearest Dec: . . .

We are leaving here about Wednesday of next week and we will stay at this lovely big house out in Maryland. I do wish you could come. We will be there until the first of October and then kind of camp around until we go to England about the 15th of October . . . Somehow I doubt if we will be so adored and such rara avis as we were before, I think everything has changed, and the Civil Rights Movement above all. No longer will it be thrilling to tell or hear the tale of Mrs. Parks and the Boycott, all of that is old hat now, and in fact she wrote me from Detroit that she and her neighbors spend the night protecting their homes . . . and were afraid of the rioters burning down their houses . . . Also Congressman [John] Conyers for whom she works and who is supposed to be a very good man, had his office completely burned down and totally destroyed and all of his records and everything concerning claims, etc. We certainly have created a monster in our midst and we did it. They just don't give a DAMN. Who can blame them but like the rest of humanity, we don't want it to hit us. I read the book you sent me, or most of it, and I do understand why, but then the next question is what to do, and I simply don't think that under our present system of government and particularly economics that it is possible to salvage the bottom group, we will have to create a new and different system entirely. But that seems a long way off at present, and all of the small things that are done are totally inadequate . . .

Lots of love dearest Dec, and do write. I do love you and miss you constantly. Devotedly, Va.

January 9, 1968
Dear Vann and Glenn:

Sorry not to see you this go-round, but you were spared our usual dose of flu . . . We had a wonderful time in England and adored every minute of it, Cliff lectured at Exeter, Oxford, Cambridge and Edinburgh, and each place was pure bliss . . . The Harkness Fellows got him over and got the Harkness Fund to pay our way . . . and as Cliff says, "our cornbread really has returned upon the waters." These were all the students who have stayed with us over the years . . . We came back refreshed and revitalized I hope for the hard Election year ahead, with George running for President and who else beside Lyndon, God alone and the Republican Party knows . . .

Tell your friend Mr. Styron we think his book* is a masterpiece, really is a work of genius. We read it while recuperating from the flu and both us thought it was superb. I am going to the Negro College here tomorrow night to hear a review of it, should be interesting. Come to see us, Lots of love, Va. Durr.

February 21, 1968
Dearest Jim [Dombrowski]:

Bob told us when he passed through that you had had another operation, for gall bladder, I believe, but got through it very well . . . I hope so. He got here the day Cliff went to the hospital with his back, another slipped disk . . . We had hoped to get down there during February or March, to visit the Ben Smiths who had asked us before we went to England, but I am afraid with this trouble of Cliff's that is out. I wish we could come, I do so long to be with people I can talk to.

England was wonderful that way, the freedom of speech is a real thing, and although people say, or some people say, that it makes no difference as nothing gets changed, it certainly is a change from here . . . where everything is whispered if talked about at all . . . The thing about England that I love so much is that people . . . call things by their right names, no euphemisms . . . and socialism and communism and fascism and democracy and dictatorship are discussed in plain terms, and of course imperialism. They think we put the British Empire to shame with our brand of imperialism. I must say that our policy of "we must destroy to save" is the worst thing I ever heard of, that is since the Crusades and the Inquisition . . .

I cannot say that I was glad to get back to Montgomery, but at least I feel at home here. We hope to move up into the country this Summer when the house gets winterized, and I rather dread that, but Cliff has

---

*William Styron, *The Confessions of Nat Turner*.

wanted to for so long and I think he is entitled to it. But as we get older the 44 miles will get longer, that is round trip but I hope we can manage for some years yet to come.

We do miss your visits. We miss Aubrey all the time. I thought the Ph.D. thesis was good. It was a fair book and he did better than I expected but . . . all the human quality and the drama and the tragedy and the comedy were left out of it entirely.

But we did do some good, even here in Alabama there is a stir and a ferment, there are now four different Democratic Parties and that in itself is a change. The Negro vote grows all the time and they are more and more taking part in politics. I don't know if things can get settled by politics but at least they are trying.

Personally I feel that I cannot vote for Lyndon under any considerations, I think he has lost his mind or something has happened to make him act so madly . . . I hope and pray that there will be someone running I can vote for, but I think the main thing is to work here at home which I try to do as difficult as it is.

Lots of love, dear Jim, do write and tell me how you are. So many of our friends are gone, dead or disappeared or changed beyond recognition. We miss Aubrey every day as I am sure you do . . . Devotedly, Va.

March 11, 1968
Dearest Otto:

I was so pleased and so proud of you when I read in the *NYT* that you had spoken at the meeting at the UN Plaza against the use of atomic weapons at Khe Sanh* or anywhere at all . . . I do think you are so wonderful to keep going and never give up and I do admire and love you very much indeed.

I have just been listening to the Foreign Relations Committee Hearing with [Dean] Rusk as witness. I must say he really is like a Buddha, never a ripple of expression and he simply pumps out the old worn and proven lies one after another, "aggression from the North" "our efforts to make peace" etc. etc. I think he is hopeless and so is the entire admin-

---

*U.S. Marine base in South Vietnam.

istration . . . I think since the last offensive there is a great deal of peace sentiment in the country, even here in Alabama you hear a different tune, although not based on any high or noble motives, simply that "our boys are dying in a foreign land for foreigners who don't care about us" and that "Lyndon Johnson cares more for those foreign people than he does for us and our boys." This is not noble but this is what they think . . . and at least they are against the war. I do not think they will end it, those in power, until they are forced to and I don't think that point has come yet . . .

All the girls are well and are working for McCarthy, Ann in Harrisburg, Lucy in Princeton, and Tilla in Washington. The young people seem to like him very much, and while I certainly do not find him dynamic, I do respect his courage and the fact that he is willing to try. I am beginning to wonder if Lyndon is even going to run for President, I think if things get worse and worse and the war goes from bad to worse, he may just not run.

Wallace is certainly running all over the place and is on the TV and in the papers daily and hourly. His wife will very likely die and that may mean he cannot use the resources of the State of Alabama to run, but at the moment he is using the personnel, the airplanes and every other thing he needs, all paid for by the taxpayers of Alabama and they make no protest. He is their God, it really is frightening to see how they adore him . . . to touch him, to honor him, he is their spokesman for whatever hunger and deep frustrations they have. As I understand it Franz Fanon* says one wins his manhood by violence, and these people too, these white Alabamians and many of the other white Southerners feel terribly frustrated, deprived, looked down on and despised and they too seem to find their manhood in looking to George Wallace to avenge them. It is terrifying to see the hold he has and is getting on the same kinds of frustrated, helpless, defeated people all over the country, arousing their fears like some Al Capone gangster and saying he will protect them.

---

*Franz Fanon (1925–1961), Francophone political philosopher and revolutionary from Martinique. Fanon's theories for the decolonization of Africa and the Third World were widely disseminated through his book *The Wretched of the Earth* (1961), which had a major influence on the Black Power movement. Its subtitle is revealing: "The Handbook for the Black Revolution that is Changing the Shape of the World." He argued that only through violence could colonized people free themselves from the psychological and material violence of colonialism.

Lots of love, dear Otto. I wish I could have heard your speech and seen you before the UN fighting against atomic weapons. I do think it is so wonderful that you do it and keep doing it in face of all kinds of disappointments.

Dr. Benjamin Spock, the famous pediatrician, Rev. William Sloane Coffin, and two other defendants were charged by the Justice Department with conspiring to counsel evasion of the draft. They were found guilty, but their convictions were later overturned on appeal. Decca wrote a book on the trial that was published in 1969.

On March 12, 1968, antiwar candidate Senator Eugene McCarthy of Minnesota won 42 percent of the vote in the New Hampshire primary to Lyndon Johnson's 49 percent. Owing to McCarthy's strong showing, Robert Kennedy entered the presidential race several days later. On March 31, Lyndon Johnson announced that he would not seek reelection.

March 18, 1968
Dearest Dec:

Your letter has just come and I am SIMPLY THRILLED over the idea of the Spock book. I think it is wonderfully exciting and I am sure you can do a great job of it. I think Spock is a superb character and the very epitome of "Americanism" in its best sense . . .

I know it will be fun to . . . work with Spock and Coffin too, but I really think you will also have to work with [Senator William J.] Fulbright and I believe Cliff does too. That the only chance to win the case is for Fulbright's thesis to become valid, which is that this is not a declared war and the President does not have the right to wage war and send troops without the express resolution of Congress and the Tonkin Bay Resolution was NOT a declaration of War . . . If you listened to the Foreign Policy Committee Hearings you would have gotten the point then, as Fulbright stressed this as THE MAIN POINT, that the Vietnamese War was an illegal war and was NOT declared by Congress . . .

I know you will be busy and I will not expect long, fascinating letters but I do hope you will keep a supply of postcards on hand unless you propose to say something you do not want the general public to hear. I am sure all postcards are read somewhere along the line . . .

We were so thrilled over McCarthy's showing but have rather mixed feelings about Bobby getting in, we think he might end up as VP on Lyndon's ticket—what do you think? . . .

Lots of love and congratulations, I do think it is wonderful that you got such a chance.

On April 4, 1968, Martin Luther King, Jr. was assassinated in Memphis, Tennessee, where he had gone to support the city's striking sanitation workers.

May 7, 1968
Dearest Dec:

I knew you were madly traveling around and never expect or look to hear from you under those circumstances. Then too we have had so much excitement here that I was too upset and busy to think of anything but getting through the . . . day ahead.

I did grieve over King's death and was shocked and horrified. I love his wife and thought she acted wonderfully and I liked him, it was just that at first I never agreed with his policies but I think he grew and grew . . . King was a great man in many ways and I watched him from the beginning and her too, who grew with him . . . I saw them grow from a young, Negro couple who lived entirely in the Negro community, were totally barred from the white community and really knew only a very few white people . . . and then saw him become a worldwide hero and it was really an amazing and remarkable career. You were wrong [to say] that I did not like him. I was constantly defending him to people like Jim [Forman] and Dinky and all the SNCC people and they were the ones who despised him so and thought he was so bourgeois and so on. I think his death is a sort of watershed, and any kind of meeting of the minds is gone. I do not expect our system nor have I ever expected it to voluntarily give over its powers or its money, no system in history has ever done so, and we are going through a lot more turmoil before anything much is changed. My objection to all this rhetorical revolution is that it is based on such weakness and that the issue is not color but our system—just as slavery was a system that had to be changed . . . and our system has to be changed, and to make it simply a color struggle to me is absurd.

I think the only victory that has been won is in the student struggle against the War which has been a struggle of both black and white, sometimes apart and sometimes together, but this is a struggle that goes to the heart of our system and I think we have won some small victory in it with the start of the Peace talks and McCarthy coming out and now Bobby [Kennedy] who I would not trust around the corner. If Humphrey gets it I will vote for Rockefeller and if Nixon gets it I won't vote at all and if he and Humphrey get it I will be prepared to flee at a moment's notice. Biggest scoundrels I know of! . . .

After the trial is over . . . do come and see us . . .

Lots of love darling Dec and do write. Devotedly, Va

On May 6, 1968, in the midst of George Wallace's vigorous campaign for the presidency on the American Independent Party ticket, Governor Lurleen Wallace died after a short battle with cancer.

May 14, 1968

Dearest Jim,

Cliff was so sorry he did not get over to Atlanta, but he was ill both with severe bronchitis and with his back and is still suffering twinges from both . . .

We have been sick on and off ever since we came back from England. I don't know if it is America or Alabama or simply we are getting old, but we were blooming with health all the time we were in England, had energy, strength, joy and life, and as soon as we come home, we react by feeling tired, getting sick, having very little joy. Living in Wallaceland is no picnic, and I do get awfully tired of it . . . We are staying more and more in the country and he loves that, and I am getting used to it, although I am a city girl at heart.

The State is still mourning Mrs. Wallace. "Lurleen" has become a symbol of all the people love best and the people love her and do mourn her and the fact that she upheld her husband in all of his vicious racism and politics means nothing to them at all, she is adored. One of the many Judkins cousins died and we went to the funeral yesterday and the cemetery was lined with flowers, all fading and wilting now, but there were thousands of them, and the sorrow and love that sent them was and is perfectly genuine. She seemed to symbolize to so many people all they think a "Southern woman" should be, pretty, small, dainty, good mother and certainly obedient wife, brave under suffering and doomed. There was and is something macabre in the recitation of the sufferings and detailed descriptions of her illness and suffering and death. I think so many Southerners especially women are in love with death and suffering and their highest ambition is to be known as "brave sufferers." I hate it.

June 3, 1968

Dearest Dec:

I did not find your letter unsatisfactory in the least. I know you do not like to analyze people's character, although I think you're a real genius in *catching* character. Joe Barnes once said to me that he thought your character sketches in *Daughters and Rebels* were superb, worthy of Jane Austen, but the *reasons* for people being the way they are you seem to hate to go into, I think you believe, like Cliff, it is an invasion of people's privacy and that each person is entitled to their own private self, which is of course directly contrary to my own mad curiosity to try and find out why people act as they do and the reasons for their behavior. And then my desire to change them if possible which I have rarely been able to do. But I do honestly believe that there is a reason for everything, I believe in a rational world, it is just that we are so ignorant of it, and know so little, and particularly in the field of human behavior. So, therefore, I do believe there is a reason for people being the way they are, it is just so hard to find out "why?" but also so absolutely fascinating. Which makes me a great gossip of course . . .

Cliff . . . thinks we are now moving into a period of "Law and Order" which is going to be very tough on dissenters, and now that Hugo has drawn the line between "action and speech" and it has been taken up, that demonstrations of all kinds are going to be harder and harder. I will say that Hugo has been that way since the Montgomery Bus Boycott, he has admonished us each time we saw him to "tell our friends to get off the streets and into the Courts" or it would be like Germany and "our friends" would get it in the neck—so really he has not changed his mind—it is only that things have become more difficult all the way around, since the Courts and the political system don't seen to answer the needs of the dissenters or even respond. But we both feel very strongly that the black separatist movement is fatal to them and is going to lead to murder or massacre—as so many have become expendable. I do not think Fanon applies to the U.S., although very well to Africa. All of which makes me a square. I know, I have been told.

On June 5, 1968, Robert F. Kennedy was assassinated in Los Angeles just after delivering a speech to supporters upon winning California's Democratic primary.

June 10, 1968

Dearest Otto: . . .

Events have been so chaotic and full of drama and tragedy that I hardly know what to say about public matters. McCarthy seems to me to be the only honest candidate or who has any real principle on the Viet Nam war, but everyone says he does not have a chance but I am for him as long as he is in the race. I did not ever go for the Kennedys but I would have voted for Bobby . . . Humphrey I have no respect for at all, nor any confidence in him, but from all we get it is going to be Humphrey–Nixon and that is a sad choice . . .

Here in Alabama, Wallace has dominated the scene so completely and is still dominating it, that we are lost in his hatred and confusion. I get sick at heart when I hear the Negroes echoing his theory that it is racism that is the main issue, and of course the report* on the riots did the same, which we know is not the case. Wallace is supported and financed and allied with the same evil forces that have kept the South in a colonial status and serving their ends and is in my opinion . . . very dangerous. If he and Nixon make a deal, which I expect them to, then we are really in the jaws of Hell. But the only alternative seems at this point to be some more hot air and hypocrisy, which Humphrey represents. But for the Civil Rights Movement and the progressive movement, what little there is, to fall for the theory that racism and racism alone is responsible for the ghettos and for the condition of the Negro, to me this is sheer insanity and simply serves the purpose of those who wish to keep people divided and hating each other.

Personally I am tired but quite well. We have been terribly distressed over the breakup of Tilla's marriage . . . Lots and lots of love, Va.

With George Wallace in control of the regular Democrats and planning a presidential race on an independent ticket, two loyalist Democratic groups formed in Alabama and elected a slate of delegates to attend the Democratic National convention in Chicago. The Alabama Independent Democratic Party supported the candidacy of Hubert H. Humphrey. Virginia was a founding member of the National Democratic Party of Al-

---

Report of the National Advisory Commission on Civil Disorders, also known as the Kerner Commission Report, issued on March 1, 1968.

abama, headed by John Cashin, and she was among the twelve delegates elected by that group and pledged to Eugene McCarthy.[6]

August 12, 1968
Dearest Clark and Mairi:

Don't you owe me a letter or is it the other way around? I know it seems a long time since I've heard from you . . .

We have had one of the hottest Summers I can ever remember, finally got an air conditioner as it was simply unbearable up in the country . . . and that has helped a lot but I hate to be all closed up . . . We have also had a lot of company but that has been very pleasant indeed as most of them have been interesting and attractive and have not stayed too long. Some Harkness Fellows, some stray foreigners, and lots of friends passing through.

I am all involved in the McCarthy fight and having a wonderful time, as you know the regular Democratic delegation is pledged to Wallace who is running on a Third Party ticket so our group which was started by Dr. [John] Cashin (Negro dentist in Huntsville) is sending a rival delegation to Chicago to contest the seats. There is also another rival delegation which is a Humphrey delegation so things are very exciting. I am simply longing to go as I am an official Delegate of the new Party and of course like an old fire horse with a fire raging, if Lulah gets back in time and Cliff continues to improve I think I may go. The Republican convention was so awful, it made me so depressed to see those FACES, so greedy, dull, lacking of all kindness and compassion . . . and then to pick that awful and horrible scoundrel Nixon, who I think is the worst. And after he had sold out to the Dixiecrats too, the paper here has printed in full the crowing of the Dixiecrat Republicans claiming how they got to him and got [Spiro] Agnew* instead of [Mark] Hatfield. Of course that horrible Nixon face grinning that horrible Nixon smile. I can't stand Humpty Dumpty† either so as long as there is even a faint chance for McCarthy I

---

*Spiro Agnew, former governor of Maryland, joined Nixon on the Republican ticket as the vice presidential candidate. Agnew's hard line in response to race riots in Baltimore that followed King's assassination the previous April was what finally sold Nixon on him. See Dan Carter, *The Politics of Rage*, 331.
†Hubert Humphrey.

will stay with it. Our delegation is very interesting, about half white and half Negro and all as friendly as can be. So far here at least I have not experienced the "Hate Whitey" and "Kill the Honky" attitude but when I say that to my Yankee liberal friends they always say it is because the Blacks here are so intimidated but I don't see that either, I can't see that they are scared of Hell or High Water, and certainly not of me or George Wallace, in fact I think they are the bravest people I know of . . .

Lots of love and do write, devotedly, Va.

At the end of August, Virginia attended the 1968 Democratic convention in Chicago as a delegate pledged to antiwar candidate Eugene McCarthy. The following letters describe her experiences as a member of one of Alabama's challenge delegations.

September 3, 1968
Dearest Dec:

So sorry you could not come to Chicago, it really was simply thrilling, rather different than the last time when you and I were "with the machine" rather than fighting it, and drove back and forth to the Cow Coliseum in the big black cars and had seats on the floor with the Texas delegation.* Horrors—just think of it now, John Connally and Lyndon, but strange to say, Maury Maverick's son was there fighting the Texas challenge so history in some strange way did repeat itself. But it was lots more fun being with the outs rather than the ins, as the outs were simply lovely, marvelous, and brave people. I never did meet Gene McCarthy but came away with even more respect for him, he is truly I believe an honest man. The kids were simply wonderful, and when the McCarthy kids at last walked across the avenue to the kids in the park it was a symbolic moment. They were weeping but both sets of kids . . . are determined to die fighting for what they believe in in this country, rather than die fighting for what they do not believe in Viet Nam . . .

Of course the Blacks (I did learn to say that, Negro now seems to be an insult) at the Convention were soul brothers, and black and white together was the theme and it was wonderful . . . all of the Mississippi, Geor-

---

*Virginia and Decca attended the national Democratic convention in 1940.

gia, and Alabama challenge got together and such great people, made us all so proud. Julian [Bond] was absolutely perfect . . . The *London Times* man . . . said he thought Julian was the best politician he had observed for some time . . . I don't know when I ever had such a good time, seeing so many old friends, feeling useful again, and once again back in the battle . . .

Lots of love darling Dec, do write and tell me the news and how the book is coming.

September 9, 1968
Dear Glenn and Vann:
You really missed it, it was simply wonderful . . . a real watershed, at least for the South. For the first time, the people who voted for years AGAINST THE DEMOCRATIC PARTY got at least some of their come-uppance. Just think of Eastland and Stennis losing the backing of the national Democratic Party and Julian Bond getting even half of Maddox's party, it really was thrilling. I am sure we will win next time and even this time we got a wonderfully good vote we thought, in spite of the whole convention being rigged.

I wish you could have been there, it was thrilling, and to hear all of those SOBs who for years have been berating the Democratic Party and . . . the Negro . . . brag about how many black people (they even said "Black" which is now the fashionable word) they had on THEIR DELEGATIONS and how they loved the Democratic Party and how they love the colored people and how there was nothing they wanted as much as to get them active in the Democratic Party, it was really a marvelous joy, and to hear the ones from Alabama cussin' out George Wallace (they are paying for it now) and bragging on how many Negroes they had on their side, the whole thing was worth a lifetime of work and worry.

Then too the Southern challenge groups all got together, young Maury Maverick . . . and Julian Bond, so handsome and elegant . . . and the wonderful people from Mississippi . . . and the Texas challengers who were terrific. Ronnie Dugger was there and is going to try and be a sort of intercom system for all of us, do you know him? You really should get his paper, the *Texas Observer*, which is I think the best political analysis in the South, he publishes it in Austin. So in spite of not getting seated, in spite of the beatings and so on, I . . . came back so encouraged.

For not only did the challengers make connection, we made connection with all of the McCarthy people, I listened to the Connecticut challenge and thought Lou Pollock did a great job and so did your friend Bill Styron, but of course they lost too and want to keep in touch with us, that is according to Anne Wexler from Westport who was wonderful to us, and so were all of the McCarthy people and so were the McGovern people. Our only enemies were the Humphrey people, and they were awful, such deceivers, such horrible hypocrites, I simply cannot stand Hubert, never could even back in Washington, always did despise him. It looks as if the choice was going to be between the worst scoundrel I ever knew and the worst hypocrite I ever knew—hard choice. But I am sure I will finally vote for the Democratic Party . . .

In spite of everyone saying what a horror it was, I thought it was wonderful, coming out of Alabama it seemed glorious to me, and I think the fact that the Southern deceivers (along with the master deceiver, Humphrey) were unmasked will help in the future. I have always thought if the South could be brought to reckoning that the Democratic Party might be saved. This is the seedbed of evil, although I think it is also caused by our dependant status and colonial economy, but I think the evil of racism is here, although it seems everywhere now.

The Black Caucus was also great, they were behind us one hundred percent, men like [John] Conyers, [Richard] Hatcher, [Carl] Stokes,* etc. this was real Black Power and on our side . . . simply a realization that their fight was our fight (black and white together) and they did come through, so did Coretta King and Abernathy and Harry Belafonte and that crowd, the only place I ran into "hate whitey" or hate "Southern whitey" was a party where I met Nelson Algren† who immediately classified me as SOUTHERN WHITE LADY which of course I am, and proceeded to be, I thought, rather nasty indeed, never even saw me before and said he had *never* been South but he knew from his maid that all

---

*John Conyers, elected to Congress in 1964, was the second black congressman to serve from Michigan. In 1967, Richard Hatcher was elected mayor of Gary, Indiana, and Carl Stokes was elected mayor of Cleveland, becoming the first two African Americans elected to mayoral office of a major city in the United States.

†Nelson Algren, a contemporary of Virginia, was a member of Chicago's literary left-wing circles and author of the classic novel *The Man with the Golden Arm* (1950).

SOUTHERN WHITE LADIES tried to get their maids to steal, by leaving money around, so they COULD SEND THEM TO JAIL. I tried nicely to tell him that most all SOUTHERN WHITE LADIES I knew wanted to keep their maids so badly that they would do most anything to keep their maids OUT OF JAIL, but this had no effect on him at all, and he went right on telling everyone at the party that this was a characteristic of ALL SOUTHERN WHITE LADIES. It did make me mad . . .

Sorry to be writing in haste, but right now there seems more to do than I have time for. We are building a house at the Pea Level, Cliff is writing a book, some Harkness Fellows coming Wednesday . . .

I am sure the South is the most interesting part of the country, it is changing the fastest.

Lots of love and do come see us, Devotedly, Va.

September 17, 1968
Dearest Dec:

You do sound as if the book is rather interrupted, and I hope you can get going on it again. I think the disorders at Chicago, the Vietnam plank, the loss of it rather, the whole election really hinges on the issues raised in the trial of Spock, et al. In fact the future of the country is going to turn on the issue of whether its citizens can oppose PRESIDENTIAL WARS without fear of jail or whether it is going to become the fact that to oppose War or Wars is going to be considered subversive and traitorous. In contrast to the prevailing mood of being "sunk" I thought Chicago was simply great. I had a wonderful time of course seeing so many old friends and being back in the harness again and feeling useful, but more than that the large, very large numbers of people I met who were opposed to the War, the entire McCarthy contingent, the kids in the park (who I thought were magnificent), the new Southern coalition, all of this was encouraging to me. After living so long in Alabama under Wallace and his kind, I suppose I am rather used to a police state and think things are actually getting better, or at least there is more opposition.

I agree with McCarthy that the really big issue is whether the PRESIDENT, whoever he may be, has the power to send troops all over the world in undeclared wars, without getting the advice and consent of the Senate or even having it debated. People now are beginning to nit-pick about McCarthy and no doubt he is not perfect but his courage and his tenacity in opposing the War is to my mind a great act, and I admire him very much. I think Hubert is such a worm . . . but think Nixon is an even bigger scoundrel but will probably get elected. Wallace may run second, he really seems to get the people, especially the poor and deprived. We have just had another English visitor, the correspondent of the *Manchester Guardian,* and he interviewed the Wallace people and saw the barrels and barrels of mail and they told him to sample the mail and he did, and said nearly all the letters were written by practically illiterate people, could not write well and could hardly spell, and yet nearly all of them enclosed some money and all of them wrote to Wallace as though he were their Savior, "you will bring God back into the schools"—"you will stop the Federal government from trying to run our lives," but he said the main burden of it was that "you will stop communism" . . . He said there was very little overt racism in the letters, he thinks they have learned the same kind of code words Wallace uses, but at the same time he thought anti-communism was the key, they equate everything they do not like with "communism"—He thought the letters were profoundly sad and pitiful and frightening. He thinks Wallace is going down the path toward Fascism (that old-fashioned word) very fast and carrying a lot of people with him. Of course he is financed by the same kinds of people, rich oil Texas money, new War Industries money, but the old money will go to him too if they need him, he preaches free enterprise constantly and States' rights and is a great supporter of the capitalist system and equates any opposition to it with "communism," subversion, and treason. He is a dangerous man.

September 28, 1968
Dear Clark and Mairi: . . .

I went to the Convention and although we did not get seated we got a good vote and . . . it really was thrilling and in spite of the violence and shenanigans . . . as for the first time for so long there was the beginnings of a new coalition, much broader, deeper and more permanent I believe than ever before since the New Deal, the McCarthy people were great I thought . . . and the young people and the SOUTH. It was so exciting to see the Solid South begin to break up, and Julian Bond emerged as the real leader of the challenge forces in the South, he really is a wonderfully able and attractive young man, and our group from Alabama was pretty good too I thought, and many from Mississippi and Texas, the South is really rising and Black and White were together and got along fine at least in our delegation and I think in most of the Southern delegations. I do wish you could stay in Atlanta and be part of the New South that is coming into being. Maynard Jackson* (Mattiwilda Dobb's nephew I believe) ran a good race and is very attractive too. I am now a firm member of the NATIONAL DEMOCRATIC PARTY OF ALABAMA, which is headed by a Negro man named Dr. John Cashin of Huntsville and I do believe we shall overcome and be seated next time, as the present Democratic Party has gone over lock, stock and barrel to Wallace—he had the entire Democratic delegation of Congressmen sitting on his platform the other night at the Rally . . .

We know Alabama will go for Wallace in a big way and I think he will get a huge vote, and he and the Republican Party will merge eventually, he is certainly destroying the two party system as he said he would. Lots of love to all of you, Devotedly, Va.

October 7, 1968
Dearest Otto:

I am glad we agree on racism, whether black or white, and also separatism . . . Of course I agree that black people should stick together, but for the purpose of becoming free and equal citizens, not for the purpose of living an all black life in an all black ghetto with all black businesses and all black schools and so on and so forth ad infinitum . . .

What astonishes me and what continually amazes me is how many good, fine, noble people . . . all think this is wonderful and great and fine and if you don't agree with it, there is something wrong with you and you are not "with it" . . . The only way I see to remove prejudice is to be in association with people. But my really big grievance against all of the "racist" school is that they do not look at the economic nor social roots of the problem. They seem to feel that "racism" is something like

---

*Maynard Jackson, 30-year-old lawyer who, in his bid for the U.S. Senate against Herman Talmadge, lost the Democratic primary but outpolled Talmadge in Atlanta. This political exposure and his impressive showing helped him build a base among liberals and black voters. In 1974, Maynard Jackson became Atlanta's first black mayor and its youngest.

original sin, and is an inborn characteristic of mankind and nothing can be done "until his heart and mind is changed" but how to do that? I think it is based very largely on the fact of economic exploitation of the Negro, and of the poor white too, which brings them into competition and the very dreadful fate of the Negro makes the white man who fears he too may go to the bottom, look on him (the Negro) as something to provide him with a cushion—there is always someone who is worse off than he is. Of course you know and I hope I know, I do not think people have prejudices and racial hatreds without some reason behind them, I do not think they are born with them, but at a time when the capitalist system is showing its weaknesses, a racial target to take off the stored-up frustration of people against their state of powerlessness, helps a lot to keep the system going . . .

What I see coming and what I am afraid of is that [Nixon] and Wallace are going to make a deal in 1972. If he can swallow Strom Thurmond,* he can swallow Wallace and the combination of Nixon Republicanism and Wallace racism is something horrible to contemplate.

In the face of this kind of possibility, the whole Black separatist movement to me is suicide and I say so all the chances I get . . .

Here in Alabama, where we are so restricted and there is so little we can do, I work with the challenge group to the regular (Wallace) party. We had a hearing before the McGovern Commission and I was on national TV and radio, CBS, but I know you neither watch TV nor listen to the radio . . .

Lots of love . . . and do write soon. I promise to be better by replying.

October 11, 1968
Dearest Dec:

I must get terribly heavy-handed when I write and flat-footed as no one ever wants to publish anything, and I am evidently not a good judge as I thought the piece on Wallace was good. Of course my point is that I

---

*Strom Thurmond, senator from South Carolina and States' Rights Party candidate for president in 1948; Thurmond switched his affiliation from the Democratic Party to the Republican Party in 1964.

don't think it is the "gogue" but the "demo" that is the thing that is important, it is the people he appeals to . . .

Wallace is no mystery down here, we are used to him and to his kind and we have been for so long, essentially he is not much different from Lyndon Johnson (very much the same) or Hugo Black or any of the poor ambitious men who had nothing when they started but brains and energy and built themselves into powerful figures, but the thing about Lyndon and Hugo (as awful as you think Lyndon is) is that they changed and stopped being racists, and stopped "niggering" as they call it, which is still considered a perfectly legitimate form of political expression. Try and get hold of a copy of a book called *Wallace* by Marshall Frady, it really is extremely good, much better than I expected . . . he . . . reveals Wallace as he is, but at the same time I don't think he tells why he has so much appeal . . .

I will write Willie Brown* and see if he can get something going on the Wallace "DEMOCRATS." He certainly fought hard for us . . . I am still working hard with the challenge group, and make speeches at least once a week. I am usually the only one, or the only one of three or four white people, all the rest black people in country churches and lodge halls. They are so kind to us and so sweet and seem so interested, no need to tell them what a menace Wallace is. Cliff seems to accept my political life, such as it is, and as long as it does not interfere with the building of the Pea Level, which is really going up in great style now and I think is going to be lovely . . .

Lots of love and do send me my Wallace piece if not lost as I value it even if no one else does. Devotedly, Va.

November 26, 1968
Dearest Clark and Mairi,

I do hope Angus [Cameron] persuaded you to write your autobiography and if you do send it on to me and I will add addenda, as so many things happened to both of us in the old SCHW . . . He asked me to do so too . . . but I do not have the time nor the money to buy the time, but maybe that is not the real explanation at all . . . There is always so much

---

*California state assemblyman from San Francisco.

to do and when I get through doing it I am too tired to sit down and write, so letters seem to be my only form of communication.

One of the things that has kept me so busy is what did happen in Alabama on November 5th. As you may know, George Wallace ran in Alabama ON THE DEMOCRATIC TICKET, although he was a candidate in the rest of the country on the American Independent Party ticket. Two groups here decided to run a separate list of Electors for the Democratic nominee, one the Alabama Independent Democratic Party, which was . . . an off shoot of the regulars, and who only ran a list of Electors under the symbol of the donkey. I did not join in with this one although I was urged to and the man who got it up, David Vann, used to be Hugo's law clerk, and is anti-Wallace and liberal BUT it seemed to me it only strengthened Wallace as it left him with the Democratic symbol and the whole machinery of the party and anyone who ran on the Democratic Party ticket had to be on it with him and they supported him and he supported them, so this as far as I could see was simply a face-saving device for the loyalists who did not want to lose all ties with Washington. So I joined the other group, the National Democratic Party of Alabama . . . This party ran candidates for all or most of the offices in the State as well as for the Senate and for the House and I was asked to be an Elector on this ticket which I was. I was also a delegate to Chicago. Well, the State of Alabama threw us off the ballot and Chuck Morgan got us back on by going to the U.S. Supreme Court, where . . . we won and they had to put us back on the ballot just two weeks before the election AND WE WON SEVENTEEN OFFICES IN ALABAMA.

They were all minor offices although one was as Chairman of the Sumter County School Board, but seventeen Negroes won office in Alabama through our party. The Probate Judge in Greene County refused to acknowledge the validity of the U.S. Supreme Court ruling and still refused to put us on the ballot, so Chuck and the ACLU have brought suit against him for contempt of Court and the Department of Justice of the U.S. has intervened. We may win some more offices there.

But what we have done now which I will admit was my idea is we have challenged the right of the men elected on the Democratic ticket who SUPPORTED GEORGE WALLACE to be seated as Democrats. They were elected, we can't keep them from that, but we may have a chance to keep them from being seated AS DEMOCRATS, and not having the Committee posts and the patronage of regular Democrats, which only makes George Wallace stronger as he can keep Alabama as his base and be both a Democrat here and something else everywhere else and it means his coattail riders and his men and his cohorts GET ALL THE DEMOCRATIC PATRONAGE, although they are fighting the Democratic Party all the time. Did you ever hear of anything so crazy?

Of course we need support and we need money. I asked Corliss to send me Peter Weiss's address as he was both in New York and did a great job for us in Chicago, but he never sent it. People who live in New York and are New Yorkers really don't think anything that happens down here amounts to much, do they? I mean they are sorry for us and would like to see things changed but they don't really think we are relevant. Of course I think we are very relevant, not in a very good way perhaps but very relevant as I think Wallace is going to get stronger and will eventually join in with the Republicans when they get discredited as I think they will, Wallace and Nixon are made for each other. Besides that, as you only too well know, the South kept the country off balance all the time we were in Washington and are still doing it. There really never has been a two-party system in this country, Wallace is only expressing what has always been, and I think it would be much healthier and happier if he could be forced to join his own party and his followers could be forced OUT OF THE DEMOCRATIC PARTY. Chuck Morgan thinks so too, but we so badly need some money and someone to do things and organize. I write millions of letters, or rather to be honest, dozens and get good responses but what we need is some really high-powered operation. I had hoped and believed and prayed that McCarthy and his crowd would take this up as a way to either purge the Democratic Party or reform it or show it up as hopeless but no response as yet from them. Lots of fun and very exciting and we will probably get the runaround as usual.

Box 300 Route 4 WETUMPKA, ALABAMA
December 18, 1968
Dearest Dec:

I am sending this on to California but am afraid you are already in Mexico, as I know you said you were going there for the holidays but what day I do not remember . . .

Please note the above address! We are MOVED, at least we are living there now and while we are still doing things to the house and will be for some time, and are still taking up little bits and pieces from 2 Felder, we are officially moved and all mail should be addressed to our country estate!

It really is awfully nice, large, simple and sunny and plenty of heat and light and electricity and big rooms and lots of windows. I long for you to see it. Cliff and his two brothers and his sister own nearly four hundred acres which they have planted in Pine trees and Cliff owns ten acres by himself, the "home place." You are right, country living is not my dish of tea but neither was Alabama living, but I am sure that both have been my salvation and I am sure I will get used to the hoot owls which still scare the daylights out of me when they start at night. I always think it is the KKK which is very big in Elmore County. As long as Cliff is there, Lulah and I are all right but when we are there alone and the owls start hooting, we nearly get scared to death . . .

I have been so absorbed in the house and getting settled that I have not done much nor have much news. Our small challenge party is still trying to unseat George Wallace's congressional delegation as Democrats . . . but we find little support for our position as most of our Northern supporters say as long as they ran as Democrats they are Democrats, and although Wallace has captured the Party for a Third Party, still they are Democrats, then too the McCarthy people are not interested in what they term "party loyalty" but it does seem they should be interested in the utter confusion and chaos of our situation, especially with all of the new voters coming on the rolls. At least they do have us to vote for and so I go out and speak each week at some Negro church (Black has not reached here yet, we are always behind) telling them about our new party and I find it very interesting and also very rewarding. Lots of strange and odd experiences which I do not have time to write about now nor you to hear I am sure.

We are well, busy, and hope you are all the same. Lots of love dearest Dec and I hope you have a fine holiday and do write and tell me about it. Remember me to Mr. Belfrage, tell him I saw Claude Williams recently, he is a member of our new party, still the same, his courage never wanes. Lots of love again, Va.

Epilogue

It was nearly 2 o'clock in the morning when the train from Chicago pulled into Montgomery's Union Station, several hours behind schedule. Cliff and Lulah waited on the platform in the hot August night. They had followed the nightly televised proceedings of the 1968 Democratic convention and were eager to hear Virginia's first hand account of what went on there. After the train stopped, Cliff watched for his wife. As he saw her stepping down to the platform he said, "She still takes my breath away." Lulah was shocked by this simple expression of passion from her 70-year-old father. It was, in its way, a striking testament to the attraction that held these two individuals together, a glimpse of the bond that sealed this remarkable partnership.[1]

At the end of 1968, Cliff and Virginia moved permanently to Wetumpka. Virginia resisted giving up their apartment in Montgomery, fearing that she would be completely isolated in the backwoods of Elmore County, but now that the house was finally finished, Cliff was determined to live there. She followed reluctantly and was soon writing about the joys of life at the Pea Level. The house was bright and airy, surrounded by long screened-in porches; even in January, Virginia described it as "lovely, warm, and full of sun." As she settled into the rhythm of life in the country, her letters included reports on the progress of her roses, the bounty of Cliff's vegetable gardens, and his efforts to plant fruit trees. "We are living in a sea of daffodils," she wrote early one spring. She promised Decca that if she came for a visit they would sit with their "feet in the creek and eat fried chicken." Mostly, she took great pleasure in Cliff's happiness. "We do love this place," she wrote Clark and Mairi in the fall of 1969. "Cliff is so happy here and he hates to leave even for the day; it is the culmination of a dream he has had for a long time."[2]

The Pea Level was an inviting place for visitors, and many of them came—out from Montgomery for Sunday lunch or an evening meal and, in the summertime, to cool off in the creek. Others came from far and wide and stayed for a night, a weekend, or sometimes longer. "Montgomery is no longer the center of attraction it used to be for travelers," Virginia wrote, "but we get plenty."[3] Often they were younger people the Durrs had met during the civil rights movement, sometimes historians and students wanting to talk about the past, and occasionally friends of friends just passing through. Once in a while, an old friend or acquaintance from New Deal days turned up, "like fish rising out of the depths of the sea."[4] Much like their house on Seminary Hill, the Pea Level became a popular gathering place where, as Lulah described it, "people came and talked." Although the stream of visitors at times got exhausting, family visits were never long enough. By 1969, all of their daughters were living outside of the South. "I know you understand the joys of having daughters arrive," she wrote Clark and Mairi, "and when they are here we are in seventh heaven."[5]

Life at the Pea Level did not eclipse Virginia's involvement in politics. Her letters include reports on her work with groups in the community and commentary on developments in Alabama and beyond, most pointedly on the continuing war in Viet Nam. She wrote to Clark Foreman early in 1969: "To see our bombers burning up villages and dropping napalm on people always makes me think of the kind of cruelty and arrogance that was visited on the slaves and while of course I make exceptions, still the fact remains that we have in our American culture this strain of using our power AGAINST THE HELPLESS and feeling strong BECAUSE THEY ARE HELPLESS and wanting to keep them that way."[6]

Virginia frequently remarked on the extraordinary changes that had taken place in the South. "To someone my age it seems like a miracle," she told John Hope Franklin. Segregation as a legal system was over and, "at least we are freer than we ever were before."[7] Still the persistence of racial discrimination remained a focus of her attention, as was abundantly evident in the deeply flawed process of school desegregation, the lack of economic opportunity for large segments of the black community, and the glaring inequities of the criminal justice system. The nature of racial prejudice and its complex history was something she continually struggled to understand. "It may be that these feelings do derive originally from economics but . . . I think a lot of it is just plain old original sin, greed, the desire to live a life of ease while someone else does the dirty work," she wrote C. Vann Woodward.[8]

The hope of the future, Virginia believed, rested in a free ballot and active participation in the political process, and she fully embraced the new possibilities created by the civil rights movement. She remained active in the National Democratic Party of Alabama, which was a force in state politics until the mid-1970s. The party elected four sheriffs in the November 1970 election, including one in Lowndes County and many minor offices at the county level. Their efforts also helped to elect two black state legislators, including civil rights lawyer Fred Gray, who ran on the Democratic Party ticket. Virginia reported with satisfaction that there were now 105 black elected officials in Alabama, the largest number to serve in the state since Reconstruction. Nationwide, Alabama ranked third in the number of black elected officials. "Isn't that amazing when you think what we started with?" she commented to Otto Nathan.[9]

George Wallace reigned supreme in Alabama, however, recapturing the governor's mansion once again in 1970, and Richard Nixon was in the White House. "O! that nasty Nixon," she complained, "just to see him on TV makes me break out with the itch."[10] Virginia watched as the scenario that she had long feared played out, with Nixon pursuing a Southern strategy that brought disaffected whites into a new Republican majority. Wallace had plowed the ground and Nixon was positioned to reap the rewards as the old New Deal coalition unraveled along racial lines and the Republican Party, with its coded appeals to white fears and resentments, became the home of white Southerners and working class voters in Northern cities. Nixon was "a high class Wallace," Virginia explained, who was "cleverly lining up all of the conservative and right wing elements and large numbers of labor people," and Wallace "whether intentionally or not helps him by making him seem respectable by contrast." She did not see how "a divided and weak Democratic Party" would be able to "stop his snakelike advance to organize the country into a reactionary majority."[11]

The Democratic Party seemed to implode in the aftermath of the riotous 1968 convention. The defeat of the antiwar plank, the nomination of Hubert Humphrey, and the police crackdown on demonstrators outside the convention hall left the Party dispirited and deeply divided. Virginia and members of other challenge groups from the South, including Julian Bond, felt guardedly hopeful in the wake of the convention. There seemed to be a chance that, in the South at least, the Democratic Party would provide a framework for blacks and whites to work together, creating an interracial politics capable of transforming the political culture of the region and energizing the national party. But, even as blacks began to win elected office in record numbers, George Wallace and a resurgent Republican Party laid claim to the future of the region's politics as shifting political allegiances followed well-worn racial patterns.[12]

Virginia faced these sobering political realities head on, but she refused to give in to the sense of futility that dominated commentary among liberals and friends on the left. "Yes, it's awful," she wrote Decca, but why must people "go on ad infinitum about it?"[13] To another friend she insisted, "The point is not how bad things are . . . the point is what to do about it? Where are the good people, the strong people, the places where we can make our defense and stand against the evil forces?" The difference between their friend Otto Nathan's "total despair and me," she told literary critic Max Geismar, "is that no matter what happens we still feel we have to fight the bastards." Virginia admitted that at times it was difficult "to hold on to the faith I profess,"[14] but the transformation she had witnessed in the South was a source of hope. "It is hard to feel discouraged down here," she wrote Vann Woodward. "There has been change and progress and things are better . . . certainly racially."[15]

She feared, though, that unless something was done to save the Democratic Party in the South from George Wallace and other latent Dixiecrats, the gains made by the civil rights movement would be greatly compromised. Lyndon Johnson, she believed, was the one person who could defeat Wallace. Johnson had helped free the South from the burden of segregation, which at least gave people a chance to learn how to live together. "He ought to defend what he did" instead of "sulking in his tent and spending all of his time justifying himself" she wrote a mutual friend.[16] In the spring of 1969, Virginia wrote to Lady Bird Johnson about a group of young loyalist Democrats in Alabama who were anxious to have the Johnsons visit and help raise the visibility of the group's efforts in the state. She continued to suggest other ways that Lyndon might lend support. "He is the only Southern politician smart enough to get him [Wallace] told," she wrote Lady Bird. "Who else," she asked in another letter, "has the will, the knowledge, and the desire to save the Democratic Party in the South?"[17]

Little came of these efforts. Lyndon Johnson, exhausted and glad to be out from under the weight of the presidency, grew his hair long, settled into the life of a rancher, and worked on establishing a library and writing his memoirs. He was finished with politics. Virginia's efforts to prod Johnson, however, did spark the renewal of her correspondence with Lyndon and Lady Bird. She never tired of trying to coax him to do something about Wallace, and she sweetened her pleas with praise for all he had done to help change the South, and for the "new look" of the Democratic Party that was evident at the 1972 convention.[18] The one topic she did not pursue in any depth in her letters was Johnson's policy on Vietnam, a subject she tried to talk about with Lady Bird when they saw each other briefly in Alabama in the summer of 1971. Afterward, she wrote Lady Bird and said that she was sorry "I asked so many questions about the war which I know must be painful to you, but I am so puzzled by it and still am."[19] She hoped that Johnson's memoir would provide some clear explanation or rationale for his pursuit of the war, but it did not. "I have read your book with great interest and care" she wrote Lyndon, "but I feel something is missing. I get the feeling you were pursing a policy that is not stated." They agreed that this discussion would have to wait until they had an opportunity to see each other and talk. That opportunity never came.[20]

Cliff and Virginia regretfully declined Johnson's invitation to attend a civil rights symposium at the Lyndon Baines Johnson Library in December 1972; Cliff was recovering from a prostate operation. Veteran civil rights leaders and activists came to Austin for the two-day affair, and for what would be Lyndon Johnson's last public appearance. Of all the records housed in the library, it was "the record of this work," he told the gathering, "that . . . holds the most of myself within it and holds for me the most intimate meaning." In an inspiring and forward-looking speech, he emphasized that the progress had been too small. The roots of racial inequality ran deep and demanded attention and continuing struggle. "Until we overcome unequal history, we cannot overcome unequal opportunity."[21] The day after the meeting ended, Johnson wrote to Cliff and Virginia and reported that he was happy with the way it all went. "I only wish that you could have been with us," he told his old friends, "because a long, long time ago you taught me so much, by precept and example, about the dignity and opportunity to which each is entitled regardless of color, birthplace, ancestry, and all the other ways in which many have been ignored and disdained."[22]

Virginia was pleased with the news of the symposium but told Johnson that she doubted she "could claim any credit for your conversion, in the first place I do not think you were a segregationist, BUT YOU HAD TO GET ELECTED BY PEOPLE WHO WERE. I have never had to be elected and never could have been." Furthermore, she felt that she could not be self-righteous about her position because "I lived so long thinking . . . I had to maintain white supremacy . . . and did not change my mind until I got to Washington." She went on to remember the people who had influenced her—Aubrey Williams, Mary McLeod Bethune, Eleanor Roosevelt. Johnson responded that her "letter was just like, or at least the next thing to the long discussions we used to have. Lady Bird and I loved reading every word and thinking about those exciting early years."[23]

The past tugged at Virginia and Cliff with greater frequency. Graduate students and historians made their way to the Pea Level "avid for information" about the "old days." All of a sudden they had become "historical relics" and people talked about the New Deal the way she remembered hearing people talk "about Gettysburg and the Civil War."[24] In 1968, Cliff signed a contract with Houghton Mifflin to write his memoirs, and Virginia later signed up with Doubleday. They shared a desire to help "set the record straight" about the New Deal years, finding very little about their own experiences reflected in the books that were being published on the period. Getting down to writing, though, was another matter. "Neither Cliff nor I have done anything on the books we are supposed to be writing," she wrote Otto Nathan. "He has been busy on the house and the place and I have been busy politicking."[25] Some variation on this theme attended any mention of their literary efforts.

For Cliff, now in his early seventies, the Pea Level absorbed much of his energy and attention. "I can't get Cliff out of the garden," she told the Formans. "He plants up to Thanksgiving and then starts again in February and he loves doing it."[26] There was always something more to be done on the house, and in the early 1970s he built a fence and a barn. When he did find time for the book, the words did not come easily. "He has this overwhelming modesty," she observed, "and simply does not seem able to write about himself."[27] And he was honest to a fault. When the words finally came, "he checks each word ten times to be sure it is absolutely truthful and exactly right and according to the evidence, [and] I think he will be writing this book for the rest of his life."[28]

Virginia had often considered writing a book but somehow never found the time and was not sure just what she should or could write about. Early in the 1970s, Doubleday offered her a contract and an advance after being advised by Studs Terkel "that I had a 'book in me.'" The working title of her book was *The Liberation of Pure White Southern Womanhood*. It would tell about her early years in Birmingham, "and how I was brought up to be utterly useless with only one aim in life, which was to get a husband." What she wanted to show "more than anything" was how segregation and class distinctions shaped people, and how events could change them. She was eager to write about life in Washington during the New Deal years. The book would "end with the death of Roosevelt as that was the most vivid and happiest and rewarding part of my life," she told Max Geismar.[29]

Virginia admitted that she could not bring herself to write about the people she had lived among in Alabama since returning in 1951. There was too much pain that she had suffered personally and "no doubt caused others to suffer." And how could she make sense of the irrationality that surrounded her? She tried to explain what she meant by referring to a book she was then reading, *The Children of Pride*, an edited collection of letters written among a slaveholding family on the eve of the Civil War. She told Geismar:

> All the characters are so familiar to me as if they were my own family and no doubt if I searched hard enough some of them will turn out to be kin. Such nice, gracious, kind, benevolent, loving and ABOVE ALL SO CHRISTIAN, and yet accepting slavery as a benevolent institution and never looking below the surface. That is what makes it so hard to write about the South and Southerners, as they are so kind, charming, benevolent and gracious and helpful if you

accepted their premises, which is that they are naturally superior by blood to other people and of course infinitely superior to Black people . . . How do you write about such people, especially your kin when they do such evil by their very attitudes? And how can I be self-righteous as I did it too for so long, and maybe still do unconsciously, how can I blame them? Do you ever suffer from these conflicting feelings?"[30]

Virginia managed to write two chapters on her early life, but it was hard to submit to the discipline of writing when there were daughters and grandchildren to visit, friends to see, and so much else to do. "I am immersed in politics," she wrote Clark Foreman in the spring of 1974, "and love it and my book suffers badly, but why write about something if you can do it?"[31] During the early 1970s, she served as chairman of an advisory committee for a federal antipoverty program in Elmore County, but most of her efforts were dedicated to working with anti-Wallace forces in and around the Democratic Party, locally and statewide. She helped organize an interracial group of Democratic women, ran for the Democratic County Committee, and was a delegate for George McGovern to the 1972 Democratic national convention. In 1974, she won a place on the Democratic State Committee. "It is so much FUN to have someone to work with and fight with and not be so alone," she wrote Clark. "I simply love being in a group that is against Wallace and who is actually putting up a fight against him. I once again feel I have allies."[32]

On May 12, 1975, just a year shy of their fiftieth wedding anniversary, Cliff died after a brief illness. He had a weak heart and had endured bouts of poor health for quite some time, but he had been fine in recent months. "His death was so sudden and I was so unprepared for it," Virginia wrote Marge Frantz. "I thought he was in good health and we had looked forward to lots more years of doing things together. He loved this place so much and enjoyed it each day and had so many plans." While "a long and happy marriage is a wonderful thing," she wrote, "the loss of it seems almost too much to bear."[33] In the immediate aftermath of Cliff's death, she said to Lulah forlornly, "no one is going to set my limits anymore."[34] Cliff had been her anchor, her best friend, her lover, her devoted husband. Life without him was almost impossible to imagine.

In the months following his death, Virginia spent much of her time trying to answer the hundreds of letters she received. "It was simply amazing," she told Decca, "how many people have written about Cliff's influence in their lives when he made so little effort to influence anyone. [He] just did what came naturally and was himself always."[35] In later years, Virginia attracted increasing attention as a figure of historical note, and her refusal to behave like a "relic" made her that much more intriguing. But as the light shone more brightly on her, she was ever conscious of drawing attention to Cliff, "one of the best men that ever lived."[36]

After Cliff died, Virginia traveled more. In the spring of 1978, she visited China with Myles Horton and a group from the Highlander Folk School, and over the years she made several trips to England, where she was wined and dined by her flock of British admirers. Her favorite destination, though, was Martha's Vineyard, where she spent every summer at the home of her daughter and son-in-law, Lucy and Sheldon Hackney. Their large old New England house, surrounded by flower gardens and over-looking Vineyard Haven Harbor, became a second home. Each year it was the scene of glorious gatherings of children and grandchildren and annual birthday parties for Virginia. "Four daughters, three sons-in-law, and ELEVEN grandchildren are quite a crowd to keep up with," she wrote with pleasure to English friends after a busy summer.[37] The Vineyard was also a place where she visited with old friends such as Lady Bird Johnson and C. Vann Woodward and made new ones. She especially enjoyed the company of fellow Southerner William Styron, who lived next door.[38]

Virginia's life, however, remained rooted in the South. There was still much to be done and as federal judge Myron Thompson put it, "she just never gave up."[39] In correspondence with John Hope Franklin in the late 1970s, she offered her assessment of life in Alabama in the post–civil rights era. For people with education, steady jobs, and money, things were much better, but "the unemployed and poor blacks have not benefited very much" from the changes. Rather than invest in job programs and schools, Alabama built prisons. "The courts are giving the most terrific sentences, simply piling [black men] up in the prisons and the jails . . . and Alabama is building five new penitentiaries. I think practically a whole generation of young men are being ruined." As in the past, the poor lacked effective legal representation and nearly all of the inmates on death row were black. "This particular horror does not seem to attract much attention," she told Franklin. Following the 1978 elections, she joined with a group of local Democratic Party activists and formed a committee against the death penalty.[40]

While Montgomery was still a very conservative and racially-divided city, there were more people who shared Virginia's interests and concerns. In the aftermath of the civil rights movement, the ACLU and Amnesty International established Alabama affiliates in Montgomery and several new organizations sprang up, most notably the Southern Poverty Law Center. Deborah Ellis, who clerked for federal judge Frank Johnson in the early 1980s and went on to join the staff of the Southern Poverty Law Center, remembered: "There was a real sense that things *can* change and . . . we were working to change them." Young lawyers worked on numerous fronts— voting rights, employment discrimination, criminal justice, and efforts to defeat the Ku Klux Klan. Virginia delighted in this new crop of activists and diligently cultivated them; they, as well, gravitated to her. Randall Williams, an early staff member of the Southern Poverty Law Center recalled, "you couldn't not know about her. She was at every [public] meeting of significance and had a vast network of contacts."[41]

Virginia remained a vibrant force in Montgomery through her later years. Her home at the Pea Level and in Montgomery, where she moved in 1983, was a gathering place where people from her various circles met— lawyers, writers, historians, journalists, movement veterans. Deborah Ellis described her as "a facilitator of conversation and community." She helped to create a supportive and nurturing environment for younger people involved in social justice work. In the late 1980s, when Bryan Stevenson began providing legal services for indigent defendants and people on death row, Virginia sought him out and offered her help. She "was quite good at integrating our work with any other progressive work she knew about," he recalled, and housed law students who came to work as interns with Stevenson and his associates in what became the Equal Justice Initiative. Virginia's sense of alarm over growing rates of incarceration and the death sentences that were imposed on exclusively poor and mostly black people, Stevenson commented, stood in bold contrast to a broader population that was largely indifferent.[42]

In 1986, Virginia published an autobiography; she had succeeded in "talking" a book. On the basis of interviews done by Sue Thrasher and Jacquelyn Hall, and other oral histories that had been conducted with her and Cliff, Hollinger Barnard worked with Virginia in creating a first-person narrative about her life and times. *Outside the Magic Circle: The Autobiography of Virginia Foster Durr,* published by the University of Alabama Press, won wide attention and received reviews in most major newspapers. Her old friend Palmer Weber hired a publicity agent in New York and provided support for a book tour, and Virginia traveled from Washington to Boston and around the South promoting the book. This generated more publicity and earned Virginia an appearance on the *Today Show,* the most widely viewed morning television program in the country. She told a *New York Times* reporter that she initially thought that "hawking a book was rather cheap and beneath me," but admitted, with a laugh, that she was having the time of her life. "I am not used to fame that comes pleasantly."[43]

After the long years of isolation and efforts to avoid publicity for fear of repercussions, going public with such acclaim was a vindication of sorts. Virginia loved the attention, the events and parties surrounding the celebration of her and her autobiography. But, even more, she was glad for the platform to speak out on the problems that loomed during the Reagan years—massive military build-up, the tightening hold of business on government, the growing gap between the rich and the poor. She wanted to know what people intended to do about it, particularly young people, and welcomed invitations to speak on college campuses. The post–civil rights generation, however, offered a striking contrast to the students who had come South in the 1960s. Their self-absorption and cynicism about politics bothered her. "Really," she exclaimed, "what they want to do is get prepared for good jobs, live a pleasant life, eat their health food, and have healthy children. They've shrunk!" She did her best to shake them up. Never content to simply tell about the past, Virginia used history "almost as a weapon," as Randall Williams observed. "She would beat you about the head and shoulders with it until you understood what you were supposed to do now."[44]

When Virginia Durr died on February 24, 1999, at the age of 95, the flag over the state capitol in Montgomery was lowered to half-staff. It was a striking gesture, one that would have hardly been imaginable when she and Cliff returned to Alabama a half century earlier. By the end of the twentieth century, however, popular culture and memory had assigned the civil rights movement to the past, to be commemorated and celebrated, much like the Civil War. In such a scenario, Virginia Durr had gone from being notorious to notable.

Praise for her participation in the movement often left Virginia uneasy and impatient; it seemed to suggest that the work was done. She never minimized the achievements of earlier struggles, particularly the gains of the 1950s and 1960s. The passage of time did not dull the feeling of hope and possibility that she had experienced during the Montgomery bus boycott, which stood as an everlasting testimony to the power of "ordinary" people to create change. Racial and economic injustice, however, were pervasive in Alabama and throughout the country, and challenged all who believed in the capacity of American democracy to advance justice and freedom. In a fitting tribute, Rev. Richard Deibert gave Virginia the last word at her memorial service. He played a recording of a 1965 interview with Studs Terkel in which Virginia turned the conversation away from the victories won by the movement and pointed to the racial inequality and cruel conditions that crushed the hopes and opportunities of many people in Terkel's hometown of Chicago. "Well, what are you all going to do?" she asked.[45]

Virginia was slightly bemused by the attention that her life and Cliff's began to attract in the years following the civil rights movement. In the late 1970s, the once blacklisted screenwriter Ring Lardner, Jr. began work on a script for a possible film about the Durrs. She doubted that they were movie material. "I cannot imagine [he] is going to make Cliff and me very thrilling," she wrote Decca.

It seems to me that we were not particularly shocking people at all. We just faced so many shocking situations—Depression, WW II, the Red Hunt, the Bomb and its aftermath, the Loyalty Oath and the race issue in the South—it seems to me that the Events themselves were the shocking things and if they had not come to us we would have stayed as we were—good Presbyterians, white supremacist, Junior League, Garden Clubs, etc. I see my friends in Alabama with whom I grew up absolutely untouched by history and living a life full of Colonial Dames, Bridge, and grandchildren. I must say they are awfully dull!! I do not regret that we were stirred up at all. It just seems to me that History was the shocker instead of us.[46]

Manuscript Collections

Hugo Black Papers. Manuscript Division, Library of Congress, Washington, D.C.

Nicholas Bosanquet Personal Papers. London, England.

Carl and Anne Braden Papers. State Historical Society of Wisconsin, Madison.

Virginia Foster Durr Papers. The Arthur and Elizabeth Schlesinger Library, Radcliffe Institute for Advanced Study, Harvard University, Cambridge, Massachusetts. (This collection includes Virginia Durr's correspondence with James Dombrowski, Clark Foreman, Corliss Lamont, Curtis MacDougall, Otto Nathan, Ava Helen Pauling.)

Maxwell Geismar Papers. Special Collections, Mugar Memorial Library, Boston University, Boston, Massachusetts.

Arthur and Elizabeth Wickenden Goldschmidt Personal Papers. In author's possession.

John Hope Franklin Personal Papers. Durham, North Carolina.

Marge Frantz Personal Papers. Santa Cruz, California.

E. Franklin Frazier Papers. Moorland-Spingarn Research Center, Howard University, Washingon, D.C.

Lyndon B. Johnson Papers. Lyndon Baines Johnson Library, Austin, Texas.

Ann Durr Lyon Personal Papers. Harrisburg, Pennsylvania.

Burke Marshall Papers. John F. Kennedy Library, Boston, Massachusetts.

Jessica Mitford Papers. The Ohio State University Libraries, Columbus, Ohio.

Eleanor Roosevelt Papers. Franklin D. Roosevelt Presidential Library, Hyde Park, New York.

Lillian Smith Papers. Hargrett Rare Book and Manuscript Collection, University of Georgia, Athens, Georgia.

C. Vann Woodward Papers. Manuscripts and Archives, Yale University Library, New Haven, Connecticut.

Notes

Introduction

1. Hollinger Barnard, ed., *Outside the Magic Circle: The Autobiography of Virginia Foster Durr* (University: University of Alabama Press, 1985), 279–80; Virginia "Tilla" Durr interview with author, January 5, 2003.
2. Marge Frantz interview with author, April 29, 2001.
3. Clifford Durr to Ann Durr, Feb. 10, 1950, Ann Durr Lyon Papers, private collection.
4. Virginia Durr to Ann Durr, April 24, 1950, Ann Durr Lyon Papers.
5. Virginia Foster, "The Emancipation of Pure, White, Southern Womanhood," *New South* 26 (1971), 51. Barnard, *Outside the Magic Circle*, 5.
6. Virginia Durr interview with author, June 9, 1992.
7. Barnard, ed., *Outside the Magic Circle*, 41.
8. Virginia Foster, "The Emancipation of Pure White Southern Womanhood," 54.
9. Barnard, *Outside the Magic Circle*, 63–65.
10. Ibid., 66–67; John A. Salmond, *The Conscience of a Lawyer: Clifford J. Durr and American Civil Liberties, 1899–1975* (Tuscaloosa: University of Alabama Press, 1990), 38.
11. Ibid., 78–79; Virginia Durr interviews with author, May 3, 1978, June 26, 1992.
12. Virginia Durr to Corliss Lamont, Feb. 16, 1933, Virginia Foster Durr Papers, Schlesinger Library, Radcliffe Institute for Advanced Study, Harvard University. Hereafter referred to as VFD Papers.
13. Virginia Durr interview with author, June 9, 1992; Alger Hiss, quoted in Katie Loucheim, *The Making of the New Deal: The Insiders Speak* (Cambridge, Mass.: Harvard University Press, 1983), 237.
14. Barnard, *Outside the Magic Circle*, 102–3.
15. Virginia Durr interview with author, June 9, 1992; *Outside the Magic Circle*, 103–4. For biographical information on Clark Foreman, see Patricia Sullivan, *Days of Hope: Race and Democracy in the New Deal Era* (Chapel Hill: University of North Carolina Press, 1996), 25–40.
16. Virginia Durr to Marge Frantz, April 15, 1982, Marge Frantz Papers, private collection.
17. Ibid.; Virginia Durr interview with author, June 9, 1992.
18. Ann Durr Lyon interview with author, May 12, 2001; Barnard, *Outside the Magic Circle*, 108.
19. Virginia Durr interview with author, June 9, 1992; Barnard, *Outside the Magic Circle*, 108–111. Virginia conflates the hearings on TCI in Birmingham, which were held in January 1937, with the hearings on Republic Steel that were held during the summer of 1938.

See Jerold Auerbach, *Labor and Liberty: The La Follette Committee and the New Deal* (Indianapolis: Bobbs-Merrill, 1966), 131–140.

20. Sullivan, *Days of Hope*, 98–100
21. Virginia Durr interview with author, June 9, 1992
22. Barnard, *Outside the Magic Circle*, 121–22.
23. Virginia Durr to C. Vann Woodward, Jan. 26, 1940, C. Vann Woodward Papers, Manuscripts and Archives, Yale University Library, Box 1.
24. Sullivan, *Days of Hope*, 115–16.
25. Marge Frantz interview with author, April 29, 2001; Jessica Mitford, *Daughters and Rebels: The Autobiography of Jessica Mitford* (Boston: Houghton Mifflin, 1960), 254–55, 257.
26. Marge Frantz interview with author, April 29, 2001; Jessica Mitford, *A Fine Old Conflict* (New York: Alfred A. Knopf, 1977), 24.
27. Virginia Durr to Jessica Mitford, July 13, 1975, Jessica Mitford Papers, Ohio State University Libraries.
28. Catherine A. Galbraith, "Virginia and Decca," unpublished essay; Catherine Galbraith interview with author, December, 2001.
29. Lucy Durr Hackney interview with author, October 14, 2002; Virginia "Tilla" Durr interview with author, January 15, 2003.
30. Mitford, *A Fine Old Conflict*, 24; Salmond, *Conscience of a Lawyer*, 57–58.
31. "A Fighting Liberal," *New Republic*, Dec. 25, 1944; Salmond, *Conscience of a Lawyer*, 72–97.
32. Salmond, *Conscience of a Lawyer*, 98–116.
33. Virginia Durr to Corliss Lamont, Feb. 1942. VFD Papers. M. J. Heale, *American Anticommunism: Combating the Enemy Within* (Baltimore: Johns Hopkins University Press, 1990) 123–29; Charles Houston, *Baltimore Afro-American*, April 12, 1947, May 3, 1947.
34. Arthur Schlesinger, "The U.S. Communist Party," *Life*, July 29, 1946, 84–85, 87, 90; Steven Gillon, *Politics and Vision: The ADA and American Liberalism, 1947–1985* (New York: Oxford University Press, 1988), 16–24.
35. Henry Steele Commager, "Washington Witch-Hunt," *Nation*, April 5, 1947, 385–88; Richard M. Freeland, *The Truman Doctrine and the Origins of McCarthyism: Foreign Policy, Domestic Policy, and Internal Security, 1946–1948* (New York: Alfred A. Knopf, 1972), 130–50.
36. "Dissenting Views of Commissioner Clifford J. Durr Re Proposed Rules Governing FCC-Loyalty Procedure," undated memorandum, VFD Papers.
37. Sullivan, *Days of Hope*, 240–43.
38. Ibid., 243–73.
39. Barnard, *Outside the Magic Circle*, 196–99; Clifford Durr to Ann Durr, Oct. 10, 1948; Nancy Marie Kucan, "A Faint Voice of Protest: The Virginia Progressive Party Campaign and the 1948 Election," senior thesis, William and Mary College, 1981.
40. Barnard, *Outside the Magic Circle*, 196–97; Salmond, *Conscience of a Lawyer*, 123–26.
41. Clement Imhoff, "Clifford Durr and the Loyalty Question, 1942–1950," *Journal of American Culture* (Fall 1989), 52; Salmond, *Conscience of a Lawyer*, 121–22; Clifford Durr, "How to Measure Loyalty," *Nation*, April 23, 1949, 470–73.
42. The case of the former Justice Department employee refers to the Judith Coplan case. Salmond, *Conscience of a Lawyer*, 135–39; Kenneth O'Reilly, *Hoover and the Un-Americans: The FBI, HUAC, and the Red Menace* (Philadelphia: Temple University Press, 1983), 130–40.
43. Clifford Durr to Ann Durr, March 13, 1949, Ann Durr Lyon Papers.
44. Virginia Durr to Mairi Foreman, n.d., VFD Papers.
45. Virginia Durr to Clark and Mairi Foreman, March 1951, VFD Papers.
46. Lyndon B. Johnson to Virginia and Cliff Durr, December 13, 1972, Lyndon B. Johnson Papers, Lyndon B. Johnson Library.
47. Sheldon Hackney, comments at memorial service for Virginia Foster Durr, Immanuel Presbyterian Church, Montgomery, Alabama, February 28, 1999.

Part 1

1. Clifford Durr to Senator John Sparkman, March 22, 1961, VFD Papers.
2. Mills Thornton, *Dividing Lines: Municipal Politics and the Struggle for Civil Rights in Montgomery, Birmingham, and Selma* (Tuscaloosa: University of Alabama Press, 2002), 20–37.

3. Virginia Durr to Clark Foreman, January 14, 1954, VFD Papers.
4. Virginia Durr to Elizabeth Wickendon Goldschmidt, May 8, 1952, Elizabeth W. Goldschmidt Papers, private collection.
5. "As Clifford J. Durr Views Washington," *Montgomery Advertiser*, October 14, 1951, C-3.
6. Virginia Durr to Corliss Lamont, February 1, 1952, VFD Papers.
7. Lucy Durr Hackney interview with author, October 14, 2002.
8. "Southern Negro: 1952: A Special Issue," *Nation*, September 27, 1952.
9. "Montgomerian Who Headed Lawyer Guild Says Group Fought McCarthy Methods," *Montgomery Advertiser*, August 30, 1953.
10. Virginia Durr to Jessica Mitford, ca. June 1954, Jessica Mitford Papers.
11. Barnard, *Outside the Magic Circle*, 271.
12. See Mitford, *A Fine Old Conflict*, 42–75, 98–138, 205–217.
13. Clifford and Virginia Durr interview, March 1, 1975, Lyndon B. Johnson Library, 36–50; New Orleans *Times Picayune*, March 10, 1954, 1; March 16, 1954, 1; March 18, 1954, 1; March 19, 1954, 1; March 20, 1954, 1.
14. Barnard, *Outside the Magic Circle*, 271.
15. Ibid., 268–29.
16. Corliss Lamont, *Yes to Life: Memoirs of Corliss Lamont* (New York: Horizon Press, 1981), 137–38.
17. Robert J. Norrell, *Reaping the Whirlwind: The Civil Rights Movement in Tuskegee* (New York: Alfred A. Knopf), 1985, 73–75, 87–88.
18. C. Vann Woodward to Virginia Durr, Dec. 9, 1955, C. Vann Woodward Papers.

Part 2

1. Virginia Durr to Jessica Mitford, February 1956, Jessica Mitford Papers.
2. Virginia Durr to Jessica Mitford, December 28, 1955, Jessica Mitford Papers.
3. Fred Gray, Clifford Durr Memorial Lecture, Auburn University, Montgomery, March 1, 1992.
4. Virginia Durr to Clark Foreman, January 7, 1956, VFD Papers.
5. Thornton, *Dividing Lines*, 96.
6. "The Southern Manifesto," March 12, 1956, reprinted in Waldo E. Martin, Jr., ed. *Brown v. Board of Education: A Brief History with Documents* (Boston: Bedford/St. Martin's, 1998), 220–23. Nineteen senators and seventy-seven representatives signed the Southern Manifesto, including Alabama's entire congressional delegation. On the black resettlement plan, see *Montgomery Advertiser*, Sept. 1, 1957, and Sept. 14, 1957.
7. Virginia Durr to Clark Foreman, Nov. 19, 1955, VFD Papers.
8. Virginia Durr to Marge Frantz, Nov. 15, 1956, Marge Frantz Papers.
9. Virginia Durr to Marge Frantz, Nov. 15, 1956, Marge Frantz Papers; Virginia Durr to Clark Foreman, Jan. 7, 1957, Feb. 28, 1957, VFD Papers; John A. Salmond, *A Southern Rebel: The Life and Times of Aubrey Willis Williams, 1890–1965* (Chapel Hill: University of North Carolina Press, 1983), 250–51.
10. *Montgomery Advertiser*, June 21, 1957, 4A.
11. *Montgomery Advertiser*, June 15, 1957, 4A; July 3, 1957, 1; July 26, 1957, 1; July 30, 1957, 1.
12. Dan T. Carter, *The Politics of Rage: George Wallace, the Origins of the New Conservatism, and the Transformation of American Politics* (New York: Simon and Schuster, 1995), 94–96; *Montgomery Advertiser*, Jan. 20, 1959, 1.
13. Quoted in Diane McWhorter, *Carry Me Home* (New York: Simon & Schuster, 2001), 104.
14. *Montgomery Advertiser*, Sept. 8, 1957, 2B.
15. "Tilla" Durr, January 14, 2003 interview with author. Barnard, *Outside the Magic Circle*, 245.
16. Virginia "Tilla" Durr interview with author, Jan. 14, 2003; Virginia Foster Durr to Hugo Black, March 5, 1971, Hugo Black Papers, Library of Congress.
17. *U.S. News and World Report*, March 7, 1960, 44–45.
18. Virginia Durr to Anne Braden, April 7, 1960, Anne Braden Papers, State Historical Society of Wisconsin, Box 34.
19. Quoted by Dan Wakefield, "Eye of the Storm: Report from the South," *Nation*, May 7, 1960, 397.
20. Norrell, *Reaping the Whirlwind*, 123–24.

21. Sarah Patton Boyle, "Spit in the Devil's Eye," *Nation,* Oct. 20, 1956, 327–29; Sarah Patton Boyle to Virginia Durr, Oct. 30, 1956, VFD Papers.
22. Lillian Smith to James Dombrowski, May 7, 1945, in Rose Gladney, *How Am I to Be Heard: The Letters of Lillian Smith* (Chapel Hill: Univerisity of North Carolina Press,) 1993, 89.
23. Marge Frantz, "We Did Overcome: The Death of the Company Town and the House Un-American Activities Committee," Paul Lubow Memorial Lecture, University of California, Santa Cruz, October 16, 1989, 18–19; Cedric Belfrage, *The American Inquisition, 1945–1960* (New York: Bobbs-Merrill, 1973), 270.
24. Norrell, *Reaping the Whirlwind,* 89–92; *Montgomery Advertiser,* June 4, 1957, 1.
25. Virginia Durr to Anne Braden, Jan. 5, 1959, Anne Braden Papers.
26. Constancia "Dinky" Romilly interview with author, Jan. 11, 2003.
27. Joan Baez, *And a Voice to Sing With: A Memoir* (New York: Summit, 1987), 56–57; Eric von Schmidt and Jim Rooney, *Baby Let Me Follow You Down: The Illustrated Story of the Cambridge Folk Years* (New York: Anchor, 1979), 64–65, 106–7.
28. Mills Thornton, *Dividing Lines,* 101–6.
29. Statement of the Emergency Civil Liberties Committee, presented by Clark Foreman, national director, and Leonard B. Boudin, general counsel—Bills considered: S. 1199, S. 810, and S. 1084, Hearings before the Subcommittee on Constitutional Rights of the Committee on the Judiciary, U.S. Senate, 86th Congress, 1st session, on Proposals to Secure, Protect, and Strengthen the Civil Rights of Persons under the Constitution and Laws of the United States, Part I, May 14, 1959, 754–58.
30. Ellen Schrecker, *No Ivory Tower: McCarthyism and the Universities* (New York: Oxford University Press, 1986), 220–21.
31. Catherine Fosl, *Subversive Southerner: Anne Braden and the Struggle for Racial Justice in the Cold War South* (New York: Palgrave, 2002), 72, 84–102, 192, 206, 220–22.
32. Lyndon Johnson to Virginia Durr, May 16, 1960, LBJ Papers.
33. Barnard, *Outside the Magic Circle,* 204–5.
34. In a recent interview, Nat Hentoff said that he had gone to Montgomery with the intention of writing about the Durrs and what their life was like as white dissenters living in the Deep South. He thought that he had protected them by changing their names, but realized afterward that this was not sufficient, and regretted the outcome. He did learn later that he and E. D. Nixon, who had picked him up at the airport and drove him to the Durrs, were followed by the police. Telephone interview with Nat Hentoff, Dec. 27, 2002.
35. Robert Cassen to author, January 6, 2003.
36. Adam Fairclough, *Race and Democracy: The Civil Rights Struggle in Louisiana, 1915–1972* (Athens: University of Georgia Press, 1995), 247–50.

Part 3

1. Harris Wofford, *Of Kennedys and Kings: Making Sense of the Sixties* (Pittsburgh: University of Pittsburgh Press, 1980), 148–49.
2. *Montgomery Advertiser,* May 7, 1961.
3. Anthony Lester interview with author, Sept. 16, 2002; Jonathon Steele, "Stopping off at the Durrs," tribute written for Virginia Durr's ninetieth birthday; Robert Cassen to author, Oct. 13, 2002.
4. Studs Terkel, interview with Clifford and Virginia Durr, November 1965, Chicago Historical Society.
5. Barnard, *Outside the Magic Circle,* 297–98.
6. *Montgomery Advertiser,* May 23, 1961, 4A.
7. Jessica Mitford, "The Longest Meeting," unpublished ms.
8. Ibid., *Montgomery Advertiser,* May 22, 1961, 1.
9. William O. Douglas to Hugo Black, June 30, 1961; Hugo Black to William O. Douglas, July 14, 1961, Hugo Black Papers.
10. Lyndon Johnson to Virginia Durr, Sept. 8, 1961, LBJ Papers.
11. Fosl, *Subversive Southerner,* 275–76.
12. Lulah Colan interview with author, February 26, 2003.
13. "JFK Told Progress of Negro Good," *Montgomery Advertiser,* February 13, 1963, 2A.
14. John Hope Franklin interview with author, April 18, 2003; review of relevant section of John Hope Franklin's autobiography, forthcoming 2004.

15. Abel A. Bartley, *Keeping the Faith: Race, Politics and Social Development in Jacksonville* (Westport, Ct.: Greenwood Press, 2000), 110–12.
16. Anthony Lester, *Justice in the American South*, Amnesty International.
17. *New York Times*, June 29, 1964, 1; George C. Herring, *America's Longest War: The United States and Vietnam, 1950–1975* (Philadelphia: Temple University Press, 1979), 117–23.
18. Quoted in Roger Newman, *Hugo Black: A Biography,* (New York, N.Y.: Pantheon Books, 1994), 548.
19. Robert Dallek, *Flawed Giant: Lyndon Johnson and His Times* (New York: Oxford University Press, 1998), 247–49.
20. Virginia Durr to Marge and Laurent Frantz, April 29, 1965, Marge Frantz Papers.
21. Clayborne Carson, *In Struggle: SNCC and the Black Awakening of the 1960s* (Cambridge: Harvard University Press, 1981), 159–61, 401–410.
22. The trial of Collie Leroy Wilkins, the first of the defendants to be tried, ended, as noted, in a hung jury. He was retried in October and acquitted. In December the three defendants were tried on federal charges of conspiracy to violate the civil rights of Viola Liuzzo, found guilty, and given the maximum sentence of ten years. See Mary Stanton, *From Selma to Sorrow: The Life and Death of Viola Liuzzo* (Athens: University of Georgia Press, 1998), chapter 5.
23. Jessica Mitford to Virginia Durr, January 19, 1965, Jessica Mitford Papers.
24. Robert Smith interview with author, January 13, 2003.
25. David Garrow, *Bearing the Cross: Martin Luther King, Jr. and the Southern Christian Leadership Conference* (New York: William Morrow, 1986), 429–30.

Part 4

1. Studs Terkel, interview with Virginia Durr, November 1965.
2. Virginia "Tilla" Durr, Introduction, "In Search of the Golden Rule," unpublished typescript; Lulah Colan interview with author, February 26, 2003.
3. Susan Youngblood Ashmore, "Carry it On: The War on Poverty and the Civil Rights Movement in Alabama, 1964–1970," Ph.D. dissertation, Auburn University, 1999, 410–26.
4. Virginia Durr to Otto Nathan, July 6, 1969, VFD Papers.
5. Dan Carter, *The Politics of Rage,* 287.
6. Ashmore, "Carry it On," 410–16.

Epilogue

1. Lulah Colon interview with author, February 26, 2003.
2. Virginia Durr to Clark and Mairi Foreman, Jan. 8, 1969; Sept. 4, 1969; June 17, 1971; March 1972, VFD Papers.
   Virginia Durr to Jessica Mitford, June 23, 1969, Jessica Mitford Papers.
3. Virginia Durr to Clark and Mairi Foreman, Sept. 4, 1969, VFD Papers.
4. Virginia Durr to Otto Nathan, Dec. 11, 1969, VFD Papers.
5. Lulah Colon interview; Virginia Durr to Clark and Mairi Foreman, Dec. 20, 1972, VFD Papers.
6. Virgina Durr to Clark Foreman, January 13, 1969, VFD Papers.
7. Virginia Durr to John Hope Franklin, May 1, 1974, John Hope Franklin, private collection, Durham, North Carolina.
8. Virginia Durr to Jessica Mitford, April 18, 1971; Virginia Durr to C. Vann Woodward, October 1, 1974, C. Vann Woodward Papers.
9. Virginia Durr to Clark and Mairi Foreman, November 7, 1970; Virginia Durr to Otto Nathan, December 10, 1970, VFD Papers.
10. Virginia Durr to Lady Bird Johnson, April 30, 1969, Lady Bird Johnson Papers, Lyndon Baines Johnson Library.
11. Virginia Durr to Clark and Mairi Foreman, October 8, 1970, VFD Papers.
12. Julian Bond interview with author, March 1, 2003.
13. Virginia Durr to Jessica Mitford, October 9, 1970, Jessica Mitford Papers.
14. Virginia Durr to Maxwell Geismar, Feb. 6, 1973; May 7, 1972, Maxwell Geismar Papers, Special Collections, Mugar Library, Boston University, Boston, MA.

15. Virginia Durr to C. Vann Woodward, January 13, 1971, C. Vann Woodward Papers.
16. Virginia Durr to Wicki Goldschmidt, January 24, 1970, in author's possession.
17. Virginia Durr to Lady Bird Johnson, April 12, 1972; October 8, 1969, Lady Bird Johnson Papers.
18. Virginia Durr to Lady Bird and Lyndon Johnson, Sept. 24, 1972, Lyndon B. Johnson Papers.
19. Virginia Durr to Lady Bird Johnson, Sept. 19, 1971, Lady Bird Johnson Papers.
20. Virginia Durr to Lyndon Johnson, Nov. 30, 1972; Dec. 19, 1972; Jan. 1, 1973; Lyndon Johnson to Virginia Durr, Dec. 5, 1972, Lyndon B. Johnson Papers.
21. Dallek, *Flawed Giant*, 621–22.
22. Lyndon Johnson to Virginia and Cliff Durr, December 13, 1972, Lyndon B. Johnson Papers.
23. Virginia Durr to Lyndon Johnson, Dec. 19, 1972; Lyndon Johnson to Virginia Durr, Dec. 29, 1972, Lyndon B. Johnson Papers.
24. Virginia Durr to Clark and Mairi Foreman, Jan. 8, 1969; Virginia Durr to Sarah and Charlie Siepmann [1978], VFD Papers.
25. Virginia Durr to Otto Nathan, Dec. 10, 1970, VFD Papers.
26. Virginia Durr to Clark and Mairi Foreman, June 21, 1972, VFD Papers.
27. Virginia Durr to Otto Nathan, Dec. 10, 1970, VFD Papers.
28. Virginia Durr to Lady Bird Johnson, Nov. 11, 1971, Lady Bird Johnson Papers
29. Virginia Durr to Max Geismar, [summer] 1972, Maxwell Geismar Papers.
30. Virginia Durr to Max Geismar, Dec. 16, 1972, Maxwell Geismar Papers; Robert Manson Myers, ed., *The Children of Pride: A True Story of Georgia and the Civil War* (New Haven: Yale University Press, 1972).
31. Virginia Durr to Clark Foreman, March 6, 1974, VFD Papers.
32. Virginia Durr to Clark Foreman, March 6, 1974, VFD Papers;Virginia Durr to C. Vann Woodward, Nov. 12, 1974, C. Vann Woodward Papers.
33. Virginia Durr to Marge Frantz, Feb. 17, 1976, Marge Frantz Papers.
34. Lulah Colan interview with author.
35. Virginia Durr to Jessica Mitford, July 1, 1975., Jessica Mitford Papers.
36. In 1992, Virginia succeeded in having an annual spring lecture series established in Cliff's honor, held at Auburn University in Montgomery, Alabama. After her death, the series was renamed "The Clifford Judkins and Virginia Foster Durr Lectures."
37. Virginia Durr to Nicholas, Ann, and Katie, and Helen Bosanquet, July 30, 1988, Nicholas Bosanquet, private collection, London, England.
38. For William Styron on Virginia Durr, see "The Women We Love," *Esquire,* June 1987.
39. Myron Thompson interview with author, April 6, 2003
40. Virginia Durr to John Hope Franklin, March 6, 1978, November, 1978, John Hope Franklin Papers; Virginia Durr to Jessica Mitford, November 2, 1978, Jessica Mitford Papers.
41. Deborah Ellis interview with author, March 24, 2003; Randall Williams interview with author, March 25, 2003; Myron Thompson interview with author.
42. Bryan Stevenson interview with author, April 14, 2003.
43. "To Be Young, Southern and Liberal," *New York Times,* Nov. 21, 1985.
44. Virginia Durr interview with author; Randall Williams interview with author.
45. Rev. Richard I. Deibert, "Lady Jeremiah:" A Service of Witness to the Resurrection of Virginia Foster Durr, 1903–1999, February 28, 1999, Immanuel Presbyterian Church, Montgomery, Alabama.
46. Virginia Durr to Jessica Mitford, June 26, 1976, Jessica Mitford Papers.

Index